Node.js Design Patterns

Second Edition

Get the best out of Node.js by mastering its most powerful
components and patterns to create modular and scalable
applications with ease

Mario Casciaro
Luciano Mammino

BIRMINGHAM - MUMBAI

Node.js Design Patterns

Second Edition

First published: December 2014

Second edition: July 2016

Production reference: 1110716

Published by Packt Publishing Ltd.

Livery Place

35 Livery Street

Birmingham B32PB, UK.

ISBN 978-1-78588-558-7

www.packtpub.com

Credits

Authors

Mario Casciaro

Luciano Mammino

Copy Editor

Safis Editing

Reviewers

Tane Piper

Joel Purra

Project Coordinator

Ulhas Kambali

Commissioning Editor

Amarabha Banerjee

Proofreader

Safis Editing

Acquisition Editor

Reshma Raman

Indexer

Mariammal Chettiyar

Content Development Editor

Onkar Wani

Graphics

Kirk D'Penha

Technical Editor

Prajakta Mhatre

Production Coordinator

Nilesh Mohite

About the Authors

Mario Casciaro is a software engineer and entrepreneur, passionate about technology, science and open source knowledge. Mario graduated with a master's degree in software engineering and started his professional career at IBM where he worked for several years on different enterprise products such as Tivoli Endpoint Manager, Cognos Insight, and SalesConnect. Next, he moved to D4H Technologies, a growing SaaS company, to lead the development of a new bleeding-edge product for managing emergency operations in real time. Currently, Mario is the co-founder and CEO of Sponsorama.com, a platform to help online projects raise funds through corporate sponsorship.

Mario is also the author of the first edition of *Node.js Design Patterns*.

Acknowledgments

When I was working on the first edition of this book I would never have thought it would become such a success. My biggest thanks go to all the readers of the first edition of this book, to those who bought it, to those who left a review, and to those who recommended it to their friends on Twitter or on other online forums. And of course, my gratitude also goes to the readers of this second edition; to you who are reading these words, you make all our efforts worthwhile. I also want you to join me in congratulating my friend Luciano, the co-author of this second edition, who did a tremendous job updating and adding new invaluable content to this book. All the merit goes to him as I only had the role of adviser in this second edition. Working on a book is not an easy task, but Luciano impressed me and all the staff at Packt for his dedication, professionalism, and technical skills, demonstrating he can achieve any goal he sets his mind to. It was a pleasure and a honor working with Luciano and I'm looking forward to other great collaborations. I also want to thank all the people who worked on the book, the folks of Packt, the technical reviewers (Tane and Joel) and all the friends who provided valuable suggestions and insights: Anton Whalley (@dhigit9), Alessandro Cinelli (@cirpo), Andrea Giuliano (@bit_shark), and Andrea Mangano (@ManganoAndrea). Thanks to all the friends who give me unconditional love, to my family, and most importantly to my girlfriend Miriam, the partner of all my adventures, who brings love and joy in every day of my life. There are still a hundred thousand adventures awaiting us.

Luciano Mammino is a software engineer born in 1987, the same year that the Nintendo released Super Mario Bros in Europe, which by chance is his favorite video-game. He started coding at the age of 12 using his father's old Intel 386, provided only with the DOS operating system and the qBasic interpreter.

After a master's degree in computer science he developed his programming skills mostly as a web developer working mainly as freelancer for companies and startups all around Italy. After a start-up parenthesis of 3 years as CTO and co-founder of Sbaam.com in Italy and in Ireland, he decided to relocate in Dublin to work as senior PHP engineer at Smartbox.

He loves developing open source libraries and working with frameworks such as Symfony and Express. He is convinced that the JavaScript fame is still at the very beginning and that this technology will have a huge impact in the future of most of the web-and mobile-related technologies. For this reason, he spends most of his free time improving his knowledge of JavaScript and playing with Node.js.

Acknowledgments

The first huge thanks go to Mario for giving me the opportunity and the trust to work alongside him on the new edition of this book. It was an amazing experience and hopefully just the beginning of a long series of collaborations.

This book was only possible thanks to the incredible and efficient work of the Packt team, especially thanks to the relentless efforts and the patience of Onkar, Reshma, and Prajakta. Also thanks to the reviewers Tane Piper and Joel Purra, their experience with Node.js was crucial to raise the quality of the content provided in this book.

A great hug (and many beers) go to my friends Anton Whalley (@dhigit9), Alessandro Cinelli (@cirpo), Andrea Giuliano (@bit_shark), and Andrea Mangano (@ManganoAndrea) for encouraging me all along the way, for sharing with me their experience as developers and for providing meaningful insights on the contents of this book.

Another great thank you goes to Ricardo, Jose, Alberto, Marcin, Nacho, David, Arthur, and all my colleagues at Smartbox for making me love my days at work and for inspiring and motivating me to get better every day as a software engineer. I couldn't ask for a better team.

My deepest gratitude goes to my family, who raised and sustained me in every possible way along my journey. Thanks, mom, for being a constant source of inspiration and strength in my life. Thanks, dad, for all the lessons, the encouragement and the advice, I really miss talking with you, I really miss you. Thanks to my brother Davide and my sister Alessia for being present in the painful and the joyful moments and making me feel part of a great family.

Thanks to Franco and his family for supporting many of my initiatives and for sharing their wisdom and life experience with me.

Kudos to my "nerd" friends Gianluca, Flavio, Antonio, Valerio, and Luca for the great time together and for constantly encouraging me to keep working on this book.

Also kudos to my "less nerdy" friends Damiano, Pietro, and Sebastiano for their friendship and all the laughs and the fun we have when we hang out together in Dublin.

Last, but definitely not least, thanks to my girlfriend Francesca. Thank you for the unconditioned love and for supporting me on every adventure, even the craziest ones. I really look forward to writing the next pages in the book of our life with you.

About the Reviewers

Tane Piper is a full stack developer based in London, UK. For over 10 years He has worked for several agencies and companies delivering software in a variety of languages such as Python, PHP, and JavaScript. He has been working with Node.js since 2010 and was one of the first people talking about server-side JavaScript in the UK and Ireland with several talks in 2011/2012. He was also an early contributor to, and advocate for the jQuery project. Currently he works at a consultancy in London delivering innovative solutions and is mostly writing React and Node applications. Outside of his professional work he is a keen scuba diver and amateur photographer.

> *I would personally like to thank my girlfriend Elina who has turned my life around in the last two years and encouraged me to take up the task of reviewing this book.*

Joel Purra started toying around with computers even before he was in his teens, seeing them as another kind of a video game device. It was not long before he took apart (sometimes broke and subsequently fixed) any computer he came across while playing the latest games on them. It was gaming that led him to discover programming in his early teens when modifying a Lunar Lander game triggered an interest in creating digital tools. Soon after getting an Internet connection at home, he developed his first e-commerce website, and thus his business started; it launched his career at an early age. At the age of 17, Joel started studying computer programming and an energy science program at a nuclear power plant's school. After graduation, he studied to become a second lieutenant telecommunications specialist in the Swedish Army before moving on to study for his master's of science degree in information technology and engineering at Linköping University. He has been involved in start-ups and other companies—both successful and unsuccessful—since 1998, and he has been a consultant since 2007. Born, raised, and educated in Sweden, Joel also enjoys the flexible lifestyle of a freelance developer, having traveled through five continents with his backpack and lived abroad for several years. A learner constantly looking for challenges, one of his goals is to build and evolve software for broad public use. You can visit his website at `http://joelpurra.com/`.

> *I'd like to thank the open source community for providing the building blocks necessary to compose both small and large software systems even as a freelance consultant. Nanos gigantum humeris insidentes. Remember to commit early, commit often!*

www.PacktPub.com

eBooks, discount offers, and more

Did you know that Packt offers eBook versions of every book published, with PDF and ePub files available? You can upgrade to the eBook version at www.PacktPub.com and as a print book customer, you are entitled to a discount on the eBook copy. Get in touch with us at customercare@packtpub.com for more details.

At www.PacktPub.com, you can also read a collection of free technical articles, sign up for a range of free newsletters and receive exclusive discounts and offers on Packt books and eBooks.

https://www2.packtpub.com/books/subscription/packtlib

Do you need instant solutions to your IT questions? PacktLib is Packt's online digital book library. Here, you can search, access, and read Packt's entire library of books.

Why subscribe?

- Fully searchable across every book published by Packt
- Copy and paste, print, and bookmark content
- On demand and accessible via a web browser

Table of Contents

Preface

Node.js is considered by many as a game-changer—the biggest shift of the decade in web development. It is loved not just for its technical capabilities, but also for the paradigm shift that it introduced in web development.

First, Node.js applications are written in JavaScript, the language of the web, the only programming language supported natively by a majority of web browsers. This aspect enables scenarios such as single-language application stacks and sharing of code between the server and the client. Node.js itself is contributing to the rise and evolution of the JavaScript language. People realize that using JavaScript on the server is not as bad as it is in the browser, and they will soon start to love it for its pragmatism and for its hybrid nature, halfway between object-oriented and functional programming.

The second revolutionizing factor is its single-threaded, asynchronous architecture. Besides obvious advantages from a performance and scalability point of view, this characteristic changed the way developers approach concurrency and parallelism. Mutexes are replaced by queues, threads by callbacks and events, and synchronization by causality.

The last and most important aspect of Node.js lies in its ecosystem: the npm package manager, its constantly growing database of modules, its enthusiastic and helpful community, and most importantly, its very own culture based on simplicity, pragmatism, and extreme modularity.

However, because of these peculiarities, Node.js development gives you a very different feel compared to the other server-side platforms, and any developer new to this paradigm will often feel unsure about how to tackle even the most common design and coding problem effectively. Common questions include: "How do I organize my code?", "What's the best way to design this?", "How can I make my application more modular?", "How do I handle a set of asynchronous calls effectively?", "How can I make sure that my application will not collapse while it grows?", or more simply "What's the right way of doing this?" Fortunately, Node.js has become a mature enough platform and most of these questions can now be easily answered with a design pattern, a proven coding technique, or a recommended practice. The aim of this book is to guide you through this emerging world of patterns, techniques, and practices, showing you what the proven solutions to the common problems are and teaching you how to use them as the starting point to building the solution to your particular problem.

By reading this book, you will learn the following:

- The "Node way":

    How to use the right point of view when approaching a Node.js design problem. You will learn, for example, how different traditional design patterns look in Node.js, or how to design modules that do only one thing.

- A set of patterns to solve common Node.js design and coding problems:

    You will be presented with a "Swiss army knife" of patterns, ready-to-use in order to efficiently solve your everyday development and design problems.

- How to write modular and efficient Node.js applications:

    You will gain an understanding of the basic building blocks and principles of writing large and well-organized Node.js applications and you will be able to apply these principles to novel problems that don't fall within the scope of existing patterns.

Throughout the book, you will be presented with several real-life libraries and technologies, such as LevelDb, Redis, RabbitMQ, ZMQ, Express, and many others. They will be used to demonstrate a pattern or technique, and besides making the example more useful, these will also give you great exposure to the Node.js ecosystem and its set of solutions.

Whether you use or plan to use Node.js for your work, your side project, or for an open source project, recognizing and using well-known patterns and techniques will allow you to use a common language when sharing your code and design, and on top of that, it will help you get a better understanding of the future of Node.js and how to make your own contributions a part of it.

What this book covers

Chapter 1, *Welcome to the Node.js Platform*, serves as an introduction to the world of Node.js application design by showing the patterns at the core of the platform itself. It covers the Node.js ecosystem and its philosophy, a short introduction to Node.js version 6, ES2015, and the reactor pattern.

Chapter 2, *Node.js Essential Patterns*, introduces the first steps towards asynchronous coding and design patterns with Node.js discussing and comparing callbacks and the event emitter (observer pattern). This chapter also introduces the Node.js module system and the related module pattern.

Chapter 3, *Asynchronous Control Flow Patterns with Callbacks*, introduces a set of patterns and techniques for efficiently handling asynchronous control flow in Node.js. This chapter teaches you how to mitigate the "callback hell" problem using plain JavaScript and the async library.

Chapter 4, *Asynchronous Control Flow Patterns with ES2015 and Beyond*, progresses with the exploration of asynchronous control flows introducing Promises, Generators, and Async-Await.

Chapter 5, *Coding with Streams*, dives deep into one of the most important patterns in Node.js: streams. It shows you how to process data with transform streams and how to combine them into different layouts.

Chapter 6, *Design Patterns*, deals with a controversial topic: traditional design patterns in Node.js. It covers the most popular conventional design patterns and shows you how unconventional they might look in Node.js. It also introduces the reader to some emerging design patterns that are specific only to JavaScript and Node.js.

Chapter 7, *Wiring Modules*, analyzes the different solutions for linking the modules of an application together. In this chapter, you will learn design patterns such as Dependency Injection and service locator.

Chapter 8, *Universal JavaScript for Web Applications*, explores one of the most interesting capabilities of modern JavaScript web applications: being able to share application code between the frontend and the backend. Across this chapter we learn the basic principles of Universal JavaScript by building a simple web application with React, Webpack, and Babel.

Chapter 9, *Advanced Asynchronous Recipes*, takes a problem-solution approach to show you how some common coding and design challenges can be solved with ready-to-use solutions.

Chapter 10, *Scalability and Architectural Patterns*, teaches you the basic techniques and patterns for scaling a Node.js application.

Chapter 11, *Messaging and Integration Patterns*, presents the most important messaging patterns, teaching you how to build and integrate complex distributed systems using ZMQ and AMQP.

What you need for this book

To experiment with the code, you will need a working installation of Node.js version 6 (or greater) and npm 3 (or greater). Some examples will require you to use a transpiler such as Babel. You will also need to be familiar with the command prompt, know how to install an npm package, and know how to run Node.js applications. You will also need a text editor to work with the code and a modern web browser.

Who this book is for

This book is for developers who have already had initial contact with Node.js and now want to get the most out of it in terms of productivity, design quality, and scalability. You are only required to have some prior exposure to the technology through some basic examples, since this book will cover some basic concepts as well. Developers with intermediate experience in Node.js will also find the techniques presented in this book beneficial.

Some background in software design theory is also an advantage to understand some of the concepts presented.

This book assumes that you have a working knowledge of web application development, JavaScript, web services, databases, and data structures.

Conventions

In this book, you will find a number of text styles that distinguish between different kinds of information. Here are some examples of these styles and an explanation of their meaning.

Code words in text, database table names, folder names, filenames, file extensions, pathnames, dummy URLs, user input, and Twitter handles are shown as follows: "ES2015 introduces the `let` keyword to declare variables that respect the block scope."

A block of code is set as follows:

```
const zmq = require('zmq')
const sink = zmq.socket('pull');
sink.bindSync("tcp://*:5001");

sink.on('message', buffer => {
  console.log(`Message from worker: ${buffer.toString()}`);
});
```

When we wish to draw your attention to a particular part of a code block, the relevant lines or items are set in bold:

```
function produce() {
  //...
  variationsStream(alphabet, maxLength)
    .on('data', combination => {
      //...
      const msg = {searchHash: searchHash, variations: batch};
      channel.sendToQueue('jobs_queue', new Buffer(JSON.stringify(msg)));
      //...
    })
  //...
}
```

Any command-line input or output is written as follows:

```
node replier
node requestor
```

New terms and **important words** are shown in bold. Words that you see on the screen, for example, in menus or dialog boxes, appear in the text like this: "To explain the problem, we will create a little **web spider**, a command-line application that takes in a web URL as the input and downloads its contents locally into a file."

Warnings or important notes appear in a box like this.

Tips and tricks appear like this.

Reader feedback

Feedback from our readers is always welcome. Let us know what you think about this book-what you liked or disliked. Reader feedback is important for us as it helps us develop titles that you will really get the most out of. To send us general feedback, simply e-mail feedback@packtpub.com, and mention the book's title in the subject of your message. If there is a topic that you have expertise in and you are interested in either writing or contributing to a book, see our author guide at www.packtpub.com/authors.

Customer support

Now that you are the proud owner of a Packt book, we have a number of things to help you to get the most from your purchase.

Downloading the example code

You can download the example code files for this book from your account at http://www.packtpub.com. If you purchased this book elsewhere, you can visit http://www.packtpub.com/support and register to have the files e-mailed directly to you.

You can download the code files by following these steps:

1. Log in or register to our website using your e-mail address and password.
2. Hover the mouse pointer on the **SUPPORT** tab at the top.
3. Click on **Code Downloads & Errata**.
4. Enter the name of the book in the **Search** box.
5. Select the book for which you're looking to download the code files.
6. Choose from the drop-down menu where you purchased this book from.
7. Click on **Code Download**.

You can also download the code files by clicking on the **Code Files** button on the book's webpage at the Packt Publishing website. This page can be accessed by entering the book's name in the **Search** box. Please note that you need to be logged into your Packt account. Once the file is downloaded, please make sure that you unzip or extract the folder using the latest version of:

* WinRAR / 7-Zip for Windows
* Zipeg / iZip / UnRarX for Mac
* 7-Zip / PeaZip for Linux

The code bundle for the book is also hosted on GitHub at `http://bit.ly/node_book_co de`. We also have other code bundles from our rich catalog of books and videos available at `https://github.com/PacktPublishing/`. Check them out!

Errata

Although we have taken every care to ensure the accuracy of our content, mistakes do happen. If you find a mistake in one of our books-maybe a mistake in the text or the code-we would be grateful if you could report this to us. By doing so, you can save other readers from frustration and help us improve subsequent versions of this book. If you find any errata, please report them by visiting `http://www.packtpub.com/submit-errata`, selecting your book, clicking on the **Errata Submission Form** link, and entering the details of your errata. Once your errata are verified, your submission will be accepted and the errata will be uploaded to our website or added to any list of existing errata under the Errata section of that title.

To view the previously submitted errata, go to `https://www.packtpub.com/books/con tent/support` and enter the name of the book in the search field. The required information will appear under the **Errata** section.

Piracy

Piracy of copyrighted material on the Internet is an ongoing problem across all media. At Packt, we take the protection of our copyright and licenses very seriously. If you come across any illegal copies of our works in any form on the Internet, please provide us with the location address or website name immediately so that we can pursue a remedy.

Please contact us at `copyright@packtpub.com` with a link to the suspected pirated material.

We appreciate your help in protecting our authors and our ability to bring you valuable content.

Questions

If you have a problem with any aspect of this book, you can contact us at `questions@packtpub.com`, and we will do our best to address the problem.

1
Welcome to the Node.js Platform

Some principles and design patterns literally define developer experience with the Node.js platform and its ecosystem; the most peculiar ones are probably its asynchronous nature and its programming style that, in its simplest incarnation, make heavy use of callbacks. It's important that we first dive into these fundamental principles and patterns, not only for writing correct code, but also to be able to take effective design decisions when it comes to solving bigger and more complex problems.

Another aspect that characterizes Node.js is its philosophy. Approaching Node.js is in fact way more than simply learning a new technology; it's also embracing a culture and a community. We will see how this greatly influences the way we design our applications and components, and the way they interact with those created by the community.

In addition to these aspects, it's worth knowing that the latest versions of Node.js introduced support for many of the features described by ES2015 (formerly ES6), which makes the language even more expressive and enjoyable to use. It is important to embrace these new syntactic and functional additions to the language in order to be able to produce more concise and readable code and come up with alternative ways to implement the design patterns that we are going to see throughout this book.

In this chapter, we will learn the following topics:

- The Node.js philosophy, the "Node way"
- Node.js version 6 and ES2015
- The reactor pattern—the mechanism at the heart of the Node.js asynchronous architecture

The Node.js philosophy

Every platform has its own philosophy—a set of principles and guidelines that are generally accepted by the community, an ideology of doing things that influences the evolution of a platform, and how applications are developed and designed. Some of these principles arise from the technology itself, some of them are enabled by its ecosystem, some are just trends in the community, and others are evolutions of different ideologies. In Node.js, some of these principles come directly from its creator, Ryan Dahl; from all the people who contributed to the core; from charismatic figures in the community; and some of the principles are inherited from the JavaScript culture or are influenced by the Unix philosophy.

None of these rules are imposed and they should always be applied with common sense; however, they can prove to be tremendously useful when we are looking for a source of inspiration while designing our programs.

 You can find an extensive list of software development philosophies on Wikipedia at `http://en.wikipedia.org/wiki/List_of_software_d evelopment_philosophies`.

Small core

The Node.js core itself has its foundations built on a few principles; one of these is having the smallest set of functionalities, leaving the rest to the so-called **userland** (or **userspace**), the ecosystem of modules living outside the core. This principle has an enormous impact on the Node.js culture, as it gives freedom to the community to experiment and iterate quickly on a broader set of solutions within the scope of the userland modules, instead of being imposed with one slowly evolving solution that is built into the more tightly controlled and stable core. Keeping the core set of functionalities to the bare minimum, then, not only becomes convenient in terms of maintainability, but also in terms of the positive cultural impact that it brings on the evolution of the entire ecosystem.

Small modules

Node.js uses the concept of a *module* as a fundamental means to structure the code of a program. It is the building block for creating applications and reusable libraries called *packages* (a package is also frequently referred to as a module since, usually, it has one single module as an entry point). In Node.js, one of the most evangelized principles is to design small modules, not only in terms of code size, but most importantly in terms of scope.

This principle has its roots in the Unix philosophy, particularly in two of its precepts, which are as follows:

- "Small is beautiful."
- "Make each program do one thing well."

Node.js brought these concepts to a whole new level. Along with the help of npm, the official package manager, Node.js helps solve the *dependency hell* problem by making sure that each installed package will have its own separate set of dependencies, thus enabling a program to depend on a lot of packages without incurring conflicts. The Node way, in fact, involves extreme levels of reusability, whereby applications are composed of a high number of small, well-focused dependencies. While this can be considered unpractical or even totally unfeasible in other platforms, in Node.js this practice is encouraged. As a consequence, it is not rare to find npm packages containing less than 100 lines of code or exposing only one single function.

Besides the clear advantage in terms of reusability, a small module is also considered to be the following:

- Easier to understand and use
- Simpler to test and maintain
- Perfect to share with the browser

Having smaller and more focused modules empowers everyone to share or reuse even the smallest piece of code; it's the **Don't Repeat Yourself** (**DRY**) principle applied to a whole new level.

Small surface area

In addition to being small in size and scope, Node.js modules usually also have the characteristic of exposing a minimal set of functionalities. The main advantage here is increased usability of the API, which means that the API becomes clearer to use and is less exposed to erroneous usage. Most of the time, in fact, the user of a component is only interested in a very limited and focused set of features, without the need to extend its functionality or tap into more advanced aspects.

In Node.js, a very common pattern for defining modules is to expose only one piece of functionality, such as a function or a constructor, while letting more advanced aspects or secondary features become properties of the exported function or constructor. This helps the user to identify what is important and what is secondary. It is not rare to find modules that expose only one function and nothing else, for the simple fact that it provides a single, unmistakably clear entry point.

Another characteristic of many Node.js modules is the fact that they are created to be used rather than extended. Locking down the internals of a module by forbidding any possibility of an extension might sound inflexible, but it actually has the advantage of reducing the use cases, simplifying its implementation, facilitating its maintenance, and increasing its usability.

Simplicity and pragmatism

Have you ever heard of the **Keep It Simple, Stupid (KISS)** principle or the famous quote:

> *"Simplicity is the ultimate sophistication."*
> *– Leonardo da Vinci*

Richard P. Gabriel, a prominentcomputer scientist, coined the term "worse is better" to describe the model, whereby less and simpler functionality is a good design choice for software. In his essay, *The Rise of "Worse is Better"*, he says:

> *"The design must be simple, both in implementation and interface. It is more important for the implementation to be simple than the interface. Simplicity is the most important consideration in a design."*

Designing simple, as opposed to perfect, fully-featured software, is a good practice for several reasons: it takes less effort to implement, allows faster shipping with fewer resources, is easier to adapt, and is easier to maintain and understand. These factors foster community contributions and allow the software itself to grow and improve.

In Node.js, this principle is also enabled by JavaScript, which is a very pragmatic language. It's not rare, in fact, to see simple functions, closures, and object literals replacing complex class hierarchies. Pure object-oriented designs often try to replicate the real world using the mathematical terms of a computer system without considering the imperfection and the complexity of the real world itself. The truth is that; our software is always an approximation of reality, and we would probably have more success in trying to get something working sooner and with reasonable complexity, instead of trying to create near-perfect software with huge effort and tons of code to maintain.

Throughout this book, we will see this principle in action many times. For example, a considerable number of traditional design patterns, such as singleton or decorator, can have a trivial, even if sometimes not foolproof, implementation and we will see how an uncomplicated, practical approach (most of the time) is preferred to a pure, flawless design.

Introduction to Node.js 6 and ES2015

At the time of writing, the latest major releases of Node.js (versions 4, 5, and 6) come with the great addition of increased language support for the new features introduced in the ECMAScript 2015 specification (in short, ES2015, and formerly known also as ES6), which aims to make the JavaScript language even more flexible and enjoyable.

Throughout this book, we will widely adopt some of these new features in the code examples. These concepts are still fresh within the Node.js community so it's worth having a quick look at the most important ES2015-specific features currently supported in Node.js. Our version of reference is Node.js version 6.

Depending on your Node.js version, some of these features will work correctly only when **strict mode** is enabled. Strict mode can be easily enabled by adding a `"use strict"` statement at the very beginning of your script. Notice that the `"use strict"` statement is a plain string and that you can either use single or double quotes to declare it. For the sake of brevity, we will not write this line in our code examples, but you should remember to add it to be able to run them correctly.

The following list is not meant to be exhaustive but just an introduction to some of the ES2015 features supported in Node.js, so that you can easily understand all the code examples in the rest of the book.

The let and const keywords

Historically, JavaScript only offered function scope and global scope to control the lifetime and the visibility of a variable. For instance, if you declare a variable inside the body of an `if` statement, the variable will be accessible even outside the statement, whether or not the body of the statement has been executed. Let's see it more clearly with an example:

```
if (false) {
    var x = "hello";
}
console.log(x);
```

This code will not fail as we might expect and it will just print `undefined` in the console. This behavior has been the cause of many bugs and a lot of frustration, and that is the reason why ES2015 introduces the `let` keyword to declare variables that respect the block scope. Let's replace `var` with `let` in our previous example:

```
if (false) {
    let x = "hello";
}
console.log(x);
```

This code will raise a `ReferenceError: x is not defined` because we are trying to print a variable that has been defined inside another block.

To give a more meaningful example we can use the `let` keyword to define a temporary variable to be used as an index for a loop:

```
for (let i=0; i < 10; i++) {
  // do something here
}
console.log(i);
```

As in the previous example, this code will raise a `ReferenceError: i is not defined` error.

This protective behavior introduced with `let` allows us to write safer code, because if we accidentally access variables that belong to another scope, we will get an error that will allow us to easily spot the bug and avoid potentially dangerous side effects.

ES2015 introduces also the `const` keyword. This keyword allows us to declare constant variables. Let's see a quick example:

```
const x = 'This will never change';
x = '...';
```

This code will raise a `TypeError: Assignment to constant variable` error because we are trying to change the value of a constant.

Anyway, it's important to underline that `const` does not behave in the same way as constant values in many other languages where this keyword allows us to define read-only variables. In fact, in ES2015, `const` does not indicate that the assigned value will be constant, but that the binding with the value is constant. To clarify this concept, we can see that with `const` in ES2015 it is still possible to do something like this:

```
const x = {};
x.name = 'John';
```

When we change a property inside the object we are actually altering the value (the object), but the binding between the variable and the object will not change, so this code will not raise an error. Conversely, if we reassign the full variable, this will change the binding between the variable and its value and raise an error:

```
x = null; // This will fail
```

Constants are extremely useful when you want to protect a scalar value from being accidentally changed in your code or, more generically, when you want to protect an assigned variable to be accidentally reassigned to another value somewhere else in your code.

It is becoming best practice to use `const` when requiring a module in a script, so that the variable holding the module cannot be accidentally reassigned:

```
const path = require('path');
// .. do stuff with the path module
let path = './some/path'; // this will fail
```

 If you want to create an immutable object, `const` is not enough, so you should use ES5's method `Object.freeze()` (https://developer.mozilla.org/it/docs/Web/JavaScript/Reference/Global_Objects/Object/freeze) or the `deep-freeze` module (https://www.npmjs.com/package/deep-freeze).

The arrow function

One of the most appreciated features introduced by ES2015 is the support for arrow functions. The arrow function is a more concise syntax for defining functions, especially useful when defining a callback. To better understand the advantages of this syntax, let's first see an example of classic filtering on an array:

```
const numbers = [2, 6, 7, 8, 1];
const even = numbers.filter(function(x) {
  return x%2 === 0;
});
```

The preceding code can be rewritten as follows using the arrow function syntax:

```
const numbers = [2, 6, 7, 8, 1];
const even = numbers.filter(x => x%2 === 0);
```

The `filter` function can be defined inline, and the keyword `function` is removed, leaving only the list of parameters, which is followed by => (the arrow), which in turn is followed by the body of the function. When the list of arguments contains more than one argument, you must surround them with parentheses and separate the argument with commas. Also, when there is no argument you must provide a set of empty parentheses before the arrow: `() => {...}`. When the body of the function is just one line, there's no need to write the `return` keyword as it is applied implicitly. If we need to add more lines of code to the body of the function, we can wrap them in curly brackets, but beware that in this case `return` is not automatically implied, so it needs to be stated explicitly, as in the following example:

```
const numbers = [2, 6, 7, 8, 1];
const even = numbers.filter(x => {
  if (x%2 === 0) {
    console.log(x + ' is even!');
    return true;
  }
});
```

But there is another important feature to know about arrow functions: arrow functions are bound to their lexical scope. This means that inside an arrow function the value of `this` is the same as in the parent block. Let's clarify this concept with an example:

```
function DelayedGreeter(name) {
  this.name = name;
}

DelayedGreeter.prototype.greet = function() {
  setTimeout( function cb() {
    console.log('Hello ' + this.name);
```

```
  }, 500);
};

const greeter = new DelayedGreeter('World');
greeter.greet(); // will print "Hello undefined"
```

In this code, we are defining a simple `greeter` prototype that accepts a name as an argument. Then we are adding the `greet` method to the prototype. This function is supposed to print `Hello` and the name defined in the current instance `500` milliseconds after it has been called. But this function is broken, because inside the timeout callback function (`cb`), the scope of the function is different from the scope of `greet` method and the value of `this` is `undefined`.

Before Node.js introduced support for arrow functions, to fix this we needed to change the `greet` function using `bind`, as follows:

```
DelayedGreeter.prototype.greet = function() {
  setTimeout( (function cb() {
    console.log('Hello' + this.name);
  }).bind(this), 500);
};
```

But since we have now arrow functions and since they are bound to their lexical scope, we can just use an arrow function as a callback to solve the issue:

```
DelayedGreeter.prototype.greet = function() {
  setTimeout( () => console.log('Hello' + this.name), 500);
};
```

This is a very handy feature; most of the time it makes our code more concise and straightforward.

Class syntax

ES2015 introduces a new syntax to leverage prototypical inheritance in a way that should sound more familiar to all the developers that come from classic object-oriented languages such as Java or C#. It's important to underline that this new syntax does not change the way objects are managed internally by the JavaScript runtime; they still inherit properties and functions through prototypes and not through classes. While this new alternative syntax can be very handy and readable, as a developer, it is important to understand that it is just syntactic sugar.

Let's see how it works with a trivial example. First of all, let's describe a `Person` function using the classic prototype-based approach:

```
function Person(name, surname, age) {
  this.name = name;
  this.surname = surname;
  this.age = age;
}

Person.prototype.getFullName = function() {
  return this.name + '' + this.surname;
};

Person.older = function(person1, person2) {
  return (person1.age >= person2.age) ? person1 : person2;
};
```

As you can see, a person has `name`, `surname`, and `age`. We are providing our prototype with a helper function that allows us to easily get the full name of a `person` object and a generic helper function accessible directly from the `Person` prototype that returns the older person between two `Person` instances given as input.

Let's see now how we can implement the same example using the new handy ES2015class syntax:

```
class Person {
  constructor (name, surname, age) {
    this.name = name;
    this.surname = surname;
    this.age = age;
  }

  getFullName () {
    return this.name + ' ' + this.surname;
  }

  static older (person1, person2) {
    return (person1.age >= person2.age) ? person1 : person2;
  }
}
```

This syntax is more readable and straightforward to understand. We are explicitly stating what the `constructor` is for the class and declaring the function `older` as a `static` method.

The two implementations are completely interchangeable, but the real killer feature of the new syntax is the possibility of extending the `Person` prototype using the `extend` and `super` keywords. Let's assume we want to create a `PersonWithMiddlename` class:

```
class PersonWithMiddlename extends Person {
  constructor (name, middlename, surname, age) {
    super(name, surname, age);
    this.middlename = middlename;
  }

  getFullName () {
    return this.name + '' + this.middlename + '' + this.surname;
  }
}
```

What is worth noticing in this third example is that the syntax really resembles what is common in other object-oriented languages. We are declaring the class from which we want to extend, we define a new constructor that can call the parent one using the keyword `super`, and we override the `getFullName` method to add support for our middle name.

Enhanced object literals

Along with the new class syntax, ES2015 introduced an enhanced object literals syntax. This syntax offers a shorthand to assign variables and functions as members of the object, allows us to define computed member names at creation time, and also handy setter and getter methods.

Let's make all of this clear with some examples:

```
const x = 22;
const y = 17;
const obj = { x, y };
```

`obj` will be an object containing the keys `x` and `y` with the values `22` and `17`, respectively.

We can do the same thing with functions:

```
module.exports = {
  square (x) {
    return x * x;
  },
  cube (x) {
    return x * x * x;
  }
};
```

In this case, we are writing a module that exports the functions `square` and `cube` mapped to properties with the same name. Notice that we don't need to specify the keyword `function`.

Let's see in another example how we can use computed property names:

```
const namespace = '-webkit-';
const style = {
  [namespace + 'box-sizing'] : 'border-box',
  [namespace + 'box-shadow'] : '10px10px5px #888888'
};
```

In this case, the resulting object will contain the properties `-webkit-box-sizing` and `-webkit-box-shadow`.

Let's see now how we can use the new setter and getter syntax by jumping directly to an example:

```
const person = {
  name : 'George',
  surname : 'Boole',

  get fullname () {
    return this.name + '' + this.surname;
  },

  set fullname (fullname) {
    let parts = fullname.split('');
    this.name = parts[0];
    this.surname = parts[1];
  }
};

console.log(person.fullname); // "George Boole"
console.log(person.fullname = 'Alan Turing'); // "Alan Turing"
console.log(person.name); // "Alan"
```

In this example we are defining three properties, two normal ones, `name` and `surname`, and a computed `fullname` property through the `set` and `get` syntax. As you can see from the result of the `console.log` calls, we can access the computed property as if it was a regular property inside the object for both reading and writing the value. It's worth noticing that the second call to `console.log` prints `Alan Turing`. This happens because by default every `set` function returns the value that is returned by the `get` function for the same property, in this case `get fullname`.

Map and Set collections

As JavaScript developers, we are used to creating hash maps using plain objects. ES2015 introduces a new prototype called `Map` that is specifically designed to leverage hash map collections in a more secure, flexible, and intuitive way. Let's see a quick example:

```
const profiles = new Map();
profiles.set('twitter', '@adalovelace');
profiles.set('facebook', 'adalovelace');
profiles.set('googleplus', 'ada');

profiles.size; // 3
profiles.has('twitter'); // true
profiles.get('twitter'); // "@adalovelace"
profiles.has('youtube'); // false
profiles.delete('facebook');
profiles.has('facebook'); // false
profiles.get('facebook'); // undefined
for (const entry of profiles) {
  console.log(entry);
}
```

As you can see, the `Map` prototype offers several handy methods, such as `set`, `get`, `has`, and `delete`, and the `size` attribute (notice how the latter differs from arrays where we use the attribute `length`). We can also iterate through all the entries using the `for...of` syntax. Every entry in the loop will be an array containing the key as first element and the value as second element. This interface is very intuitive and self-explanatory.

But what makes maps really interesting is the possibility of using functions and objects as keys of the map, and this is something that is not entirely possible using plain objects, because with objects all the keys are automatically cast to strings. This opens new opportunities; for example, we can build a micro testing framework leveraging this feature:

```
const tests = new Map();
tests.set(() => 2+2, 4);
tests.set(() => 2*2, 4);
tests.set(() => 2/2, 1);

for (const entry of tests) {
  console.log((entry[0]() === entry[1]) ? 'PASS' : 'FAIL');
}
```

As you can see in this last example, we are storing functions as keys and expected results as values. Then we can iterate through our hash map and execute all the functions. It's also worth noticing that when we iterate through the map, all the entries respect the order in which they have been inserted; this is also something that was not always guaranteed with plain objects.

Along with `Map`, ES2015 also introduces the `Set` prototype. This prototype allows us to easily construct sets, which means lists with unique values:

```
const s = new Set([0, 1, 2, 3]);
s.add(3); // will not be added
s.size; // 4
s.delete(0);
s.has(0); // false

for (const entry of s) {
  console.log(entry);
}
```

As you can see, in this example the interface is quite similar to the one we have just seen for `Map`. We have the methods `add` (instead of `set`), `has`, and `delete` and the property `size`. We can also iterate through the set and in this case every entry is a value, in our example it will be one of the numbers in the set. Finally, sets can also contain objects and functions as values.

WeakMap and WeakSet collections

ES2015 also defines a "weak" version of the `Map` and the `Set` prototypes called `WeakMap` and `WeakSet`.

`WeakMap` is quite similar to `Map` in terms of interface; however, there are two main differences you should be aware of: there is no way to iterate all over the entries, and it only allows having objects as keys. While this might seem like a limitation, there is a good reason behind it. In fact, the distinctive feature of `WeakMap` is that it allows objects used as keys to be garbage collected when the only reference left is inside `WeakMap`. This is extremely useful when we are storing some metadata associated with an object that might get deleted during the regular lifetime of the application. Let's see an example:

```
let obj = {};
const map = new WeakMap();
map.set(obj, {key: "some_value"});
console.log(map.get(obj)); // {key: "some_value"}
obj = undefined; // now obj and the associated data in the map
```

```
// will be cleaned up in the next gc cycle
```

In this code, we are creating a plain object called `obj`. Then we store some metadata for this object in a new `WeakMap` called `map`. We can access this metadata with the `map.get` method. Later, when we cleanup the object by assigning its variable to `undefined`, the object will be correctly garbage collected and its metadata removed from the map.

Similar to `WeakMap`, `WeakSet` is the weak version of `Set`: it exposes the same interface of `Set` but it only allows storing objects and cannot be iterated. Again, the difference with `Set` is that `WeakSet` allows objects to be garbage collected when their only reference left is in the weak set:

```
let obj1= {key: "val1"};
let obj2= {key: "val2"};
const set= new WeakSet([obj1, obj2]);
console.log(set.has(obj1)); // true
obj1= undefined; // now obj1 will be removed from the set
console.log(set.has(obj1)); // false
```

It's important to understand that `WeakMap` and `WeakSet` are not better or worse than `Map` and `Set`, they are simply more suitable for different use cases.

Template literals

ES2015 offers a new alternative and more powerful syntax to define strings: the `template literals`. This syntax uses back ticks (`` ` ``) as delimiters and offers several benefits compared to regular quoted (') or double-quoted (") delimited strings. The main benefits are that template literal syntax can interpolate variables or expressions using `${expression}` inside the string (this is the reason why this syntax is called "template") and that a single string can finally be easily written in multiple lines. Let's see a quick example:

```
const name = "Leonardo";
const interests = ["arts", "architecture", "science", "music",
                   "mathematics"];
const birth = { year : 1452, place : 'Florence' };
const text = `${name} was an Italian polymath
 interested in many topics such as
 ${interests.join(', ')}.He was born
 in ${birth.year} in ${birth.place}.`;
console.log(text);
```

This code will print the following:

```
Leonardo was an Italian polymath interested in many topics
such as arts, architecture, science, music, mathematics.
He was born in 1452 in Florence.
```

Downloading the example code

Detailed steps to download the code bundle are mentioned in the *Preface* of this book. Have a look.

The code bundle for the book is also hosted on GitHub at: http://bit.ly/node_book_code.

We also have other code bundles from our rich catalog of books and videos available at: https://github.com/PacktPublishing/.

Other ES2015 features

Another extremely interesting feature added in ES2015 and available since Node.js version 4 is **Promise**. We will discuss Promise in detail in Chapter 4, *Asynchronous Control Flow Patterns with ES2015 and Beyond*.

Other interesting ES2015 features introduced in Node.js version 6 are as follows:

- Default function parameters
- Rest parameters
- Spread operator
- Destructuring
- new.target (we will talk about this in Chapter 2, *Node.js Essential Patterns*)
- Proxy (we will talk about this in Chapter 6, *Design Patterns*)
- Reflect
- Symbols

A more extended and up-to-date list of all the supported ES2015 features is available in the official Node.js documentation: https://nodejs.org/en/docs/es6/.

The reactor pattern

In this section, we will analyze the reactor pattern, which is the heart of the asynchronous nature of Node.js. We will go through the main concepts behind the pattern, such as the single-threaded architecture and the non-blocking I/O, and we will see how this creates the foundation for the entire Node.js platform.

I/O is slow

I/O is definitely the slowest among the fundamental operations of a computer. Accessing the RAM is in the order of nanoseconds (10E-9 seconds), while accessing data on the disk or the network is in the order of milliseconds (10E-3 seconds). For the bandwidth, it is the same story; RAM has a transfer rate consistently in the order of GB/s, while disk and network varies from MB/s to, optimistically, GB/s. I/O is usually not expensive in terms of CPU, but it adds a delay between the moment the request is sent and the moment the operation completes. On top of that, we also have to consider the human factor; often, the input of an application comes from a real person, for example, the click of a button or a message sent in a real-time chat application, so the speed and frequency of I/O doesn't only depend on technical aspects and it can be many orders of magnitude slower than the disk or network.

Blocking I/O

In traditional blocking I/O programming, the function call corresponding to an I/O request will block the execution of the thread until the operation completes. This can go from a few milliseconds, in the case of disk access, to minutes or even more, in case the data is generated from user actions, such as pressing a key. The following pseudocode shows a typical blocking thread performed against a socket:

```
//blocks the thread until the data is available
data = socket.read();
//data is available
print(data);
```

It is trivial to notice that a web server that is implemented using blocking I/O will not be able to handle multiple connections in the same thread; each I/O operation on a socket will block the processing of any other connection. For this reason, the traditional approach to handling concurrency in web servers is to kick off a thread or a process (or to reuse one taken from a pool) for each concurrent connection that needs to be handled. This way, when a thread gets blocked for an I/O operation it will not impact the availability of the other requests, because they are handled in separate threads.

The following image illustrates this scenario:

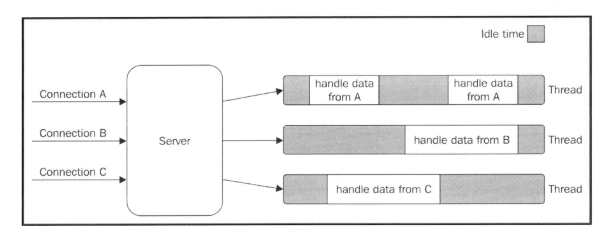

The preceding image lays emphasis on the amount of time each thread is idle, waiting for new data to be received from the associated connection. Now, if we also consider that any type of I/O can possibly block a request, for example, while interacting with databases or with the filesystem, we soon realize how many times a thread has to block in order to wait for the result of an I/O operation. Unfortunately, a thread is not cheap in terms of system resources; it consumes memory and causes context switches, so having a long-running thread for each connection and not using it for most of the time is not the best compromise in terms of efficiency.

Non-blocking I/O

In addition to blocking I/O, most modern operating systems support another mechanism to access resources called non-blocking I/O. In this operating mode, the system call always returns immediately without waiting for the data to be read or written. If no results are available at the moment of the call, the function will simply return a predefined constant, indicating that there is no data available to return at that moment.

For example, in Unix operating systems, the `fcntl()` function is used to manipulate an existing file descriptor to change its operating mode to non-blocking (with the `O_NONBLOCK` flag). Once the resource is in non-blocking mode, any read operation will fail with the return code `EAGAIN`, in case the resource doesn't have any data ready to be read.

The most basic pattern for accessing this kind of non-blocking I/O is to actively poll the resource within a loop until some actual data is returned; this is called **busy-waiting**. The following pseudocode shows you how it's possible to read from multiple resources using non-blocking I/O and a polling loop:

```
resources = [socketA, socketB, pipeA];
while(!resources.isEmpty()) {
  for(i = 0; i < resources.length; i++) {
    resource = resources[i];
    //try to read
    let data = resource.read();
    if(data === NO_DATA_AVAILABLE)
      //there is no data to read at the moment
      continue;
    if(data === RESOURCE_CLOSED)
      //the resource was closed, remove it from the list
      resources.remove(i);
    else
      //some data was received, process it
      consumeData(data);
  }
}
```

You can see that, with this simple technique, it is already possible to handle different resources in the same thread, but it's still not efficient. In fact, in the preceding example, the loop will only consume precious CPU for iterating over resources that are unavailable most of the time. Polling algorithms usually result in a huge amount of wasted CPU time.

Event demultiplexing

Busy-waiting is definitely not an ideal technique for processing non-blocking resources, but luckily, most modern operating systems provide a native mechanism to handle concurrent, non-blocking resources in an efficient way; this mechanism is called **synchronous event demultiplexer** or **event notification interface**. This component collects and queues I/O events that come from a set of watched resources, and block until new events are available to process. The following is the pseudocode of an algorithm that uses a generic synchronous event demultiplexer to read from two different resources:

```
socketA, pipeB;
watchedList.add(socketA, FOR_READ);                    //[1]
watchedList.add(pipeB, FOR_READ);
while(events = demultiplexer.watch(watchedList)) {      //[2]
  //event loop
  foreach(event in events) {                           //[3]
    //This read will never block and will always return data
    data = event.resource.read();
    if(data === RESOURCE_CLOSED)
      //the resource was closed, remove it from the watched list
      demultiplexer.unwatch(event.resource);
    else
      //some actual data was received, process it
      consumeData(data);
  }
}
```

These are the important steps of the preceding pseudocode:

1. The resources are added to a data structure, associating each one of them with a specific operation, in our example, read.

2. The event notifier is set up with the group of resources to be watched. This call is synchronous and blocks until any of the watched resources are ready for read. When this occurs, the event demultiplexer returns from the call and a new set of events is available to be processed.

3. Each event returned by the event demultiplexer is processed. At this point, the resource associated with each event is guaranteed to be ready to read and to not block during the operation. When all the events are processed, the flow will block again on the event demultiplexer until new events are again available to be processed. This is called the **event loop**.

It's interesting to see that with this pattern, we can now handle several I/O operations inside a single thread, without using a busy-waiting technique. The following image shows us how a web server would be able to handle multiple connections using a synchronous event demultiplexer and a single thread:

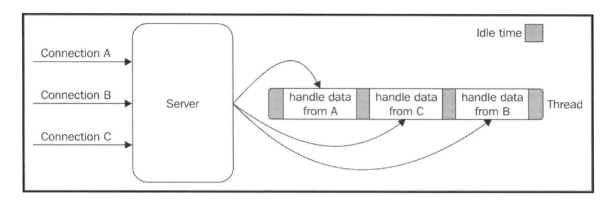

The previous image helps us understand how concurrency works in a single-threaded application using a synchronous event demultiplexer and non-blocking I/O. We can see that using only one thread does not impair our ability to run multiple I/O bound tasks concurrently. The tasks are spread over time, instead of being spread across multiple threads. This has the clear advantage of minimizing the total idle time of the thread, as clearly shown in the image. This is not the only reason for choosing this model. To have only a single thread, in fact, also has a beneficial impact on the way programmers approach concurrency in general. Throughout the book, we will see how the absence of in-process race conditions and multiple threads to synchronize allows us to use much simpler concurrency strategies.

In the next chapter, we will have the opportunity to talk more about the concurrency model of Node.js.

Introducing the reactor pattern

We can now introduce the reactor pattern, which is a specialization of the algorithms presented in the previous section. The main idea behind it is to have a handler (which in Node.js is represented by a `callback` function) associated with each I/O operation, which will be invoked as soon as an event is produced and processed by the event loop. The structure of the reactor pattern is shown in the following image:

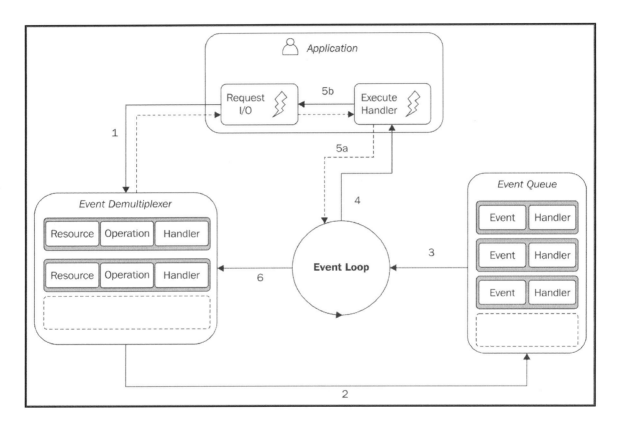

This is what happens in an application using the reactor pattern:

1. The application generates a new I/O operation by submitting a request to the **Event Demultiplexer**. The application also specifies a handler, which will be invoked when the operation completes. Submitting a new request to the **Event Demultiplexer** is a non-blocking call and it immediately returns control to the application.
2. When a set of I/O operations completes, the **Event Demultiplexer** pushes the new events into the **Event Queue**.
3. At this point, the **Event Loop** iterates over the items of the **Event Queue**.
4. For each event, the associated handler is invoked.
5. The handler, which is part of the application code, will give back control to the **Event Loop** when its execution completes (**5a**). However, new asynchronous operations might be requested during the execution of the handler (**5b**), causing new operations to be inserted in the **Event Demultiplexer** (**1**), before control is given back to the **Event Loop**.
6. When all the items in the **Event Queue** are processed, the loop will block again on the **Event Demultiplexer** which will then trigger another cycle when a new event is available.

The asynchronous behavior is now clear: the application expresses the interest to access a resource at one point in time (without blocking) and provides a handler, which will then be invoked at another point in time when the operation completes.

 A Node.js application will exit automatically when there are no more pending operations in the Event Demultiplexer, and no more events to be processed inside the **Event Queue**.

We can now define the pattern at the heart of Node.js:

Pattern (reactor) handles I/O by blocking until new events are available from a set of observed resources, and then reacts by dispatching each event to an associated handler.

The non-blocking I/O engine of Node.js-libuv

Each operating system has its own interface for the **Event Demultiplexer:** epoll on Linux, kqueue on Mac OS X, and the **I/O Completion Port** (**IOCP**) API on Windows. Besides that, each I/O operation can behave quite differently depending on the type of the resource, even within the same OS. For example, in Unix, regular filesystem files do not support non-blocking operations, so, in order to simulate non-blocking behavior, it is necessary to use a separate thread outside the Event Loop. All these inconsistencies across and within the different operating systems required a higher-level abstraction to be built for the Event Demultiplexer. This is exactly why the Node.js core team created a C library called **libuv**, with the objective to make Node.js compatible with all the major platforms and normalize the non-blocking behavior of the different types of resource; libuv today represents the low-level I/O engine of Node.js.

Besides abstracting the underlying system calls, libuv also implements the reactor pattern, thus providing an API for creating event loops, managing the event queue, running asynchronous I/O operations, and queuing other types of task.

 A great resource to learn more about libuv is the free online book created by Nikhil Marathe, which is available at:
`http://nikhilm.github.io/uvbook/`

The recipe for Node.js

The reactor pattern and libuv are the basic building blocks of Node.js, but we need the following three other components to build the full platform:

- A set of bindings responsible for wrapping and exposing libuv and other low-level functionality to JavaScript.
- **V8**, the JavaScript engine originally developed by Google for the Chrome browser. This is one of the reasons why Node.js is so fast and efficient. V8 is acclaimed for its revolutionary design, its speed, and for its efficient memory management.
- A core JavaScript library (called **node-core**) that implements the high-level Node.js API.

Finally, this is the recipe of Node.js, and the following image represents its final architecture:

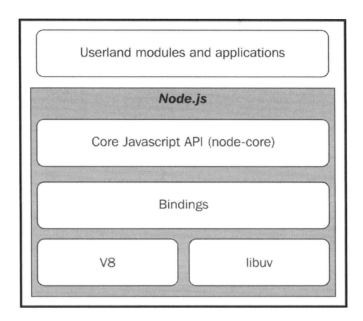

Summary

In this chapter, we have seen how the Node.js platform is based on a few important principles that provide the foundation to build efficient and reusable code. The philosophy and the design choices behind the platform have, in fact, a strong influence on the structure and behavior of every application and module we create. Often, for a developer moving from another technology, these principles might seem unfamiliar and the usual instinctive reaction is to fight the change by trying to find more familiar patterns inside a world which, in reality, requires a real shift in the mindset.

On one hand, the asynchronous nature of the reactor pattern requires a different programming style made of callbacks and things that happen at a later time, without worrying too much about threads and race conditions. On the other hand, the module pattern and its principles of simplicity and minimalism create interesting new scenarios in terms of reusability, maintenance, and usability.

Finally, besides the obvious technical advantages of being fast, efficient, and based on JavaScript, Node.js is attracting so much interest because of the principles we have just discovered. For many, grasping the essence of this world feels like returning to the origins, to a more humane way of programming in both size and complexity, and that's why developers end up falling in love with Node.js. The introduction of ES2015 makes things even more interesting and opens new scenarios in which we can embrace all these advantages with an even more expressive syntax.

In the next chapter, we will get deep into the two basic asynchronous patterns used in Node.js: the callback pattern and the event emitter. We will also understand the difference between synchronous and asynchronous code and how to avoid writing unpredictable functions.

2
Node.js Essential Patterns

Embracing the asynchronous nature of Node.js is not trivial at all, especially if coming from a language such as PHP where it is not usual to deal with asynchronous code.

In synchronous programming, we are used to the concept of imagining code as a series of consecutive computing steps defined to solve a specific problem. Every operation is blocking, which means that only when an operation is completed is it possible to execute the next one. This approach makes the code easy to understand and debug.

Instead, in asynchronous programming, some operations, such as reading a file or performing a network request, can be executed as an operation in the background. When an asynchronous operation is invoked, the next one is executed immediately, even if the previous operation has not finished yet. The operations pending in the background can complete at any time, and the whole application should be programmed to react in the proper way when an asynchronous call finishes.

While this non-blocking approach could almost always guarantee superior performance compared to an always-blocking scenario, it provides a paradigm that could be hard to reason about and that can get really cumbersome when dealing with more advanced applications that require complex control flows.

Node.js offers a series of tools and design patterns to deal optimally with asynchronous code. It's important to learn how to use them to gain confidence and write applications that are both performant and easy to understand and debug.

In this chapter, we will see two of the most important asynchronous patterns: callback and event emitter.

The callback pattern

Callbacks are the materialization of the handlers of the reactor pattern, which we introduced in the previous chapter. They are one of those imprints that give Node.js its distinctive programming style. Callbacks are functions that are invoked to propagate the result of an operation and this is exactly what we need when dealing with asynchronous operations. They do replace the use of the `return` instruction that always executes synchronously. JavaScript is a great language to represent callbacks, because as we have seen, functions are first class objects and can be easily assigned to variables, passed as arguments, returned from another function invocation or stored into data structures. Another ideal construct for implementing callbacks is **closures**. With closures, we can in fact reference the environment in which a function was created; we can always maintain the context in which the asynchronous operation was requested, no matter when or where its callback is invoked.

If you need to refresh your knowledge about closures, you can refer to the article on the Mozilla Developer Network at `https://developer.mozilla.org/en-US/docs/Web/JavaScript/Guide/Closures`.

In this section, we will analyze this particular style of programming that's made of callbacks instead of x return instructions.

The continuation-passing style

In JavaScript, a callback is a function that is passed as an argument to another function and is invoked with the result when the operation completes. In functional programming, this way of propagating the result is called **continuation-passing style** (**CPS**). It is a general concept, and it is not always associated with asynchronous operations. In fact, it simply indicates that a result is propagated by passing it to another function (the callback), instead of directly returning it to the caller.

Synchronous continuation-passing style

To clarify the concept, let's take a look at a simple synchronous function:

```
function add(a, b) {
  return a + b;
}
```

There is nothing special here; the result is passed back to the caller using the `return` instruction; this is also called **direct style**, and it represents the most common way of returning a result in synchronous programming. The equivalent continuation-passing style of the preceding function would be as follows:

```
function add(a, b, callback) {
  callback(a + b);
}
```

The `add()` function is a synchronous CPS function, which means that it will return a value only when the callback completes its execution. The following code demonstrates this statement:

```
console.log('before');
add(1, 2, result => console.log('Result: ' + result));
console.log('after');
```

Since `add()` is synchronous, the previous code will trivially print the following:

```
before
Result: 3
after
```

Asynchronous continuation-passing style

Now, let's consider a case where the `add()` function is asynchronous, as follows:

```
function additionAsync(a, b, callback) {
  setTimeout(() => callback(a + b), 100);
}
```

In the previous code, we used `setTimeout()` to simulate an asynchronous invocation of the callback. Now, let's try to use `additionAsync` and see how the order of the operations changes:

```
console.log('before');
additionAsync(1, 2, result => console.log('Result: ' + result));
console.log('after');
```

The preceding code will print the following output:

```
before
after
Result: 3
```

Since `setTimeout()` triggers an asynchronous operation, it will not wait for the callback to be executed, but instead, it returns immediately, giving the control back to `additionAsync()`, and then back to its caller. This property in Node.js is crucial, as it gives control back to the event loop as soon as an asynchronous request is sent, thus allowing a new event from the queue to be processed.

The following image shows how this works:

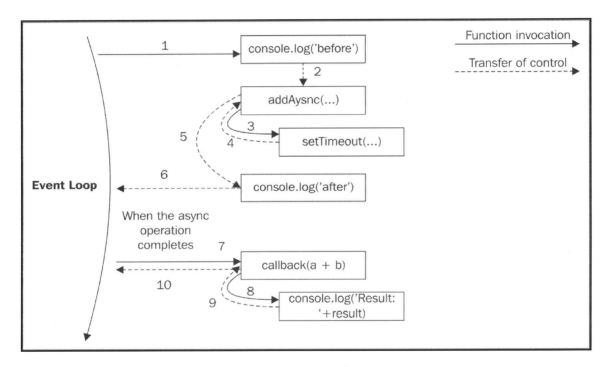

When the asynchronous operation completes, the execution is then resumed starting from the callback provided to the asynchronous function that caused the unwinding. The execution will start from the **Event Loop**, so it will have a fresh stack. This is where JavaScript comes in really handy. Thanks to closures, it is trivial to maintain the context of the caller of the asynchronous function, even if the callback is invoked at a different point in time and from a different location.

A synchronous function blocks until it completes its operations. An asynchronous function returns immediately and the result is passed to a handler (in our case, a callback) at a later cycle of the event loop.

Non-continuation-passing style callbacks

There are several circumstances in which the presence of a callback argument might make us think that a function is asynchronous or is using a continuation-passing style; that's not always true. Let's take, for example, the map() method of an Array object:

```
const result = [1, 5, 7].map(element => element - 1);
console.log(result); // [0, 4, 6]
```

Clearly, the callback is used just to iterate over the elements of the array, and not to pass the result of the operation. In fact, the result is returned synchronously using a direct style. The intent of a callback is usually clearly stated in the documentation of the API.

Synchronous or asynchronous?

We have seen how the order of the instructions changes radically depending on the nature of a function-synchronous or asynchronous. This has strong repercussions on the flow of the entire application, both in correctness and efficiency. The following is an analysis of these two paradigms and their pitfalls. In general, what must be avoided is creating inconsistency and confusion around the nature of an API, as doing so can lead to a set of problems which might be very hard to detect and reproduce. To drive our analysis, we will take as an example the case of an inconsistently asynchronous function.

An unpredictable function

One of the most dangerous situations is to have an API that behaves synchronously under certain conditions and asynchronously under others. Let's take the following code as an example:

```
const fs = require('fs');
const cache = {};
function inconsistentRead(filename, callback) {
  if(cache[filename]) {
    //invoked synchronously
    callback(cache[filename]);
  } else {
    //asynchronous function
    fs.readFile(filename, 'utf8', (err, data) => {
      cache[filename] = data;
      callback(data);
    });
  }
}
```

The preceding function uses the `cache` variable to store the results of different file read operations. Bear in mind that this is just an example, it does not have error management, and the caching logic itself is suboptimal. Besides this, the preceding function is dangerous because it behaves asynchronously if the cache is not set-which is not until the `fs.readFile()` function returns its results-but it will also be synchronous for all the subsequent requests for a file already in the cache-triggering an immediate invocation of the callback.

Unleashing Zalgo

Now, let's see how the use of an unpredictable function, such as the one that we defined previously, can easily break an application. Consider the following code:

```
function createFileReader(filename) {
  const listeners = [];
  inconsistentRead(filename, value => {
    listeners.forEach(listener => listener(value));
  });

  return {
    onDataReady: listener => listeners.push(listener)
  };
}
```

When the preceding function is invoked, it creates a new object that acts as a notifier, allowing us to set multiple listeners for a file read operation. All the listeners will be invoked at once when the read operation completes and the data is available. The preceding function uses our `inconsistentRead()` function to implement this functionality. Let's now try to use the `createFileReader()` function:

```
const reader1 = createFileReader('data.txt');
reader1.onDataReady(data => {
  console.log('First call data: ' + data);

  //...sometime later we try to read again from
  //the same file
  const reader2 = createFileReader('data.txt');
  reader2.onDataReady( data => {
    console.log('Second call data: ' + data);
  });
});
```

The preceding code will print the following output:

```
First call data: some data
```

As you can see, the callback of the second operation is never invoked. Let's see why:

- During the creation of `reader1`, our `inconsistentRead()` function behaves asynchronously, because there is no cached result available. Therefore, we have all the time in the world to register our listener, as it will be invoked later in another cycle of the event loop, when the read operation completes.
- Then, `reader2` is created in a cycle of the event loop in which the cache for the requested file already exists. In this case, the inner call to `inconsistentRead()` will be synchronous. So, its callback will be invoked immediately, which means that all the listeners of `reader2` will be invoked synchronously as well. However, we are registering the listeners after the creation of `reader2`, so they will never be invoked.

The callback behavior of our `inconsistentRead()` function is really unpredictable, as it depends on many factors, such as the frequency of its invocation, the filename passed as argument, and the amount of time taken to load the file.

The bug that we've just seen might be extremely complicated to identify and reproduce in a real application. Imagine using a similar function in a web server, where there can be multiple concurrent requests; imagine seeing some of those requests hanging, without any apparent reason and without any error being logged. This definitely falls under the category of *nasty defects*.

Isaac Z. Schlueter, creator of npm and former Node.js project lead, in one of his blog posts compared the use of this type of unpredictable functions to *unleashing Zalgo*.

Zalgo is an Internet legend about an ominous entity believed to cause insanity, death, and destruction of the world. If you're not familiar with Zalgo, you are invited to find out what it is.

You can find Isaac Z. Schlueter's original post at `http://blog.izs.me/post/59142742143/designing-apis-for-asynchrony`.

Using synchronous APIs

The lesson to learn from the unleashing Zalgo example is that it is imperative for an API to clearly define its nature: either synchronous or asynchronous.

One suitable fix for our `inconsistentRead()` function is to make it totally synchronous. This is possible because Node.js provides a set of synchronous direct style APIs for most basic I/O operations. For example, we can use the `fs.readFileSync()` function in place of its asynchronous counterpart. The code would now be as follows:

```
const fs = require('fs');
const cache = {};
function consistentReadSync(filename) {
  if(cache[filename]) {
    return cache[filename];
  } else {
    cache[filename] = fs.readFileSync(filename, 'utf8');
    return cache[filename];
  }
}
```

We can see that the entire function was also converted to a direct style. There is no reason for a function to have a continuation-passing style if it is synchronous. In fact, we can state that it is always best practice to implement a synchronous API using a direct style; this will eliminate any confusion around its nature and will also be more efficient from a performance perspective.

Pattern
Prefer the direct style for purely synchronous functions.

Bear in mind that changing an API from CPS to a direct style, or from asynchronous to synchronous or vice versa might also require a change to the style of all the code using it. For example, in our case, we will have to totally change the interface of our `createFileReader()` API and adapt it to always work synchronously.

Also, using a synchronous API instead of an asynchronous one has some caveats:

- A synchronous API for a specific functionality might not always be available.
- A synchronous API will block the event loop and put the concurrent requests on hold. It does break the JavaScript concurrency model, slowing down the whole application. We will see later in the book what this really means for our applications.

In our `consistentReadSync()` function, the risk of blocking the event loop is partially mitigated because the synchronous I/O API is invoked only once per filename, while the cached value will be used for all the subsequent invocations. If we have a limited number of static files, then using `consistentReadSync()` won't have a big effect on our event loop. Things can change quickly if we have to read many files and only once. Using synchronous I/O in Node.js is strongly discouraged in many circumstances; however, in some situations, this might be the easiest and most efficient solution. Always evaluate your specific use case in order to choose the right alternative. Just to make a real use case example: it makes perfect sense to use a synchronous blocking API to load a configuration file while bootstrapping an application.

Use blocking API only when they don't affect the ability of the application to serve concurrent requests.

Deferred execution

Another alternative for fixing our `inconsistentRead()` function is to make it purely asynchronous. The trick here is to schedule the synchronous callback invocation to be executed "in the future" instead of being run immediately in the same event loop cycle. In Node.js, this is possible using `process.nextTick()`, which defers the execution of a function until the next pass of the event loop. Its functioning is very simple; it takes a callback as an argument and pushes it to the top of the event queue, in front of any pending I/O event, and returns immediately. The callback will then be invoked as soon as the event loop runs again.

Let's apply this technique to fix our `inconsistentRead()` function as follows:

```
const fs = require('fs');
const cache = {};
function consistentReadAsync(filename, callback) {
  if(cache[filename]) {
    process.nextTick(() => callback(cache[filename]));
  } else {
    //asynchronous function
    fs.readFile(filename, 'utf8', (err, data) => {
      cache[filename] = data;
      callback(data);
    });
  }
}
```

Now, our function is guaranteed to invoke its callback asynchronously, under any circumstances.

Another API for deferring the execution of code is `setImmediate()`. While their purposes are very similar, their semantics are quite different. Callbacks deferred with `process.nextTick()` run before any other I/O event is fired, while with `setImmediate()`, the execution is queued behind any I/O event that is already in the queue. Since `process.nextTick()` runs before any already scheduled I/O, it might cause I/O starvation under certain circumstances, for example, a recursive invocation; this can never happen with `setImmediate()`. We will learn to appreciate the difference between these two APIs when we analyze the use of deferred invocation for running synchronous CPU-bound tasks later in the book.

Pattern

We guarantee that a callback is invoked asynchronously by deferring its execution using `process.nextTick()`.

Node.js callback conventions

In Node.js, continuation-passing style APIs and callbacks follow a set of specific conventions. These conventions apply to the Node.js core API but they are also followed by the vast majority of the userland modules and applications. So, it's very important that we understand them and make sure that we comply whenever we need to design an asynchronous API.

Callbacks come last

In all core Node.js methods, the standard convention is that when a function accepts a callback in input, this has to be passed as the last argument. Let's take the following Node.js core API as an example:

```
fs.readFile(filename, [options], callback)
```

As we can see from the signature of the preceding function, the callback is always put in the last position, even in the presence of optional arguments. The reason for this convention is that the function call is more readable in case the callback is defined in place.

Error comes first

In CPS, errors are propagated as any other type of result, which means using callbacks. In Node.js, any error produced by a CPS function is always passed as the first argument of the callback, and any actual result is passed starting from the second argument. If the operation succeeds without errors, the first argument will be null or undefined. The following code shows you how to define a callback complying with this convention:

```
fs.readFile('foo.txt', 'utf8', (err, data) => {
  if(err)
    handleError(err);
  else
    processData(data);
});
```

It is best practice to always check for the presence of an error, as not doing so will make it harder for us to debug our code and discover the possible points of failure. Another important convention to take into account is that the error must always be of type Error. This means that simple strings or numbers should never be passed as error objects.

Propagating errors

Propagating errors in synchronous, direct style functions is done with the well-known throw statement, which causes the error to jump up in the call stack until it is caught.

In asynchronous CPS however, proper error propagation is done by simply passing the error to the next callback in the chain. The typical pattern looks as follows:

```
const fs = require('fs');
function readJSON(filename, callback) {
  fs.readFile(filename, 'utf8', (err, data) => {
    let parsed;
    if(err)
      //propagate the error and exit the current function
      return callback(err);

    try {
      //parse the file contents
      parsed = JSON.parse(data);
    } catch(err) {
      //catch parsing errors
      return callback(err);
    }
    //no errors, propagate just the data
    callback(null, parsed);
```

```
    });
  };
```

The detail you should notice in the previous code is how the callback is invoked when we want to pass a valid result and when we want to propagate an error. Also notice that when we are propagating an error we use the `return` statement. We do so to exit from the function as soon as the callback function is invoked and to avoid executing the next lines in `readJSON`.

Uncaught exceptions

You might have seen in the `readJSON()` function, that was used in order to avoid any exception being thrown into the `fs.readFile()` callback, we put a `try...catch` block around `JSON.parse()`. Throwing inside an asynchronous callback will cause the exception to jump up to the event loop and never be propagated to the next callback.

In Node.js, this is an unrecoverable state and the application will simply shut down printing the error to the `stderr` interface. To demonstrate this, let's try to remove the `try...catch` block from the `readJSON()` function defined previously:

```
const fs = require('fs');
function readJSONThrows(filename, callback) {
  fs.readFile(filename, 'utf8', (err, data) => {
    if(err) {
      return callback(err);
    }
    //no errors, propagate just the data
    callback(null, JSON.parse(data));
  });
};
```

Now, in the function we just defined, there is no way of catching an eventual exception coming from `JSON.parse()`. If we try to parse an invalid JSON file with the following code:

```
readJSONThrows('nonJSON.txt', err => console.log(err));
```

This would result in the application being abruptly terminated with the following exception being printed on the console:

```
SyntaxError: Unexpected token d
    at Object.parse (native)
    at [...]
    at fs.js:266:14
    at Object.oncomplete (fs.js:107:15)
```

Now, if we look at the preceding stack trace, we will see that it starts somewhere from the `fs.js` module, exactly from the point at which the native API has completed reading and returned its result back to the `fs.readFile()` function, via the event loop. This clearly shows us that the exception traveled from our callback into the stack and then straight into the event loop, where it's finally caught and thrown in the console.

This also means that wrapping the invocation of `readJSONThrows()` with a `try...catch` block will not work, because the stack in which the block operates is different from the one in which our callback is invoked. The following code shows the anti-pattern that we just described:

```
try {
  readJSONThrows('nonJSON.txt', function(err, result) {
    //...
  });
} catch(err) {
  console.log('This will not catch the JSON parsing exception');
}
```

The preceding `catch` statement will never receive the JSON parsing exception, as it will travel back to the stack in which the exception was thrown. We just saw that the stack ends up in the event loop and not with the function that triggers the asynchronous operation.

As said before, the application aborts the moment an exception reaches the event loop; however, we still have a chance to perform some cleanup or logging before the application terminates. In fact, when this happens, Node.js emits a special event called `uncaughtException` just before exiting the process. The following code shows a sample use case:

```
process.on('uncaughtException', (err) => {
  console.error('This will catch at last the ' +
    'JSON parsing exception: ' + err.message);
  // Terminates the application with 1 (error) as exit code:
  // without the following line, the application would continue
  process.exit(1);
});
```

It's important to understand that an uncaught exception leaves the application in a state that is not guaranteed to be consistent, which can lead to unforeseeable problems. For example, there might still be incomplete I/O requests running or closures might have become inconsistent. That's why it is always advised, especially in production, to exit from the application after an uncaught exception is received anyway.

The module system and its patterns

Modules are the bricks for structuring non-trivial applications, but also the main mechanism to enforce information hiding by keeping private all the functions and variables that are not explicitly marked to be exported. In this section, we will introduce the Node.js module system and its most common usage patterns.

The revealing module pattern

One of the major problems with JavaScript is the absence of namespacing. Programs that run in the global scope polluting it with data that comes from both internal application code and dependencies. A popular technique to solve this problem is called the revealing module pattern, and it looks like the following:

```
const module = (() => {
  const privateFoo = () => {...};
  const privateBar = [];

  const exported = {
    publicFoo: () => {...},
    publicBar: () => {...}
  };

  return exported;
})();
console.log(module);
```

This pattern leverages a self-invoking function to create a private scope, exporting only the parts that are meant to be public. In the preceding code, the `module` variable contains only the exported API, while the rest of the module content is practically inaccessible from outside. As we will see in a moment, the idea behind this pattern is used as a base for the Node.js module system.

Node.js modules explained

CommonJS is a group with the aim to standardize the JavaScript ecosystem, and one of their most popular proposals is called **CommonJS modules**. Node.js built its module system on top of this specification, with the addition of some custom extensions. To describe how it works, we can make an analogy with the revealing module pattern, where each module runs in a private scope, so that every variable that is defined locally does not pollute the global namespace.

A homemade module loader

To explain how this works, let's build a similar system from scratch. The code that follows creates a function that mimics a subset of the functionality of the original `require()` function of Node.js.

Let's start by creating a function that loads the content of a module, wraps it into a private scope, and evaluates it:

```
function loadModule(filename, module, require) {
  const wrappedSrc=`(function(module, exports, require) {
      ${fs.readFileSync(filename, 'utf8')}
    })(module, module.exports, require);`;
  eval(wrappedSrc);
}
```

The source code of a module is essentially wrapped into a function, as it was for the revealing module pattern. The difference here is that we pass a list of variables to the module, in particular, `module`, `exports`, and `require`. Make a note of how the `exports` argument of the wrapping function is initialized with the content of `module.exports`, as we will talk about this later.

 Bear in mind that this is only an example, and you will rarely need to evaluate some source code in a real application. Features such as `eval()` or the functions of the `vm` module (`http://nodejs.org/api/vm.html`) can be easily used in the wrong way or with the wrong input, thus opening a system to code injection attacks. They should always be used with extreme care or avoided altogether.

Let's now see what these variables contain by implementing our `require()` function:

```
const require = (moduleName) => {
  console.log(`Require invoked for module: ${moduleName}`);
  const id = require.resolve(moduleName);        //[1]
  if(require.cache[id]) {                         //[2]
    return require.cache[id].exports;
  }

  //module metadata
  const module = {                                //[3]
    exports: {},
    id: id
  };
  //Update the cache
  require.cache[id] = module;                     //[4]

  //load the module
  loadModule(id, module, require);                //[5]

  //return exported variables
  return module.exports;                          //[6]
};
require.cache = {};
require.resolve = (moduleName) => {
  /* resolve a full module id from the moduleName */
};
```

The previous function simulates the behavior of the original `require()` function of Node.js, which is used to load a module. Of course, this is just for educative purposes and it does not accurately or completely reflect the internal behavior of the real `require()` function, but it's great to understand the internals of the Node.js module system, how a module is defined, and loaded. What our homemade module system does is explained as follows:

1. A module name is accepted as input, and the very first thing that we do is resolve the full path of the module, which we call `id`. This task is delegated to `require.resolve()`, which implements a specific resolving algorithm (we will talk about it later).
2. If the module has already been loaded in the past, it should be available in the cache. In this case, we just return it immediately.
3. If the module was not loaded yet, we set up the environment for the first load. In particular, we create a `module` object that contains an `exports` property initialized with an empty object literal. This property will be used by the code of the module to export any public API.

4. The `module` object is cached.

5. The module source code is read from its file and the code is evaluated, as we have seen before. We provide the module with the `module` object that we just created, and a reference to the `require()` function. The module exports its public API by manipulating or replacing the `module.exports` object.

6. Finally, the content of `module.exports`, which represents the public API of the module, is returned to the caller.

As we see, there is nothing magical behind the workings of the Node.js module system; the trick is all in the wrapper we create around a module's source code and the artificial environment in which we run it.

Defining a module

By looking at how our custom `require()` function works, we should now know how to define a module. The following code gives us an example:

```
//load another dependency
const dependency = require('./anotherModule');

//a private function
function log() {
  console.log(`Well done ${dependency.username}`);
}

//the API to be exported for public use
module.exports.run = () => {
  log();
};
```

The essential concept to remember is that everything inside a module is private unless it's assigned to the `module.exports` variable. The content of this variable is then cached and returned when the module is loaded using `require()`.

Defining globals

Even if all the variables and functions that are declared in a module are defined in its local scope, it is still possible to define a global variable. In fact, the module system exposes a special variable called `global`, which can be used for this purpose. Everything that is assigned to this variable will end up automatically in the global scope.

> Polluting the global scope is considered bad practice and nullifies the advantage of having a module system. So, use it only if you really know what you are doing.

module.exports versus exports

For many developers who are not yet familiar with Node.js, a common source of confusion is the difference between using `exports` and `module.exports` to expose a public API. The code of our custom `require` function should again clear any doubt. The variable `exports` is just a reference to the initial value of `module.exports`; we have seen that such a value is essentially a simple object literal created before the module is loaded.

This means that we can only attach new properties to the object referenced by the `exports` variable, as shown in the following code:

```
exports.hello = () => {
  console.log('Hello');
}
```

Reassigning the `exports` variable doesn't have any effect, because it doesn't change the content of `module.exports`; it will only reassign the variable itself. The following code is therefore wrong:

```
exports = () => {
  console.log('Hello');
}
```

If we want to export something other than an object literal, such as a function, an instance, or even a string, we have to reassign `module.exports` as follows:

```
module.exports = () => {
  console.log('Hello');
}
```

The require function is synchronous

Another important detail that we should take into account is that our homemade `require` function is synchronous. In fact, it returns the module contents using a simple direct style, and no callback is required. This is true for the original Node.js `require()` function too. As a consequence, any assignment to `module.exports` must be synchronous as well. For example, the following code is incorrect:

```
setTimeout(() => {
  module.exports = function() {...};
}, 100);
```

This property has important repercussions in the way we define modules, as it limits us to mostly using synchronous code during the definition of a module. This is actually one of the most important reasons why the core Node.js libraries offer synchronous APIs as an alternative to most of the asynchronous ones.

If we need some asynchronous initialization steps for a module, we can always define and export an uninitialized module that is initialized asynchronously at a later time. The problem with this approach, though, is that loading such a module using `require` does not guarantee that it's ready to be used. In `Chapter 9`, *Advanced Asynchronous Recipes*, we will analyze this problem in detail and present some patterns to solve this issue elegantly.

For the sake of curiosity, you might want to know that in its early days, Node.js used to have an asynchronous version of `require()`, but it was soon removed because it was overcomplicating a functionality that was actually meant to be used only at initialization time and where asynchronous I/O brings more complexities than advantages.

The resolving algorithm

The term *dependency hell* describes a situation whereby the dependencies of software in turn depend on a shared dependency, but require different incompatible versions. Node.js solves this problem elegantly by loading a different version of a module depending on where the module is loaded from. All the merits of this feature go to npm, and also to the resolving algorithm used in the `require` function.

Let's now give a quick overview of this algorithm. As we saw, the `resolve()` function takes a module name (which we will call here, `moduleName`) as input and it returns the full path of the module. This path is then used to load its code and also to identify the module uniquely. The resolving algorithm can be divided into the following three major branches:

- **File modules**: If `moduleName` starts with `/`, it is already considered an absolute path to the module and it's returned as it is. If it starts with `./`, then `moduleName` is considered a relative path, which is calculated starting from the requiring module.
- **Core modules**: If `moduleName` is not prefixed with `/` or `./`, the algorithm will first try to search within the core Node.js modules.
- **Package modules**: If no core module is found matching `moduleName`, then the search continues by looking for a matching module in the first `node_modules` directory that is found navigating up in the directory structure starting from the requiring module. The algorithm continues to search for a match by looking into the next `node_modules` directory up in the directory tree, until it reaches the root of the filesystem.

For file and package modules, both the individual files and directories can match `moduleName`. In particular, the algorithm will try to match the following:

- `<moduleName>.js`
- `<moduleName>/index.js`
- The directory/file specified in the `main` property of `<moduleName>/package.json`

The complete, formal documentation of the resolving algorithm can be found at http://nodejs.org/api/modules.html#modules_all_together.

The `node_modules` directory is actually where npm installs the dependencies of each package. This means that, based on the algorithm we just described, each package can have its own private dependencies. For example, consider the following directory structure:

```
myApp
├── foo.js
└── node_modules
    ├── depA
    │   └── index.js
    ├── depB
    │   ├── bar.js
    │   └── node_modules
    │       └── depA
```

```
|                └── index.js
└── depC
    ├── foobar.js
    └── node_modules
        └── depA
            └── index.js
```

In the previous example, `myApp`, `depB`, and `depC` all depend on `depA`; however, they all have their own private version of the dependency! Following the rules of the resolving algorithm, using `require('depA')` will load a different file depending on the module that requires it, for example:

- Calling `require('depA')` from `/myApp/foo.js` will load
  `/myApp/node_modules/depA/index.js`
- Calling `require('depA')` from `/myApp/node_modules/depB/bar.js` will
  load `/myApp/node_modules/depB/node_modules/depA/index.js`
- Calling `require('depA')` from `/myApp/node_modules/depC/foobar.js` will
  load `/myApp/node_modules/depC/node_modules/depA/index.js`

The resolving algorithm is the core part behind the robustness of the Node.js dependency management, and is what makes it possible to have hundreds or even thousands of packages in an application without having collisions or problems of version compatibility.

The resolving algorithm is applied transparently for us when we invoke `require()`; however, if needed, it can still be used directly by any module by simply invoking `require.resolve()`.

The module cache

Each module is only loaded and evaluated the first time it is required, since any subsequent call of `require()` will simply return the cached version. This should be clear by looking at the code of our homemade `require` function. Caching is crucial for performance, but it also has some important functional implications:

- It makes it possible to have cycles within module dependencies
- It guarantees, to some extent, that the same instance is always returned when requiring the same module from within a given package

The module cache is exposed via the `require.cache` variable, so it is possible to directly access it if needed. A common use case is to invalidate any cached module by deleting the relative key in the `require.cache` variable, a practice very useful during testing but very dangerous if applied in normal circumstances.

Circular dependencies

Many consider circular dependencies an intrinsic design issue, but it is something which might actually happen in a real project, so it's useful for us to know at least how this works in Node.js. If we look again at our homemade `require()` function, we immediately get a glimpse of how this might work and what its caveats are.

Suppose we have two modules defined as follows:

- Module `a.js`:

```
exports.loaded = false;
const b = require('./b');
module.exports = {
  bWasLoaded: b.loaded,
  loaded: true
};
```

- Module `b.js`:

```
exports.loaded = false;
const a = require('./a');
module.exports = {
  aWasLoaded: a.loaded,
  loaded: true
};
```

Now, let's try to load these from another module, `main.js`, as follows:

```
const a = require('./a');
const b = require('./b');
console.log(a);
console.log(b);
```

The preceding code will print the following output:

```
{ bWasLoaded: true, loaded: true }
{ aWasLoaded: false, loaded: true }
```

This result reveals the caveats of circular dependencies. While both the modules are completely initialized the moment they are required from the `main` module, the `a.js` module will be incomplete when it is loaded from `b.js`. In particular, its state will be the one that it reached the moment it required `b.js`. This behavior should ring another bell, which will be confirmed if we swap the order in which the two modules are required in `main.js`.

If you try it, you will see that this time it will be the module a.js that will receive an incomplete version of b.js. We understand now that this can become quite a fuzzy business if we lose control of which module is loaded first, which can happen quite easily if the project is big enough.

Module definition patterns

The module system, besides being a mechanism for loading dependencies, is also a tool for defining APIs. As for any other problem related to API design, the main factor to consider is the balance between private and public functionality. The aim is to maximize information hiding and API usability, while balancing these with other software qualities such as *extensibility* and *code reuse*.

In this section, we will analyze some of the most popular patterns for defining modules in Node.js; each one has its own balance of information hiding, extensibility, and code reuse.

Named exports

The most basic method for exposing a public API is using **named exports**, which consists of assigning all the values we want to make public to properties of the object referenced by exports (or module.exports). In this way, the resulting exported object becomes a container or namespace for a set of related functionality.

The following code shows a module implementing this pattern:

```
//file logger.js
exports.info = (message) => {
  console.log('info: ' + message);
};

exports.verbose = (message) => {
  console.log('verbose: ' + message);
};
```

The exported functions are then available as properties of the loaded module, as shown in the following code:

```
//file main.js
const logger = require('./logger');
logger.info('This is an informational message');
logger.verbose('This is a verbose message');
```

Most of the Node.js core modules use this pattern.

The CommonJS specification only allows the use of the `exports` variable to expose public members. Therefore, the named exports pattern is the only one that is really compatible with the CommonJS specification. The use of `module.exports` is an extension provided by Node.js to support a broader range of module definition patterns, as those we are going to see next.

Exporting a function

One of the most popular module definition patterns consists of reassigning the whole `module.exports` variable to a function. Its main strength is the fact that it exposes only a single functionality, which provides a clear entry point for the module, making it simpler to understand and use; it also honors the principle of *small surface* area very well. This way of defining modules is also known in the community as the **substack pattern**, after one of its most prolific adopters, James Halliday (nickname substack). Have a look at this pattern in the following example:

```
//file logger.js
module.exports = (message) => {
  console.log(`info: ${message}`);
};
```

A possible extension of this pattern is using the exported function as namespace for other public APIs. This is a very powerful combination, because it still gives the module the clarity of a single entry point (the main exported function). This approach also allows us to expose other functionalities that have secondary or more advanced use cases. The following code shows you how to extend the module we defined previously by using the exported function as a namespace:

```
module.exports.verbose = (message) => {
  console.log(`verbose: ${message}`);
};
```

This code demonstrates how to use the module that we just defined:

```
//file main.js
const logger = require('./logger');
logger('This is an informational message');
logger.verbose('This is a verbose message');
```

Even though just exporting a function might seem like a limitation, in reality it's a perfect way to put the emphasis on a single functionality, the most important one for the module, while giving less visibility to secondary or internal aspects, which are instead exposed as properties of the exported function itself. The modularity of Node.js heavily encourages the adoption of the **Single Responsibility Principle (SRP)**: every module should have responsibility over a single functionality and that responsibility should be entirely encapsulated by the module.

> **Pattern (substack)**
> Expose the main functionality of a module by exporting only one function. Use the exported function as namespace to expose any auxiliary functionality.

Exporting a constructor

A module that exports a constructor is a specialization of a module that exports a function. The difference is that with this new pattern we allow the user to create new instances using the constructor, but we also give them the ability to extend its prototype and forge new classes. The following is an example of this pattern:

```
//file logger.js
function Logger(name) {
  this.name = name;
}

Logger.prototype.log = function(message) {
  console.log(`[${this.name}] ${message}`);
};

Logger.prototype.info = function(message) {
  this.log(`info: ${message}`);
};

Logger.prototype.verbose = function(message) {
  this.log(`verbose: ${message}`);
};

module.exports = Logger;
```

And, we can use the preceding module as follows:

```
//file main.js
const Logger = require('./logger');
const dbLogger = new Logger('DB');
dbLogger.info('This is an informational message');
```

```
const accessLogger = new Logger('ACCESS');
accessLogger.verbose('This is a verbose message');
```

In the same fashion we can easily export an ES2015 class:

```
class Logger {
  constructor(name) {
    this.name = name;
  }

  log(message) {
    console.log(`[${this.name}] ${message}`);
  }

  info(message) {
    this.log(`info: ${message}`);
  }

  verbose(message) {
    this.log(`verbose: ${message}`);
  }
}

module.exports = Logger;
```

Given that ES2015 classes are just syntactic sugar for prototypes, the usage of this module will be exactly the same as its prototype-based alternative.

Exporting a constructor or a class still provides a single entry point for the module, but compared to the substack pattern, it exposes a lot more of the module internals; however, on the other hand it allows much more power when it comes to extending its functionality.

A variation of this pattern consists of applying a guard against invocations that doesn't use the new instruction. This little trick allows us to use our module as a *factory*. Let's see how this works:

```
function Logger(name) {
  if(!(this instanceof Logger)) {
    return new Logger(name);
  }
  this.name = name;
};
```

The trick is simple: we check whether `this` exists and is an instance of `Logger`. If any of these conditions is false, it means that the `Logger()` function was invoked without using `new`, we then proceed with creating the `new` instance properly and returning it to the caller. This technique allows us to use the module also as a factory:

```
//file logger.js
const Logger = require('./logger');
const dbLogger = Logger('DB');
accessLogger.verbose('This is a verbose message');
```

A much cleaner approach to implement the guard is offered by the ES2015 `new.target` syntax which is available starting from Node.js version 6. This syntax exposes the `new.target` property which is a "meta property" made available inside all the functions and that evaluates to true at runtime if the function was called using the `new` keyword.

We can use this syntax to rewrite our logger factory:

```
function Logger(name) {
  if(!new.target) {
    return new LoggerConstructor(name);
  }
  this.name = name;
}
```

This code is totally equivalent to the previous one, so we can say that this `new.target` syntax is more helpful ES2015 syntactic sugar that makes our code much more readable and natural.

Exporting an instance

We can leverage the caching mechanism of `require()` to easily define stateful instances with a state created from a constructor or a factory, which can be shared across different modules. The following code shows an example of this pattern:

```
//file logger.js
function Logger(name) {
  this.count = 0;
  this.name = name;
}
Logger.prototype.log = function(message) {
  this.count++;
  console.log('[' + this.name + '] ' + message);
};
module.exports = new Logger('DEFAULT');
```

This newly defined module can then be used as follows:

```
//file main.js
const logger = require('./logger');
logger.log('This is an informational message');
```

Because the module is cached, every module that requires the `logger` module will actually always retrieve the same instance of the object, thus sharing its state. This pattern is very much like creating a **singleton**; however, it does not guarantee the uniqueness of the instance across the entire application, as it happens in the traditional singleton pattern. When analyzing the resolving algorithm, we have seen in fact, that a module might be installed multiple times inside the dependency tree of an application. This results in multiple instances of the same logical module, all running in the context of the same Node.js application. In `Chapter 7`, *Wiring Modules*, we will analyze the consequences of exporting stateful instances and some alternative patterns.

An extension to the pattern we just described, consists of exposing the constructor used to create the instance, in addition to the instance itself. This allows the user to create new instances of the same object, or even to extend it if necessary. To enable this, we just need to assign a new property to the instance, as shown in the following line of code:

```
module.exports.Logger = Logger;
```

Then, we can use the exported constructor to create other instances of the class:

```
const customLogger = new logger.Logger('CUSTOM');
customLogger.log('This is an informational message');
```

From the usability perspective, this is similar to using an exported function as a namespace; the module exports the default instance of an object—the piece of functionality we might want to use most of the time, while more advanced features, such as the ability to create new instances or extend the object, are still available through less exposed properties.

Modifying other modules or the global scope

A module can even export nothing. This can look a bit out of place; however, we should not forget that a module can modify the global scope and any object in it, including other modules in the cache. Please note that these are in general considered bad practices, but since this pattern can be useful and safe under some circumstances (for example, for testing) and is sometimes used in the wild, it is worth knowing and understanding it. We said a module can modify other modules or objects in the global scope; well, this is called **monkey patching**. It generally refers to the practice of modifying the existing objects at runtime to change or extend their behavior or to apply temporary fixes.

The following example shows you how we can add a new function to another module:

```
//file patcher.js

// ./logger is another module
require('./logger').customMessage = () => console.log('This is a new
  functionality');
```

Using our new `patcher` module would be as easy as writing the following code:

```
//file main.js

require('./patcher');
const logger = require('./logger');
logger.customMessage();
```

In the preceding code, `patcher` must be required before using the `logger` module for the first time in order to allow the patch to be applied.

The techniques described here are all dangerous ones to apply. The main concern is that having a module that modifies the global namespace or other modules is an operation with side effects. In other words, it affects the state of entities outside their scope, which can have consequences that aren't predictable, especially when multiple modules interact with the same entities. Imagine having two different modules trying to set the same global variable, or modifying the same property of the same module; the effects might be unpredictable (which module wins?), but most importantly it would have repercussions in the entire application.

The observer pattern

Another important and fundamental pattern used in Node.js is the observer pattern. Together with the reactor, callbacks, and modules, the observer pattern is one of the pillars of the platform and an absolute prerequisite for using many node-core and userland modules.

Observer is an ideal solution for modeling the reactive nature of Node.js and a perfect complement for callbacks. Let's give a formal definition as follows:

Pattern (observer) defines an object (called subject), which can notify a set of observers (or listeners), when a change in its state happens.

The main difference from the callback pattern is that the subject can actually notify multiple observers, while a traditional continuation-passing style callback will usually propagate its result to only one listener, the callback.

The EventEmitter class

In traditional object-oriented programming, the observer pattern requires interfaces, concrete classes, and a hierarchy; in Node.js, all becomes much simpler. The observer pattern is already built into the core and is available through the EventEmitter class. The EventEmitter class allows us to register one or more functions as listeners, which will be invoked when a particular event type is fired. The following image visually explains the concept:

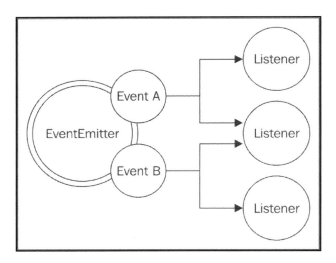

The EventEmitter is a prototype and it is exported from the events core module. The following code shows how we can obtain a reference to it:

```
const EventEmitter = require('events').EventEmitter;
const eeInstance = new EventEmitter();
```

The essential methods of the EventEmitter are given as follows:

- on(event, listener): This method allows you to register a new listener (a function) for the given event type (a string)
- once(event, listener): This method registers a new listener, which is then removed after the event is emitted for the first time

- `emit(event, [arg1], [...])`: This method produces a new event and provides additional arguments to be passed to the listeners
- `removeListener(event, listener)`: This method removes a listener for the specified event type

All the preceding methods will return the `EventEmitter` instance to allow chaining. The listener function has the signature `function([arg1], [...])`, so it simply accepts the arguments provided the moment the event is emitted. Inside the listener, this refers to the instance of the `EventEmitter` that produces the event.

We can already see that there is a big difference between a listener and a traditional Node.js callback; in particular, the first argument is not an error, but it can be any data passed to `emit()` at the moment of its invocation.

Creating and using EventEmitter

Let's see how we can use an `EventEmitter` in practice. The simplest way is to create a new instance and use it immediately. The following code shows a function that uses an `EventEmitter` to notify its subscribers in real time when a particular pattern is found in a list of files:

```
const EventEmitter = require('events').EventEmitter;
const fs = require('fs');

function findPattern(files, regex) {
  const emitter = new EventEmitter();
  files.forEach(function(file) {
    fs.readFile(file, 'utf8', (err, content) => {
      if(err)
        return emitter.emit('error', err);

      emitter.emit('fileread', file);
      let match;
      if(match = content.match(regex))
        match.forEach(elem => emitter.emit('found', file, elem));
    });
  });
  return emitter;
}
```

The EventEmittercreated by the preceding function will produce three events:

- fileread: This event occurs when a file is read
- found: This event occurs when a match has been found
- error: This event occurs when an error has occurred during the reading of the file

Let's see now how our findPattern() function can be used:

```
findPattern(
    ['fileA.txt', 'fileB.json'],
    /hello \w+/g
)
.on('fileread', file => console.log(file + ' was read'))
.on('found', (file, match) => console.log('Matched "' + match +
    '" in file ' + file))
.on('error', err => console.log('Error emitted: ' + err.message));
```

In the preceding example, we registered a listener for each of the three event types produced by the EventEmitter which was created by our findPattern() function.

Propagating errors

The EventEmitter, as it happens for callbacks, cannot just throw exceptions when an error condition occurs, as they would be lost in the event loop if the event is emitted asynchronously. Instead, the convention is to emit a special event, called error, and to pass an Error object as an argument. That's exactly what we are doing in the findPattern() function that we defined earlier.

It is always best practice to register a listener for the error event, as Node.js will treat it in a special way and will automatically throw an exception and exit from the program if no associated listener is found.

Making any object observable

Sometimes, creating a new observable object directly from the EventEmitter class is not enough, as this makes it impractical to provide functionality that goes beyond the mere production of new events. It is more common, in fact, to have the need to make a generic object observable; this is possible by extending the EventEmitter class.

To demonstrate this pattern, let's try to implement the functionality of the findPattern() function in an object as follows:

```
const EventEmitter = require('events').EventEmitter;
const fs = require('fs');

class FindPattern extends EventEmitter {
  constructor (regex) {
    super();
    this.regex = regex;
    this.files = [];
  }

  addFile (file) {
    this.files.push(file);
    return this;
  }

  find () {
    this.files.forEach( file => {
      fs.readFile(file, 'utf8', (err, content) => {
        if (err) {
          return this.emit('error', err);
        }

        this.emit('fileread', file);

        let match = null;
        if (match = content.match(this.regex)) {
          match.forEach(elem => this.emit('found', file, elem));
        }
      });
    });
    return this;
  }
}
```

The `FindPattern` prototype that we defined extends `EventEmitter` using the `inherits()` function provided by the core module `util`. In this way it becomes a fully-fledged observable class. The following is an example of its usage:

```
const findPatternObject = new FindPattern(/hello \w+/);
findPatternObject
  .addFile('fileA.txt')
  .addFile('fileB.json')
  .find()
  .on('found', (file, match) => console.log(`Matched "${match}"
    in file ${file}`))
  .on('error', err => console.log(`Error emitted ${err.message}`));
```

We can now see how the `FindPattern` object has a full set of methods, in addition to being observable, by inheriting the functionality of `EventEmitter`.

This is a pretty common pattern in the Node.js ecosystem, for example, the `Server` object of the core HTTP module defines methods such as `listen()`, `close()`, `setTimeout()`, and internally it also inherits from the `EventEmitter` function, thus allowing it to produce events, such as `request`, when a new request is received; or `connection`, when a new connection is established; or `closed`, when the server is closed.

Other notable examples of objects extending `EventEmitter` are Node.js streams. We will analyze streams in more detail in `Chapter 5`, *Coding with Streams*.

Synchronous and asynchronous events

As with callbacks, events can be emitted synchronously or asynchronously. It is crucial that we never mix the two approaches in the same `EventEmitter`, but even more important, when emitting the same event type, to avoid producing the same problems that we described in the *Unleashing Zalgo* section.

The main difference between emitting synchronous and asynchronous events lies in the way listeners can be registered. When the events are emitted asynchronously, the program has all the time to register new listeners even after `EventEmitter` is initialized, because the events are guaranteed not to be fired until the next cycle of the event loop. That's exactly what is happening in the `findPattern()` function. We defined this function previously and it represents a common approach that is used in most Node.js modules.

On the contrary, emitting events synchronously requires that all the listeners are registered before the `EventEmitter` function starts to emit any event. Let's look at an example:

```
const EventEmitter = require('events').EventEmitter;

class SyncEmit extends EventEmitter {
  constructor() {
    super();
    this.emit('ready');
  }
}

const syncEmit = new SyncEmit();
syncEmit.on('ready', () => console.log('Object is ready to be  used'));
```

If the `ready` event was emitted asynchronously, then the previous code would have worked perfectly; however, the event is produced synchronously and the listener is registered after the event was already sent, so the result is that the listener is never invoked; the code will print nothing to the console.

There are situations where using an `EventEmitter` function in a synchronous fashion makes sense, given its different purpose. For this reason, it's very important to clearly highlight the behavior of our `EventEmitter` in its documentation to avoid confusion, and potentially incorrect usage.

EventEmitter versus callbacks

A common dilemma when defining an asynchronous API is to check whether to use an `EventEmitter` or simply accept a callback. The general differentiating rule is semantic: callbacks should be used when a result must be returned in an asynchronous way; events should instead be used when there is a need to communicate that something has just happened.

But besides this simple principle, a lot of confusion is generated from the fact that the two paradigms are, most of the time, equivalent and allow you to achieve the same results. Consider the following code as an example:

```
function helloEvents() {
  const eventEmitter= new EventEmitter();
  setTimeout(() => eventEmitter.emit('hello', 'hello world'), 100);
  return eventEmitter;
}

function helloCallback(callback) {
  setTimeout(() => callback('hello world'), 100);
}
```

The two functions `helloEvents()` and `helloCallback()` can be considered equivalent in terms of functionality; the first communicates the completion of the timeout using an event, the second uses a callback to notify the caller instead, passing the event type as an argument. But what really differentiates them is the readability, the semantics, and the amount of code that is required to be implemented or used. While we cannot give a deterministic set of rules to choose between one style or the other, we can certainly provide some hints to help you take a decision.

As a first observation, we can say that callbacks have some limitations when it comes to supporting different types of events. In fact, we can still differentiate between multiple events by passing the type as an argument of the callback, or by accepting several callbacks, one for each supported event. However, this cannot exactly be considered an elegant API. In this situation, `EventEmitter` can give a better interface and leaner code.

Another case where `EventEmitter` might be preferable is when the same event can occur multiple times, or not occur at all. A callback, in fact, is expected to be invoked exactly once, whether the operation is successful or not. The fact that we have a possibly repeating circumstance should let us think again about the semantic nature of the occurrence, which is more similar to an event that has to be communicated rather than a result; in this case `EventEmitter` is the preferred choice.

Lastly, an API using callbacks can notify only a particular callback, while using an `EventEmitter` function is possible for multiple listeners to receive the same notification.

Combining callbacks and EventEmitter

There are also some circumstances where EventEmitter can be used in conjunction with a callback. This pattern is extremely useful when we want to implement the principle of *small surface area* by exporting a traditional asynchronous function as the main functionality, while still providing richer features and more control by returning EventEmitter. One example of this pattern is offered by the node-glob module (https://npmjs.org/packa ge/glob), a library that performs glob-style file searches. The main entry point of the module is the function it exports, which has the following signature:

```
glob(pattern, [options], callback)
```

The function takes pattern as the first argument, a set of options, and a callback function that is invoked with the list of all the files matching the provided pattern. At the same time, the function returns EventEmitter that provides a more fine-grained report over the state of the process. For example, it is possible to be notified in real-time when a match occurs by listening to the match event, to obtain the list of all the matched files with the end event, or to know whether the process was manually aborted by listening to the abort event. The following code shows how this looks:

```
const glob = require('glob');
glob('data/*.txt', (error, files) => console.log(`All files found:
  ${JSON.stringify(files)}`))
  .on('match', match => console.log(`Match found: ${match}`));
```

As we can see, the practice of exposing a simple, clean, and minimal entry point while still providing more advanced or less important features with secondary means is quite common in Node.js, and combining EventEmitter with traditional callbacks is one of the ways to achieve that.

Pattern
Create a function that accepts a callback and returns EventEmitter, thus providing a simple and clear entry point for the main functionality, while emitting more fine-grained events using EventEmitter.

Summary

In this chapter, we first learnt the difference between synchronous and asynchronous code. Then we explored how to use the callback and the event emitter patterns to deal with some basic asynchronous scenarios. We also learned the main differences between the two patterns and when one is more suitable than the other to address a specific problem. We just made the first steps toward more advanced asynchronous patterns.

In the next chapter we will have a look at more complex scenarios, learning how to leverage the callback and the event emitter patterns to deal with advanced asynchronous control flows.

3
Asynchronous Control Flow Patterns with Callbacks

Moving from a synchronous programming style to a platform such as Node.js, where continuation-passing style and asynchronous APIs are the norm, can be frustrating. Writing asynchronous code can be a different experience, especially when it comes to control flow. Asynchronous code might make it hard to predict the order in which statements are executed within Node.js applications, so simple problems such as iterating over a set of files, executing tasks in sequence, or waiting for a set of operations to complete require the developer to take new approaches and techniques to avoid ending up writing inefficient and unreadable code. One common mistake is to fall into the trap of the callback hell problem and see the code growing horizontally rather than vertically, with a nesting that makes even simple routines hard to read and maintain.

In this chapter, we will see how it's actually possible to tame callbacks and write clean, manageable asynchronous code by using some discipline and with the aid of some patterns. We will see how control flow libraries, such as `async`, can significantly simplify our problems making our code much more readable and maintainable.

The difficulties of asynchronous programming

Losing control of asynchronous code in JavaScript is undoubtedly easy. Closures and in-place definitions of anonymous functions allow a smooth programming experience that doesn't require the developer to jump to other points in the code base. This is perfectly in line with the KISS principle; it's simple, it keeps the code flowing, and we get it working in less time. Unfortunately, sacrificing qualities such as modularity, reusability, and maintainability will sooner or later lead to the uncontrolled proliferation of callback nesting, the growth in the size of functions, and will lead to poor code organization. Most of the time, creating closures is not functionally needed, so it's more a matter of discipline than a problem related to asynchronous programming. Recognizing that our code is becoming unwieldy, or even better, knowing in advance that it might become unwieldy and then acting accordingly with the most adequate solution is what differentiates a novice from an expert.

Creating a simple web spider

To explain the problem, we will create a little web spider, a command-line application that takes in a web URL as input and downloads its contents locally into a file. In the code presented in this chapter, we are going to use a few npm dependencies:

- `request`: A library to streamline HTTP calls
- `mkdirp`: A small utility to create directories recursively

Also, we will often refer to a local module named `./utilities`, which contains some helpers which we will be using in our application. We omit the contents of this file for brevity, but you can find the full implementation, along with a `package.json` file containing the full list of dependencies, in the download pack for this book available at:

`http://www.packtpub.com`.

The core functionality of our application is contained inside a module named `spider.js`. Let's see how it looks. To start with, let's load all the dependencies that we are going to use:

```
const request = require('request');
const fs = require('fs');
const mkdirp = require('mkdirp');
const path = require('path');
const utilities = require('./utilities');
```

Next, we create a new function named `spider()`, which takes in the URL to download and a callback function that will be invoked when the download process completes:

```
function spider(url, callback) {
  const filename = utilities.urlToFilename(url);
  fs.exists(filename, exists => {                    //[1]
    if(!exists) {
      console.log(`Downloading ${url}`);
      request(url, (err, response, body) => {        //[2]
        if(err) {
          callback(err);
        } else {
          mkdirp(path.dirname(filename), err => {    //[3]
            if(err) {
              callback(err);
            } else {
              fs.writeFile(filename, body, err => {  //[4]
                if(err) {
                  callback(err);
                } else {
                  callback(null, filename, true);
                }
              });
            }
          });
        }
      });
    } else {
      callback(null, filename, false);
    }
  });
}
```

The preceding function executes the following tasks:

1. Checks if the URL was already downloaded by verifying that the corresponding file was not already created:

   ```
   fs.exists(filename, exists => ...
   ```

2. If the file is not found, the URL is downloaded using the following line of code:

   ```
   request(url, (err, response, body) => ...
   ```

3. Then, we make sure whether the directory that will contain the file exists or not:

```
mkdirp(path.dirname(filename), err => ...
```

4. Finally, we write the body of the HTTP response to the filesystem:

```
fs.writeFile(filename, body, err => ...
```

To complete our web spider application, we just need to invoke the `spider()` function by providing a URL as an input (in our case, we read it from the command-line arguments):

```
spider(process.argv[2], (err, filename, downloaded) => {
  if(err) {
    console.log(err);
  } else if(downloaded){
    console.log(`Completed the download of "${filename}"`);
  } else {
    console.log(`"${filename}" was already downloaded`);
  }
});
```

Now we are ready to try our web spider application, but first, make sure you have the `utilities.js` module and the `package.json` containing the full list of dependencies in your `project` directory. Then, install all the dependencies by running the following command:

```
npm install
```

Next, we can execute the `spider` module to download the contents of a web page, with a command like this:

```
node spider http://www.example.com
```

 Our web spider application requires that we always include the protocol (for example, `http://`) in the URL we provide. Also, do not expect HTML links to be rewritten or resources such as images to be downloaded as this is just a simple example to demonstrate how asynchronous programming works.

The callback hell

Looking at the `spider()` function we defined earlier, we can surely notice that even though the algorithm we implemented is really straightforward, the resulting code has several levels of indentation and is very hard to read. Implementing a similar function with a direct style blocking API would be straightforward, and there would be very few chances to make it look so wrong. However, using asynchronous CPS is another story, and making bad use of closures can lead to incredibly bad code.

The situation where the abundance of closures and in-place callback definitions transform the code into an unreadable and unmanageable blob is known as **callback hell**. It's one of the most well recognized and severe anti-patterns in Node.js and JavaScript in general. The typical structure of a code affected by this problem looks like the following:

```
asyncFoo( err => {
  asyncBar( err => {
    asyncFooBar( err => {
      //...
    });
  });
});
```

We can see how code written in this way assumes the shape of a pyramid due to the deep nesting and that's why it is also colloquially known as the **pyramid of doom**.

The most evident problem with code such as the preceding snippet, is the poor readability. Due to the nesting being too deep, it's almost impossible to keep track of where a function ends and where another one begins.

Another issue is caused by the overlapping of the variable names used in each scope. Often, we have to use similar or even identical names to describe the content of a variable. The best example is the error argument received by each callback. Some people often try to use variations of the same name to differentiate the object in each scope, for example, `err`, `error`, `err1`, `err2`, and so on; others prefer to just hide the variable defined in the scope by always using the same name; for example, `err`. Both alternatives are far from perfect, and cause confusion and increase the probability of introducing defects.

Also, we have to keep in mind that closures come at a small price in terms of performance and memory consumption. In addition, they can create memory leaks that are not so easy to identify because we shouldn't forget that any context referenced by an active closure is retained from garbage collection.

 For a great introduction to how closures work in V8 you can refer to the blog post by Vyacheslav Egorov, a software engineer at Google working on V8, at `http://mrale.ph/blog/2012/09/23/grokking-v8-closures-for-fun.html`.

If we look at our `spider()` function, we will notice that it clearly represents a callback hell situation and has all the problems we just described. That's exactly what we are going to fix with the patterns and techniques we will learn in this chapter.

Using plain JavaScript

Now that we have met our first example of callback hell, we know what we should definitely avoid; however, that's not the only concern when writing asynchronous code. In fact, there are several situations where controlling the flow of a set of asynchronous tasks requires the use of specific patterns and techniques, especially if we are only using plain JavaScript without the aid of any external library. For example, iterating over a collection by applying an asynchronous operation in sequence is not as easy as invoking `forEach()` over an array, but it actually requires a technique similar to a recursion.

In this section, we will learn not only about how to avoid callback hell but also how to implement some of the most common control flow patterns using only simple and plain JavaScript.

Callback discipline

When writing asynchronous code, the first rule to keep in mind is to not abuse closures when defining callbacks. It can be tempting to do so, because it does not require any additional thinking for problems such as modularization and reusability; however, we have seen how this can have more disadvantages than advantages. Most of the time, fixing the callback hell problem does not require any libraries, fancy techniques, or change of paradigm, but just some common sense.

These are some basic principles that can help us keep the nesting level low and improve the organization of our code in general:

- You must exit as soon as possible. Use `return`, `continue`, or `break`, depending on the context, to immediately exit the current statement instead of writing (and nesting) complete `if...else` statements. This will help keep our code shallow.
- You need to create named functions for callbacks, keeping them out of closures and passing intermediate results as arguments. Naming our functions will also make them look better in stack traces.
- You need to modularize the code. Split the code into smaller, reusable functions whenever it's possible.

Applying the callback discipline

To demonstrate the power of the earlier mentioned principles, let's apply them to fix the callback hell problem in our web spider application.

For the first step, we can refactor our error-checking pattern by removing the `else` statement. This is made possible by returning from the function immediately after we receive an error. So, instead of having code such as the following:

```
if(err) {
  callback(err);
} else {
  //code to execute when there are no errors
}
```

We can improve the organization of our code by writing the following one instead:

```
if(err) {
  return callback(err);
}
//code to execute when there are no errors
```

With this simple trick, we immediately have a reduction of the nesting level of our functions; it is easy and doesn't require any complex refactoring.

A common mistake when executing the optimization we just described is forgetting to terminate the function after the callback is invoked. For the error-handling scenario, the following code is a typical source of defects:

```
if(err) {
    callback(err);
} //code to execute when there are no errors.
```

We should never forget that the execution of our function will continue even after we invoke the callback. It is then important to insert a return instruction to block the execution of the rest of the function. Also note that it doesn't really matter what output is returned by the function; the real result (or error) is produced asynchronously and passed to the callback. The return value of the asynchronous function is usually ignored. This property allows us to write shortcuts such as the following:

```
return callback(...)
```

Otherwise we'd have to write slightly more verbose ones such as the following:

```
callback(...)
return;
```

As a second optimization for our `spider()` function, we can try to identify reusable pieces of code. For example, the functionality that writes a given string to a file can be easily factored out into a separate function as follows:

```
function saveFile(filename, contents, callback) {
  mkdirp(path.dirname(filename), err => {
    if(err) {
      return callback(err);
    }
    fs.writeFile(filename, contents, callback);
  });
}
```

Following the same principle, we can create a generic function named `download()` which takes a URL and a filename as input, and downloads the URL into the given file. Internally, we can use the `saveFile()` function we created earlier.

```
function download(url, filename, callback) {
  console.log(`Downloading ${url}`);
  request(url, (err, response, body) => {
    if(err) {
      return callback(err);
    }
```

```
    saveFile(filename, body, err => {
      if(err) {
        return callback(err);
      }
      console.log(`Downloaded and saved: ${url}`);
      callback(null, body);
    });
  });
}
```

For the last step, we modify the `spider()` function, which, thanks to our changes, will now look like the following:

```
function spider(url, callback) {
  const filename = utilities.urlToFilename(url);
  fs.exists(filename, exists => {
    if(exists) {
      return callback(null, filename, false);
    }
    download(url, filename, err => {
      if(err) {
        return callback(err);
      }
      callback(null, filename, true);
    })
  });
}
```

The functionality and the interface of the `spider()` function remain exactly the same; what changed is only the way the code was organized. By applying the basic principles that we discussed, we were able to drastically reduce the nesting of our code and at the same time increase its reusability and testability. In fact, we could think of exporting both `saveFile()` and `download()`, so that we can reuse them in other modules. This also allows us to test their functionality more easily.

The refactoring we carried out in this section clearly demonstrates that most of the time, all we need is just some discipline to make sure we do not abuse closures and anonymous functions. It works brilliantly, requires minimal effort, and just uses plain JavaScript.

Sequential execution

We now begin our exploration of the asynchronous control flow patterns. We will start by analyzing the sequential execution flow.

Executing a set of tasks in sequence means running them one at a time, one after the other. The order of execution matters and must be preserved, because the result of a task in the list may affect the execution of the next. The following image illustrates this concept:

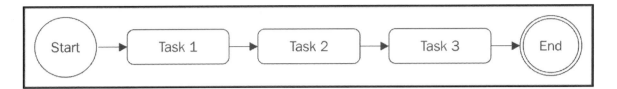

There are different variations of this flow:

- Executing a set of known tasks in sequence, without chaining or propagating results
- Using the output of a task as the input for the next (also known as *chain*, *pipeline*, or *waterfall*)
- Iterating over a collection while running an asynchronous task on each element, one after the other

Sequential execution, despite being trivial when implemented using the direct style blocking API, is usually the main cause of the callback hell problem when using asynchronous CPS.

Executing a known set of tasks in sequence

We already met a sequential execution while implementing the `spider()` function in the previous section. By applying the simple rules that we studied, we were able to organize a set of known tasks in a sequential execution flow. Taking that code as a guideline, we can then generalize the solution with the following pattern:

```
function task1(callback) {
  asyncOperation(() => {
    task2(callback);
  });
}

function task2(callback) {
  asyncOperation(result () => {
    task3(callback);
  });
}
```

```
function task3(callback) {
  asyncOperation(() => {
    callback(); //finally executes the callback
  });
}

task1(() => {
  //executed when task1, task2 and task3 are completed
  console.log('tasks 1, 2 and 3 executed');
});
```

The preceding pattern shows how each task invokes the next upon the completion of a generic asynchronous operation. The pattern puts the emphasis on the modularization of tasks, showing how closures are not always necessary to handle asynchronous code.

Sequential iteration

The pattern we described earlier works perfectly if we know in advance what and how many tasks are to be executed. This allows us to hardcode the invocation of the next task in the sequence; but what happens if we want to execute an asynchronous operation for each item in a collection? In cases such as this, we cannot hardcode the task sequence anymore; instead, we have to build it dynamically.

Web spider version 2

To show an example of sequential iteration, let's introduce a new feature to the web spider application. We now want to download all the links contained in a web page recursively. To do that, we are going to extract all the links from the page and then trigger our web spider on each one of them recursively and in sequence.

The first step is modifying our spider() function so that it triggers a recursive download of all the links of a page by using a function named spiderLinks(), which we are going to create shortly.

Also, instead of checking if the file already exists, we now try to read it, and start spidering its links; this way, we are able to resume interrupted downloads. As a final change, we make sure we propagate a new parameter, nesting, which helps us limit the recursion depth. The resultant code is as follows:

```
function spider(url, nesting, callback) {
  const filename = utilities.urlToFilename(url);
  fs.readFile(filename, 'utf8', (err, body) => {
    if(err) {
      if(err.code ! == 'ENOENT') {
        return callback(err);
      }

      return download(url, filename, (err, body) => {
        if(err) {
          return callback(err);
        }
        spiderLinks(url, body, nesting, callback);
      });
    }

    spiderLinks(url, body, nesting, callback);
  });
}
```

Sequential crawling of links

Now we can create the core of this new version of our web spider application, the spiderLinks() function, which downloads all the links of an HTML page using a sequential asynchronous iteration algorithm. Pay attention to the way we are going to define that in the following code block:

```
function spiderLinks(currentUrl, body, nesting, callback) {
  if(nesting === 0) {
    return process.nextTick(callback);
  }
  const links = utilities.getPageLinks(currentUrl, body);  //[1]
  function iterate(index) {                                 //[2]
    if(index === links.length) {
      return callback();
    }

    spider(links[index], nesting - 1, err => {              //[3]
      if(err) {
        return callback(err);
      }
```

```
        iterate(index + 1);
      });
  }
  iterate(0);                                            //[4]
}
```

The important steps to understand from this new function are as follows:

1. We obtain the list of all the links contained in the page using the `utilities.getPageLinks()` function. This function returns only the links pointing to an internal destination (same hostname).
2. We iterate over the links using a local function called `iterate()`, which takes the index of the next link to analyze. In this function, the first thing we do is check if the index is equal to the length of the `links` array, in which case we immediately invoke the `callback()` function, as it means we processed all the items.
3. At this point, everything should be ready for processing the link. We invoke the `spider()` function by decreasing the nesting level and invoking the next step of the iteration when the operation completes.
4. As the last step in the `spiderLinks()` function, we bootstrap the iteration by invoking `iterate(0)`.

The algorithm we just presented allows us to iterate over an array by executing an asynchronous operation in sequence, which in our case is the `spider()` function.

We can now try this new version of the spider application and watch it download all the links of a web page recursively, one after the other. To interrupt the process, which can take a while if there are many links, remember that we can always use *Ctrl + C*. If we then decide to resume it, we can do so by launching the spider application and providing the same URL we used for the first run.

 Now that our web spider application might potentially trigger the download of an entire website, please consider using it carefully. For example, do not set a high nesting level or leave the spider running for more than a few seconds. It is not polite to overload a server with thousands of requests. In some circumstances this can also be considered illegal. Spider responsibly!

The pattern

The code of the `spiderLinks()` function that we showed previously is a clear example of how it's possible to iterate over a collection while applying an asynchronous operation. We can also notice that it's a pattern that can be adapted to any other situation where we have the need to iterate asynchronously in sequence over the elements of a collection or in general over a list of tasks. This pattern can be generalized as follows:

```
function iterate(index) {
  if(index === tasks.length)  {
    return finish();
  }
  const task = tasks[index];
  task(function() {
    iterate(index + 1);
  });
}

function finish() {
  //iteration completed
}

iterate(0);
```

 It's important to notice that these types of algorithm become really recursive if `task()` is a synchronous operation. In such a case, the stack will not unwind at every cycle and there might be a risk of hitting the maximum call stack size limit.

The pattern we just presented is very powerful as it can adapt to several situations; for example, we can map the values of an array or we can pass the results of an operation to the next one in the iteration to implement a reduce algorithm, we can quit the loop prematurely if a particular condition is met, or we can even iterate over an infinite number of elements.

We could also choose to generalize the solution even further by wrapping it into a function having a signature such as the following:

```
iterateSeries(collection, iteratorCallback, finalCallback)
```

We leave this to you as an exercise.

Pattern (sequential iterator)
Execute a list of tasks in sequence by creating a function named `iterator`, which invokes the next available task in the collection and makes sure to invoke the next step of the iteration when the current task completes.

Parallel execution

There are some situations where the order of execution of a set of asynchronous tasks is not important and all we want is just to be notified when all those running tasks are completed. Such situations are better handled using a parallel execution flow, as shown in the following diagram:

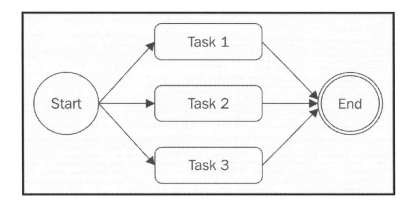

This may sound strange if we consider that Node.js is single threaded, but if we remember what we discussed in `Chapter 1`, *Welcome to the Node.js Platform*, we realize that even though we have just one thread, we can still achieve concurrency, thanks to the non-blocking nature of Node.js. In fact, the word *parallel* is used improperly in this case, as it does not mean that the tasks run simultaneously, but rather that their execution is carried out by an underlying non-blocking API and interleaved by the event loop.

As we know, a task gives control back to the event loop when it requests a new asynchronous operation allowing the event loop to execute another task. The proper word to use for this kind of flow is *concurrency*, but we will still use parallel for simplicity.

The following diagram shows how two asynchronous tasks can run in parallel in a Node.js program:

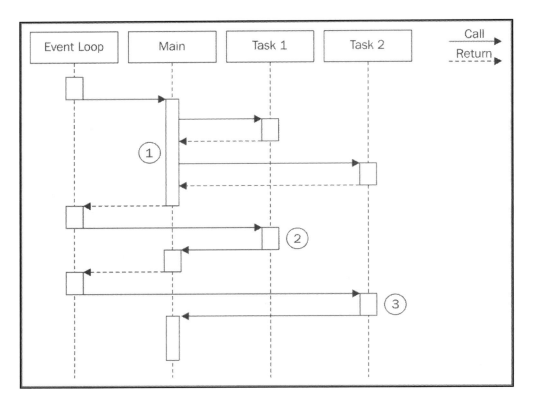

In the previous image, we have a **Main** function that executes two asynchronous tasks:

1. The **Main** function triggers the execution of **Task 1** and **Task 2**. As these trigger an asynchronous operation, they immediately return the control back to the **Main** function, which then returns it to the event loop.

2. When the asynchronous operation of **Task 1** is completed, the event loop gives control to it. When **Task 1** completes its internal synchronous processing as well, it notifies the **Main** function.

3. When the asynchronous operation triggered by **Task 2** is completed, the event loop invokes its callback, giving the control back to **Task 2**. At the end of **Task 2**, the **Main** function is again notified. At this point, the **Main** function knows that both **Task 1** and **Task 2** are complete, so it can continue its execution or return the results of the operations to another callback.

In short, this means that in Node.js, we can only execute in parallel asynchronous operations, because their concurrency is handled internally by the non-blocking APIs. In Node.js, synchronous (blocking) operations cannot run concurrently unless their execution is interleaved with an asynchronous operation, or deferred with `setTimeout()` or `setImmediate()`. We will see this in more detail in `Chapter 9`, *Advanced Asynchronous Recipes*.

Web spider version 3

Our web spider application seems like a perfect candidate to apply the concept of parallel execution. So far, our application is executing the recursive download of the linked pages in a sequential fashion. We can easily improve the performance of this process by downloading all the linked pages in parallel.

To do that, we just need to modify the `spiderLinks()` function to make sure to spawn all the `spider()` tasks at once, and then invoke the final callback only when all of them have completed their execution. So let's modify our `spiderLinks()` function as follows:

```
function spiderLinks(currentUrl, body, nesting, callback) {
  if(nesting === 0) {
    return process.nextTick(callback);
  }
  const links = utilities.getPageLinks(currentUrl, body);
  if(links.length === 0) {
    return process.nextTick(callback);
  }

  let completed = 0, hasErrors = false;

  function done(err) {
    if(err) {
      hasErrors = true;
      return callback(err);
    }
    if(++completed === links.length && !hasErrors) {
      return callback();
    }
  }

  links.forEach(link => {
    spider(link, nesting - 1, done);
  });
}
```

Let's explain what we changed. As we mentioned earlier, the `spider()` tasks are now started all at once. This is possible by simply iterating over the links array and starting each task without waiting for the previous one to finish:

```
links.forEach(link => {
  spider(link, nesting - 1, done);
});
```

Then, the trick to make our application wait for all the tasks to complete is to provide the `spider()` function with a special callback, which we call `done()`. The `done()` function increases a counter when a `spider` task completes. When the number of completed downloads reaches the size of the `links` array, the final callback is invoked:

```
function done(err) {
  if(err) {
    hasErrors = true;
    return callback(err);
  }
  if(++completed === links.length && !hasErrors) {
    callback();
  }
}
```

With these changes in place, if we now try to run our spider against a web page, we will notice a huge improvement in the speed of the overall process, as every download is carried out in parallel without waiting for the previous link to be processed.

The pattern

Also, for the parallel execution flow, we can extract our nice little pattern, which we can adapt and reuse for different situations. We can represent a generic version of the pattern with the following code:

```
const tasks = [ /* ... */ ];
let completed = 0;
tasks.forEach(task => {
  task(() => {
    if(++completed === tasks.length) {
      finish();
    }
  });
});

function finish() {
  //all the tasks completed
```

```
}
```

With small modifications, we can adapt the pattern to accumulate the results of each task into a collection, to filter or map the elements of an array, or to invoke the finish() callback as soon as one or a given number of tasks complete (this last situation in particular is called **competitive race**).

 Pattern (unlimited parallel execution)
Run a set of asynchronous tasks in parallel by spawning them all at once, and then wait for all of them to complete by counting the number of times their callbacks are invoked.

Fixing race conditions with concurrent tasks

Running a set of tasks in parallel can cause issues when using blocking I/O in combination with multiple threads. However, we have just seen that in Node.js this is a totally different story; running multiple asynchronous tasks in parallel is in fact straightforward and cheap in terms of resources. This is one of the most important strengths for Node.js, because it makes parallelization a common practice rather than a complex technique to only use when strictly necessary.

Another important characteristic of the concurrency model of Node.js is the way we deal with task synchronization and race conditions. In multithreaded programming, this is usually done using constructs such as locks, mutexes, semaphores, and monitors, and it can be one of the most complex aspects of parallelization, which has considerable impact on performances as well. In Node.js, we usually don't need a fancy synchronization mechanism, as everything runs on a single thread! However, this doesn't mean that we can't have race conditions; on the contrary, they can be quite common. The root of the problem is the delay between the invocation of an asynchronous operation and the notification of its result. To make a concrete example, we can refer again to our web spider application, in particular, the last version we created, which actually contains a race condition (can you spot it?).

The problem we are talking about lies in the spider() function, where we check if a file already exists, before starting to download the corresponding URL:

```
function spider(url, nesting, callback) {
  const filename = utilities.urlToFilename(url);
  fs.readFile(filename, 'utf8', (err, body) => {
    if(err) {
      if(err.code !== 'ENOENT') {
        return callback(err);
      }
```

```
        return download(url, filename, function(err, body) {
//...
```

The problem is that, two `spider` tasks operating on the same URL might invoke `fs.readFile()` on the same file before one of the two tasks completes the download and creates a file, causing both tasks to start a download. This situation is shown in the following diagram:

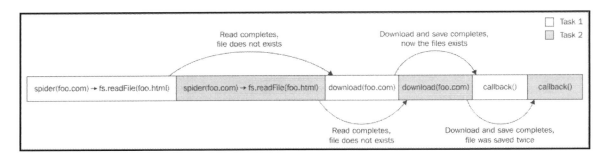

The preceding diagram shows how **Task 1** and **Task 2** are interleaved in the single thread of Node.js and how an asynchronous operation can actually introduce a race condition. In our case, the two `spider` tasks end up downloading the same file.

How can we fix that? The answer is much simpler than we might think. In fact, all we need is a variable to mutually exclude multiple `spider()` tasks running on the same URL. This can be achieved with some code such as the following:

```
const spidering = new Map();
function spider(url, nesting, callback) {
  if(spidering.has(url)) {
    return process.nextTick(callback);
  }
  spidering.set(url, true);

//...
```

The fix does not require many comments. We simply exit the function immediately if the flag for the given `url` is set in the `spidering` map; otherwise, we set the flag and continue with the download. For our case, we don't need to release the lock, as we are not interested in downloading a URL twice, even if the `spider` tasks are executed at two completely different points in time.

Race conditions can cause many problems, even if we are in a single-threaded environment. In some circumstances, they can lead to data corruption and are usually very hard to debug because of their ephemeral nature. So, it's always good practice to double check for this type of situation when running tasks in parallel.

Limited parallel execution

Often, spawning parallel tasks without control can lead to an excessive load. Imagine having thousands of files to read, URLs to access, or database queries to run in parallel. A common problem in such situations is running out of resources, for example, by utilizing all the file descriptors available for an application when trying to open too many files at once. In a web application, it may also create a vulnerability that is exploitable with **Denial of Service (DoS)** attacks. In all such situations, it is a good idea to limit the number of tasks that can run at the same time. This way, we can add some predictability to the load of our server and also make sure that our application will not run out of resources. The following diagram describes a situation where we have five tasks that run in parallel with a concurrency limit of 2:

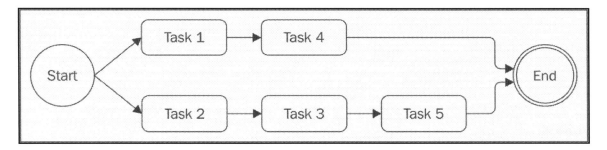

From the preceding figure, it should be clear how our algorithm will work:

1. Initially, we spawn as many tasks as we can without exceeding the concurrency limit.
2. Then, every time a task is completed, we spawn one or more tasks until we don't reach the limit again.

Limiting the concurrency

We now present a pattern to execute a set of given tasks in parallel with limited concurrency:

```
const tasks = ...
let concurrency = 2, running = 0, completed = 0, index = 0;
function next() {                                              //[1]
  while(running < concurrency && index < tasks.length) {
    task = tasks[index++];
    task(() => {                                              //[2]
      if(completed === tasks.length) {
        return finish();
      }
      completed++, running--;
      next();
    });
    running++;
  }
}
next();

function finish() {
  //all tasks finished
}
```

This algorithm can be considered a mix between a sequential execution and a parallel execution. In fact, we might notice similarities with both the patterns we presented earlier in the chapter:

1. We have an `iterator` function, which we called `next()`, and then an inner loop that spawns in parallel as many tasks as possible while staying within the concurrency limit.
2. The next important part is the callback we pass to each task, which checks if we completed all the tasks in the list. If there are still tasks to run, it invokes `next()` to spawn another bunch of tasks.

Pretty simple, isn't it?

Globally limiting the concurrency

Our web spider application is perfect for applying what we learned about limiting the concurrency of a set of tasks. In fact, to avoid the situation in which we have thousands of links crawled at the same time, we can enforce a limit on the concurrency of this process by adding some predictability on the number of concurrent downloads.

 Node.js versions before 0.11 already limit the number of concurrent HTTP connections per host to 5. This can, however, be changed to accommodate our needs. Find out more in the official docs at `http://nodejs.org/docs/v0.10.0/api/http.html#http_agent_m axsockets`. Starting from Node.js 0.11, there is no default limit on the number of concurrent connections.

We could apply the pattern we just learned to our `spiderLinks()` function, but what we would obtain is only limiting the concurrency of a set of links found within one single page. If we chose, for example, a concurrency of 2, we would have at most two links downloaded in parallel for each page. However, as we can download multiple links at once, each page would then spawn another two downloads, causing the grand total of download operations to grow exponentially anyway.

Queues to the rescue

What we really want then, is to limit the global number of download operations we can have running in parallel. We could slightly modify the pattern showed before, but we prefer to leave this as an exercise for you, as we want to take this opportunity to introduce another mechanism, which makes use of **queues** to limit the concurrency of multiple tasks. Let's see how this works.

We are now going to implement a simple class named `TaskQueue`, which will combine a queue with the algorithm we presented before. Let's create a new module named `taskQueue.js`:

```
class TaskQueue {
  constructor(concurrency) {
    this.concurrency = concurrency;
    this.running = 0;
    this.queue = [];
  }

  pushTask(task) {
    this.queue.push(task);
    this.next();
  }
```

```
next() {
  while(this.running < this.concurrency && this.queue.length) {
    const task = this.queue.shift();
    task(() => {
      this.running--;
      this.next();
    });
    this.running++;
  }
}
};
```

The constructor of this class takes as input only the concurrency limit, but besides that, it initializes the variables `running` and `queue`. The former variable is a counter used to keep track of all the running tasks, while the latter is the array that will be used as a queue to store the pending tasks.

The `pushTask()` method simply adds a new task to the queue and then bootstraps the execution of the worker by invoking `this.next()`.

The `next()` method spawns a set of tasks from the queue, ensuring that it does not exceed the concurrency limit.

We might notice that this method has some similarities with the pattern that limits the concurrency we presented earlier. It essentially starts as many tasks from the queue as possible, without exceeding the concurrency limit. When each task is complete, it updates the count of running tasks and then starts another round of tasks by invoking `next()` again. The interesting property of the `TaskQueue` class is that it allows us to dynamically add new items to the queue. The other advantage is that now we have a central entity responsible for the limitation of the concurrency of our tasks, which can be shared across all the instances of a function's execution. In our case, it's the `spider()` function, as we will see in a moment.

Web spider version 4

Now that we have our generic queue to execute tasks in a limited parallel flow, let's use it straightaway in our web spider application. Let's first load the new dependency and create a new instance of the `TaskQueue` class by setting the concurrency limit to 2:

```
const TaskQueue = require('./taskQueue');
const downloadQueue = new TaskQueue(2);
```

Next, we need to update the `spiderLinks()` function so that it can use the newly created `downloadQueue`:

```
function spiderLinks(currentUrl, body, nesting, callback) {
  if(nesting === 0) {
    return process.nextTick(callback);
  }

  const links = utilities.getPageLinks(currentUrl, body);
  if(links.length === 0) {
    return process.nextTick(callback);
  }

  let completed = 0, hasErrors = false;
  links.forEach(link => {
    downloadQueue.pushTask(done => {
      spider(link, nesting - 1, err => {
        if(err) {
          hasErrors= true;
          return callback(err);
        }
        if(++completed === links.length && !hasErrors) {
          callback();
        }
        done();
      });
    });
  });
}
```

This new implementation of the function is extremely easy, and it's very similar to the algorithm for unlimited parallel execution, which we presented earlier in the chapter. This is because we are delegating the concurrency control to the `TaskQueue` object, and the only thing we have to do is to check when all our tasks are complete. The only interesting part in the preceding code is how we defined our tasks:

- We run the `spider()` function by providing a custom callback.
- In the callback, we check if all the tasks relative to this execution of the `spiderLinks()` function are completed. When this condition is `true`, we invoke the final callback of the `spiderLinks()` function.
- At the end of our task, we invoke the `done()` callback so that the queue can continue its execution.

After we have applied these small changes, we can now try to run the `spider` module again. This time, we should notice that no more than two downloads will be active at the same time.

The async library

If we take a look for a moment at every control flow pattern we have analyzed so far, we can see that they could be used as a base to build reusable and more generic solutions. For example, we could wrap the unlimited parallel execution algorithm into a function which accepts a list of tasks, runs them in parallel, and invokes the given callback when all of them are complete. This way of wrapping control flow algorithms into reusable functions can lead to a more declarative and expressive way to define asynchronous control flows, and that's exactly what `async` (`https://npmjs.org/package/async`) does. The `async` library is a very popular solution, in Node.js and JavaScript in general, to deal with asynchronous code. It offers a set of functions that greatly simplify the execution of a set of tasks in different configurations and it also provides useful helpers for dealing with collections asynchronously. Even though there are several other libraries with a similar goal, `async` is a de facto standard in Node.js due to its popularity.

Let's try it straightaway to demonstrate its capabilities.

Sequential execution

The `async` library can help us immensely when implementing complex asynchronous control flows, but one difficulty with it is choosing the right helper for the problem at hand. For example, for the case of the sequential execution flow, there are around 20 different functions to choose from, including `eachSeries()`, `mapSeries()`, `filterSeries()`, `rejectSeries()`, `reduce()`, `reduceRight()`, `detectSeries()`, `concatSeries()`, `series()`, `whilst()`, `doWhilst()`, `until()`, `doUntil()`, `forever()`, `waterfall()`, `compose()`, `seq()`, `applyEachSeries()`, `iterator()`, and `timesSeries()`.

Choosing the right function is an important step in writing more compact and readable code, but this also requires some experience and practice. In our examples, we are going to cover just a few of these situations, but they will still provide a solid base to understand and efficiently use the rest of the library.

Now, to show in practice how `async` works, we are going to adapt our web spider application. Let's start directly with version 2, the one that downloads all the links recursively in sequence.

However, first let's make sure we install the `async` library into our current project:

```
npm install async
```

Then we need to load the new dependency from the `spider.js` module:

```
const async = require('async');
```

Sequential execution of a known set of tasks

Let's modify the `download()` function first. As we have already seen, it executes the following three tasks in sequence:

1. Download the contents of a URL.
2. Create a new directory if it doesn't exist yet.
3. Save the contents of the URL into a file.

The ideal function to use with this flow is definitely `async.series()`, which has the following signature:

```
async.series(tasks, [callback])
```

It takes a list of `tasks` and a `callback` function that is invoked when all the tasks have been completed. Each task is just a function that accepts a `callback` function, which must be invoked when the task completes its execution:

```
function task(callback) {}
```

The nice thing about `async` is that it uses the same callback conventions of Node.js, and it automatically handles error propagation. So, if any of the tasks invoke its callback with an error, `async` will skip the remaining tasks in the list and jump directly to the final callback.

With this in mind, let's see how the `download()` function would change by using `async`:

```
function download(url, filename, callback) {
  console.log(`Downloading ${url}`);
  let body;

  async.series([
    callback => {                                      //[1]
      request(url, (err, response, resBody) => {
        if(err) {
          return callback(err);
        }
        body = resBody;
```

```
      callback();
    });
  },

  mkdirp.bind(null, path.dirname(filename)),        //[2]

  callback => {                                      //[3]
    fs.writeFile(filename, body, callback);
  }
], err => {                                          //[4]
  if(err) {
    return callback(err);
  }
  console.log(`Downloaded and saved: ${url}`);
  callback(null, body);
});
}
```

If we remember the callback hell version of this code, we will surely appreciate the way `async` allows us to organize our tasks. There is no need to nest callbacks anymore, as we just have to provide a flat list of tasks, usually one for each asynchronous operation, which `async` will then execute in sequence. This is how we define each task:

1. The first task involves the download of the URL. Also, we save the `response` body into a closure variable (`body`) so that it can be shared with the other tasks.

2. In the second task, we want to create the directory that will hold the downloaded page. We do this by performing a partial application of the `mkdirp()` function, binding the path of the directory to be created. This way, we can save a few lines of code and increase its readability.

3. At last, we write the contents of the downloaded URL to a file. In this case, we could not perform a partial application (as we did for the second task), because the variable, `body`, is only available after the first task in the series completes. However, we can still save some lines of code by exploiting the automatic error management of `async` by simply passing the callback of the task directly to the `fs.writeFile()` function.

4. After all the tasks are complete, the final callback of `async.series()` is invoked. In our case, we are simply doing some error management and then returning the `body` variable to `callback` of the `download()` function.

For this specific situation, a possible alternative to `async.series()` would be `async.waterfall()`, which still executes the tasks in sequence but in addition, it also provides the output of each task as input to the next. In our situation, we could use this feature to propagate the `body` variable until the end of our sequence. As an exercise, you can try to implement the same function using the waterfall flow and then take a look at the differences.

Sequential iteration

We saw in the previous paragraph how we can execute a set of known tasks in sequence; we used `async.series()` to do that. We could use the same functionality to implement the `spiderLinks()` function of our web spider version 2; however, `async` offers a more appropriate helper for the specific situation in which we have to iterate over a collection; this helper is `async.eachSeries()`. Let's use it then to reimplement our `spiderLinks()` function (version 2, download in series) as follows:

```
function spiderLinks(currentUrl, body, nesting, callback) {
  if(nesting === 0) {
    return process.nextTick(callback);
  }

  const links = utilities.getPageLinks(currentUrl, body);
  if(links.length === 0) {
    return process.nextTick(callback);
  }

  async.eachSeries(links, (link, callback) => {
    spider(link, nesting - 1, callback);
  }, callback);
}
```

If we compare the preceding code, which uses `async`, with the code of the same function implemented with plain JavaScript patterns, we will notice the big advantage that `async` gives us in terms of code organization and readability.

Parallel execution

The `async` library doesn't lack functions to handle parallel flows; among them we can find `each()`, `map()`, `filter()`, `reject()`, `detect()`, `some()`, `every()`, `concat()`, `parallel()`, `applyEach()`, and `times()`. They follow the same logic as the functions we have already seen for sequential execution, with the difference being that the tasks provided are executed in parallel.

To demonstrate that, we can try to apply one of these functions to implement version 3 of our web spider application, the one performing the downloads using an unlimited parallel flow.

If we remember the code we used earlier to implement the sequential version of the `spiderLinks()` function, adapting it to make it work in parallel is a trivial task:

```
function spiderLinks(currentUrl, body, nesting, callback) {
  // ...
  async.each(links, (link, callback) => {
    spider(link, nesting - 1, callback);
  }, callback);
}
```

The function is exactly the same one that we used for the sequential download, but this time we used `async.each()` instead of `async.eachSeries()`. This clearly demonstrates the power of abstracting the asynchronous flow with a library such as `async`. The code is not bound to a particular execution flow anymore; there is no code specifically written for that. Most of it is just application logic.

Limited parallel execution

If you are wondering if `async` can also be used to limit the concurrency of parallel tasks, the answer is yes, it can! We have a few functions we can use for that, namely, `eachLimit()`, `mapLimit()`, `parallelLimit()`, `queue()`, and `cargo()`.

Let's try to exploit one of them to implement version 4 of the web spider application, the one executing the download of the links in parallel with limited concurrency. Fortunately, `async` has `async.queue()`, which works in a similar way to the `TaskQueue` class we created earlier in the chapter. The `async.queue()` function creates a new queue, which uses a `worker()` function to execute a set of tasks with a specified `concurrency` limit:

```
const q = async.queue(worker, concurrency);
```

The `worker()` function receives, as input, `task` to run and a `callback` function to invoke, when the task completes:

```
function worker(task, callback)
```

We should notice that `task` in this case can be anything, not just a function. In fact, it's the responsibility of the worker to handle a task in the most appropriate way. New tasks can be added to the queue by using `q.push(task, callback)`. The callback associated to a task has to be invoked by the worker after the task has been processed.

Now, let's modify our code again to implement a parallel globally limited execution flow, using `async.queue()`. First of all, we need to create a new queue:

```
const downloadQueue = async.queue((taskData, callback) => {
  spider(taskData.link, taskData.nesting - 1, callback);
}, 2);
```

The code is really straightforward. We are just creating a new queue with a concurrency limit of 2, having a worker that simply invokes our `spider()` function with the data associated with a task. Next, we implement the `spiderLinks()` function:

```
function spiderLinks(currentUrl, body, nesting, callback) {
  if(nesting === 0) {
    return process.nextTick(callback);
  }
  const links = utilities.getPageLinks(currentUrl, body);
  if(links.length === 0) {
    return process.nextTick(callback);
  }
  const completed = 0, hasErrors = false;
  links.forEach(function(link) {
    const taskData = {link: link, nesting: nesting};
    downloadQueue.push(taskData, err => {
      if(err) {
        hasErrors = true;
        return callback(err);
      }
      if(++completed === links.length&& !hasErrors) {
        callback();
      }
    });
  });
}
```

The preceding code should look very familiar, as it's almost the same as the one we used to implement the same flow using the `TaskQueue` object. Also, in this case, the important part to analyze is where we push a new task into the queue. At that point, we ensure that we pass a callback that enables us to check if all the download tasks for the current page are completed, and eventually invoke the final callback.

Thanks to `async.queue()`, we could easily replicate the functionality of our `TaskQueue` object, again demonstrating that with `async`, we can really avoid writing asynchronous control flow patterns from scratch, reducing our efforts and saving precious lines of code.

Summary

At the beginning of this chapter, we said that Node.js programming can be tough because of its asynchronous nature, especially for people used to developing on other platforms. However, throughout this chapter we showed how asynchronous APIs can be bent to our will, starting with plain JavaScript, which provided us the foundation for the analysis of more sophisticated techniques. We then saw that the tools at our disposal are indeed variegated and provide good solutions to most of our problems, in addition to offering a programming style for every taste; for example, we may choose `async` to simplify the most common flows.

This chapter served as an introduction to more advanced techniques, such as promises and generators, that will be the main focus of the next chapter. When you know all these techniques, you will be able to choose the best solution for your needs or use many of them together in the same project.

4

Asynchronous Control Flow Patterns with ES2015 and Beyond

In the previous chapter, we learned how to deal with asynchronous code using callbacks and how they can have a bad impact on our code, generating issues such as **callback hell**. Callbacks are the building blocks of asynchronous programming in JavaScript and in Node.js, but over the years, other alternatives have emerged. Those alternatives are more sophisticated in order to be able to deal with asynchronous code in ways that are more convenient.

In this chapter, we are going to explore some of the most famous alternatives, **promises** and **generators**. We will also explore **async await**, an innovative syntax that will be available in JavaScript as part of the release of ECMAScript 2017.

We will see how these alternatives can simplify the way we deal with asynchronous control flows. Finally, we will compare all these approaches in order to understand all the pros and cons of each of them and be able to wisely choose the approach that best suits the requirements of our next Node.js project.

Promise

We mentioned in the previous chapters that **Continuation Passing Style** (**CPS**) is not the only way to write asynchronous code. In fact, the JavaScript ecosystem provides interesting alternatives to the traditional callback pattern. One of the most famous alternatives is promise, which is getting more and more attention, especially now that it is part of ECMAScript 2015 and has been natively available in Node.js since version 4.

What is a promise?

In very simple terms, promise is an abstraction that allows a function to return an object called `promise`, which represents the eventual result of an asynchronous operation. In the promises jargon, we say that a promise is **pending** when the asynchronous operation is not yet complete, it's **fulfilled** when the operation successfully completes, and **rejected** when the operation terminates with an error. Once a promise is either fulfilled or rejected, it's considered **settled**.

To receive the fulfillment value or the error (*reason*) associated with the rejection, we can use the `then()` method of the promise. The following is its signature:

```
promise.then([onFulfilled], [onRejected])
```

In the preceding code, `onFulfilled()` is a function that will eventually receive the fulfillment value of the promise, and `onRejected()` is another function that will receive the reason for the rejection (if any). Both functions are optional.

To have an idea of how promises can transform our code, let's consider the following:

```
asyncOperation(arg, (err, result) => {
  if(err) {
    //handle error
  }
  //do stuff with result
});
```

Promises allow us to transform this typical CPS code into a better structured and more elegant code, such as the following:

```
asyncOperation(arg)
  .then(result => {
    //do stuff with result
  }, err => {
    //handle error
  });
```

One crucial property of the `then()` method is that it synchronously returns another promise. If any of the `onFulfilled()` or `onRejected()` functions return a value *x*, the promise returned by the `then()` method will be as follows:

- Fulfill with *x* if *x* is a value
- Fulfill with the fulfillment value of *x* if *x* is a promise or a thenable
- Reject with the eventual rejection reason of *x* if *x* is a promise or a thenable

 A **thenable** is a promise-like object with a `then()` method. This term is used to indicate a promise that is *foreign* to the particular promise implementation in use.

This feature allows us to build chains of promises, allowing easy aggregation and arrangement of asynchronous operations in several configurations. Also, if we don't specify an `onFulfilled()` or `onRejected()` handler, the fulfillment value or rejection reasons are automatically forwarded to the next promise in the chain. This allows us, for example, to automatically propagate errors across the whole chain until caught by an `onRejected()` handler. With a promise chain, sequential execution of tasks suddenly becomes a trivial operation:

```
asyncOperation(arg)
  .then(result1 => {
    //returns another promise
    return asyncOperation(arg2);
  })
  .then(result2 => {
    //returns a value
    return 'done';
  })
  .then(undefined, err => {
    //any error in the chain is caught here
  });
```

The following diagram provides another perspective on how a promise chain works:

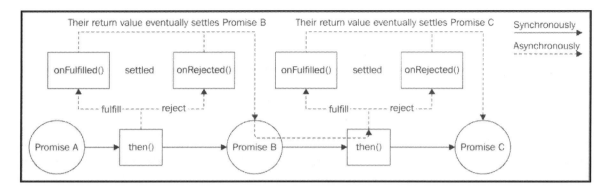

Another important property of promises is that the onFulfilled() and onRejected() functions are guaranteed to be invoked asynchronously, even if we resolve the promise synchronously with a value, as we did in the preceding example, where we returned the string done in the last then() function of the chain. This behavior shields our code against all those situations where we could unintentionally release Zalgo (see Chapter 2, *Node.js Essential Patterns*), making our asynchronous code more consistent and robust with no effort.

Now comes the best part. If an exception is thrown (using the throw statement) in the onFulfilled() or onRejected() handler, the promise returned by the then() method will automatically reject, with the exception thrown as the rejection reason. This is a tremendous advantage over CPS, as it means that with promises, exceptions will propagate automatically across the chain, and that the throw statement is finally usable.

Historically, there have been many different implementations of promise libraries, and most of the time they were not compatible between each other, meaning that it was not possible to create thenable chains between promise objects coming from libraries that were using different promise implementations.

The JavaScript community worked very hard to sort out this limitation and these efforts lead to the creation of the **Promises/A+** specification. This specification details the behavior of the then method, providing an interoperable base, which makes promise objects from different libraries able to work with each other out of the box.

For a detailed description of the **Promises/A+** specification, you can refer to the official website, https://promisesaplus.com.

Promises/A+ implementations

In JavaScript, and also in Node.js, there are several libraries implementing the Promises/A+ specification. The following are the most popular:

- Bluebird (`https://npmjs.org/package/bluebird`)
- Q (`https://npmjs.org/package/q`)
- RSVP (`https://npmjs.org/package/rsvp`)
- Vow (`https://npmjs.org/package/vow`)
- When.js (`https://npmjs.org/package/when`)
- ES2015 promises

What really differentiates them is the additional set of features they provide on top of the Promises/A+ standard. As we said, the standard defines the behavior of the `then()` method and the promise resolution procedure, but it does not specify other functionalities, for example, how a promise is created from a callback-based asynchronous function.

In our examples, we will use the set of APIs implemented by the ES2015 promises, as they have been natively available in Node.js since version 4 without the support of any external libraries.

For reference, here is the list of the APIs provided by ES2015 promises:

Constructor (new Promise(function(resolve, reject) {})): This creates a new promise that fulfills or rejects based on the behavior of the function passed as an argument. The arguments of the constructor are explained as follows:

- `resolve(obj)`: This will resolve the promise with a fulfillment value, which will be `obj` if `obj` is a value. It will be the fulfillment value of `obj` if `obj` is a promise or a thenable.
- `reject(err)`: This rejects the promise with the reason `err`. It is a convention for `err` to be an instance of `Error`.

Static methods of the Promise object:

- `Promise.resolve(obj)`: This creates a new promise from a thenable or a value.
- `Promise.reject(err)`: This creates a promise that rejects with err as the reason.
- `Promise.all(iterable)`: This creates a promise that fulfills with an iterable of fulfillment values when every item in the iterable object fulfills, and rejects with the first rejection reason if any item rejects. Each item in the iterable object can be a promise, a generic thenable, or a value.
- `Promise.race(iterable)`: This returns a promise that resolves or rejects as soon as one of the promises in the iterable resolves or rejects, with the value or reason from that promise.

Methods of a promise instance:

- `promise.then(onFulfilled, onRejected)`: This is the essential method of a promise. Its behavior is compatible with the Promises/A+ standard we described before.
- `promise.catch(onRejected)`: This is just syntactic sugar for `promise.then(undefined, onRejected)`.

 It is worth mentioning that some promise implementations offer another mechanism to create new promises, called **deferreds**. We are not going to describe it here, because it's not part of the ES2015 standard, but if you want to know more, you can read the documentation for Q (`https://github.com/kriskowal/q#using-deferreds`) or When.js (`https://github.com/cujojs/when/wiki/Deferred`).

Promisifying a Node.js style function

In JavaScript, not all the asynchronous functions and libraries support promises out-of-the-box. Most of the time, we have to convert a typical callback-based function into one that returns a promise; this process is also known as **promisification**.

Fortunately, the callback conventions used in Node.js allow us to create a reusable function that we can utilize to promisify any Node.js style API. We can do this easily by using the constructor of the Promise object. Let's then create a new function called promisify() and include it into the utilities.js module (so we can use it later in our web spider application):

```
module.exports.promisify = function(callbackBasedApi) {
  return function promisified() {
    const args = [].slice.call(arguments);
    return new Promise((resolve, reject) => {        //[1]
      args.push((err, result) => {                   //[2]
        if(err) {
          return reject(err);                        //[3]
        }
        if(arguments.length <= 2) {                  //[4]
          resolve(result);
        } else {
          resolve([].slice.call(arguments, 1));
        }
      });
      callbackBasedApi.apply(null, args);            //[5]
    });
  }
};
```

The preceding function returns another function called promisified(), which represents the promisified version of the callbackBasedApi given in the input. This is how it works:

1. The promisified() function creates a new promise using the Promise constructor and immediately returns it to the caller.
2. In the function passed to the Promise constructor, we make sure to pass to callbackBasedApi, a special callback. As we know that the callback always comes last, we simply append it to the argument list (args) provided to the promisified() function.
3. In the special callback, if we receive an error, we immediately reject the promise.
4. If no error is received, we resolve the promise with a value or an array of values, depending on how many results are passed to the callback.
5. Finally, we simply invoke the callbackBasedApi with the list of arguments we have built.

Most of the promise implementations already provide, out-of-the-box, some sort of helper to convert a Node.js style API to one returning a promise. For example, Q has `Q.denodeify()` and `Q.nbind()`, Bluebird has `Promise.promisify()`, and When.js has `node.lift()`.

Sequential execution

After a little bit of necessary theory, we are now ready to convert our web spider application to use promises. Let's start directly from version 2, the one downloading the links of a web page in sequence.

In the `spider.js` module, the very first step required is to load our promises implementation (we will use it later) and promisify the callback-based functions that we plan to use:

```
const utilities = require('./utilities');

const request = utilities.promisify(require('request'));
const mkdirp = utilities.promisify(require('mkdirp'));
const fs = require('fs');
const readFile = utilities.promisify(fs.readFile);
const writeFile = utilities.promisify(fs.writeFile);
```

Now, we can start converting the `download()` function:

```
function download(url, filename) {
  console.log(`Downloading ${url}`);
  let body;
  return request(url)
    .then(response => {
      body = response.body;
      return mkdirp(path.dirname(filename));
    })
    .then(() => writeFile(filename, body))
    .then(() => {
      console.log(`Downloaded and saved: ${url}`);
      return body;
    });
}
```

The important thing to notice here is that we also registered an `onRejected()` function for the promise returned by `readFile()` to handle cases where a page has not been downloaded (file does not exist). Also, it's interesting to see how we were able to use `throw` to propagate the error from within the handler.

Now that we have converted our `spider()` function as well, we can modify its main invocation as follows:

```
spider(process.argv[2], 1)
  .then(() => console.log('Download complete'))
  .catch(err => console.log(err));
```

Note how we used, for the first time, the syntactic sugar `catch` to handle any error situations originating from the `spider()` function. If we look again at all the code we have written so far, we would be pleasantly surprised by the fact that we haven't included any error propagation logic, as we would be forced to do when using callbacks. This is clearly an enormous advantage, as it greatly reduces the boilerplate in our code and the chances of missing any asynchronous errors.

Now, the only missing bit to complete version 2 of our web spider application is the `spiderLinks()` function, which we are going to implement in a moment.

Sequential iteration

So far, the web spider codebase was mainly an overview of what promises are and how they are used, demonstrating how simple and elegant it is to implement a sequential execution flow using promises. However, the code we considered until now only involves the execution of a known set of asynchronous operations. So, the missing piece that will complete our exploration of sequential execution flows is to see how we can implement an iteration using promises. Again, the `spiderLinks()` function of web spider version 2 is a perfect example to show that.

Let's add the missing piece:

```
function spiderLinks(currentUrl, body, nesting) {
  let promise = Promise.resolve();
  if(nesting === 0) {
    return promise;
  }
  const links = utilities.getPageLinks(currentUrl, body);
  links.forEach(link => {
    promise = promise.then(() => spider(link, nesting - 1));
  });
}
```

```
    return promise;
  }
```

To iterate asynchronously over all the links of a web page, we had to dynamically build a chain of promises:

1. First, we defined an "empty" promise, resolving to `undefined`. This promise is just used as a starting point to build our chain.
2. Then, in a loop, we updated the `promise` variable with a new promise obtained by invoking `then()` on the previous promise in the chain. This is actually our asynchronous iteration pattern using promises.

This way, at the end of the loop, the `promise` variable will contain the promise of the last `then()` invocation in the loop, so it will resolve only when all the promises in the chain have been resolved.

With this, we completely converted our web spider version 2 to use promises. We should now be able to try it out again.

Sequential iteration – the pattern

To conclude this section on sequential execution, let's extract the pattern to iterate over a set of promises in sequence:

```
let tasks = [ /* ... */ ]
let promise = Promise.resolve();
tasks.forEach(task => {
  promise = promise.then(() => {
    return task();
  });
});
promise.then(() => {
  //All tasks completed
});
```

An alternative to using the `forEach()` loop is the `reduce()` function, allowing an even more compact code:

```
let tasks = [ /* ... */ ]
let promise = tasks.reduce((prev, task) => {
  return prev.then(() => {
    return task();
  });
}, Promise.resolve());
```

```
promise.then(() => {
  //All tasks completed
});
```

As always, with simple adaptations of this pattern, we could collect all the tasks' results in an array; we could implement a mapping algorithm, or build a filter, and so on.

 Pattern (sequential iteration with promises):
This pattern dynamically builds a chain of promises using a loop.

Parallel execution

Another execution flow that becomes trivial with promises is the parallel execution flow. In fact, all that we need to do is use the built-in `Promise.all()`. This helper function creates another promise, which fulfills only when all the promises received in an input are fulfilled. That's essentially a parallel execution because no order between the various promises' resolutions is enforced.

To demonstrate this, let's consider version 3 of our web spider application, which downloads all the links in page in parallel. Let's update the `spiderLinks()` function again to implement a parallel flow, using promises:

```
function spiderLinks(currentUrl, body, nesting) {
  if(nesting === 0) {
    return Promise.resolve();
  }

  const links = utilities.getPageLinks(currentUrl, body);
  const promises = links.map(link => spider(link, nesting - 1));

  return Promise.all(promises);
}
```

The pattern here consists of starting the `spider()` tasks all at once in the `elements.map()` loop, which also collects all their promises. This time, in the loop, we are not waiting for the previous download to complete before starting a new one: all the download tasks are started in the loop at once, one after the other. Afterwards, we leverage the `Promise.all()` method, which returns a new promise that will be fulfilled when all the promises in the array are fulfilled. In other words, it fulfills when all the download tasks have completed; this is exactly what we wanted.

Limited parallel execution

Unfortunately, the ES2015 Promise API does not provide a native way to limit the number of concurrent tasks, but we can always rely on what we learned about limiting the concurrency with plain JavaScript. In fact, the pattern we implemented inside the `TaskQueue` class can be easily adapted to support tasks that return a promise. This can easily be done by modifying the `next()` method:

```
next() {
  while(this.running < this.concurrency && this.queue.length) {
    const task = this.queue.shift();
    task().then(() => {
      this.running--;
      this.next();
    });
    this.running++;
  }
}
```

Instead of handling the task with a callback, we simply invoke `then()` on the promise it returns. The rest of the code is basically identical to the old version of `TaskQueue`.

Let's go back to the `spider.js` module, and modify it to support our new version of the `TaskQueue` class. First, we make sure to define a new instance of `TaskQueue`:

```
const TaskQueue = require('./taskQueue');
const downloadQueue = new TaskQueue(2);
```

Then, it's the turn of the `spiderLinks()` function again. The change here is also pretty straightforward:

```
function spiderLinks(currentUrl, body, nesting) {
  if(nesting === 0) {
    return Promise.resolve();
  }

  const links = utilities.getPageLinks(currentUrl, body);
  //we need the following because the Promise we create next
  //will never settle if there are no tasks to process
  if(links.length === 0) {
    return Promise.resolve();
  }

  return new Promise((resolve, reject) => {
    let completed = 0;
    let errored = false;
    links.forEach(link => {
```

```
        let task = () => {
          return spider(link, nesting - 1)
            .then(() => {
              if(++completed === links.length) {
                resolve();
              }
            })
            .catch(() => {
              if (!errored) {
                errored = true;
                reject();
              }
            });
        };
        downloadQueue.pushTask(task);
      });
    });
}
```

There are a couple of things in the previous code that deserve our attention:

- First, we needed to return a new promise created using the `Promise` constructor. As we will see, this enables us to resolve the promise manually, when all of the tasks in the queue are completed.
- Second, we should look at how we defined the task. What we did is attach an `onFulfilled()` callback to the promise returned by `spider()`, so we could count the number of completed downloaded tasks. When the amount of completed downloads matches the number of links in the current page, we know that we are done processing, so we can invoke the `resolve()` function of the outer promise.

 The Promises/A+ specification states that the `onFulfilled()` and `onRejected()` callbacks of the `then()` method have to be invoked only once and exclusively (only one or the other is invoked). A compliant promises implementation makes sure that even if we call `resolve` or `reject` multiple times, the promise is either fulfilled or rejected only once.

Version 4 of the web spider application using promises should now be ready to try out. We might notice once again how the download tasks now run in parallel, with a concurrency limit of 2.

Exposing callbacks and promises in public APIs

As we have learned in the previous paragraphs, promises can be used as a nice replacement for callbacks. They turn out to be very useful for making our code more readable and easy to reason about. While promises bring many advantages, they also require the developer to understand many non-trivial concepts in order to be used correctly and proficiently. For this and other reasons, in some cases it might be more practical to prefer callbacks to promises.

Now let's imagine for a moment that we want to build a public library that performs asynchronous operations. What do we do? Do we create a callback-oriented API or a promise-oriented one? Do we need to be opinionated on one side or another or there are ways to support both and make everyone happy?

This is a problem that many well-known libraries face and there are at least two approaches that are worth mentioning that allow us to provide a versatile API.

The first approach, used by libraries such as `request`, `redis`, and `mysql`, consists of offering a simple API that is only based on callbacks and leave the developer the option to promisify the exposed functions if needed. Some of these libraries provide helpers to be able to promisify all the asynchronous functions they offer, but the developer still needs to somehow convert the exposed API to be able to use promises.

The second approach is more transparent. It also offers a callback-oriented API, but it makes the callback argument optional. Whenever the callback is passed as an argument, the function will behave normally, executing the callback on completion or on failure.When the callback is not passed, the function will immediately return a `Promise` object. This approach effectively combines callbacks and promises in a way that allows the developer to choose at call time what interface to adopt, without any need to promisify the function in advance. Many libraries, such as `mongoose` and `sequelize`, support this approach.

Let's see a simple implementation of this approach with an example. Let's assume we want to implement a dummy module that executes divisions asynchronously:

```
module.exports = function asyncDivision (dividend, divisor, cb) {
  return new Promise((resolve, reject) => {                 // [1]

    process.nextTick(() => {
      const result = dividend / divisor;
      if (isNaN(result) || !Number.isFinite(result)) {
        const error = new Error('Invalid operands');
        if (cb) { cb(error); }                              // [2]
        return reject(error);
      }
```

```
    if (cb) { cb(null, result); }                          // [3]
    resolve(result);
  });

});
};
```

The code of the module is very straightforward, but there are some details that are worth underlining:

- First, were return a new promise created using the `Promise` constructor. We define the whole logic inside the function passed as argument to the constructor.
- In the case of an error, we reject the promise, but if the callback was passed at call time, we also execute the callback to propagate the error.
- After we calculate the result we resolve the promise, but again, if there's a callback, we propagate the result to the callback as well.

Let's see now how we can use this module with both callbacks and promises:

```
// callback oriented usage
asyncDivision(10, 2, (error, result) => {
  if (error) {
    return console.error(error);
  }
  console.log(result);
});

// promise oriented usage
asyncDivision(22, 11)
  .then(result => console.log(result))
  .catch(error => console.error(error));
```

It should be clear that with very little effort, the developers who are going to use our new module will be able to easily choose the style that best suits their needs, without having to introduce an external promisification function whenever they want to leverage promises.

Generators

The ES2015 specification introduces another mechanism that, besides other things, can be used to simplify the asynchronous control flow of our Node.js applications. We are talking about **generators**, also known as **semi-coroutines**. They are a generalization of subroutines, where there can be different entry points. In a normal function, in fact, we can have only one entry point, which corresponds to the invocation of the function itself. A generator is similar to a function, but in addition, it can be suspended (using the `yield` statement) and then resumed at a later time. Generators are particularly useful when implementing iterators, and this should ring a bell, as we already discussed how iterators can be used to implement important asynchronous control flow patterns such as sequential and limited parallel execution.

The basics of generators

Before we explore the use of generators for asynchronous control flow, it's important we learn some basic concepts. Let's start from the syntax; a generator function can be declared by appending the * (asterisk) operator after the `function` keyword:

```
function* makeGenerator() {
  //body
}
```

Inside the `makeGenerator()` function, we can pause the execution using the keyword `yield` and return to the caller the value passed to it:

```
function* makeGenerator() {
  yield 'Hello World';
  console.log('Re-entered');
}
```

In the preceding code, the generator yields a string, `Hello World`, by putting the execution of the function on pause. When the generator is resumed, the execution will start from `console.log('Re-entered')`.

The `makeGenerator()` function is essentially a factory that, when invoked, returns a new generator object:

```
const gen = makeGenerator();
```

The most important method of the generator object is `next()`, which is used to start/resume the execution of the generator and returns an object in the following form:

```
{
  value: <yielded value>
  done: <true if the execution reached the end>
}
```

This object contains the value yielded by the generator (`value`) and a flag to indicate if the generator has completed its execution (`done`).

A simple example

To demonstrate generators, let's create a new module called `fruitGenerator.js`:

```
function* fruitGenerator() {
    yield 'apple';
    yield 'orange';
    return 'watermelon';
}

const newFruitGenerator = fruitGenerator();
console.log(newFruitGenerator.next());     //[1]
console.log(newFruitGenerator.next());     //[2]
console.log(newFruitGenerator.next());     //[3]
```

The preceding code will print the following output:

```
{ value: 'apple', done: false }
{ value: 'orange', done: false }
{ value: 'watermelon', done: true }
```

This is a short explanation of what happened:

- The first time `newFruitGenerator.next()` was invoked, the generator started its execution until it reached the first `yield` command, which put the generator on pause and returned the value `apple` to the caller.
- At the second invocation of `newFruitGenerator.next()`, the generator resumed, starting from the second `yield` command, which in turn put the execution on pause again, while returning the value `orange` to the caller.
- The last invocation of `newFruitGenerator.next()` caused the execution of the generator to resume from its last instruction, a `return` statement, which terminates the generator, returns the value `watermelon`, and sets the `done` property to `true` in the `result` object.

Generators as iterators

To better understand why generators are so useful for implementing iterators, let's build one. In a new module, which we will call `iteratorGenerator.js`, let's write the following code:

```
function* iteratorGenerator(arr) {
  for(let i = 0; i <arr.length; i++) {
    yield arr[i];
  }
}

const iterator = iteratorGenerator(['apple', 'orange',  'watermelon']);
let currentItem = iterator.next();
while(!currentItem.done) {
  console.log(currentItem.value);
  currentItem = iterator.next();
}
```

This code should print the list of the items in the array as follows:

```
apple
orange
watermelon
```

In this example, each time we call `iterator.next()`, we resume the `for` loop of the generator, which runs another cycle by yielding the next item in the array. This demonstrates how the state of the generator is maintained across invocations. When resumed, the loop and all the variables are exactly the same as when the execution was put on pause.

Passing values back to a generator

To conclude our exploration of the basic functionality of generators, we will now learn how to pass values back to a generator. This is actually very simple; what we need to do is just provide an argument to the `next()` method, and that value will be provided as the return value of the `yield` statement inside the generator.

To show this, let's create a new simple module:

```
function* twoWayGenerator() {
  const what = yield null;
  console.log('Hello ' + what);
}
```

```
const twoWay = twoWayGenerator();
twoWay.next();
twoWay.next('world');
```

When executed, the preceding code will print `Hello world`. This means that the following has happened:

- The first time the `next()` method is invoked, the generator reaches the first `yield` statement and is then put on pause.
- When `next('world')` is invoked, the generator resumes from the point where it was put on pause, which is on the `yield` instruction, but this time we have a value that is passed back to the generator. This value will then be set into the `what` variable. The generator then executes the `console.log()` instruction and terminates.

In a similar way, we can force a generator to throw an exception. This is possible by using the `throw` method of the generator, as shown in the following example:

```
const twoWay = twoWayGenerator();
twoWay.next();
twoWay.throw(new Error());
```

Using this last code snippet, the `twoWayGenerator()` function will throw an exception the moment the `yield` function returns. This works exactly as if an exception was thrown from inside the generator, and this means that it can be caught and handled like any other exception using a `try...catch` block.

Asynchronous control flow with generators

You must be wondering how generators can help us with handling asynchronous operations. We can demonstrate this by creating a special function that accepts a generator as an argument and allows us to use asynchronous code inside the generator. This function takes care to resume the execution of the generator when the asynchronous operation completes. We will call this function `asyncFlow()`:

```
function asyncFlow(generatorFunction) {
  function callback(err) {
    if(err) {
      return generator.throw(err);
    }
    const results = [].slice.call(arguments, 1);
    generator.next(results.length> 1 ? results : results[0]);
  }
```

```
const generator = generatorFunction(callback);
generator.next();
}
```

The preceding function takes a generator as input, instantiates it, and then immediately starts its execution:

```
const generator = generatorFunction(callback);
generator.next();
```

The `generatorFunction()` receives as input, a special `callback` function that invokes `generator.throw()` if an error is received; otherwise, it resumes the execution of the generator by passing back the results received in the `callback` function:

```
if(err) {
  return generator.throw(err);
}
const results = [].slice.call(arguments, 1);
generator.next(results.length> 1 ? results : results[0]);
```

To demonstrate the power of this simple function, let's create a new module called `clone.js`, which, for no meaningful reason, creates a clone of itself. Paste the `asyncFlow()` function we just created, followed by the core of the program:

```
const fs = require('fs');
const path = require('path');

asyncFlow(function* (callback) {
  const fileName = path.basename(__filename);
  const myself = yield fs.readFile(fileName, 'utf8', callback);
  yield fs.writeFile(`clone_of_${filename}`, myself, callback);
  console.log('Clone created');
});
```

Remarkably, with the help of the `asyncFlow()` function, we were able to write asynchronous code using a linear approach, as we were using blocking functions! The magic behind this result should be clear by now. The callback passed to each asynchronous function will in turn resume the generator as soon as the asynchronous operation is complete. Nothing complicated, but the outcome is surely impressive.

There are two other variations of this technique, one involving the use of promises and the other using thunks.

> A **thunk** used in the generator-based control flow is just a function that partially applies all the arguments of the original function except its callback. The `return` value is another function that only accepts the callback as an argument. For example, the thunkified version of `fs.readFile()` would be as follows:
>
> ```
> function readFileThunk(filename, options) {
>   return function(callback){
>     fs.readFile(filename, options, callback);
>   }
> }
> ```

Both thunks and promises allow us to create generators that do not need a callback to be passed as an argument; for example, a version of `asyncFlow()` using thunks might be the following:

```
function asyncFlowWithThunks(generatorFunction) {
  function callback(err) {
    if(err) {
      return generator.throw(err);
    }
    const results = [].slice.call(arguments, 1);
    const thunk = generator.next(results.length> 1 ? results :
                  results[0]).value;
    thunk && thunk(callback);
  }
  const generator = generatorFunction();
  const thunk = generator.next().value;
  thunk && thunk(callback);
}
```

The trick is to read the return value of `generator.next()`, which contains the thunk. The next step is to invoke the thunk itself by injecting our special callback. Simple! This allows us to write the following code:

```
asyncFlowWithThunks(function* () {
  const fileName = path.basename(__filename);
  const myself = yield readFileThunk(__filename, 'utf8');
  yield writeFileThunk(`clone_of_${fileName}`, myself);
  console.log("Clone created");
});
```

In the same way, we could implement a version of `asyncFlow()` that accepts a promise as yieldable. We leave this as an exercise as its implementation requires only a minimal change to the `asyncFlowWithThunks()` function. We may also implement an `asyncFlow()` function that accepts both promises and thunks as yieldables, using the same principles.

Generator-based control flow using co

As you may guess, the Node.js ecosystem provides some solutions to handle asynchronous control flows using generators, for example, suspend (`https://npmjs.org/package/sus pend`) is one of the oldest and supports promises, thunks, Node.js-style callbacks, as well as *raw* callbacks. Also, most of the promise libraries we analyzed earlier in the chapter provide helpers to use promises with generators.

All these solutions are based on the same principles we demonstrated with the `asyncFlow()` function; so, we may want to reuse one of these instead of writing one ourselves.

For the examples in this section, we chose to use co (`https://npmjs.org/package/co`). It supports several types of yieldables, some of which are:

- Thunks
- Promises
- Arrays (parallel execution)
- Objects (parallel execution)
- Generators (delegation)
- Generator functions (delegation)

co also has its own ecosystem of packages including the following:

- Web frameworks, the most popular being koa (`https://npmjs.org/package/koa`)
- Libraries implementing specific control flow patterns
- Libraries wrapping popular APIs to support co

We will use co to re-implement our web spider application using generators.

While converting Node.js-style functions to thunks, we are going to use a little library called thunkify (`https://npmjs.org/package/thunkify`).

Sequential execution

Let's start our practical exploration of generators and co by modifying version 2 of the web spider application. The very first thing we have to do is to load our dependencies and generate a thunkified version of the functions we are going to use. These will go at the top of the `spider.js` module:

```
const thunkify = require('thunkify');
const co = require('co');

const request = thunkify(require('request'));
const fs = require('fs');
const mkdirp = thunkify(require('mkdirp'));
const readFile = thunkify(fs.readFile);
const writeFile = thunkify(fs.writeFile);
const nextTick = thunkify(process.nextTick);
```

Looking at the preceding code, we can surely notice some similarities with the code we used earlier in the chapter to promisify some APIs. In this regard, it is interesting to point out that if we decided to use the promisified version of our functions instead of their thunkified alternative, the code would remain exactly the same, thanks to the fact that co supports both thunks and promises as yieldable objects. In fact, if we want, we could even use both thunks and promises in the same application, even in the same generator. This is a tremendous advantage in terms of flexibility, as it allows us to use a generator-based control flow with whatever solution we already have at our disposal.

Okay, now let's start transforming the `download()` function into a generator:

```
function* download(url, filename) {
  console.log(`Downloading ${url}`);
  const response = yield request(url);
  const body = response[1];
  yield mkdirp(path.dirname(filename));
  yield writeFile(filename, body);
  console.log(`Downloaded and saved ${url}`);
  return body;
}
```

By using generators and co, our `download()` function suddenly becomes trivial. All we had to do is convert it into a generator function and use `yield` wherever we had an asynchronous function (as `thunk`) to invoke.

Next, it's the turn of the `spider()` function:

```
function* spider(url, nesting) {
  const filename = utilities.urlToFilename(url);
  let body;
  try {
    body = yield readFile(filename, 'utf8');
  } catch(err) {
    if(err.code !== 'ENOENT') {
      throw err;
    }
    body = yield download(url, filename);
  }
  yield spiderLinks(url, body, nesting);
}
```

The interesting detail to notice from this last fragment of code is how we were able to use a `try...catch` block to handle exceptions. Also, we can now use `throw` to propagate errors! Another remarkable line is where we yield the `download()` function, which is not a thunk nor a promisified function, but just another generator. This is possible, thanks to co, which also supports other generators as yieldables.

Finally, we can also convert `spiderLinks()`, where we implemented an iteration to download the links of a web page in sequence. With generators, this becomes trivial as well:

```
function* spiderLinks(currentUrl, body, nesting) {
  if(nesting === 0) {
    return nextTick();
  }

  const links = utilities.getPageLinks(currentUrl, body);
  for(let i = 0; i <links.length; i++) {
    yield spider(links[i], nesting - 1);
  }
}
```

There is little to explain from the previous code. There is no pattern to show for the sequential iteration; generators and co are doing all the dirty work for us, so we were able to write the asynchronous iteration as if we were using blocking, direct style APIs.

Now comes the most important part, the entry point of our program:

```
co(function* () {
  try {
    yield spider(process.argv[2], 1);
    console.log('Download complete');
  } catch(err) {
```

```
        console.log(err);
    }
});
```

This is the only place where we have to invoke `co(...)` to wrap a generator. In fact, once we do that, `co` will automatically wrap any generator we pass to a `yield` statement, and this will happen recursively, so the rest of the program is totally agnostic to the fact we are using `co`, even though it's under the hood.

Now it should be possible to run our generator-based web spider application.

Parallel execution

The bad news about generators is that they are great for writing sequential algorithms, but they can't be used to parallelize the execution of a set of tasks, at least not just using yield and generators. In fact, the pattern to use in these circumstances is to simply rely on a callback-based or promise-based function, which in turn can easily be yielded and used with generators.

Luckily, for the specific case of the unlimited parallel execution, co already allows us to obtain it natively by simply yielding an array of promises, thunks, generators, or generator functions.

With this in mind, version 3 of our web spider application can be implemented simply by rewriting the `spiderLinks()` function as follows:

```
function* spiderLinks(currentUrl, body, nesting) {
  if(nesting === 0) {
    return nextTick();
  }

  const links = utilities.getPageLinks(currentUrl, body);
  const tasks = links.map(link => spider(link, nesting - 1));
  yield tasks;
}
```

What we did was just to collect all the download tasks, which are essentially generators, and then yield on the resulting array. All these tasks will be executed by co in parallel and then the execution of our generator (`spiderLinks`) will be resumed when all the tasks finish running.

If you think we cheated by exploiting the feature of co that allows us to yield on an array, it is possible to demonstrate how the same parallel flow can be achieved using a callback-based solution similar to what we have already used earlier in the chapter. Let's use this technique to rewrite spiderLinks() once again:

```
function spiderLinks(currentUrl, body, nesting) {
  if(nesting === 0) {
    return nextTick();
  }

  //returns a thunk
  return callback => {
    let completed = 0, hasErrors = false;
    const links = utilities.getPageLinks(currentUrl, body);
    if(links.length === 0) {
      return process.nextTick(callback);
    }

    function done(err, result) {
      if(err && !hasErrors) {
        hasErrors = true;
        return callback(err);
      }
      if(++completed === links.length && !hasErrors) {
        callback();
      }
    }

    for(let i = 0; i < links.length; i++) {
      co(spider(links[i], nesting - 1)).then(done);
    }
  }
}
```

To run the spider() function in parallel, we use co, which executes the generator and returns a promise. This way, we are able to wait for the promise to be resolved and call the done() function. Usually, all the libraries for generator-based control flows have similar features, so you can always transform a generator into a callback-based or a promise-based function if needed.

To start multiple download tasks in parallel, we just reused the callback-based pattern for parallel execution defined earlier in the chapter. We should also notice that we transformed the `spiderLinks()` function to a thunk (it's not even a generator anymore.) This enabled us to have a `callback` function to invoke when all the parallel tasks are completed.

 Pattern (generator-to-thunk)
It converts a generator to a thunk in order to be able to run it in parallel or utilize it for taking advantage of other callback- or promise-based control flow algorithms.

Limited parallel execution

Now that we know what to do with nonsequential execution flows, it should be easy to plan the implementation of version 4 of our web spider application, the one imposing a limit on the number of concurrent download tasks. We have several options we can use to do that; some of them are as follows:

- Use the callback-based version of the previously implemented `TaskQueue` class. We would need to just thunkify its functions and any generator we want to use as a task.
- Use the promises-based version of the `TaskQueue` class, and just make sure that each generator we want to use as a task is converted into a function returning a promise.
- Use `async`, and thunkify any helper we plan to use, in addition to converting any generator to a callback-based function that can be used by the library.
- Use a library from the co ecosystem, specifically designed for this type of flow, such as, **co-limiter** (`https://npmjs.org/package/co-limiter`).
- Implement a custom algorithm based on the producer-consumer pattern, the same that co-limiter uses internally.

For educational purposes, we are going to choose the last option, so we can dive into a pattern that is often associated with coroutines (but also threads and processes).

Producer-consumer pattern

The goal is to leverage a queue to feed a fixed number of workers, as many as the concurrency level we want to set. To implement this algorithm, we are going to take as a starting point, the `TaskQueue` class we defined earlier in the chapter:

```
class TaskQueue {
  constructor(concurrency) {
    this.concurrency = concurrency;
    this.running = 0;
    this.taskQueue = [];
    this.consumerQueue = [];
    this.spawnWorkers(concurrency);
  }

  pushTask(task) {
    if (this.consumerQueue.length !== 0) {
      this.consumerQueue.shift()(null, task);
    } else {
      this.taskQueue.push(task);
    }
  }

  spawnWorkers(concurrency) {
    const self = this;
    for(let i = 0; i < concurrency; i++) {
      co(function* () {
        while(true) {
          const task = yield self.nextTask();
          yield task;
        }
      });
    }
  }

  nextTask() {
    return callback => {
      if(this.taskQueue.length !== 0) {
        return callback(null, this.taskQueue.shift());
      }

      this.consumerQueue.push(callback);
    }
  }
}
```

Let's start to analyze this new implementation of `TaskQueue`. The first thing to underline is in the constructor. Notice the invocation of `this.spawnWorkers()`, as this is the method in charge of starting the workers.

Our workers are very simple; they are just generators wrapped around `co()` and executed immediately so that each one can run in parallel. Internally, each worker is running an infinite loop that blocks (`yield`) waiting for a new task to be available in the queue (`yield self.nextTask()`), and when this happens, it yields the task (which is any valid yieldable) waiting for its completion. You may be wondering how we can actually wait for the next task to be queued. The answer is in the `nextTask()` method. Let's see in greater detail what happens within this method:

```
nextTask() {
  return callback => {
    if(this.taskQueue.length !== 0) {
      return callback(null, this.taskQueue.shift());
    }
    this.consumerQueue.push(callback);
  }
}
```

Let's see what happens in this method, which is the core of the pattern:

1. The method returns a thunk, which is a valid yieldable for `co`.
2. The callback of the returned thunk is invoked by providing the next task in the `taskQueue` function (if there is any available). This will immediately unblock a worker, providing the next task to yield on.
3. If there are no tasks in the queue, the callback itself is pushed into `consumerQueue`. By doing this, we are basically putting a worker in *idle* mode. The callbacks in the `consumerQueue` function will be invoked as soon as we have a new task to process, which will resume the corresponding worker.

Now, to understand how the idle workers in the `consumerQueue` function are resumed, we need to analyze the `pushTask()` method. The `pushTask()` method invokes the first callback in the `consumerQueue` function if available, which in turn will unblock a worker. If no callback is available, it means that all the workers are busy, so we simply add a new item to the `taskQueue` function.

In the `TaskQueue` class, the workers have the role of consumers, while whoever uses `pushTask()` can be considered a producer. This pattern shows us how a generator can be very similar to a thread (or a process). In fact, the producer-consumer interaction is probably the most common problem presented when studying inter-process communication techniques, but as we already mentioned, it is also a common use case for coroutines.

Limiting the download tasks concurrency

Now that we have implemented a limited parallel algorithm using generators and the producer-consumer pattern, we can apply it to limit the concurrency of the download tasks of our web spider application (version 4). First, let's load and initialize a `TaskQueue` object:

```
const TaskQueue = require('./taskQueue');
const downloadQueue = new TaskQueue(2);
```

Next, let's modify the `spiderLinks()` function. Its body is almost identical to the one we just used to implement the unlimited parallel execution flow, so we will only show the changed parts here:

```
function spiderLinks(currentUrl, body, nesting) {
  //...
  return (callback) => {
    //...
    function done(err, result) {
      //...
    }
    links.forEach(function(link) {
      downloadQueue.pushTask(function *() {
        yield spider(link, nesting - 1);
        done();
      });
    });
  }
}
```

In each of the tasks, we invoke the `done()` function just after a download completes, so we can count how many links were downloaded and then notify the callback of the thunk when all are complete.

As an exercise, you can try to implement version 4 of the web spider application, using the other four methods we presented at the beginning of this section.

Async await using Babel

Callbacks, promises, and generators turn out to be the weapons at our disposal to deal with asynchronous code in JavaScript and in Node.js. As we have seen, generators are very interesting because they offer a way to actually suspend the execution of a function and resume it at a later stage. Now we can adopt this feature to write asynchronous code that allows developers to write functions that "appear" to block at each asynchronous operation, waiting for the results before continuing with the following statement.

The problem is that generator functions are designed to deal mostly with iterators and their usage with asynchronous code feels a bit cumbersome. It might be hard to understand, leading to code that is hard to read and maintain.

But there is hope that there will be a cleaner syntax sometime in the near future. In fact, there is an interesting proposal that will be introduced with the ECMAScript 2017 specification that defines the `async` function's syntax.

 You can read more about the current status of the async await proposal at `https://tc39.github.io/ecmascript-asyncawait/`.

The `async` function specification aims to dramatically improve the language-level model for writing asynchronous code by introducing two new keywords into the language: `async` and `await`.

To clarify how these keywords are meant to be used and why they are useful, let's see a very quick example:

```
const request = require('request');

function getPageHtml(url) {
  return new Promise(function(resolve, reject) {
    request(url, function(error, response, body) {
      resolve(body);
    });
  });
}

async function main() {
  const html = await getPageHtml('http://google.com');
  console.log(html);
}

main();
```

```
console.log('Loading...');
```

In this code,there are two functions: `getPageHtml` and `main`. The first one is a very simple function that fetches the HTML code of a remote web page given its URL. It's worth noticing that this function returns a promise.

The `main` function is the most interesting one because it's where the new `async` and `await` keywords are used. The first thing to notice is that the function is prefixed with the `async` keyword. This means that the function executes asynchronous code and allows it to use the `await` keyword within its body. The `await` keyword before the call to `getPageHtml` tells the JavaScript interpreter to "await" the resolution of the promise returned by `getPageHtml` before continuing to the next instruction. This way, the `main` function is internally suspended until the asynchronous code completes without blocking the normal execution of the rest of the program. In fact, we will see the string `Loading...` in the console and, after a moment, the HTML code of the Google landing page.

Isn't this approach much more readable and easy to understand?

Unfortunately, this proposal is not yet final, and even if it will be approved we will need to wait for the next version of the ECMAScript specification to come out and be integrated in Node.js to be able to use this new syntax natively.

So what do we do today? Just wait? No, of course not! We can already leverage async await in our code thanks to transpilers such as Babel.

Installing and running Babel

Babel is a JavaScript compiler (or transpiler) that is able to convert JavaScript code into other JavaScript code using syntax transformers. Syntax transformers allows the use of new syntax such as ES2015, ES2016, JSX, and others to produce backward compatible equivalent code that can be executed in modern JavaScript runtimes, such as browsers or Node.js.

You can install Babel in your project using npm with the following command:

```
npm install --save-dev babel-cli
```

We also need to install the extensions to support async await parsing and transformation:

```
npm install --save-dev babel-plugin-syntax-async-functions
babel-plugin-transform-async-to-generator
```

Now let's assume we want to run our previous example (called `index.js`). We need to launch the following command:

```
node_modules/.bin/babel-node --plugins
"syntax-async-functions,transform-async-to-generator"index.js
```

This way, we are transforming the source code in `index.js` on the fly, applying the transformers to support async await. This new backward compatible code is stored in memory and then executed on the fly on the Node.js runtime.

Babel can also be configured to act as a build processor that stores the generated code into files so that you can easily deploy and run the generated code.

 You can read more about how to install and configure Babel on the official website at `https://babeljs.io`.

Comparison

At this point, we should have a better understanding of the options we have to tame the asynchronous nature of JavaScript. Each one of the solutions presented has its own pros and cons. Let's summarize them in the following table:

Solutions	Pros	Cons
Plain JavaScript	• Does not require any additional libraries or technology • Offers the best performance • Provides the best level of compatibility with third-party libraries • Allows the creation of ad hoc and more advanced algorithms	**Might require extra code and relatively complex algorithms**
Async (library)	• Simplifies the most common control flow patterns • Is still a callback-based solution • Good performance	• Introduces an external dependency • Might still not be enough for advanced flows

Solutions	Pros	Cons
Promises	• Greatly simplifies the most common control flow patterns • Robust error handling • Part of the ES2015 specification • Guarantees deferred invocation of `onFulfilled` and `onRejected`	• Requires promisify callback-based APIs • Introduces a small performance hit
Generators	• Makes non-blocking API look like a blocking one • Simplifies error handling • Part of ES2015 specification	• Requires a complementary control flow library • Still requires callbacks or promises to implement non-sequential flows • Requires thunkify or promisify nongenerator-based APIs
Async await	• Makes non-blocking API look like blocking • Clean and intuitive syntax	• Not yet available in JavaScript and Node.js natively • Requires Babel or other transpilers and some configuration to be used today

 It is worth mentioning that we chose to present in this chapter only the most popular solutions to handle asynchronous control flow, or the ones receiving a lot of momentum, but it's good to know that there are a few more options you might want to look at, for example, `Fibers` (`https://npmjs.org/package/fibers`) and `Streamline` (`https://npmjs.org/package/streamline`).

Summary

Throughout this chapter, we analyzed some alternative approaches of dealing with asynchronous control flows considering promises, generators, and the upcoming async await syntax.

We learned how to use these approaches to write asynchronous code that is more concise, cleaner and easier to reason about. We discussed some of the most important advantages and drawbacks of these approaches and realized that even if they are very useful they need some time to be mastered. That's why they should not be seen as a complete replacement of callbacks which are still very useful in many scenarios. As a developer, you should now be able to decide which solution best suits the problem you are facing. If you are building a public library that performs asynchronous operations, you should provide an interface that is easy to use, even for developers who only want to use callbacks.

In the next chapter we will explore another fascinating topic relevant to asynchronous code execution and which is another fundamental building block in the whole Node.js ecosystem: streams.

5
Coding with Streams

Streams are one of the most important components and patterns of Node.js. There is a motto in the community that says "stream all the things!" and this alone should be enough to describe the role of streams in Node.js. Dominic Tarr, a top contributor to the Node.js community, defines streams as node's best and most misunderstood idea. There are different reasons that make Node.js streams so attractive; again, it's not just related to technical properties, such as performance or efficiency, but it's more about their elegance and the way they fit perfectly into the Node.js philosophy.

In this chapter, you will learn about the following topics:

- Why streams are so important in Node.js
- Using and creating streams
- Streams as a programming paradigm: leveraging their power in many different contexts and not just for I/O
- Piping patterns and connecting streams together in different configurations

Discovering the importance of streams

In an event-based platform such as Node.js, the most efficient way to handle I/O is in real time, consuming the input as soon as it is available and sending the output as soon as it is produced by the application.

In this section, we are going to give an initial introduction to Node.js streams and their strengths. Please bear in mind that this is only an overview, as a more detailed analysis on how to use and compose streams will follow later in the chapter.

Buffering versus streaming

Almost all the asynchronous APIs that we've seen so far in the book work using *buffer mode*. For an input operation, buffer mode causes all the data coming from a resource to be collected into a buffer; it is then passed to a callback as soon as the entire resource is read. The following diagram shows a visual example of this paradigm:

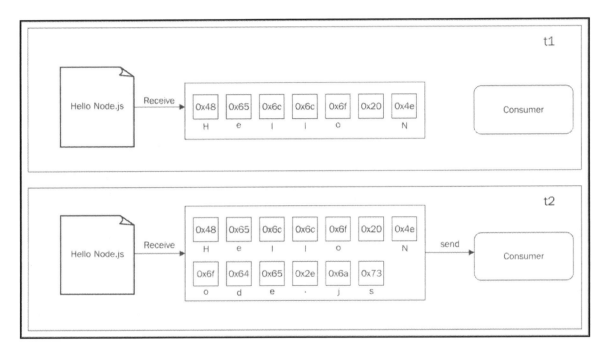

In the preceding figure, we can see that, at the time **t1**, some data is received from the resource and saved into the buffer. At the time **t2**, another data chunk is received—the final one—that completes the read operation and causes the entire buffer to be sent to the consumer.

On the other side, streams allow you to process the data as soon as it arrives from the resource. This is shown in the following diagram:

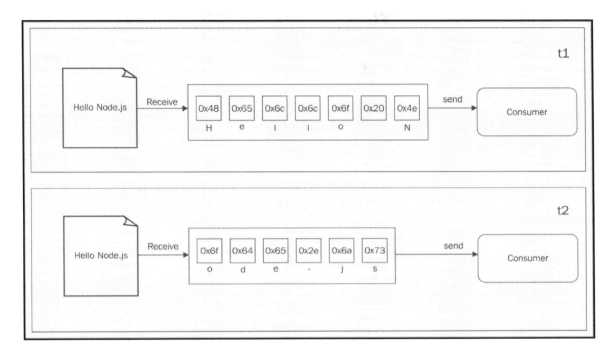

This time, the diagram shows you how each new chunk of data is received from the resource and is immediately provided to the consumer, who now has the chance to process it straight away without waiting for all the data to be collected in the buffer.

But what are the differences between the two approaches? We can summarize them in two major categories:

- Spatial efficiency
- Time efficiency

However, Node.js streams have another important advantage: **composability**. Let's now see what impact these properties have in the way we design and write our applications.

Spatial efficiency

First of all, streams allow us to do things that would not be possible, by buffering data and processing it all at once. For example, consider the case in which we have to read a very big file, let's say, in the order of hundreds of megabytes or even gigabytes. Clearly, using an API that returns a big buffer when the file is completely read is not a good idea. Imagine reading a few of these big files concurrently; our application will easily run out of memory. Besides that, buffers in V8 cannot be bigger than *0x3FFFFFFF* bytes (a little bit less than 1GB). So, we might hit a wall way before running out of physical memory.

Gzipping using a buffered API

To make a concrete example, let's consider a simple **command-line interface** (**CLI**) application that compresses a file using the Gzip format. Using a buffered API, such an application will look like the following in Node.js (error handling is omitted for brevity):

```
const fs = require('fs');
const zlib = require('zlib');

const file = process.argv[2];

fs.readFile(file, (err, buffer) => {
  zlib.gzip(buffer, (err, buffer) => {
    fs.writeFile(file + '.gz', buffer, err => {
      console.log('File successfully compressed');
    });
  });
});
```

Now, we can try to put the preceding code in a file named `gzip.js` and then run it with the following command:

```
node gzip <path to file>
```

If we choose a file that is big enough, let's say a little bit bigger than 1GB, we will receive a nice error message saying that the file that we are trying to read is bigger than the maximum allowed buffer size, such as the following:

```
RangeError: File size is greater than possible Buffer: 0x3FFFFFFF bytes
```

That's exactly what we expected, and it's a symptom of using the wrong approach.

Gzipping using streams

The simplest way we have to fix our Gzip application and make it work with big files is to use a streaming API. Let's see how this can be achieved; let's replace the contents of the module we just created with the following code:

```
const fs = require('fs');
const zlib = require('zlib');
const file = process.argv[2];

fs.createReadStream(file)
  .pipe(zlib.createGzip())
  .pipe(fs.createWriteStream(file + '.gz'))
  .on('finish', () => console.log('File successfully compressed'));
```

"Is that it?" you may ask. Yes; as we said, streams are amazing also because of their interface and composability, thus allowing clean, elegant, and concise code. We will see this in a while in more detail, but for now the important thing to realize is that the program will run smoothly against files of any size, ideally with constant memory utilization. Try it yourself (but consider that compressing a big file might take a while).

Time efficiency

Let's now consider the case of an application that compresses a file and uploads it to a remote HTTP server, which in turn decompresses it and saves it on the filesystem. If our client was implemented using a buffered API, the upload would start only when the entire file has been read and compressed. On the other hand, the decompression will start on the server only when all the data has been received. A better solution to achieve the same result involves the use of streams. On the client machine, streams allows you to compress and send the data chunks as soon as they are read from the filesystem, whereas on the server, it allows you to decompress every chunk as soon as it is received from the remote peer. Let's demonstrate this by building the application that we mentioned earlier, starting from the server side.

Let's create a module named gzipReceive.js containing the following code:

```
const http = require('http');
const fs = require('fs');
const zlib = require('zlib');

const server = http.createServer((req, res) => {
  const filename = req.headers.filename;
  console.log('File request received: ' + filename);
```

```
    req
      .pipe(zlib.createGunzip())
      .pipe(fs.createWriteStream(filename))
      .on('finish', () => {
        res.writeHead(201, {'Content-Type': 'text/plain'});
        res.end('That's it\n');
        console.log(`File saved: ${filename}`);
      });
});

server.listen(3000, () => console.log('Listening'));
```

The server receives the data chunks from the network, decompresses them, and saves them as soon as they are received, thanks to Node.js streams.

The client side of our application will go into a module named `gzipSend.js`, and it looks like the following:

```
const fs = require('fs');
const zlib = require('zlib');
const http = require('http');
const path = require('path');
const file = process.argv[2];
const server = process.argv[3];

const options = {
  hostname: server,
  port: 3000,
  path: '/',
  method: 'PUT',
  headers: {
    filename: path.basename(file),
    'Content-Type': 'application/octet-stream',
    'Content-Encoding': 'gzip'
  }
};

const req = http.request(options, res => {
  console.log('Server response: ' + res.statusCode);
});

fs.createReadStream(file)
  .pipe(zlib.createGzip())
  .pipe(req)
  .on('finish', () => {
    console.log('File successfully sent');
  });
```

In the preceding code, we are again using streams to read the data from the file, and then compressing and sending each chunk as soon as it is read from the filesystem.

Now, to try out the application, let's first start the server using the following command:

```
node gzipReceive
```

Then, we can launch the client by specifying the file to send and the address of the server (for example, `localhost`):

```
node gzipSend <path to file> localhost
```

If we choose a file big enough, we will see more easily how the data flows from the client to the server, but why exactly is this paradigm, where we have flowing data, more efficient compared to using a buffered API? The following diagram should give us a hint:

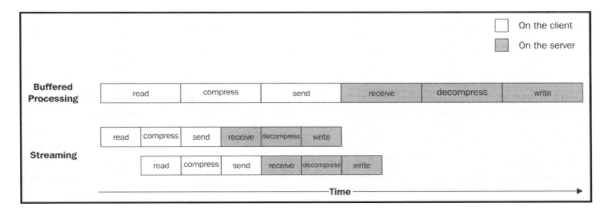

When a file is processed it goes through a set of sequential stages:

1. [Client] Read from the filesystem.
2. [Client] Compress the data.
3. [Client] Send it to the server.
4. [Server] Receive from the client.
5. [Server] Decompress the data.
6. [Server] Write the data to disk.

To complete the processing, we have to go through each stage like in an assembly line, in sequence, until the end. In the preceding figure, we can see that, using a buffered API, the process is entirely sequential. To compress the data, we first have to wait for the entire file to be read, then, to send the data, we have to wait for the entire file to be both read and compressed, and so on. When instead we are using streams, the assembly line is kicked off as soon as we receive the first chunk of data, without waiting for the entire file to be read. But more amazingly, when the next chunk of data is available, there is no need to wait for the previous set of tasks to be completed; instead, another assembly line is launched in parallel. This works perfectly because each task that we execute is asynchronous, so it can be parallelized by Node.js; the only constraint is that the order in which the chunks arrive in each stage must be preserved (and Node.js streams take care of this for us).

As we can see from the previous figure, the result of using streams is that the entire process takes less time, because we waste no time waiting for all the data to be read and processed all at once.

Composability

The code we have seen so far has already given us an overview of how streams can be composed thanks to the `pipe()` method, which allows us to connect the different processing units, each being responsible for one single functionality in perfect Node.js style. This is possible because streams have a uniform interface, and they can understand each other in terms of API. The only prerequisite is that the next stream in the pipeline has to support the data type produced by the previous stream, which can be either binary, text, or even objects, as we will see later in the chapter.

To take a look at another demonstration of the power of this property, we can try to add an encryption layer to the `gzipReceive`/`gzipSend` application that we built previously.

To do this, we only need to update the client by adding another stream to the pipeline; to be precise, the stream returned by `crypto.createChipher()`. The resulting code should be as follows:

```
const crypto = require('crypto');
// ...
fs.createReadStream(file)
  .pipe(zlib.createGzip())
  .pipe(crypto.createCipher('aes192', 'a_shared_secret'))
  .pipe(req)
  .on('finish', () => console.log('File succesfully sent'));
```

In a similar way, we can update the server so that the data is decrypted before being decompressed:

```
const crypto = require('crypto');
// ...
const server = http.createServer((req, res) => {
  // ...
  req
    .pipe(crypto.createDecipher('aes192', 'a_shared_secret'))
    .pipe(zlib.createGunzip())
    .pipe(fs.createWriteStream(filename))
    .on('finish', () => { /* ... */ });
});
```

With very little effort (just a few lines of code), we added an encryption layer to our application; we simply had to reuse an already available transform stream by including it in the pipeline that we already had. In a similar way, we can add and combine other streams, as if we were playing with Lego bricks.

Clearly, the main advantage of this approach is reusability, but as we can see from the code we presented so far, streams also enable cleaner and more modular code. For these reasons, streams are often used not just to deal with pure I/O, but also as a means to simplify and modularize the code.

Getting started with streams

In the previous section, we learned why streams are so powerful, but also that they are everywhere in Node.js, starting from its core modules. For example, we have seen that the `fs` module has `createReadStream()` for reading from a file and `createWriteStream()` for writing to a file, the HTTP `request` and `response` objects are essentially streams, and the `zlib` module allows us to compress and decompress data using a streaming interface.

Now that we know why streams are so important, let's take a step back and start to explore them in more detail.

Anatomy of streams

Every stream in Node.js is an implementation of one of the four base abstract classes available in the `stream` core module:

- `stream.Readable`
- `stream.Writable`
- `stream.Duplex`
- `stream.Transform`

Each `stream` class is also an instance of `EventEmitter`. Streams, in fact, can produce several types of event, such as `end`, when a Readable stream has finished reading, or `error`, when something goes wrong.

 Please note that, for brevity, in the examples presented in this chapter, we will often omit proper error management. However, in production applications it is always advised to register an `error` event listener for all your streams.

One of the reasons why streams are so flexible is the fact that they can not only handle binary data, but almost any JavaScript value; in fact, they can support two operating modes:

- **Binary mode**: This mode is where data is streamed in the form of chunks, such as buffers or strings
- **Object mode**: This mode is where the streaming data is treated as a sequence of discrete objects (allowing us to use almost any JavaScript value)

These two operating modes allow us to use streams not only for I/O, but also as a tool to elegantly compose processing units in a functional fashion, as we will see later in the chapter.

 In this chapter, we will mainly use the Node.js stream interface, also known as **Version 3**, which was introduced in Node.js 0.11. For further details about the differences with the old interfaces, please refer to this excellent blog post by StrongLoop at `https://strongloop.com/strong blog/whats-new-io-js-beta-streams3/`.

Readable streams

A Readable stream represents a source of data; in Node.js, it's implemented using the `Readable`abstract class that is available in the `stream` module.

Reading from a stream

There are two ways to receive the data from a Readable stream: **non-flowing** and **flowing**. Let's analyze these modes in more detail.

The non-flowing mode

The default pattern for reading from a Readable stream consists of attaching a listener for the `readable` event that signals the availability of new data to read. Then, in a loop, we read all the data until the internal buffer is emptied. This can be done using the `read()` method, which synchronously reads from the internal buffer and returns a `Buffer` or `String` object representing the chunk of data. The `read()` method has the following signature:

```
readable.read([size])
```

Using this approach, the data is explicitly pulled from the stream on demand.

To show how this works, let's create a new module named `readStdin.js`, which implements a simple program that reads from the standard input (a Readable stream) and echoes everything back to the standard output:

```
process.stdin
  .on('readable', () => {
    let chunk;
    console.log('New data available');
    while((chunk = process.stdin.read()) !== null) {
      console.log(
        `Chunk read: (${chunk.length}) "${chunk.toString()}"`
      );
    }
  })
  .on('end', () => process.stdout.write('End of stream'));
```

The `read()` method is a synchronous operation that pulls a data chunk from the internal buffers of the Readable stream. The returned chunk is, by default, a `Buffer` object if the stream is working in binary mode.

 In a Readable stream working in binary mode, we can read strings instead of buffers by calling `setEncoding(encoding)` on the stream, and provide a valid encoding format (for example, `utf8`).

The data is read exclusively from within the `readable` listener, which is invoked as soon as new data is available. The `read()` method returns `null` when there is no more data available in the internal buffers; in such a case, we have to wait for another `readable` event to be fired, telling us that we can read again or wait for the end event that signals the end of the stream. When a stream is working in binary mode, we can also specify that we are interested in reading a specific amount of data by passing a `size` value to the `read()` method. This is particularly useful when implementing network protocols or when parsing specific data formats.

Now, we are ready to run the `readStdin` module and experiment with it. Let's type some characters in the console and then press *Enter* to see the data echoed back into the standard output. To terminate the stream and hence generate a graceful end event, we need to insert an EOF (end-of-file) character (using *Ctrl + Z* on Windows or *Ctrl + D* on Linux).

We can also try to connect our program with other processes; this is possible using the pipe operator (|), which redirects the standard output of a program to the standard input of another. For example, we can run a command such as the following:

```
cat <path to a file> | node readStdin
```

This is an amazing demonstration of how the streaming paradigm is a universal interface, which enables our programs to communicate, regardless of the language they are written in.

Flowing mode

Another way to read from a stream is by attaching a listener to the data event; this will switch the stream into using **flowing mode**, where the data is not pulled using `read()`, but instead it's pushed to the data listener as soon as it arrives. For example, the `readStdin` application that we created earlier will look like this using flowing mode:

```
process.stdin
  .on('data', chunk => {
    console.log('New data available');
```

```
console.log(
  `Chunk read: (${chunk.length}) "${chunk.toString()}"`
);
})
.on('end', () => process.stdout.write('End of stream'));
```

Flowing mode is an inheritance of the old version of the stream interface (also known as **Streams1**), and offers less flexibility to control the flow of data. With the introduction of the **Streams2** interface, flowing mode is not the default working mode; to enable it, it's necessary to attach a listener to the data event or explicitly invoke the `resume()` method. To temporarily stop the stream from emitting data events, we can then invoke the `pause()` method, causing any incoming data to be cached in the internal buffer.

Calling `pause()` does not cause the stream to switch back to non-flowing mode.

Implementing Readable streams

Now that we know how to read from a stream, the next step is to learn how to implement a new Readable stream. To do this, it's necessary to create a new class by inheriting the prototype of `stream.Readable`. The concrete stream must provide an implementation of the `_read()` method, which has the following signature:

```
readable._read(size)
```

The internals of the `Readable` class will call the `_read()` method, which in turn will start to fill the internal buffer using `push()`:

```
readable.push(chunk)
```

Please note that `read()` is a method called by the stream consumers, while `_read()` is a method to be implemented by a stream subclass and should never be called directly. The underscore usually indicates that the method is not public and should not be called directly.

To demonstrate how to implement new Readable streams, we can try to implement a stream that generates random strings. Let's create a new module called `randomStream.js` that will contain the code of our string generator:

```
const stream = require('stream');
const Chance = require('chance');
```

```
const chance = new Chance();

class RandomStream extends stream.Readable {
  constructor(options) {
    super(options);
  }

  _read(size) {
    const chunk = chance.string();                        //[1]
    console.log(`Pushing chunk of size: ${chunk.length}`);
    this.push(chunk, 'utf8');                             //[2]
    if(chance.bool({likelihood: 5})) {                   //[3]
      this.push(null);
    }
  }
}

module.exports = RandomStream;
```

At the top of the file, we will load our dependencies. There is nothing special here, except that we are loading a npm module called chance (https://npmjs.org/package/chance), which is a library for generating all sorts of random values, from numbers to strings to entire sentences.

The next step is to create a new class called RandomStream and that specifies stream.Readable as its parent. In the preceding code, we call the constructor of the parent class to initialize its internal state, and forward the options argument received as input. The possible parameters passed through the options object include the following:

- The encoding argument that is used to convert Buffers to Strings (defaults to null)
- A flag to enable object mode (objectMode defaults to false)
- The upper limit of the data stored in the internal buffer, after which no more reading from the source should be done (highWaterMark defaults to 16KB)

Okay, now let's explain the _read() method:

- The method generates a random string using chance.
- It pushes the string into the internal reading buffer. Note that since we are pushing String, we also specify the encoding, utf8 (this is not necessary if the chunk is simply a binary Buffer).

- It terminates the stream randomly, with a likelihood of 5 percent, by pushing `null` into the internal buffer to indicate an EOF situation or, in other words, the end of the stream.

We can also see that the `size` argument given in input to the `_read()` function is ignored, as it is an advisory parameter. We can simply just push all the available data, but if there are multiple pushes inside the same invocation, then we should check whether `push()` returns `false`, as this would mean that the internal buffer has reached the `highWaterMark` limit and we should stop adding more data to it.

That's it for `RandomStream`; we are now ready to use it. Let's create a new module named `generateRandom.js` in which we instantiate a new `RandomStream` object and pull some data from it:

```
const RandomStream = require('./randomStream');
const randomStream = new RandomStream();

randomStream.on('readable', () => {
  let chunk;
  while((chunk = randomStream.read()) !== null) {
    console.log(`Chunk received: ${chunk.toString()}`);
  }
});
```

Now, everything is ready for us to try our new custom stream. Simply execute the `generateRandom` module as usual and watch a random set of strings flowing on the screen.

Writable streams

A Writable streamrepresents a data destination; in Node.js, it's implemented using the `Writable` abstract class, which is available in the stream module.

Writing to a stream

Pushing some data down a Writable stream is a straightforward business; all we need to do is to use the `write()` method, which has the following signature:

```
writable.write(chunk, [encoding], [callback])
```

The `encoding` argument is optional and can be specified if `chunk` is `String` (it defaults to `utf8`, and is ignored if `chunk` is `Buffer`); the `callback` function instead is called when the chunk is flushed into the underlying resource and is optional as well.

To signal that no more data will be written to the stream, we have to use the `end()` method:

```
writable.end([chunk], [encoding], [callback])
```

We can provide a final chunk of data through the `end()` method; in this case, the `callback` function is equivalent to registering a listener to the `finish` event, which is fired when all the data written in the stream has been flushed into the underlying resource.

Now, let's show how this works by creating a small HTTP server that outputs a random sequence of strings:

```
const Chance = require('chance');
const chance = new Chance();

require('http').createServer((req, res) => {
  res.writeHead(200, {'Content-Type': 'text/plain'});       //[1]
  while(chance.bool({likelihood: 95})) {                     //[2]
    res.write(chance.string() + '\n');                      //[3]
  }
  res.end('\nThe end...\n');                                 //[4]
  res.on('finish', () => console.log('All data was sent'));  //[5]
}).listen(8080, () => console.log('Listening on http://localhost:8080'));
```

The HTTP server that we created writes into the `res` object, which is an instance of `http.ServerResponse` and also a Writable stream. What happens is explained as follows:

1. We first write the head of the HTTP response. Note that `writeHead()` is not a part of the Writable interface; in fact, it's an auxiliary method exposed by the `http.ServerResponse` class.
2. We start a loop that terminates with a likelihood of 5% (we instruct `chance.bool()` to return `true` 95% of the time).
3. Inside the loop, we write a random string into the stream.
4. Once we are out of the loop, we call `end()` on the stream, indicating that no more data will be written. Also, we provide a final string to be written into the stream before ending it.
5. Finally, we register a listener for the `finish` event, which will be fired when all the data has been flushed into the underlying socket.

We can call this small module `entropyServer.js`, and then execute it. To test the server, we can open a browser at the address `http://localhost:8080`, or use `curl` from the terminal as follows:

curl localhost:8080

At this point, the server should start sending random strings to the HTTP client that you chose (please bear in mind that some browsers might buffer the data, and the streaming behavior might not be apparent).

Back-pressure

Similar to a liquid flowing in a real piping system, Node.js streams can also suffer from bottlenecks, where data is written faster than the stream can consume it. The mechanism to cope with this problem consists of buffering the incoming data; however, if the stream doesn't give any feedback to the writer, we might incur a situation where more and more data is accumulated into the internal buffer, leading to undesired levels of memory usage.

To prevent this from happening, writable.write() will return false when the internal buffer exceeds the highWaterMark limit. Writable streams have a highWaterMark property, which is the limit of the internal buffer size beyond which the write() method starts returning false, indicating that the application should now stop writing. When the buffer is emptied, the drain event is emitted, communicating that it's safe to start writing again. This mechanism is called **back-pressure**.

 The mechanism described in this section is similarly applicable to Readable streams. In fact, back-pressure exists in Readable streams too, and it's triggered when the push() method, which is invoked inside _read(), returns false. However, it's a problem specific to stream implementers, so we will deal with it less frequently.

We can quickly demonstrate how to take into account the back-pressure of a Writable stream by modifying the entropyServer that we created before:

```
const Chance = require('chance');
const chance = new Chance();

require('http').createServer((req, res) => {
  res.writeHead(200, {'Content-Type': 'text/plain'});

  function generateMore() {                          //[1]
    while(chance.bool({likelihood: 95})) {
      let shouldContinue = res.write(
      chance.string({length: (16 * 1024) - 1})        //[2]
    );
      if(!shouldContinue) {                           //[3]
        console.log('Backpressure');
        return res.once('drain', generateMore);
      }
    }
  }
```

```
      res.end('\nThe end...\n',() => console.log('All data was sent'));
   }
   generateMore();
}).listen(8080, () => console.log('Listening on http://localhost:8080'));
```

The most important steps of the previous code can be summarized as follows:

1. We wrapped the main logic in a function called `generateMore()`.

2. To increase the chances of receiving some back-pressure, we increased the size of the data chunk to 16 KB-1 Byte, which is very close to the default `highWaterMark` limit.

3. After writing a chunk of data, we check the return value of `res.write()`; if we receive `false`, it means that the internal buffer is full and we should stop sending more data. In this case, we exit from the function, and register another cycle of writes for when the `drain` event is emitted.

If we now try to run the server again, and then generate a client request with `curl`, there is a high probability that there will be some back-pressure, as the server produces data at a very high rate, faster than the underlying socket can handle.

Implementing Writable streams

We can implement a new Writable stream by inheriting the prototype of stream.Writable and providing an implementation for the `_write()` method. Let's try to do it immediately while discussing the details along the way.

Let's build a Writable stream that receives objects in the following format:

```
{
  path: <path to a file>
  content: <string or buffer>
}
```

For each one of these objects, our stream has to save the content part into a file created at the given path. We can immediately see that the inputs of our stream are objects, and not strings or buffers; this means that our stream has to work in `object` mode.

Let's call the module `toFileStream.js`:

```
const stream = require('stream');
const fs = require('fs');
const path = require('path');
const mkdirp = require('mkdirp');
```

```
class ToFileStream extends stream.Writable {
  constructor() {
    super({objectMode: true});
  }

  _write (chunk, encoding, callback) {
    mkdirp(path.dirname(chunk.path), err => {
      if (err) {
        return callback(err);
      }
      fs.writeFile(chunk.path, chunk.content, callback);
    });
  }
}
module.exports = ToFileStream;
```

As the first step, let's load all the dependencies that we are going to use. Beware that we are requiring the module `mkdirp` and, as you should know from the previous chapters, it should be installed with NPM.

We created a new class for our new stream, which extends from `stream.Writable`.

We had to invoke the parent constructor to initialize its internal state; we also provide an `options` object that specifies that the stream works in object mode (`objectMode: true`). Other options accepted by `stream.Writable` are as follows:

- `highWaterMark` (the default is 16 KB): This controls the back-pressure limit.
- `decodeStrings` (defaults to `true`): This enables the automatic decoding of strings into binary buffers before passing them to the `_write()` method. This option is ignored in object mode.

Finally, we provided an implementation for the `_write()` method. As you can see, the method accepts a data chunk, an encoding (which makes sense only if we are in binary mode and the stream option `decodeStrings` is set to `false`). Also, the method accepts a `callback` function, which needs to be invoked when the operation completes; it's not necessary to pass the result of the operation but, if needed, we can still pass an error that will cause the stream to emit an `error` event.

Now, to try the stream that we just built, we can create a new module called, for example, `writeToFile.js`, and perform some write operations against the stream:

```
const ToFileStream = require('./toFileStream.js');
const tfs = new ToFileStream();

tfs.write({path: "file1.txt", content: "Hello"});
```

```
tfs.write({path: "file2.txt", content: "Node.js"});
tfs.write({path: "file3.txt", content: "Streams"});
tfs.end(() => console.log("All files created"));
```

With this, we created and used our first custom Writable stream. Run the new module as usual to check its output; you will see that after the execution, three new files will be created.

Duplex streams

A Duplex stream is a stream that is both Readable and Writable. It is useful when we want to describe an entity that is both a data source and a data destination, such as network sockets, for example. Duplex streams inherit the methods of both stream.Readable and stream.Writable, so this is nothing new to us. This means that we can read() or write() data, or listen for both the readable and drain events.

To create a custom Duplex stream, we have to provide an implementation for both _read() and _write(); the options object passed to the Duplex() constructor is internally forwarded to both the Readable and Writable constructors. The options are the same as those we already discussed in the previous sections, with the addition of a new one called allowHalfOpen (defaults to true) that if set to false will cause both the parts (Readable and Writable) of the stream to end if only one of them does.

> To have a Duplex stream working in object mode on one side and binary mode on the other, we need to manually set the following properties from within the stream constructor:
> this._writableState.objectMode
> this._readableState.objectMode

Transform streams

The Transform streams are a special kind of Duplex stream that are specifically designed to handle data transformations.

In a simple Duplex stream, there is no immediate relationship between the data read from the stream and the data written into it (at least, the stream is agnostic to such a relationship). Think about a TCP socket, which just sends and receives data to and from the remote peer; the socket is not aware of any relationship between the input and output. The following diagram illustrates the data flow in a Duplex stream:

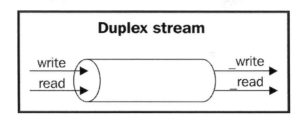

On the other side, `Transform` streams apply some kind of transformation to each chunk of data that they receive from their Writable side and then make the transformed data available on their Readable side. The following diagram shows how the data flows in a Transform stream:

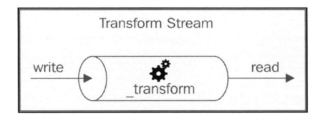

From the outside, the interface of a `Transform` stream is exactly like that of a Duplex stream. However, when we want to build a new Duplex stream, we have to provide the `_read()` and `_write()` methods while, for implementing a new `Transform` stream, we have to fill in another pair of methods: `_transform()` and `_flush()`.

Let's show how to create a new `Transform` stream with an example.

Implementing Transform streams

Let's implement a `Transform` stream that replaces all the occurrences of a given string. To do this, we have to create a new module named `replaceStream.js`. Let's jump directly to the implementation:

```
const stream = require('stream');
const util = require('util');

class ReplaceStream extends stream.Transform {
  constructor(searchString, replaceString) {
    super();
    this.searchString = searchString;
```

```
    this.replaceString = replaceString;
    this.tailPiece = '';
  }

  _transform(chunk, encoding, callback) {
    const pieces = (this.tailPiece + chunk)            //[1]
      .split(this.searchString);
    const lastPiece = pieces[pieces.length - 1];
    const tailPieceLen = this.searchString.length - 1;

    this.tailPiece = lastPiece.slice(-tailPieceLen);    //[2]
    pieces[pieces.length - 1] = lastPiece.slice(0,-tailPieceLen);

    this.push(pieces.join(this.replaceString));         //[3]
    callback();
  }

  _flush(callback) {
    this.push(this.tailPiece);
    callback();
  }
}

module.exports = ReplaceStream;
```

As always, we will start building the module from its dependencies. This time we are not using third-party modules.

Then we created a new class extending from the `stream.Transform` base class. The constructor of the class accepts two arguments: `searchString` and `replaceString`. As you can imagine, they allow us to define the text to match and the string to use as a replacement. We also initialize an internal `tailPiece` variable that will be used by the `_transform()` method.

Now, let's analyze the `_transform()` method, which is the core of our new class. The `_transform()` method has practically the same signature as that of the `_write()` method of the Writable stream but, instead of writing data into an underlying resource, it pushes it into the internal buffer using `this.push()`, exactly as we would do in the `_read()` method of a Readable stream. This confirms how the two sides of a `Transform` stream are actually connected.

The `_transform()` method of `ReplaceStream` implements the core of our algorithm. To search and replace a string in a buffer is an easy task; however, it's a totally different story when the data is streaming, and possible matches might be distributed across multiple chunks. The procedure followed by the code can be explained as follows:

1. Our algorithm splits the chunk using the `searchString` function as a separator.
2. Then, it takes the last item of the array generated by the operation and extracts the last *searchString.length – 1* characters. The result is saved into the `tailPiece` variable and it will be prepended to the next chunk of data.
3. Finally, all the pieces resulting from `split()` are joined together using `replaceString` as a separator and pushed into the internal buffer.

When the stream ends, we might still have a last `tailPiece` variable not pushed into the internal buffer. That's exactly what the `_flush()` method is for; it is invoked just before the stream is ended, and this is where we have one final chance to finalize the stream or push any remaining data before completely ending the stream.

The `_flush()` method only takes in a callback that we have to make sure to invoke when all the operations are complete, causing the stream to be terminated. With this, we have completed our `ReplaceStream` class.

Now, it's time to try the new stream. We can create another module called `replaceStreamTest.js` that writes some data and then reads the transformed result:

```
const ReplaceStream = require('./replaceStream');

const rs = new ReplaceStream('World', 'Node.js');
rs.on('data', chunk => console.log(chunk.toString()));

rs.write('Hello W');
rs.write('orld!');
rs.end();
```

To make life a little bit harder for our stream, we spread the search term (which is `World`) across two different chunks; then, using flowing mode, we read from the same stream, logging each transformed chunk. Running the preceding program should produce the following output:

```
Hel
lo Node.js
!
```

 There is a fifth type of stream that is worth mentioning: `stream.PassThrough`. Unlike the other stream classes that we presented, `PassThrough` is not abstract and can be instantiated straightaway without the need to implement any method. It is, in fact, a `Transform` stream that outputs every data chunk without applying any transformation.

Connecting streams using pipes

The concept of Unix pipes was invented by Douglas McIlroy; this enabled the output of a program to be connected to the input of the next. Take a look at the following command:

```
echo Hello World! | sed s/World/Node.js/g
```

In the preceding command, `echo` will write `Hello World!` to its standard output, which is then redirected to the standard input of the `sed` command (thanks to the pipe `|` operator); then `sed` replaces any occurrence of `World` with Node.js and prints the result to its standard output (which, this time, is the console).

In a similar way, Node.js streams can be connected together using the `pipe()` method of the Readable stream, which has the following interface:

```
readable.pipe(writable, [options])
```

Very intuitively, the `pipe()` method takes the data that is emitted from the `readable` stream and pumps it into the provided `writable` stream. Also, the `writable` stream is ended automatically when the `readable` stream emits an `end` event (unless we specify `{end: false}` as `options`). The `pipe()` method returns the `writable` stream passed as an argument, allowing us to create chained invocations if such a stream is also Readable (such as a `Duplex` or `Transform` stream).

Piping two streams together will create a *suction* which allows the data to flow automatically to the `writable` stream, so there is no need to call `read()` or `write()`; but most importantly there is no need to control the back-pressure anymore, because it's automatically taken care of.

To make a quick example (there will be tons of them coming), we can create a new module called `replace.js` that takes a text stream from the standard input, applies the *replace* transformation, and then pushes the data back to the standard output:

```
const ReplaceStream = require('./replaceStream');
process.stdin
  .pipe(new ReplaceStream(process.argv[2], process.argv[3]))
  .pipe(process.stdout);
```

The preceding program pipes the data that comes from the standard input into a `ReplaceStream` and then back to the standard output. Now, to try this small application, we can leverage a Unix pipe to redirect some data into its standard input, as shown in the following example:

```
echo Hello World! | node replace World Node.js
```

This should produce the following output:

```
Hello Node.js
```

This simple example demonstrates that streams (and in particular text streams) are a universal interface, and pipes are the way to compose and interconnect almost magically all these interfaces.

The `error` events are not propagated automatically through the pipeline. Take, for example, this code fragment:
```
stream1
  .pipe(stream2)
  .on('error', function() {});
```
In the preceding pipeline, we will catch only the errors coming from `stream2`, which is the stream that we attached the listener to. This means that, if we want to catch any error generated from `stream1`, we have to attach another error listener directly to it. We will later see a pattern that mitigates this inconvenience (combining streams). Also, we should notice that if the destination stream emits an error it gets automatically unpiped from the source stream, causing the pipeline to break.

Through and from for working with streams

The way we created custom streams so far does not exactly follow the *Node* way; in fact, inheriting from a base stream class violates the small surface area principle and requires some boilerplate code. This does not mean that the streams were badly designed; in fact, we should not forget that since they are a part of the Node.js core they must be as flexible as possible in order to enable userland modules to extend them for a broad range of purposes.

However, most of the time we don't need all the power and extensibility that prototypal inheritance can give, but usually what we want is just a quick and an expressive way to define new streams. The Node.js community, of course, created a solution also for this. A perfect example is through2 (`https://npmjs.org/package/through2`), a small library which simplifies the creation of `Transform` streams. With `through2`, we can create a new `Transform` stream by invoking a simple function:

```
const transform = through2([options], [_transform], [_flush])
```

In a similar way, `from2` (`https://npmjs.org/package/from2`) allows us to easily and succinctly create Readable streams with code such as the following:

```
const readable = from2([options], _read)
```

The advantages of using these little libraries will be immediately clear as soon as we start showing their usage in the rest of the chapter.

 The packages `through` (`https://npmjs.org/package/through`) and `from` (`https://npmjs.org/package/from`) are the original libraries built on top of Streams1.

Asynchronous control flow with streams

Going through the examples that we have presented so far, it should be clear that streams can be useful not only to handle I/O, but also as an elegant programming pattern that can be used to process any kind of data. But the advantages do not end at the simple appearance; streams can also be leveraged to turn the asynchronous control flow into flow control, as we will see in this section.

Sequential execution

By default, streams will handle data in a sequence; for example, a `_transform()` function of a `Transform` stream will never be invoked again with the next chunk of data, until the previous invocation completes by executing `callback()`. This is an important property of streams, crucial for processing each chunk in the right order, but it can also be exploited to turn streams into an elegant alternative to the traditional control flow patterns.

Some code is always better than too much explanation, so let's work on an example to demonstrate how we can use streams to execute asynchronous tasks in a sequence. Let's create a function that concatenates a set of files received as input, making sure to honor the order in which they are provided. Let's create a new module called `concatFiles.js` and define its contents starting from its dependencies:

```
const fromArray = require('from2-array');
const through = require('through2');
const fs = require('fs');
```

We will be using `through2` to simplify the creation of `Transform` streams and `from2-array` in order to create a Readable stream from an array of objects.

Next, we can define the `concatFiles()` function:

```
function concatFiles(destination, files, callback) {
  const destStream = fs.createWriteStream(destination);
  fromArray.obj(files)                          //[1]
    .pipe(through.obj((file, enc, done) => {    //[2]
      const src = fs.createReadStream(file);
      src.pipe(destStream, {end: false});
      src.on('end', done)                       //[3]
    }))
    .on('finish', () => {                       //[4]
      destStream.end();
      callback();
    });
}
module.exports = concatFiles;
```

The preceding function implements a sequential iteration over the `files` array by transforming it into a stream. The procedure followed by the `function` is explained as follows:

1. First, we use `from2-array` to create a Readable stream from the `files` array.
2. Next, we create a `through` (`Transform`) stream to handle each file in the sequence. For each file, we create a Readable stream and we pipe it into `destStream`, which represents the output file. We make sure not to close `destStream` after the source file finishes reading, by specifying `{end: false}` into the `pipe()` options.
3. When all the contents of the source file have been piped into `destStream`, we invoke the `done` function, which is exposed by `through.obj` to communicate the completion of the current processing, which in our case is necessary to trigger the processing of the next file.
4. When all the files have been processed, the `finish` event is fired; we can finally end `destStream` and invoke the `callback()` function of `concatFiles()`, which signals the completion of the whole operation.

We can now try to use the little module we just created. Let's do that in a new file, called `concat.js`:

```
const concatFiles = require('./concatFiles');
concatFiles(process.argv[2], process.argv.slice(3), () => {
  console.log('Files concatenated successfully');
});
```

We can now run the preceding program by passing the destination file as the first command-line argument followed by a list of files to concatenate, for example:

```
node concatallTogether.txtfile1.txtfile2.txt
```

This should create a new file called `allTogether.txt` containing, in order, the contents of `file1.txt` and `file2.txt`.

With the `concatFiles()` function, we were able to obtain an asynchronous sequential iteration using only streams. As we saw in Chapter 3, *Asynchronous Control Flow Patterns with Callbacks*, this would have required the use of an iterator, if implemented with pure JavaScript, or an external library such as `async`. We have now provided another option for achieving the same result, which as we see is also very compact and elegant.

Pattern
Use a stream, or combination of streams, to easily iterate over a set of asynchronous tasks in sequence.

Unordered parallel execution

We just saw that streams process each data chunk in a sequence, but sometimes this can be a bottleneck as we would not make the most of the Node.js concurrency. If we have to execute a slow asynchronous operation for every data chunk, it can be advantageous to parallelize the execution and speed up the overall process. Of course, this pattern can only be applied if there is no relationship between each chunk of data, which might happen frequently for object streams, but very rarely for binary streams.

Caution
Parallel streams cannot be used when the order in which the data is processed is important.

To parallelize the execution of a `Transform` stream, we can apply the same patterns that we learned in `Chapter 3`, *Asynchronous Control Flow Patterns with Callbacks*, but with some adaptations to get them working with streams. Let's see how this works.

Implementing an unordered parallel stream

Let's demonstrate this immediately with an example; let's create a module called `parallelStream.js` and define a generic `Transform` stream that executes a given transform function in parallel:

```
const stream = require('stream');

class ParallelStream extends stream.Transform {
  constructor(userTransform) {
    super({objectMode: true});
    this.userTransform = userTransform;
    this.running = 0;
    this.terminateCallback = null;
  }

  _transform(chunk, enc, done) {
    this.running++;
    this.userTransform(chunk, enc, this.push.bind(this),
```

```
        this._onComplete.bind(this));
      done();
    }

    _flush(done) {
      if(this.running> 0) {
        this.terminateCallback = done;
      } else {
        done();
      }
    }

    _onComplete(err) {
      this.running--;
      if(err) {
        return this.emit('error', err);
      }
      if(this.running === 0) {
        this.terminateCallback && this.terminateCallback();
      }
    }

  }

  module.exports = ParallelStream;
```

Let's analyze this new class. As you can see, the constructor accepts a userTransform() function, which is then saved as an instance variable; we also invoke the parent constructor and for convenience we enable the object mode by default.

Next, it is the turn of the _transform() method. In this method, we execute the userTransform() function, then we increment the count of running tasks; finally, we notify that the current transformation step is complete by invoking done(). The trick for triggering the processing of another item in parallel is exactly this; we are not waiting for the userTransform() function to complete before invoking done(); instead, we do it immediately. On the other hand, we provide a special callback to userTransform(), which is the this._onComplete() method; this allows us to get notified when the userTransform() completes.

The _flush() method is invoked just before the stream terminates, so if there are still tasks running we can put on hold the release of the finish event by not invoking the done() callback immediately; instead, we assign it to the this.terminateCallback variable. To understand how the stream is then properly terminated, we have to look into the _onComplete() method. This last method is invoked every time an asynchronous task completes. It checks whether there are any more tasks running and, if there are none, it invokes the this.terminateCallback() function, which will cause the stream to end, releasing the finish event that was put on hold in the _flush() method.

The ParallelStream class we just built allows us to easily create a Transform stream that executes its tasks in parallel, but there is a caveat: it does not preserve the order of the items as they are received. In fact, asynchronous operations can complete and push data at any time, regardless of when they are started. We immediately understand that this property does not play well with binary streams where the order of data usually matters, but it can surely be useful with some types of object streams.

Implementing a URL status monitoring application

Now, let's apply our ParallelStream to a concrete example. Let's imagine that we wanted to build a simple service to monitor the status of a big list of URLs. Let's imagine all these URLs are contained in a single file and are newline separated.

Streams can offer a very efficient and elegant solution to this problem, especially if we use our ParallelStream class to parallelize the checking of the URLs.

Let's build this simple application immediately in a new module called checkUrls.js:

```
const fs = require('fs');
const split = require('split');
const request = require('request');
const ParallelStream = require('./parallelStream');

fs.createReadStream(process.argv[2])                     //[1]
  .pipe(split())                                          //[2]
  .pipe(new ParallelStream((url, enc, push, done) => {    //[3]
    if(!url) return done();
    request.head(url, (err, response) => {
      push(url + ' is ' + (err ? 'down' : 'up') + '\n');
      done();
    });
  }))
  .pipe(fs.createWriteStream('results.txt'))    //[4]
  .on('finish', () => console.log('All urls were checked'));
```

As we can see, with streams our code looks very elegant and straightforward; let's see how it works:

1. First, we create a Readable stream from the file given as input.

2. We pipe the contents of the input file through `split` (`https://npmjs.org/pac kage/split`), a `Transform` stream that ensures outputting each line on a different chunk.

3. Then, it's the time to use our `ParallelStream` to check the URL. We do this by sending a `head` request and waiting for a response. When the callback is invoked, we push the result of the operation down the stream.

4. Finally, all the results are piped into a file, `results.txt`.

Now, we can run the `checkUrls` module with a command such as this:

```
node checkUrlsurlList.txt
```

Here the file `urlList.txt` contains a list of URLs, for example:

- `http://www.mariocasciaro.me`
- `http://loige.co`
- `http://thiswillbedownforsure.com`

When the command finishes running, we will see that a file, `results.txt`, was created. This contains the results of the operation, for example:

```
http://thiswillbedownforsure.com is down
http://loige.co is up
http://www.mariocasciaro.me is up
```

There is a good probability that the order in which the results are written is different from the order in which the URLs were specified in the input file. This is clear evidence that our stream executes its tasks in parallel, and it does not enforce any order between the various data chunks in the stream.

 For the sake of curiosity, we might want to try replacing `ParallelStream` with a normal `through2` stream, and compare the behavior and performances of the two (you might want to do this as an exercise). We will see that using `through2` is way slower, because each URL would be checked in a sequence, but also that the order of the results in the file `results.txt` would be preserved.

Unordered limited parallel execution

If we try to run the `checkUrls` application against a file that contains thousands or millions of URLs, we will surely run into trouble. Our application will create an uncontrolled number of connections all at once, sending a considerable amount of data in parallel and potentially undermining the stability of the application and the availability of the entire system. As we already know, the solution to keep the load and resource usage under control is to limit the concurrency of the parallel tasks.

Let's see how this works with streams by creating a `limitedParallelStream.js` module, which is an adaptation of `parallelStream.js` that we created in the previous section.

Let's see what it looks like, starting from its constructor (we will highlight the changed parts):

```
class LimitedParallelStream extends stream.Transform {
  constructor(concurrency, userTransform) {
    super({objectMode: true});
    this.concurrency = concurrency;
    this.userTransform = userTransform;
    this.running = 0;
    this.terminateCallback = null;
    this.continueCallback = null;
  }
//...
```

We need a `concurrency` limit to be taken as the input, and this time we are going to save two callbacks, one for any pending `_transform` method (`continueCallback`) and another one for the callback of the `_flush` method (`terminateCallback`).

Next is the `_transform()` method:

```
_transform(chunk, enc, done) {
  this.running++;
  this.userTransform(chunk, enc, this._onComplete.bind(this));
  if(this.running < this.concurrency) {
    done();
  } else {
    this.continueCallback = done;
  }
}
```

This time in the `_transform()` method, we have to check whether we have any free execution slots before we invoke `done()` and trigger the processing of the next item. If we have already reached the maximum number of concurrent running streams, we can simply save the `done()` callback into the `continueCallback` variable, so that it can be invoked as soon as a task finishes.

The `_flush()` method remains exactly the same as in the `ParallelStream` class, so let's move directly to implementing the `_onComplete()` method:

```
_onComplete(err) {
  this.running--;
  if(err) {
    return this.emit('error', err);
  }
  const tmpCallback = this.continueCallback;
  this.continueCallback = null;
  tmpCallback && tmpCallback();
  if(this.running === 0) {
    this.terminateCallback && this.terminateCallback();
  }
}
```

Every time a task completes we invoke any saved `continueCallback()` that will cause the stream to unblock, triggering the processing of the next item.

That's it for the `limitedParallelStream` module; we can now use it in the `checkUrls` module in place of `parallelStream` and have the concurrency of our tasks limited to the value that we set.

Ordered parallel execution

The parallel streams that we created previously might shuffle the order of the emitted data, but there are situations where this is not acceptable; sometimes, in fact, it is necessary to have each chunk emitted in the same order in which it was received. However, not all hopes is lost, we can still run the transform function in parallel; all we have to do is to sort the data emitted by each task so that it follows the same order in which the data was received.

This technique involves the use of a buffer to reorder the chunks while they are emitted by each running task. For brevity, we are not going to provide an implementation of such a stream, as it's quite verbose for the scope of this book; what we are going to do instead is reuse one of the available packages on NPM built for this specific purpose, for example, `through2-parallel` (`https://npmjs.org/package/through2-parallel`).

We can quickly check the behavior of an ordered parallel execution by modifying our existing `checkUrls` module. Let's say that we want our results to be written in the same order as the URLs in the input file, while executing our checks in parallel. We can do this using `through2-parallel`:

```
//...
const throughParallel = require('through2-parallel');

fs.createReadStream(process.argv[2])
  .pipe(split())
  .pipe(throughParallel.obj({concurrency: 2},(url, enc, done) => {
      //...
    })
  )
  .pipe(fs.createWriteStream('results.txt'))
  .on('finish', () => console.log('All urls were checked'));
```

As we can see, the interface of `through2-parallel` is very similar to that of `through2`; the only difference is that we can also specify a concurrency limit for the transform function that we provide. If we try to run this new version of `checkUrls`, we will now see that the `results.txt` file lists the results in the same order as the URLs appear in the input file.

 It is important to see that, even though the order of the output is the same as the input, the asynchronous tasks still run in parallel and can possibly complete in any order.

With this, we conclude our analysis of the asynchronous control flow with streams; next, we are going to focus on some piping patterns.

Piping patterns

As in real-life plumbing, Node.js streams also can be piped together following different patterns; we can, in fact, merge the flow of two different streams into one, split the flow of one stream into two or more pipes, or redirect the flow based on a condition. In this section, we are going to explore the most important plumbing techniques that can be applied to Node.js streams.

Combining streams

In this chapter, we have stressed a lot on the fact that streams provide a simple infrastructure to modularize and reuse our code, but there is one last piece missing in this puzzle: what if we want to modularize and reuse an entire pipeline? What if we want to combine multiple streams so that they look like one from the outside? The following figure shows what this means:

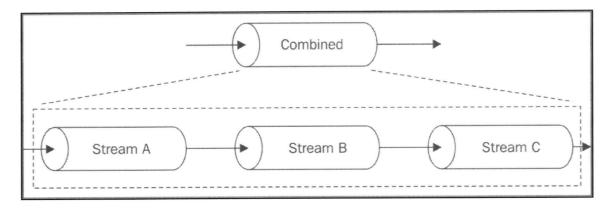

From the preceding diagram, we should already get a hint of how this works:

- When we write into the combined stream, we are actually writing into the first stream of the pipeline
- When we read from the combined stream, we are actually reading from the last stream of the pipeline

A combined stream is usually a Duplex stream, which is built by connecting the first stream to its Writable side and the last stream to its Readable side.

> To create a Duplex stream out of two different streams, one Writable and one Readable, we can use an npm module such as duplexer2 (https://npmjs.org/package/duplexer2).

But that's not enough; in fact, another important characteristic of a combined stream is that it has to capture all the errors that are emitted from any stream inside the pipeline. As we already mentioned, any error event is not automatically propagated down the pipeline; so, if we want to have proper error management (and we should), we will have to explicitly attach an error listener to each stream. However, if the combined stream is really a black box, which means that we don't have access to any of the streams in the middle of the pipeline, so it's crucial for the combined stream to also act as an *aggregator* for all the errors coming from any stream in the pipeline.

To recap, a combined stream has two major advantages:

- We can redistribute it as a black box by hiding its internal pipeline
- We have simplified error management, as we don't have to attach an error listener to each stream in the pipeline, but just to the combined stream itself

Combining streams is a pretty generic and common practice, so if we don't have any particular need we might just want to reuse an existing solution such as multipipe (https://www.npmjs.org/package/multipipe) or combine-stream (https://www.npmjs.org/package/combine-stream), just to name two.

Implementing a combined stream

To illustrate a simple example, let's consider the case of the following two transform streams:

- One that both compresses and encrypts the data
- One that both decrypts and decompresses the data

Using a library such as multipipe, we can easily build these streams by combining some of the streams that we already have available from the core libraries (file combinedStreams.js):

```
const zlib = require('zlib');
const crypto = require('crypto');
const combine = require('multipipe');

module.exports.compressAndEncrypt = password => {
  return combine(
    zlib.createGzip(),
    crypto.createCipher('aes192', password)
  );
};
```

```
module.exports.decryptAndDecompress = password => {
  return combine(
    crypto.createDecipher('aes192', password),
    zlib.createGunzip()
  );
};
```

We can now use these combined streams as if they were black boxes, for example, to create a small application that archives a file by compressing and encrypting it. Let's do that in a new module named `archive.js`:

```
const fs = require('fs');
const compressAndEncryptStream =
  require('./combinedStreams').compressAndEncrypt;

fs.createReadStream(process.argv[3])
  .pipe(compressAndEncryptStream(process.argv[2]))
  .pipe(fs.createWriteStream(process.argv[3] + ".gz.enc"));
```

We can further improve the preceding code by building a combined stream out of the pipeline that we created, this time not to obtain a reusable black box but only to take advantage of its aggregated error management. In fact, as we have already mentioned many times, writing something such as the following will only catch the errors that are emitted by the last stream:

```
fs.createReadStream(process.argv[3])
  .pipe(compressAndEncryptStream(process.argv[2]))
  .pipe(fs.createWriteStream(process.argv[3] + ".gz.enc"))
  .on('error', err => {
    //Only errors from the last stream
    console.log(err);
  });
```

However, by combining all the streams together, we can fix the problem elegantly. Let's then rewrite the `archive.js` file as follows:

```
const combine = require('multipipe');
const fs = require('fs');
const compressAndEncryptStream =
  require('./combinedStreams').compressAndEncrypt;

combine(
  fs.createReadStream(process.argv[3])
  .pipe(compressAndEncryptStream(process.argv[2]))
  .pipe(fs.createWriteStream(process.argv[3] + ".gz.enc"))
).on('error', err => {
  //this error may come from any stream in the pipeline
```

```
  console.log(err);
});
```

As we can see, we can now attach an error listener directly to the combined stream and it will receive any `error` event that is emitted by any of its internal streams.

Now, to run the `archive` module, simply specify a password and a file in the command-line argument:

node archive mypassword /path/to/a/file.txt

With this example, we have clearly demonstrated how important it is to combine streams; from one aspect, it allows us to create reusable compositions of streams, and from another, it simplifies the error management of a pipeline.

Forking streams

We can perform a *fork* of a stream by piping a single Readable stream into multiple Writable streams. This is useful when we want to send the same data to different destinations, for example, two different sockets or two different files. It can also be used when we want to perform different transformations on the same data, or when we want to split the data based on some criteria. The following figure gives us a graphical representation of this pattern:

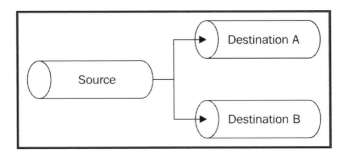

Forking a stream in Node.js is a trivial matter; let's see why by working on an example.

Implementing a multiple checksum generator

Let's create a small utility that outputs both the `sha1` and `md5` hashes of a given file. Let's call this new module `generateHashes.js` and let's start by initializing our checksum streams:

```
const fs = require('fs');
const crypto = require('crypto');

const sha1Stream = crypto.createHash('sha1');
sha1Stream.setEncoding('base64');

const md5Stream = crypto.createHash('md5');
md5Stream.setEncoding('base64');
```

Nothing special so far; the next part of the module is actually where we will create a Readable stream from a file and fork it to two different streams in order to obtain two other files, one containing the `sha1` hash and the other containing the `md5` checksum:

```
const inputFile = process.argv[2];
const inputStream = fs.createReadStream(inputFile);
inputStream
  .pipe(sha1Stream)
  .pipe(fs.createWriteStream(inputFile + '.sha1'));

inputStream
  .pipe(md5Stream)
  .pipe(fs.createWriteStream(inputFile + '.md5'));
```

Very simple, right? The `inputStream` variable is piped into `sha1Stream` on one side and `md5Stream` on the other. There are a couple of things to note, though, that happen behind the scenes:

- Both `md5Stream` and `sha1Stream` will be ended automatically when `inputStream` ends, unless we specify `{end: false}` as an option when invoking `pipe()`
- The two forks of the stream will receive the same data chunks, so we must be very careful when performing side-effect operations on the data, as that would affect every stream that we are forking to
- Back-pressure will work out-of-the-box; the flow coming from `inputStream` will go as fast as the slowest branch of the fork!

Merging streams

Merging is the opposite operation to forking and consists of piping a set of Readable streams into a single Writable stream, as shown in the following figure:

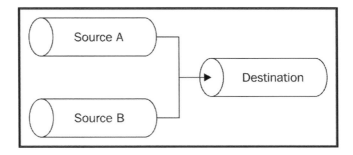

Merging multiple streams into one is in general a simple operation; however, we have to pay attention to the way we handle the end event, as piping using the auto end option will cause the destination stream to be ended as soon as one of the sources ends. This can often lead to an error situation, as the other active sources will still continue to write to an already terminated stream. The solution to this problem is to use the option {end: false} when piping multiple sources to a single destination and then invoke end() on the destination only when all the sources have completed reading.

Creating a tarball from multiple directories

To make a simple example, let's implement a small program that creates a tarball from the contents of two different directories. For this purpose, we are going to introduce two new NPM packages:

- tar (https://npmjs.org/package/tar): a streaming library to create tarballs
- fstream (https://npmjs.org/package/fstream): a library to create object streams from filesystem files

Our new module is going to be called `mergeTar.js`; let's define its contents starting from some initialization steps:

```
const tar = require('tar');
const fstream = require('fstream');
const path = require('path');

const destination = path.resolve(process.argv[2]);
const sourceA = path.resolve(process.argv[3]);
const sourceB = path.resolve(process.argv[4]);
```

In the preceding code, we are just loading all the dependencies and initializing the variables that contain the name of the destination file and the two source directories (`sourceA` and `sourceB`).

Next, we will create the `tar` stream and pipe it into its destination:

```
const pack = tar.Pack();
pack.pipe(fstream.Writer(destination));
```

Now it's time to initialize the `source` streams:

```
let endCount = 0;
function onEnd() {
  if(++endCount === 2) {
    pack.end();
  }
}

const sourceStreamA = fstream.Reader({type: "Directory", path: sourceA})
  .on('end', onEnd);

const sourceStreamB = fstream.Reader({type: "Directory", path: sourceB})
  .on('end', onEnd);
```

In the preceding code, we created the streams that read from both the two source directories (`sourceStreamA` and `sourceStreamB`); then for each source stream we attach an `end` listener, which will terminate the `pack` stream only when both the directories are read completely.

Finally, it is time to perform the real merge:

```
sourceStreamA.pipe(pack, {end: false});
sourceStreamB.pipe(pack, {end: false});
```

We pipe both the sources into the `pack` stream and take care to disable the auto ending of the destination stream by providing the option `{end: false}` to the two `pipe()` invocations.

With this, we have completed our simple TAR utility. We can try this utility by providing the destination file as the first command-line argument, followed by the two source directories:

node mergeTar dest.tar /path/to/sourceA /path/to/sourceB

To conclude this section, it's worth mentioning that, on npm, we can find a few modules that can simplify the merging of streams, for example:

- `merge-stream` (https://npmjs.org/package/merge-stream)
- `multistream-merge` (https://npmjs.org/package/multistream-merge)

As for the last comment on the stream merge pattern, it's worth reminding that the data piped into the destination stream is randomly intermingled; this is a property that can be acceptable in some types of object streams (as we saw in the last example) but it is often an undesired effect when dealing with binary streams.

However, there is one variation of the pattern that allows us to merge streams in order; it consists of consuming the source streams one after the other, when the previous one ends, the next one starts emitting chunks (it is like *concatenating* the output of all the sources). As always, on NPM we can find some packages that also deal with this situation. One of them is `multistream` (https://npmjs.org/package/multistream).

Multiplexing and demultiplexing

There is a particular variation of the merge stream pattern in which we don't really want to just join multiple streams together but, instead, use a shared channel to deliver the data of a set of streams. This is a conceptually different operation because the source streams remain logically separated inside the shared channel, which allows us to split the stream again once the data reaches the other end of the shared channel. The following figure clarifies the situation:

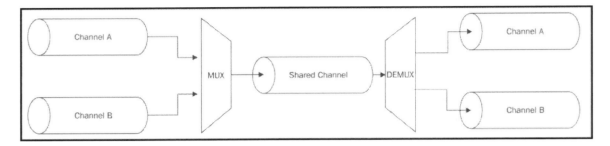

The operation of combining multiple streams together (in this case, also known as **channels**) to allow transmission over a single stream is called **multiplexing**, while the opposite operation, namely reconstructing the original streams from the data received from a shared stream, is called **demultiplexing**. The *devices* that perform these operations are called **multiplexer** (or **mux**) and **demultiplexer** (or **demux**) respectively. This is a widely studied area in computer science and telecommunications in general, as it is one of the foundations of almost any type of communication media such as telephony, radio, TV, and of course the Internet itself. For the scope of this book, we will not go too far with the explanations, as this is a vast topic.

What we want to demonstrate in this section, instead, is how it's possible to use a shared Node.js stream in order to convey multiple logically separated streams that are then split again at the other end of the shared stream.

Building a remote logger

Let's use an example to drive our discussion. We want to have a small program that starts a child process and redirects both its standard output and standard error to a remote server, which in turn saves the two streams into two separate files. So, in this case, the shared medium is a TCP connection, while the two channels to be multiplexed are the `stdout` and `stderr` of a child process. We will leverage a technique called **packet switching**, the same technique that is used by protocols such as IP, TCP, or UDP and that consists of wrapping the data into *packets* allowing us to specify various meta information, useful for multiplexing, routing, controlling the flow, checking for corrupted data, and so on. The protocol that we are going to implement for our example is very minimalist; in fact, we will simply wrap our data into packets with the following structure:

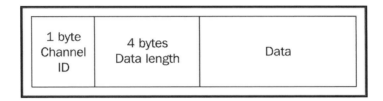

As shown in the preceding figure, the packet contains the actual data, but also a header (*Channel ID + Data length*), which will make it possible to differentiate the data of each stream and enable the demultiplexer to route the packet to the right channel.

Client side – multiplexing

Let's start to build our application from the client side. With a lot of creativity, we will call the module `client.js`; this represents the part of the application that is responsible for starting a child process and multiplexing its streams.

So, let's start by defining the module. First, we need some dependencies:

```
const child_process = require('child_process');
const net = require('net');
```

Then, let's implement a function that performs the multiplexing of a list of sources:

```
function multiplexChannels(sources, destination) {
  let totalChannels = sources.length;
  for(let i = 0; i <sources.length; i++) {
    sources[i]
      .on('readable', function() {                        //[1]
        let chunk;
        while((chunk = this.read()) !== null) {
          const outBuff = new Buffer(1 + 4 + chunk.length);  //[2]
          outBuff.writeUInt8(i, 0);
          outBuff.writeUInt32BE(chunk.length, 1);
          chunk.copy(outBuff, 5);
          console.log('Sending packet to channel: ' + i);
          destination.write(outBuff);                     //[3]
        }
      })
      .on('end', () => {                                   //[4]
        if(--totalChannels === 0) {
          destination.end();
        }
      });
  }
}
```

The `multiplexChannels()` function takes in as input the source streams to be multiplexed and the destination channel, and then it performs the following steps:

1. For each source stream, it registers a listener for the `readable` event where we read the data from the stream using the non-flowing mode.
2. When a chunk is read, we wrap it into a packet that contains in order: 1 byte (UInt8) for the channel ID, 4 bytes (UInt32BE) for the packet size, and then the actual data.
3. When the packet is ready, we write it into the destination stream.
4. Finally, we register a listener for the `end` event so that we can terminate the destination stream when all the source streams are ended.

 Our protocol is to be able to multiplex up to 256 different source streams because we only have 1 byte to identify the channel.

Now the last part of our client becomes very easy:

```
const socket = net.connect(3000, () => {              //[1]
  const child = child_process.fork(                   //[2]
  process.argv[2],
  process.argv.slice(3),
    {silent: true}
  );
  multiplexChannels([child.stdout, child.stderr], socket);  //[3]
});
```

In this last code fragment, we perform the following operations:

1. We create a new TCP client connection to the address `localhost:3000`.
2. We start the child process by using the first command-line argument as the path, while we provide the rest of the `process.argv` array as arguments for the child process. We specify the option `{silent: true}`, so that the child process does not inherit `stdout` and `stderr` of the parent.
3. Finally, we take `stdout` and `stderr` of the child process and we multiplex them into socket using the `mutiplexChannels()` function.

Server side – demultiplexing

Now we can take care of creating the server side of the application (`server.js`), where we demultiplex the streams from the remote connection and pipe them into two different files. Let's start by creating a function called `demultiplexChannel()`:

```
const net = require('net');
const fs = require('fs');

function demultiplexChannel(source, destinations) {
  let currentChannel = null;
  let currentLength = null;

  source
    .on('readable', () => {                            //[1]
      let chunk;
      if(currentChannel === null) {                    //[2]
        chunk = source.read(1);
        currentChannel = chunk && chunk.readUInt8(0);
      }

      if(currentLength === null) {                     //[3]
        chunk = source.read(4);
        currentLength = chunk && chunk.readUInt32BE(0);
```

```
      if(currentLength === null) {
        return;
      }
    }

    chunk = source.read(currentLength);                      // [4]
    if(chunk === null) {
      return;
    }
    console.log('Received packet from: ' + currentChannel);
    destinations[currentChannel].write(chunk);               // [5]
    currentChannel = null;
    currentLength = null;
  })
  .on('end', ()=> {                                          // [6]
    destinations.forEach(destination => destination.end());
    console.log('Source channel closed');
  });
}
```

The preceding code might look complicated but it is not; thanks to the pull nature of Node.js Readable streams, we can easily implement the demultiplexing of our little protocol as follows:

1. We start reading from the stream using the non-flowing mode.
2. First, if we have not read the channel ID yet, we try to read 1 byte from the stream and then transform it into a number.
3. The next step is to read the length of the data. We need 4 bytes for that, so it's possible (even if unlikely) that we don't have enough data in the internal buffer, which will cause the this.read() invocation to return null. In such a case, we simply interrupt the parsing and retry at the next readable event.
4. When we finally can also read the data size, we know how much data to pull from the internal buffer, so we try to read it all.
5. When we read all the data, we can write it to the right destination channel, making sure that we reset the currentChannel and currentLength variables (these will be used to parse the next packet).
6. Lastly, we make sure to end all the destination channels when the source channel ends.

Now that we can demultiplex the source stream, let's put our new function to work:

```
net.createServer(socket => {
  const stdoutStream = fs.createWriteStream('stdout.log');
  const stderrStream = fs.createWriteStream('stderr.log');
  demultiplexChannel(socket, [stdoutStream, stderrStream]);
}).listen(3000, () => console.log('Server started'));
```

In the preceding code, we first start a TCP server on the port 3000, then for each connection that we receive, we will create two Writable streams pointing to two different files, one for the standard output and another for the standard error; these are our destination channels. Finally, we use demultiplexChannel() to demultiplex the socket stream into stdoutStream and stderrStream.

Running the mux/demux application

Now, we are ready to try our new mux/demux application, but first let's create a small Node.js program to produce some sample output; let's call it generateData.js:

```
console.log("out1");
console.log("out2");
console.error("err1");
console.log("out3");
console.error("err2");
```

Okay, now we are ready to try our remote logging application. First, let's start the server:

node server

Then the client, by providing the file that we want to start as child process:

node client generateData.js

The client will run almost immediately, but at the end of the process the standard input and standard output of the generateData application have traveled through one single TCP connection and then, on the server, have been demultiplexed into two separate files.

 Please make a note that, as we are using child_process.fork() (http://nodejs.org/api/child_process.html#child_process_ch ild_process_fork_modulepath_args_options), our client will be able to launch only other Node.js modules.

Multiplexing and demultiplexing object streams

The example that we have just shown demonstrated how to multiplex and demultiplex a binary/text stream, but it's worth mentioning that the same rules apply also to object streams. The greatest difference is that, using objects, we already have a way to transmit the data using atomic messages (the objects), so multiplexing would be as easy as setting a property `channelID` into each object, while demultiplexing would simply involve reading the `channelID` property and routing each object towards the right destination stream.

Another pattern involving only demultiplexing consists of routing the data coming from a source depending on some condition. With this pattern, we can implement complex flows, such as the one shown in the following diagram:

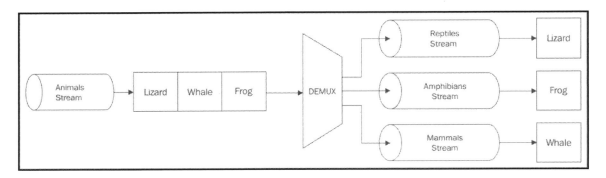

The demultiplexer used in the system described by the preceding diagram, takes a stream of objects representing *animals* and distributes each of them to the right destination stream based on the class of the animal: *reptiles*, *amphibians*, and *mammals*.

Using the same principle, we can also implement an `if...else` statement for streams; for some inspiration, take a look at the `ternary-stream` package (`https://npmjs.org/package/ternary-stream`) that allows us to do exactly that.

Summary

In this chapter, we have shed some light on Node.js streams and their use case, but at the same time this should have thrown open a door to a programming paradigm with virtually unlimited possibilities. We learned why streams are so acclaimed by the Node.js community and we mastered their basic functionality, enabling us to discover more and navigate comfortably in this new world. We analyzed some advanced patterns and started to understand how to connect streams together in different configurations, grasping the importance of interoperability which is what makes streams so versatile and powerful.

If we can't do something with one stream, we probably can do it by connecting other streams together, and this works great with the *one thing per module* philosophy. At this point, it should be clear that streams are not just a *good to know* feature of Node.js; they are, instead, an essential part of this, a crucial pattern to handle binary data, strings, and objects. It's not by chance that an entire chapter was dedicated to them.

In the next chapter, we will focus on the traditional object-oriented design patterns. But don't be fooled; even though JavaScript is to some extent an object-oriented language, in Node.js the functional or hybrid approach is often preferred. Get rid of every prejudice before reading the next chapter.

6
Design Patterns

A design pattern is a reusable solution to a recurring problem; the term is really broad in its definition and can span multiple domains of an application. However, the term is often associated with a well-known set of object-oriented patterns that were popularized in the 90s by the book, *Design Patterns: Elements of Reusable Object-Oriented Software, Pearson Education*, by the almost legendary **Gang of Four** (**GoF**): Erich Gamma, Richard Helm, Ralph Johnson, and John Vlissides. We will often refer to these specific sets of patterns as *traditional* design patterns, or GoF design patterns.

Applying this set of object-oriented design patterns in JavaScript is not as linear and formal as it would be in a classical object-oriented language. As we know, JavaScript is multi-paradigm, object-oriented, and prototype-based, and has dynamic typing; it treats functions as first-class citizens, and allows functional programming styles. These characteristics make JavaScript a very versatile language, which gives tremendous power to the developer but at the same time it causes a fragmentation of programming styles, conventions, techniques, and ultimately the patterns of its ecosystem. There are so many ways to achieve the same result using JavaScript that everybody has their own opinion on what the best way is to approach a problem. A clear demonstration of this phenomenon is the abundance of frameworks and opinionated libraries in the JavaScript ecosystem; probably no other language has ever seen so many, especially now that Node.js has given new astonishing possibilities to JavaScript and has created so many new scenarios.

In this context, the traditional design patterns are affected by the nature of JavaScript too. There are so many ways in which they can be implemented that their traditional, strongly object-oriented implementation means they cease to be patterns. In some cases, they are not even possible, because JavaScript, as we know, doesn't have *real* classes or abstract interfaces. What doesn't change though is the original idea at the base of each pattern, the problem it solves, and the concepts at the heart of the solution.

In this chapter, we will see how some of the most important GoF design patterns apply to Node.js and its philosophy, thus rediscovering their importance from another perspective. Among these traditional patterns, we will also have a look at some "less traditional" design patterns generated within the JavaScript ecosystem.

The design patterns explored in this chapter are as follows:

- Factory
- Revealing constructor
- Proxy
- Decorator
- Adapter
- Strategy
- State
- Template
- Middleware
- Command

 This chapter assumes that the reader has some notion of how inheritance works in JavaScript. Please also be advised that throughout this chapter we will often use generic and more intuitive diagrams to describe a pattern in place of standard UML, since many patterns can have an implementation based not only on classes, but also on objects and even functions.

Factory

We begin our journey starting from what is probably the most simple and common design pattern in Node.js: **factory**.

A generic interface for creating objects

We already stressed the fact that, in JavaScript, the functional paradigm is often preferred to a purely object-oriented design, for its simplicity, usability, and *small surface area*. This is especially true when creating new object instances. In fact, invoking a factory, instead of directly creating a new object from a prototype using the `new` operator or `Object.create()`, is so much more convenient and flexible in several respects.

First and foremost, a factory allows us to separate the object creation from its implementation; essentially, a factory wraps the creation of a new instance giving us more flexibility and control in the way we do it. Inside the factory, we can create a new instance leveraging closures, using a prototype and the `new` operator, using `Object.create()`, or even returning a different instance based on a particular condition. The consumer of the factory is totally agnostic about how the creation of the instance is carried out. The truth is that, by using `new`, we are binding our code to one specific way of creating an object, while in JavaScript we can have much more flexibility, almost for free. As a quick example, let's consider a simple factory that creates an `Image` object:

```
function createImage(name) {
  return new Image(name);
}
const image = createImage('photo.jpeg');
```

The `createImage()` factory might look totally unnecessary; why not instantiate the `Image` class by using the `new` operator directly? Something like the following line of code:

```
const image = new Image(name);
```

As we already mentioned, using `new` binds our code to one particular type of object; in the preceding case, to objects of type `Image`. A factory instead gives us much more flexibility; imagine that we want to refactor the `Image` class, splitting it into smaller classes, one for each image format that we support. If we exposed a factory as the only means to create new images, we can simply rewrite it as follows, without breaking any of the existing code:

```
function createImage(name) {
  if(name.match(/\.jpeg$/)) {
    return new JpegImage(name);
  } else if(name.match(/\.gif$/)) {
    return new GifImage(name);
  } else if(name.match(/\.png$/)) {
    return new PngImage(name);
  } else {
    throw new Exception('Unsupported format');
  }
}
```

Our factory also allows us to not expose the constructors of the objects it creates, and prevents them from being extended or modified (remember the principle of small surface area?). In Node.js, this can be achieved by exporting only the factory, while keeping each constructor private.

A mechanism to enforce encapsulation

A factory can also be used as an encapsulation mechanism, thanks to closures.

 Encapsulation refers to the technique of controlling the access to some internal details of an object by preventing the external code from manipulating them directly. The interaction with the object happens only through its public interface, isolating the external code from the changes in the implementation details of the object. This practice is also referred to as **information hiding**. Encapsulation is also a fundamental principle of object-oriented design, together with inheritance, polymorphism, and abstraction.

As we know, in JavaScript, we don't have *access level modifiers* (for example, we can't declare a private variable), so the only way to enforce encapsulation is through function scopes and closures. A factory makes it straightforward to enforce private variables; consider the following code for example:

```
function createPerson(name) {
  const privateProperties = {};

  const person = {
    setName: name => {
      if(!name) throw new Error('A person must have a name');
      privateProperties.name = name;
    },
    getName: () => {
      return privateProperties.name;
    }
  };

  person.setName(name);
  return person;
}
```

In the preceding code, we leverage closures to create two objects: a `person` object which represents the public interface returned by the factory, and a group of `privateProperties` that are inaccessible from the outside and that can be manipulated only through the interface provided by the `person` object. For example, in the preceding code, we make sure that a person's `name` is never empty; this would not be possible to enforce if `name` was just a property of the `person` object.

Factories are only one of the techniques that we have for creating private members; in fact, other possible approaches are as follows:

Defining private variables in a constructor (as recommended by Douglas Crockford: http://javascript.crockford.com/private.html).

Using conventions, for example, prefixing the name of a property with an underscore "_" or the dollar sign "$" (this however, does not technically prevent a member from being accessed from the outside)

Using ES2015 WeakMaps: (http://fitzgeraldnick.com/weblog/53/).

A very complete article on this subject was published by Mozilla: https://developer.mozilla.org/en-US/Add-ons/SDK/Guides/Contributor_s_Guide/Private_Properties.

Building a simple code profiler

Now, let's work on a complete example using a factory. Let's build a simple *code profiler*, an object with the following properties:

- A start() method that triggers the start of a profiling session
- An end() method to terminate the session and log its execution time to the console

Let's start by creating a file named profiler.js, which will have the following content:

```
class Profiler {
  constructor(label) {
    this.label = label;
    this.lastTime = null;
  }

  start() {
    this.lastTime = process.hrtime();
  }

  end() {
    const diff = process.hrtime(this.lastTime);
    console.log(
      `Timer "${this.label}" took ${diff[0]} seconds and ${diff[1]}
      nanoseconds.`
    );
  }
}
```

There is nothing fancy in the preceding class; we simply use the default high resolution timer to save the current time when `start()` is invoked, and then calculate the elapsed time when `end()` is executed, printing the result to the console.

Now, if we are going to use such a profiler in a real-world application to calculate the execution time of the different routines, we can easily imagine the huge amount of logging we will generate to the standard output, especially in a production environment. What we might want to do instead is redirect the profiling information to another source, for example, a database, or alternatively, disable the profiler altogether if the application is running in production mode. It's clear that if we were to instantiate a `Profiler` object directly by using the `new` operator, we would need some extra logic in the client code or in the `Profiler` object itself in order to switch between the different logics. We can instead use a factory to abstract the creation of the `Profiler` object, so that, depending on whether the application runs in production or development mode, we can return a fully working `Profiler` object, or alternatively, a mock object with the same interface, but with empty methods. Let's do this then in the `profiler.js` module, instead of exporting the `Profiler` constructor, we will export only a function, our factory. The following is its code:

```
module.exports = function(label) {
  if(process.env.NODE_ENV === 'development') {
    return new Profiler(label);                      //[1]
  } else if(process.env.NODE_ENV === 'production') {
    return {                                         //[2]
      start: function() {},
      end: function() {}
    }
  } else {
    throw new Error('Must set NODE_ENV');
  }
};
```

The factory that we created abstracts the creation of a `Profiler` object from its implementation:

- If the application is running in development mode, we return a new, fully functional `Profiler` object
- If instead the application is running in production mode, we return a mock object where the `start()` and `stop()` methods are empty functions

The nice feature to highlight is that, thanks to JavaScript dynamic typing, we were able to return an object instantiated with the `new` operator in one circumstance and a simple object literal in the other (this is also known as **duck typing** `https://en.wikipedia.org/wiki/Duck_typing`). Our factory is doing its job perfectly; we really can create objects in any way that we like inside the factory function, and we can execute additional initialization steps or return a different type of object based on particular conditions, and all of this while isolating the consumer of the object from all these details. We can easily understand the power of this simple pattern.

Now we can play with our profiler; this is a possible use case for the factory that we just created earlier:

```
const profiler = require('./profiler');

function getRandomArray(len) {
  const p = profiler('Generating a ' + len + ' items long array');
  p.start();
  const arr = [];
  for(let i = 0; i < len; i++) {
    arr.push(Math.random());
  }
  p.end();
}

getRandomArray(1e6);
console.log('Done');
```

The `p` variable contains the instance of our `Profiler` object, but we don't know how it's created and what its implementation is at this point in the code.

If we include the preceding code in a file named `profilerTest.js`, we can easily test these assumptions. To try the program with profiling enabled, run the following command:

`export NODE_ENV=development; node profilerTest`

The preceding command enables the real profiler and prints the profiling information to the console. If we want to try the mock profiler instead, we can run the following command:

`export NODE_ENV=production; node profilerTest`

The example that we just presented is just a simple application of the factory function pattern, but it clearly shows the advantages of separating an object's creation from its implementation.

Composable factory functions

Now that we have a good idea about how factory functions can be implemented in Node.js, we are ready to introduce a new advanced pattern that has recently been getting traction in the JavaScript community. We are talking about **composable factory functions**, which represent a particular type of factory function that can be "composed" together to build new enhanced factory functions. They are especially useful for allowing us to construct objects that "inherit" behaviors and properties from different sources without the need for building complex class hierarchies.

We can clarify this concept with a simple and effective example. Let's assume we want to build a videogame in which the characters on the screen can have a number of different behaviors: they can *move* on the screen; they can *slash* and *shoot*. And yes, to be a character they should have some basic properties such as life points, position on the screen, and name.

We want to define several types of character, one for every specific behavior:

- **Character**: base character that has life points, a position, and a name
- **Mover**: character that is able to move
- **Slasher**: character that is able to slash
- **Shooter**: character that is able to shoot (as long as it has bullets!)

Ideally we would be able to define new types of characters, combining different behaviors from the existing ones. We want absolute freedom and, for example, we would like to define these new types on top of the existing ones:

- **Runner**: a character that can move
- **Samurai**: a character that can move and slash
- **Sniper**: a character that can shoot (it doesn't move)
- **Gunslinger**: a character that can move and shoot
- **Western Samurai**: a character that can move, slash, and shoot

As you can see, we want total freedom in combining the features of every basic type, so it should now be obvious that we cannot easily model this problem using classes and inheritance.

So instead, we are going to use composable factory functions and in particular we are going to use the **stamp specification**as implemented by the `stampit` module: (`https://www.np mjs.com/package/stampit`).

This module offers an intuitive interface for defining factory functions that can be composed together to build new factory functions. Basically, it allows us to define factory functions that will generate objects with a specific set of properties and methods, by using a handy fluent interface to describe them.

Let's see how easily we can define our basic types for our game. We will start with the basic character type:

```
const stampit = require('stampit');

const character = stampit().
  props({
    name: 'anonymous',
    lifePoints: 100,
    x: 0,
    y: 0
  });
```

In the previous snippet of code, we defined the `character` factory function, which can be used to create new instances of basic characters. Every character will have these properties: name, `lifePoints`, x, and y and the default values will be respectively anonymous, 100, 0, and 0. The `props` method of `stampit` allows us to define these properties. To use this factory function, we can do something like this:

```
const c = character();
c.name = 'John';
c.lifePoints = 10;
console.log(c); // { name: 'John', lifePoints: 10, x:0, y:0 }
```

Now let's define our `mover` factory function:

```
const mover = stampit()
  .methods({
    move(xIncr, yIncr) {
      this.x += xIncr;
      this.y += yIncr;
      console.log(`${this.name} moved to [${this.x}, ${this.y}]`);
    }
  });
```

In this case, we are using the `methods` function of `stampit` to declare all the methods available in the objects produced by this factory function. For our `Mover` definition, we have a `move` function that can increase the `x` and the `y` position of the instance. Notice that we can access instance properties with the keyword `this` from inside a method.

Now that we have understood the basic concepts, we can easily add the factory function definitions for the slasher and shooter types:

```
const slasher = stampit()
  .methods({
    slash(direction) {
      console.log(`${this.name} slashed to the ${direction}`);
    }
  });

const shooter = stampit()
  .props({
    bullets: 6
  })
  .methods({
    shoot(direction) {
      if (this.bullets > 0) {
        --this.bullets;
          console.log(`${this.name} shoot to the ${direction}`);
      }
    }
  });
```

Notice how we are using both `props` and `methods` to define our `shooter` factory function.

Ok, now that we have all our base types defined, we are ready to compose them to create new powerful and expressive factory functions:

```
const runner = stampit.compose(character, mover);
const samurai = stampit.compose(character, mover, slasher);
const sniper = stampit.compose(character, shooter);
const gunslinger = stampit.compose(character, mover, shooter);
const westernSamurai = stampit.compose(gunslinger, samurai);
```

The method `stampit.compose` defines a new composed factory function that will produce an object based on the methods and properties of the composed factory functions. As you can tell, this is a powerful mechanism that gives us a lot of freedom and allows us to reason in terms of behaviors rather than in terms of classes.

To wrap up our example, let's instantiate and use a new westernSamurai.

```
const gojiro = westernSamurai();
gojiro.name = 'Gojiro Kiryu';
gojiro.move(1,0);
gojiro.slash('left');
gojiro.shoot('right');
```

This will produce the following output:

```
Yojimbo moved to [1, 0]
Yojimbo slashed to the left
Yojimbo shoot to the right
```

 More details about the stamp specification and the ideas behind it can be found in this post written by Eric Elliot, the original author of the specification: https://medium.com/javascript-scene/introducing -the-stamp-specification-77f8911c2fee.

In the wild

As we said, factories are very popular in Node.js. Many packages offer only a factory for creating new instances; some examples are the following:

- Dnode (https://npmjs.org/package/dnode): This is a **Remote Procedure Call (RPC)** system for Node.js. If we look into its source code, we will see that its logic is implemented into a class named D; however, this is never exposed to the outside as the only exported interface is a factory, which allows us to create new instances of the class. You can take a look at its source code at: https://github.com/substack/dnode/blob/34d1c9aa9696f13bdf8fb99d 9d039367ad873f90/index.js#L7-9.

- Restify (https://npmjs.org/package/restify): This is a framework for building REST APIs that allow us to create new instances of a server using the restify.createServer() factory, which internally creates a new instance of the Server class (which is not exported). You can take a look at its source code at: https://github.com/mcavage/node- restify/blob/5f31e2334b38361ac7ac1a5e5d852b7206ef7d94/lib/index .js#L91-116.

Other modules expose both a class and a factory, but document the factory as the main method—or the most convenient way—to create new instances; some of the examples are as follows:

- `http-proxy` (`https://npmjs.org/package/http-proxy`): This is a programmable proxying library, where new instances are created with `httpProxy.createProxyServer(options)`
- The core Node.js HTTP server: This is where new instances are mostly created using `http.createServer()`, even though this is essentially a shortcut for `new http.Server()`
- `bunyan` (`https://npmjs.org/package/bunyan`): This is a popular logging library; in its readme file the contributors propose a factory, `bunyan.createLogger()`, as the main method to create new instances, even though this would be equivalent to running `new bunyan()`

Some other modules provide a factory to wrap the creation of other components. Popular examples are `through2` and `from2` (we saw them in `Chapter 5`, *Coding with Streams*), which allow us to simplify the creation of new streams using a factory approach, freeing the developer from explicitly using inheritance and the `new` operator.

Finally, to see some packages that are using the stamp specification and composable factory functions internally, you can have a look at `react-stampit` (`https://www.npmjs.com/package/react-stampit`), which brings the power of composable factory functions to the frontend allowing you to easily compose widget behaviors and `remitter` (`https://www.npmjs.com/package/remitter`), a pub/sub module based on Redis.

Revealing constructor

The revealing constructor pattern is a relatively new pattern that is gaining traction in the Node.js community and in JavaScript, especially because it's used within some core libraries such as `Promise`.

We have already implicitly seen this pattern in `Chapter 4`, *Asynchronous Control Flow Patterns with ES2015 and Beyond*, while exploring promises, but let's get back to it and analyze the `Promise` constructor to embrace it in greater detail:

```
const promise = new Promise(function (resolve, reject) {
  // ...
});
```

As you can see, `Promise` accepts a function as a constructor argument, which is called the **executor function**. This function is called by the internal implementation of the `Promise` constructor and it is used to allow the constructing code to manipulate only a limited part of the internal state of the promise under construction. In other words, it serves as a mechanism to expose the `resolve` and `reject` functions so that they can be invoked to change the internal state of the object.

The advantage of this is that only the constructing code has access to `resolve` and `reject` and once the `promise` object is constructed, it can be passed around safely; no other code will be able to call `reject` or `resolve` and change the internal state of the promise.

That is exactly the reason why this pattern has been named "revealing constructor" by Domenic Denicola in one of his blog posts.

The full post by Domenic is extremely interesting and also analyzes the historical origins of the pattern and compares some aspects of this pattern with the template pattern used by node streams, or with other construction patterns used by earlier implementation, of the `Promise` libraries. You can read it here: `https://blog.domenic.me/the-reveal ing-constructor-pattern/`.

A read-only event emitter

In this paragraph, we are going to use the revealing constructor pattern to build a *read-only event emitter*, a special kind of event emitter in which is not possible to call the `emit` method (apart from within the function passed to the constructor).

Let's write the code for the `Roee` (read-only event emitter) class in a file called `roee.js`:

```
const EventEmitter = require('events');

module.exports = class Roee extends EventEmitter {
  constructor (executor) {
    super();
    const emit = this.emit.bind(this);
    this.emit = undefined;
    executor(emit);
  }
};
```

In this simple class, we are extending the core `EventEmitter` class and accepting an `executor` function as the only constructor argument.

Inside the constructor, we invoke the `super` function to be sure to initialize the event emitter properly by calling its parent constructor, then we save a backup of the `emit` function and we remove it by assigning `undefined` to it.

Finally, we call the `executor` function by passing the `emit` method backup as argument.

What is important to understand here is that after `undefined` is assigned to the `emit` method, it won't be possible to call it anymore from other parts of our code. Our backup version of `emit` is defined as a local variable that will be forwarded only to the `executor` function. This mechanism allows us to be able to use `emit` only within the executor function.

Now let's use this new class to create a simple ticker, a class that emits a *tick* every second and keeps the count of all the *ticks* emitted. This will be the content of our new `ticker.js` module:

```
const Roee = require('./roee');

const ticker = new Roee((emit) => {
  let tickCount = 0;
  setInterval(() => emit('tick', tickCount++), 1000);
});

module.exports = ticker;
```

As you can see here, the code is very trivial. We instantiate a new `Roee` and we pass the logic of event emission within the executor function. Our executor function receives `emit` as argument so we can use it to emit a new tick event every second.

Now let's see a quick example on how to use this ticker module:

```
const ticker = require('./ticker');

ticker.on('tick', (tickCount) => console.log(tickCount, 'TICK'));
// ticker.emit('something', {}); <-- This will fail
```

We use the `ticker` object the same as any other event emitter-based object, and we can attach any number of listeners with the `on` method, but in this case, if we try to use the `emit` method, our code will fail by triggering a `TypeError: ticker.emit is not a function` error.

Even if this example plays a nice role in showing how the revealing constructor pattern can be used, it is worth mentioning that this read-only functionality for the event emitter is not completely bulletproof and it is still possible to bypass it in several ways. For example, we can still emit an event on our `ticker` instance by using the original `emit` prototype directly, as follows:
```
require('events').prototype.emit.call(ticker,
'someEvent', {});
```

In the wild

Even if this pattern is quite interesting and clever, it is really hard to find common use cases apart from the `Promise` constructor.

It's worth mentioning that there is a new specification for streams under development that tries to adopt this pattern as a better alternative to the currently used template pattern to be able to describe the behavior of various stream objects: `https://streams.spec.whatwg.org`.

Also it's important to point out that we already used this pattern in `Chapter 5`, *Coding with Streams* when we implemented the `ParallelStream` class. This class accepts as constructor argument the `userTransform` function (the executor function).

Even if in this case the executor function is not called at construction time, but in the internal `_transform` method of the stream, the general concept of the pattern remains valid. In fact, this approach allows us to expose some internals of the stream (for example, the `push` function) only to the specific logic of the transformation that we want to specify at construction time when creating a new instance of `ParallelStream`.

Proxy

A proxy is an object that controls access to another object, called a **subject**. The proxy and the subject have an identical interface and this allows us to transparently swap one for the other; in fact, the alternative name for this pattern is **surrogate**. A proxy intercepts all or some of the operations that are meant to be executed on the subject, augmenting or complementing their behavior. The following figure shows a diagrammatic representation:

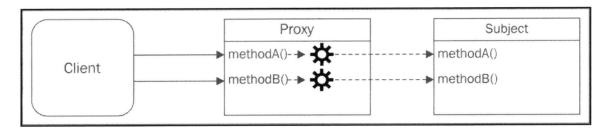

The preceding figure shows us how the **Proxy** and the **Subject** have the same interface, and how this is totally transparent to the client, who can use one or the other interchangeably. The **Proxy** forwards each operation to the subject, enhancing its behavior with additional pre-processing or post-processing.

It's important to observe that we are not talking about proxying between classes; the proxy pattern involves wrapping actual instances of the subject, thus preserving its state.

A proxy is useful in several circumstances; for example, consider the following ones:

- **Data validation**: The proxy validates the input before forwarding it to the subject
- **Security**: The proxy verifies that the client is authorized to perform the operation and it passes the request to the subject only if the outcome of the check is positive
- **Caching**: The proxy keeps an internal cache so that the operations are executed on the subject only if the data is not yet present in the cache
- **Lazy initialization**: If the creation of the subject is expensive, the proxy can delay it to when it's really necessary
- **Logging**: The proxy intercepts the method invocations and the relative parameters, recoding them as they happen
- **Remote objects**: A proxy can take an object that is located remotely, and make it appear local

Of course, there are many more applications for the proxy pattern, but these should give us an idea of the extent of its purpose.

Techniques for implementing proxies

When proxying an object, we can decide to intercept all of its methods or only some of them, while delegating the rest of them directly to the subject. There are several ways in which this can be achieved; let's analyze some of them.

Object composition

Composition is a technique whereby an object is combined with another object for the purpose of extending or using its functionality. In the specific case of the proxy pattern, a new object with the same interface as the subject is created, and a reference to the subject is stored internally in the proxy in the form of an instance variable or a closure variable. The subject can be injected from the client at creation time or created by the proxy itself.

The following is one example of this technique using a pseudo class and a factory:

```
function createProxy(subject) {
  const proto = Object.getPrototypeOf(subject);

  function Proxy(subject) {
    this.subject = subject;
  }

  Proxy.prototype = Object.create(proto);

  //proxied method
  Proxy.prototype.hello = function(){
    return this.subject.hello() + ' world!';
  };

  //delegated method
  Proxy.prototype.goodbye = function(){
    return this.subject.goodbye
      .apply(this.subject, arguments);
  };

  return new Proxy(subject);
}
module.exports = createProxy;
```

To implement a proxy using composition, we have to intercept the methods that we are interested in manipulating (such as `hello()`), while simply delegating the rest of them to the subject (as we did with `goodbye()`).

The preceding code also shows the particular case where the subject has a prototype and we want to maintain the correct prototype chain, so that executing `proxy instanceof Subject` will return `true`; we used **pseudo-classical inheritance** to achieve this.

This is just an extra step, required only if we are interested in maintaining the prototype chain, which can be useful in order to improve the compatibility of the proxy with code initially meant to work with the subject.

However, as JavaScript has dynamic typing, most of the time we can avoid using inheritance and use more immediate approaches. For example, an alternative implementation of the proxy presented in the preceding code might just use an object literal and a factory:

```
function createProxy(subject) {
  return {
    //proxied method
    hello: () => (subject.hello() + ' world!'),

    //delegated method
    goodbye: () => (subject.goodbye.apply(subject, arguments))
  };
}
```

> If we want to create a proxy that delegates most of its methods, it would be convenient to generate these automatically using a library, such as `delegates` (`https://npmjs.org/package/delegates`).

Object augmentation

Object augmentation (or **monkey patching**) is probably the most pragmatic way of proxying individual methods of an object and consists of modifying the subject directly by replacing a method with its proxied implementation; consider the following example:

```
function createProxy(subject) {
  const helloOrig = subject.hello;
  subject.hello = () => (helloOrig.call(this) + ' world!');

  return subject;
}
```

This technique is definitely the most convenient one when we need to proxy only one or a few methods, but it has the drawback of modifying the `subject` object directly.

A comparison of the different techniques

Composition can be considered the *safest* way of creating a proxy, because it leaves the subject untouched without mutating its original behavior. Its only drawback is that we have to manually delegate all the methods, even if we want to proxy only one of them. If needed, we might also have to delegate the access to the properties of the subject.

 The object properties can be delegated using `Object.defineProperty()`. Find out more at: `https://developer.mozilla.org/en-US/docs/Web/JavaScript/Reference/Global_Objects/Object/defineProperty`.

Object augmentation, on the other hand, modifies the subject, which might not always be what we want, but it does not present the various inconveniences related to delegation. For this reason, object augmentation is definitely the most pragmatic way to implement proxies in JavaScript, and it's the preferred technique in all those circumstances where modifying the subject is not a big concern.

However, there is at least one situation where composition is almost necessary; this is when we want to control the initialization of the subject, to, for example, create it only when needed (*lazy initialization*).

 It is worth pointing out that by using a factory function (`createProxy()` in our examples), we can shield our code from the technique used to generate the proxy.

Creating a logging Writable stream

To see the proxy pattern in a real example, we will now build an object that acts as a proxy to a Writable stream, by intercepting all the calls to the `write()` method and logging a message every time this happens. We will use an object composition to implement our proxy; this is how the `loggingWritable.js` file looks:

```
function createLoggingWritable(writableOrig) {
  const proto = Object.getPrototypeOf(writableOrig);

  function LoggingWritable(writableOrig) {
```

```
      this.writableOrig = writableOrig;
    }

    LoggingWritable.prototype = Object.create(proto);

    LoggingWritable.prototype.write = function(chunk, encoding, callback) {
      if(!callback && typeof encoding === 'function') {
        callback = encoding;
        encoding = undefined;
      }
      console.log('Writing ', chunk);
      return this.writableOrig.write(chunk, encoding, function() {
        console.log('Finished writing ', chunk);
        callback && callback();
      });
    };

    LoggingWritable.prototype.on = function() {
      return this.writableOrig.on
        .apply(this.writableOrig, arguments);
    };

    LoggingWritable.prototype.end = function() {
      return this.writableOrig.end
        .apply(this.writableOrig, arguments);
    };

    return new LoggingWritable(writableOrig);
  }
```

In the preceding code, we created a factory that returns a proxied version of the `writable` object passed as an argument. We provide an override for the `write()` method that logs a message to the standard output every time it is invoked and every time the asynchronous operation completes. This is also a good example of creating proxies of asynchronous functions, which makes proxying the callback necessary as well; this is an important detail to be considered in a platform such as Node.js. The remaining methods, `on()` and `end()`, are simply delegated to the original `writable` stream (to keep the code leaner we are not considering the other methods of the writable interface).

We can now include a few more lines of code into the `loggingWritable.js` module to test the proxy that we just created:

```
const fs = require('fs');

const writable = fs.createWriteStream('test.txt');
const writableProxy = createLoggingWritable(writable);
```

```
writableProxy.write('First chunk');
writableProxy.write('Second chunk');
writable.write('This is not logged');
writableProxy.end();
```

The proxy did not change the original interface of the stream or its external behavior, but if we run the preceding code, we will now see that every chunk that is written into the stream is transparently logged to the console.

Proxy in the ecosystem – function hooks and AOP

In its numerous forms, proxy is quite a popular pattern in Node.js, as well as in the ecosystem. In fact, we can find several libraries that allow us to simplify the creation of proxies, most of the time leveraging object augmentation as an implementation approach. In the community, this pattern can also be referred to as **function hooking**, or sometimes as **Aspect-Oriented Programming (AOP)**, which is actually a common area of application for proxies. In AOP, these libraries usually allow the developer to set *pre-* or *post-*execution hooks for a specific method (or a set of methods) that allow us to execute custom code before and after the execution of the advised method, respectively.

Sometimes proxies are also called **middleware**, because, as it happens in the middleware pattern (which we will see later in the chapter), they allow us to pre-process and post-process the input/output of a function. Sometimes, they also allow the registering of multiple hooks for the same method using a middleware-like pipeline.

There are several libraries on npm that allow us to implement function hooks with little effort. Among them there are hooks (https://npmjs.org/package/hooks), hooker (https://npmjs.org/package/hooker), and meld (https://npmjs.org/package/meld).

ES2015 Proxy

The ES2015 specification introduced a global object called Proxy, which is available in Node.js starting from version 6.

The Proxy API contains a Proxy constructor that accepts a target and a handler as arguments:

```
const proxy = new Proxy(target, handler);
```

Here, `target` represents the object on which the proxy is applied (the **subject** for our canonical definition), while `handler` is a special object that defines the behavior of the proxy.

The `handler` object contains a series of optional methods with predefined names called **trap methods** (for example, `apply`, `get`, `set`, and `has`) that are automatically called when the corresponding operations are performed on the proxy instance.

To better understand how this API works, let's see an example:

```
const scientist = {
  name: 'nikola',
  surname: 'tesla'
};

const uppercaseScientist = new Proxy(scientist, {
  get: (target, property) => target[property].toUpperCase()
});

console.log(uppercaseScientist.name, uppercaseScientist.surname);
  // prints NIKOLA TESLA
```

In this example, we are using the Proxy API to intercept all access to the properties of the `target` object, `scientist`, and convert the original value of the property to an uppercase string.

If you look carefully at this example, you can probably notice something very peculiar about this API: it allows us to intercept access to the generic attribute in the `target` object. This is possible because the API is not just a simple wrapper to facilitate the creation of proxy objects, like the ones we defined in the previous sections of this chapter; instead it is a feature deeply integrated into the JavaScript language itself, which enables developers to intercept and customize many operations that can be performed on objects. This characteristic opens up new interesting scenarios that were not easily achievable before such as *meta-programming, operator overloading,* and *object virtualization.*

Let's see another example to clarify this concept:

```
const evenNumbers = new Proxy([], {
  get: (target, index) => index * 2,
  has: (target, number) => number % 2 === 0
});

console.log(2 in evenNumbers); // true
console.log(5 in evenNumbers); // false
console.log(evenNumbers[7]);   // 14
```

In this example, we are creating a virtual array that contains all the even numbers. It can be used as a regular array, which means we can access items in the array with the regular array syntax (for example, evenNumbers[7]), or check the existence of an element in the array with the in operator (for example, 2 in evenNumbers). The array is considered *virtual* because we never store data in it.

Looking at the implementation, this proxy uses an empty array as the target and then defines the traps get and has in the handler:

- The get trap intercepts access to the array elements, returning the even number for the given index
- The has trap instead intercepts the usage of the in operator and checks whether the given number is even or not

The Proxy API supports a number of other interesting traps such as set, delete, and construct, and allows us to create proxies that can be revoked on demand, disabling all the traps and restoring the original behavior of the target object.

Analyzing all these features goes beyond the scope of this chapter; what is important here is understanding that the Proxy API provides a powerful foundation for taking advantage of the Proxy design pattern when you need it.

 If you are curious to know more about the Proxy API and discover all its capabilities and trap methods, you can read more in this article by Mozilla: https://developer.mozilla.org/it/docs/Web/JavaScript/Reference/Global_Objects/Proxy. Another good source is this detailed article from Google: https://developers.google.com/web/updates/2016/02/es2015-proxies.

In the wild

Mongoose (http://mongoosejs.com) is a popular **Object-Document Mapping (ODM)** library for MongoDB. Internally, it uses the hooks package (https://npmjs.org/package/hooks) to provide pre-and post-execution hooks for the init, validate, save, and remove methods of its Document objects. Find out more with the official documentation at http://mongoosejs.com/docs/middleware.html.

Decorator

Decorator is a structural pattern that consists of dynamically augmenting the behavior of an existing object. It's different from classical inheritance, because the behavior is not added to all the objects of the same class, but only to the instances that are explicitly decorated.

Implementation-wise, it is very similar to the Proxy pattern, but instead of enhancing or modifying the behavior of the existing interface of an object, it augments it with new functionalities, as described in the following figure:

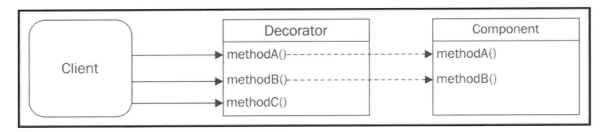

In the previous figure, the `Decorator` object is extending the `Component` object by adding the `methodC()` operation. The existing methods are usually delegated to the decorated object, without further processing. Of course, if necessary we can easily combine the Proxy pattern so that the calls to the existing methods can be intercepted and manipulated as well.

Techniques for implementing Decorators

Although Proxy and Decorator are conceptually two different patterns with different intents, they practically share the same implementation strategies. Let's review them.

Composition

Using composition, the decorated component is wrapped around a new object that usually inherits from it. The Decorator in this case simply needs to define the new methods, while delegating the existing ones to the original component:

```
function decorate(component) {
  const proto = Object.getPrototypeOf(component);

  function Decorator(component) {
    this.component = component;
  }
```

```
Decorator.prototype = Object.create(proto);

//new method
Decorator.prototype.greetings = function() {
  return 'Hi!';
};

//delegated method
Decorator.prototype.hello = function() {
  return this.component.hello.apply(this.component, arguments);
};

return new Decorator(component);
}
```

Object augmentation

Object decoration can also be achieved by simply attaching new methods directly to the decorated object, as follows:

```
function decorate(component) {
  //new method
  component.greetings = () => {
    //...
  };
  return component;
}
```

The same caveats discussed during the analysis of the Proxy pattern are also valid for Decorator. Let's now practice the pattern with a working example!

Decorating a LevelUP database

Before we start coding the next example, let's say a few words about **LevelUP**, the module that we are now going to work with.

Introducing LevelUP and LevelDB

LevelUP (https://npmjs.org/package/levelup) is a Node.js wrapper around Google's **LevelDB**, a key/value store originally built to implement IndexedDB in the Chrome browser, but it's much more than that. LevelDB has been defined by Dominic Tarr as the "Node.js of databases" because of its minimalism and extensibility. Like Node.js, LevelDB provides blazingly fast performance and only the most basic set of features, allowing developers to build any kind of database on top of it.

The Node.js community, and in this case Rod Vagg, did not miss the chance to bring the power of this database into Node.js by creating LevelUP. Born as a wrapper for LevelDB, it then evolved to support several kinds of backend, from in-memory stores, to other NoSQL databases such as Riak and Redis, to web storage engines such as IndexedDB and localStorage, allowing us to use the same API on both the server and the client, opening up some really interesting scenarios.

Today, there is a fully-fledged ecosystem around LevelUP made of plugins and modules that extend the tiny core to implement features such as replication, secondary indexes, live updates, query engines, and more. Also, complete databases were built on top of LevelUP, including CouchDB clones such as PouchDB (https://npmjs.org/package/pouchdb) and CouchUP (https://npmjs.org/package/couchup), and even a graph database, levelgraph (https://npmjs.org/package/levelgraph), which can work both on Node.js and the browser!

 Find out more about the LevelUP ecosystem at:
https://github.com/rvagg/node-levelup/wiki/Modules.

Implementing a LevelUP plugin

In the next example, we are going to show how we can create a simple plugin for LevelUP using the Decorator pattern, and in particular, the object augmentation technique, which is the simplest but nevertheless the most pragmatic and effective way to decorate objects with additional capabilities.

 For convenience, we are going to use the level package
(http://npmjs.org/package/level), which bundles both levelup and the default adapter called leveldown, which uses LevelDB as the backend.

What we want to build is a plugin for LevelUP that allows us to receive notifications every time an object with a certain pattern is saved into the database. For example, if we subscribe to a pattern such as {a: 1}, we want to receive a notification when objects such as {a: 1, b: 3} or {a: 1, c: 'x'} are saved into the database.

Let's start to build our small plugin by creating a new module called levelSubscribe.js. We will then insert the following code:

```
module.exports = function levelSubscribe(db) {

  db.subscribe = (pattern, listener) => {        //[1]
    db.on('put', (key, val) => {                 //[2]
      const match = Object.keys(pattern).every(
        k => (pattern[k] === val[k])             //[3]
      );
      if(match) {
        listener(key, val);                      //[4]
      }
    });
  };

  return db;
};
```

That's it for our plugin, it's extremely simple. Let's briefly see what happens in the preceding code:

1. We decorated the db object with a new method named subscribe(). We simply attached the method directly to the provided db instance (object augmentation).
2. We listened for any put operation performed on the database.
3. We performed a very simple pattern-matching algorithm, which verified that all the properties in the provided pattern are also available on the data being inserted.
4. If we have a match, we notify the listener.

Let's now create some code—in a new file named levelSubscribeTest.js—to try out our new plugin:

```
const level = require('level');                         //[1]
const levelSubscribe = require('./levelSubscribe');     //[2]

let db = level(__dirname + '/db', {valueEncoding: 'json'});
db = levelSubscribe(db);

db.subscribe(
```

```
    {doctype: 'tweet', language: 'en'},                          //[3]
    (k, val) => console.log(val)
);
db.put('1', {doctype: 'tweet', text: 'Hi', language: 'en'}); //[4]
db.put('2', {doctype: 'company', name: 'ACME Co.'});
```

This is what we did in the preceding code:

1. First, we initialize our LevelUP database, choosing the directory where the files will be stored and the default encoding for the values.
2. Then, we attach our plugin, which decorates the original db object.
3. At this point, we are ready to use the new feature provided by our plugin, the subscribe() method, where we specify that we are interested in all the objects with doctype: 'tweet' and language: 'en'.
4. Finally, we save some values in the database using put. The first call will trigger the callback associated to our subscription and we will see the stored object printed in the console. This is because in this case the object matches the subscription. Instead, the second call will not generate any output because the stored object will not match the subscription criteria.

This example shows a real application of the decorator pattern in its simplest implementation: object augmentation. It might look like a trivial pattern, but it has undoubted power if used appropriately.

 For simplicity, our plugin will work only in combination with the put operations, but it can be easily expanded to work even with the batch operations (https://github.com/rvagg/node-levelup#batch).

In the wild

For more examples of how Decorator is used in the real world, we might want to inspect the code of some more LevelUP plugins:

- level-inverted-index (https://github.com/dominictarr/level-inverted-index): This is a plugin that adds inverted indexes to a LevelUP database, allowing us to perform simple text searches across the values stored in the database
- level-plus (https://github.com/eugeneware/levelplus): This is a plugin that adds atomic updates to a LevelUP database

Adapter

The Adapter pattern allows us to access the functionality of an object using a different interface. As the name suggests, it adapts an object so that it can be used by components expecting a different interface. The following diagram clarifies the situation:

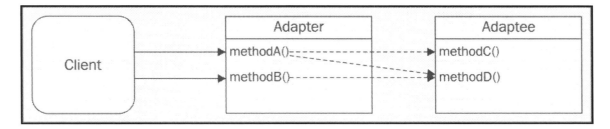

The preceding diagram shows how the Adapter is essentially a wrapper for the Adaptee, exposing a different interface. The diagram also highlights the fact that the operations of the Adapter can also be a composition of one or more method invocations on the Adaptee. From an implementation perspective, the most common technique is composition, where the methods of the Adapter provide a bridge to the methods of the Adaptee. This pattern is pretty straightforward, so let's immediately work on an example.

Using LevelUP through the filesystem API

We are now going to build an Adapter around the LevelUP API, transforming it into an interface that is compatible with the core `fs` module. In particular, we will make sure that every call to `readFile()` and `writeFile()` will translate into calls to `db.get()` and `db.put()`; this way we will be able to use a LevelUP database as a storage backend for simple filesystem operations.

Let's start by creating a new module named `fsAdapter.js`. We will begin by loading the dependencies and exporting the `createFsAdapter()` factory that we are going to use to build the adapter:

```
const path = require('path');

module.exports = function createFsAdapter(db) {
  const fs = {};
  //...continues with the next code fragments
```

Next, we will implement the readFile() function inside the factory and ensure that its interface is compatible with one of the original functions from the fs module:

```
fs.readFile = (filename, options, callback) => {
  if(typeof options === 'function') {
    callback = options;
    options = {};
  } else if(typeof options === 'string') {
    options = {encoding: options};
  }

  db.get(path.resolve(filename), {                    //[1]
      valueEncoding: options.encoding
    },
    (err, value) => {
      if(err) {
        if(err.type === 'NotFoundError') {            //[2]
          err = new Error(`ENOENT, open "${filename}"`);
          err.code = 'ENOENT';
          err.errno = 34;
          err.path = filename;
        }
        return callback && callback(err);
      }
      callback && callback(null, value);              //[3]
    }
  );
};
```

In the preceding code, we had to do some extra work to make sure that the behavior of our new function is as close as possible to the original fs.readFile() function. The steps performed by the function are described as follows:

1. To retrieve a file from the db class, we invoke db.get(), using filename as a key, by making sure to always use its full path (using path.resolve()). We set the value of valueEncoding used by the database to be equal to any eventual encoding option received as an input.

2. If the key is not found in the database, we create an error with ENOENT as the error code, which is the code used by the original fs module to indicate a missing file. Any other type of error is forwarded to callback (for the scope of this example, we are adapting only the most common error condition).

3. If the key/value pair is retrieved successfully from the database, we will return the value to the caller using the callback.

As we can see, the function that we created is quite rough; it does not want to be a perfect replacement for the `fs.readFile()` function, but it definitely does its job in the most common situations.

To complete our small adapter, let's now see how to implement the `writeFile()` function:

```
fs.writeFile = (filename, contents, options, callback) => {
  if(typeof options === 'function') {
    callback = options;
    options = {};
  } else if(typeof options === 'string') {
    options = {encoding: options};
  }

  db.put(path.resolve(filename), contents, {
    valueEncoding: options.encoding
  }, callback);
}
```

Also, in this case, we don't have a perfect wrapper; we will ignore some options such as file permissions (`options.mode`), and we will forward any error that we receive from the database as it is.

Finally, we only have to return the `fs` object and close the factory function using the following line of code:

```
  return fs;
}
```

Our new adapter is now ready; if we now write a small test module, we can try to use it:

```
const fs = require('fs');

fs.writeFile('file.txt', 'Hello!', () => {
  fs.readFile('file.txt', {encoding: 'utf8'}, (err, res) => {
    console.log(res);
  });
});

//try to read a missing file
fs.readFile('missing.txt', {encoding: 'utf8'}, (err, res) => {
  console.log(err);
});
```

The preceding code uses the original `fs` API to perform a few read and write operations on the filesystem, and should print something like the following to the console:

```
{ [Error: ENOENT, open 'missing.txt'] errno: 34, code: 'ENOENT', path:
'missing.txt' }
Hello!
```

Now, we can try to replace the `fs` module with our adapter, as follows:

```
const levelup = require('level');
const fsAdapter = require('./fsAdapter');
const db = levelup('./fsDB', {valueEncoding: 'binary'});
const fs = fsAdapter(db);
```

Running our program again should produce the same output, except for the fact that no parts of the file that we specified is read or written using the filesystem; instead, any operation performed using our adapter will be converted into an operation performed on a LevelUP database.

The adapter that we just created might look silly; what's the purpose of using a database in place of the real filesystem? However, we should remember that LevelUP itself has adapters that enable the database to also run in the browser; one of these adapters is `level.js` (`https://npmjs.org/package/level-js`). Now our adapter should make perfect sense; we can think of using it to share with the browser code, which relies on the `fs` module! For example, the web spider that we created in Chapter 3, *Asynchronous Control Flow Patterns with Callbacks*, uses the `fs` API to store the web pages downloaded during its operations; our adapter will allow it to run in the browser by applying only minor modifications! We will soon realize that Adapter is also an extremely important pattern when it comes to sharing code with the browser, as we will see in more detail in Chapter 8, *Universal JavaScript for Web Applications*.

In the wild

There are plenty of real-world examples of the Adapter pattern: we list some of the most notable examples here for you to explore and analyze:

- We already know that LevelUP is able to run with different storage backends, from the default LevelDB to IndexedDB in the browser. This is made possible by the various adapters that are created to replicate the internal (private) LevelUP API. Take a look at some of them to see how they are implemented: `https://github.com/rvagg/node-levelup/wiki/Modules#storage-back-ends`.

- `jugglingdb` is a multi-database ORM and of course, multiple adapters are used to make it compatible with different databases. Take a look at some of them at: `https://github.com/1602/jugglingdb/tree/master/lib/adapters`.
- The perfect complement to the example that we created is `level-filesystem` (`https://www.npmjs.org/package/level-filesystem`), which is the proper implementation of the `fs` API on top of LevelUP.

Strategy

The Strategy pattern enables an object, called the *Context*, to support variations in its logic by extracting the *variable* parts into separate, interchangeable objects called *Strategies*. The context implements the common logic of a family of algorithms, while a strategy implements the mutable parts, allowing the context to adapt its behavior depending on different factors such as an input value, a system configuration, or user preferences. The strategies are usually part of a family of solutions and all of them implement the same interface, which is the one that is expected by the context. The following figure shows the situation we just described:

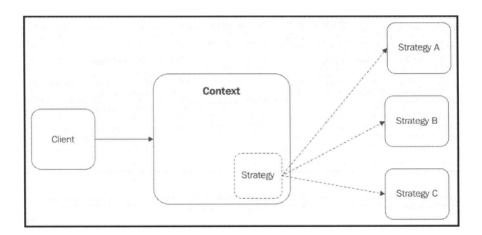

The preceding figure shows how the context object can plug different strategies into its structure, as if they were replaceable parts of a piece of machinery. Imagine a car; its tires can be considered its strategy for adapting to the different road conditions. We can fit winter tires to go on snowy roads thanks to their studs, while we can decide to fit high-performance tires for traveling mainly on motorways, for a long trip. On the one hand, we don't want to change the entire car for this to be possible, and on the other, we don't want a car with eight wheels so that it can go on every possible road.

We quickly understand how powerful this pattern is; not only does it help with separating the concerns within an algorithm, but it also enables it to have better flexibility and adapt to different variations of the same problem.

The Strategy pattern is particularly useful in all those situations where supporting variations of an algorithm requires complex conditional logic (lots of if...else or switch statements), or mixing together different algorithms of the same family. Imagine an object called Order that represents an online order of an e-commerce website. The object has a method called pay() that, as it says, finalizes the order and transfers the funds from the user to the online store.

To support different payment systems, we have a couple of options, as follows:

- Use an if...else statement in the pay() method to complete the operation-based on the chosen payment option
- Delegate the logic of the payment to a strategy object that implements the logic for the specific payment gateway selected by the user

In the first solution, our Order object cannot support other payment methods unless its code is modified. Also, this can become quite complex when the number of payment options grows. Instead, using the Strategy pattern enables the Order object to support a virtually unlimited number of payment methods and keeps its scope limited to only managing the details of the user, the purchased items, and relative price, while delegating the job of completing the payment to another object.

Let's now demonstrate this pattern with a simple, realistic example.

Multi-format configuration objects

Let's consider an object called Config that holds a set of configuration parameters used by an application, such as the database URL, the listening port of the server, and so on. The Config object should be able to provide a simple interface to access these parameters, but also a way to import and export the configuration using a persistent storage, such as a file. We want to be able to support different formats to store the configuration, for example, JSON, INI, or YAML.

By applying what we learned about the Strategy pattern, we can immediately identify the variable part of the Config object, which is the functionality that allows us to serialize and deserialize the configuration. This is going to be our strategy.

Let's create a new module called `config.js`, and let's define the *generic* part of our configuration manager:

```
const fs = require('fs');
const objectPath = require('object-path');

class Config {
  constructor(strategy) {
    this.data = {};
    this.strategy = strategy;
  }

  get(path) {
    return objectPath.get(this.data, path);
  }
//... rest of the class
```

In the preceding code, we encapsulate the configuration data into an instance variable (`this.data`) and then we provide the `set()` and `get()` methods that allow us to access the configuration properties using a dotted path notation (for example, `property.subProperty`) by leveraging npm library called `object-path` (`https://npmjs.org/package/object-path`). In the constructor, we also take in a `strategy` as input, which represents an algorithm for parsing and serializing the data.

Let's now see how we are going to use `strategy`, by writing the remaining part of the `Config` class:

```
  set(path, value) {
    return objectPath.set(this.data, path, value);
  }

  read(file) {
    console.log(`Deserializing from ${file}`);
    this.data = this.strategy.deserialize(fs.readFileSync(file, 'utf-8'));
  }

  save(file) {
    console.log(`Serializing to ${file}`);
    fs.writeFileSync(file, this.strategy.serialize(this.data));
  }
}
module.exports = Config;
```

In the previous code, when reading the configuration from a file, we delegate the deserialization task to the `strategy`; then, when we want to save the configuration into a file, we use `strategy` to serialize the configuration. This simple design allows the `Config` object to support different file formats when loading and saving its data.

To demonstrate this, let's create a couple of strategies in a file called `strategies.js`. Let's start with a strategy for parsing and serializing JSON data:

```
module.exports.json = {
  deserialize: data => JSON.parse(data),
  serialize: data => JSON.stringify(data, null, '  ')
}
```

Nothing really complicated! Our strategy simply implements the agreed interface, so that it can be used by the `Config` object.

Similarly, the next strategy we are going to create allows us to support the INI file format:

```
const ini = require('ini'); //-> https://npmjs.org/package/ini
module.exports.ini = {
  deserialize: data => ini.parse(data),
  serialize: data => ini.stringify(data)
}
```

Now, to show you how everything comes together, let's create a file named `configTest.js`, and let's try to load and save a sample configuration using different formats:

```
const Config = require('./config');
const strategies = require('./strategies');

const jsonConfig = new Config(strategies.json);
jsonConfig.read('samples/conf.json');
jsonConfig.set('book.nodejs', 'design patterns');
jsonConfig.save('samples/conf_mod.json');

const iniConfig = new Config(strategies.ini);
iniConfig.read('samples/conf.ini');
iniConfig.set('book.nodejs', 'design patterns');
iniConfig.save('samples/conf_mod.ini');
```

Our test module reveals the properties of the Strategy pattern. We defined only one `Config` class, which implements the common parts of our configuration manager, while changing the strategy used for serializing and deserializing allowed us to create different `Config` instances supporting different file formats.

The preceding example shows only one of the possible alternatives that we had for selecting the strategy. Other valid approaches might have been the following:

- Creating two different strategy families: one for the deserialization and the other for the serialization. This would have allowed reading from a format and saving into another.
- Dynamically selecting the strategy, depending on the extension of the file provided; the `Config` object could have maintained a map `extension->strategy` and used it to select the right algorithm for the given extension.

As we can see, there are several options for selecting the strategy to use and the right one only depends on our requirements and the trade-off in terms of features/simplicity we want to obtain.

Also, the implementation of the pattern itself can vary a lot; for example, in its simplest form, the context and the strategy can both be simple functions:

```
function context(strategy) {...}
```

Even though the preceding situation might seem insignificant, it should not be underestimated in a programming language, such as JavaScript, where functions are first-class citizens and used as much as fully-fledged objects.

Between all these variations, though, what does not change is the idea behind the pattern; as always the implementation can slightly change but the core concepts that drive the pattern are always the same.

In the wild

`Passport.js` (`http://passportjs.org`) is an authentication framework for Node.js which allows support for different authentication schemes on a web server. With Passport, we can provide a *login with Facebook* or *login with Twitter* functionality to our web application with minimal effort. Passport uses the Strategy pattern to separate the common logic required during an authentication process from the parts that can change, namely the actual authentication step. For example, we might want to use OAuth in order to obtain an access token to access a Facebook or Twitter profile, or simply use a local database to verify a username/password pair. For Passport, these are all different strategies for completing the authentication process and, as we can imagine, this allows the library to support a virtually unlimited number of authentication services. Take a look at the number of different authentication providers supported at `http://passportjs.org/guide/providers` to get an idea of what the strategy pattern can do.

State

State is a variation of the Strategy pattern where the strategy changes depending on the state of the context. We have seen in the previous section how a strategy can be selected based on different variables such as user preferences, a configuration parameter, and the input provided, and once this selection is done, the strategy stays unchanged for the rest of the lifespan of the context.

Instead, in the State pattern, the strategy (also called *state* in this circumstance) is dynamic and can change during the lifetime of the context, thus allowing its behavior to adapt depending on its internal state, as shown in the following figure:

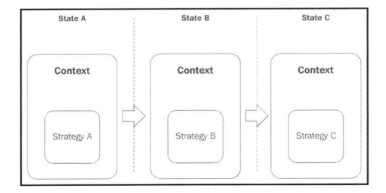

Imagine that we have a hotel booking system and an object called `Reservation` that models a room reservation. This is a classical situation where we have to adapt the behavior of an object based on its state. Consider the following series of events:

1. When the reservation is initially created, the user can confirm (using `confirm()`) the reservation; of course, they cannot cancel it (using `cancel()`), because it's still not confirmed. They can however delete it (using `delete()`) if they change their mind before buying.
2. Once the reservation is confirmed, using the `confirm()` function again does not make any sense; however, now it should be possible to cancel the reservation but no longer delete it, because it has to be kept for the record.
3. On the day before the reservation date, it should not be possible to cancel the reservation; it's too late for that.

Now, imagine that we have to implement the reservation system that we described in one monolithic object; we can already picture all the `if...else` or `switch` statements that we would have to write to enable/disable each action depending on the state of the reservation.

The State pattern instead is perfect in this situation: there will be three strategies, all implementing the three methods described (`confirm()`, `cancel()`, and `delete()`) and each one implementing only one behavior, the one corresponding to the modeled state. By using this pattern, it should be very easy for the `Reservation` object to switch from one behavior to another; this will simply require the *activation* of a different strategy on each state change.

The state transition can be initiated and controlled by the context object, by the client code, or by the `State` objects themselves. This last option usually provides the best results in terms of flexibility and decoupling, as the context does not have to know about all the possible states and how to transition between them.

Implementing a basic fail-safe socket

Let's now work on a concrete example so that we can apply what we learned about the State pattern. Let's build a client TCP socket that does not fail when the connection with the server is lost; instead, we want to queue all the data sent during the time in which the server is offline and then try to send it again as soon as the connection is re-established. We want to leverage this socket in the context of a simple monitoring system, where a set of machines sends some statistics about their resource utilization at regular intervals; if the server that collects these resources goes down, our socket will continue to queue the data locally until the server comes back online.

Let's start by creating a new module called `failsafeSocket.js` that represents our context object:

```
const OfflineState = require('./offlineState');
const OnlineState = require('./onlineState');

class FailsafeSocket{
  constructor (options) {                              //[1]
    this.options = options;
    this.queue = [];
    this.currentState = null;
    this.socket = null;
    this.states = {
      offline: new OfflineState(this),
      online: new OnlineState(this)
    };
    this.changeState('offline');
  }

  changeState (state) {                                //[2]
    console.log('Activating state: ' + state);
    this.currentState = this.states[state];
    this.currentState.activate();
  }

  send(data) {                                         //[3]
    this.currentState.send(data);
  }
}

module.exports = options => {
  return new FailsafeSocket(options);
};
```

The `FailsafeSocket` class is made of three main elements:

1. The constructor initializes various data structures, including the queue that will contain any data sent while the socket is offline. Also, it creates a set of two `states`, one for implementing the behavior of the socket while it's offline, and another one when the socket is online.
2. The `changeState()` method is responsible for transitioning from one state to another. It simply updates the `currentState` instance variable and calls `activate()` on the target state.
3. The `send()` method is the functionality of the socket this is where we want to have a different behavior based on the offline/online state. As we can see, this is done by delegating the operation to the currently active state.

Let's now see what the two states look like, starting from the `offlineState.js` module:

```
const jot = require('json-over-tcp');              //[1]

module.exports = class OfflineState {

  constructor (failsafeSocket) {
    this.failsafeSocket = failsafeSocket;
  }

  send(data) {                                     //[2]
    this.failsafeSocket.queue.push(data);
  }

  activate() {                                     //[3]
    const retry = () => {
      setTimeout(() => this.activate(), 500);
    }

    this.failsafeSocket.socket = jot.connect(
      this.failsafeSocket.options,
      () => {
        this.failsafeSocket.socket.removeListener('error', retry);
        this.failsafeSocket.changeState('online');
      }
    );
    this.failsafeSocket.socket.once('error', retry);
  }
};
```

The module that we created is responsible for managing the behavior of the socket while it's offline; this is how it works:

1. Instead of using a raw TCP socket, we will use a little library called `json-over-tcp` (https://npmjs.org/package/json-over-tcp), which will allow us to easily send JSON objects over a TCP connection.
2. The `send()` method is only responsible for queuing any data it receives; we are assuming that we are offline, so that's all we need to do.
3. The `activate()` method tries to establish a connection with the server using `json-over-tcp`. If the operation fails, it tries again after 500 milliseconds. It continues trying until a valid connection is established, in which case the state of `failsafeSocket` is transitioned to `online`.

Next, let's implement the `onlineState.js` module, and then let's implement the `onlineState` strategy, as follows:

```
module.exports = class OnlineState {
  constructor(failsafeSocket) {
    this.failsafeSocket = failsafeSocket;
  }

  send(data) {                                    //[1]
    this.failsafeSocket.socket.write(data);
  };

  activate() {                                    //[2]
    this.failsafeSocket.queue.forEach(data => {
      this.failsafeSocket.socket.write(data);
    });
    this.failsafeSocket.queue = [];

    this.failsafeSocket.socket.once('error', () => {
      this.failsafeSocket.changeState('offline');
    });
  }
};
```

The `OnlineState` strategy is very simple and is explained as follows:

1. The `send()` method writes the data directly into the socket, as we assume we are online.
2. The `activate()` method flushes any data that was queued while the socket was offline and it also starts listening for any `error` events; we will take this as a symptom that the socket went offline (for simplicity). When this happens, we transition to the `offline` state.

That's it for our `failsafeSocket`; now we are ready to build a sample client and a server to try it out. Let's put the server code in a module named `server.js`:

```
const jot = require('json-over-tcp');
const server = jot.createServer(5000);
server.on('connection', socket => {
  socket.on('data', data => {
    console.log('Client data', data);
  });
});
server.listen(5000, () => console.log('Started'));
```

Then the client-side code, which is what we are really interested in, goes into `client.js`:

```
const createFailsafeSocket = require('./failsafeSocket');
const failsafeSocket = createFailsafeSocket({port: 5000});

setInterval(() => {
  //send current memory usage
  failsafeSocket.send(process.memoryUsage());
}, 1000);
```

Our server simply prints any JSON message it receives to the console, while our clients are sending a measurement of their memory utilization every second, leveraging a `FailsafeSocket` object.

To try the small system that we built, we should run both the client and the server, then we can test the features of `failsafeSocket` by stopping and then restarting the server. We should see that the state of the client changes between `online` and `offline` and that any memory measurement collected while the server is offline is queued and then resent as soon as the server goes back online.

This sample should be a clear demonstration of how the State pattern can help increase the modularity and readability of a component that has to adapt its behavior depending on its state.

The `FailsafeSocket` class that we built in this section is only for demonstrating the state pattern and doesn't want to be a complete and 100%-reliable solution for handling connectivity issues within TCP sockets. For example, we are not verifying that all the data written into the socket stream is received by the server, which would require some more code not strictly related to the pattern that we wanted to describe.

Template

The next pattern that we are going to analyze is called **Template** and it also has a lot in common with the Strategy pattern. Template consists of defining an abstract pseudo class that represents the skeleton of an algorithm, where some of its steps are left undefined. Subclasses can then *fill* the gaps in the algorithm by implementing the missing steps, called **template methods**. The intent of this pattern is to make it possible to define a family of classes that are all variations of a similar algorithm. The following UML diagram shows the structure that we just described:

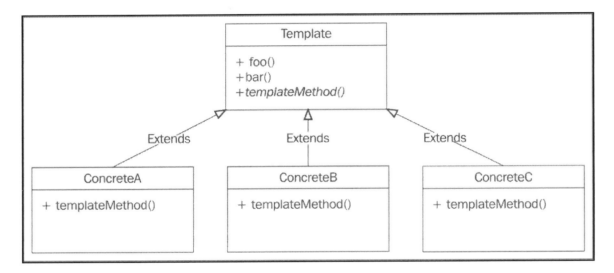

The three concrete classes shown in the previous diagram, extend Template and provide an implementation for `templateMethod()`, which is *abstract* or *pure virtual*, to use the C++ terminology; in JavaScript this means that the method is left undefined or is assigned to a function that always throws an exception, indicating the fact that the method has to be implemented. The Template pattern can be considered more classically object-oriented than the other patterns we have seen so far, because inheritance is a core part of its implementation.

The purpose of Template and Strategy is very similar, but the main difference between the two lies in their structure and implementation. Both allow us to change some parts of an algorithm while reusing the common parts; however, while Strategy allows us to do it *dynamically* and possibly at runtime, with Template the complete algorithm is determined the moment the concrete class is defined. Under these assumptions, the Template pattern might be more suitable in those circumstances where we want to create prepackaged variations of an algorithm. As always, the choice between one pattern and the other is up to the developer, who has to consider the various pros and cons for each use case.

A configuration manager template

To have a better idea of the differences between Strategy and Template, let's now re-implement the `Config` object that we defined in the section about the Strategy pattern, but this time using Template. Like in the previous version of the `Config` object, we want to have the ability to load and save a set of configuration properties using different file formats.

Let's start by defining the template class; we will call it `ConfigTemplate`:

```
const fs = require('fs');
const objectPath = require('object-path');

class ConfigTemplate {

  read(file) {
    console.log(`Deserializing from ${file}`);
    this.data = this._deserialize(fs.readFileSync(file, 'utf-8'));
  }

  save(file) {
    console.log(`Serializing to ${file}`);
    fs.writeFileSync(file, this._serialize(this.data));
  }

  get(path) {
    return objectPath.get(this.data, path);
  }

  set(path, value) {
    return objectPath.set(this.data, path, value);
  }

  _serialize() {
    throw new Error('_serialize() must be implemented');
```

```
    }

    _deserialize() {
      throw new Error('_deserialize() must be implemented');
    }
}
module.exports = ConfigTemplate;
```

The new `ConfigTemplate` class defines two template methods: `_deserialize()` and `_serialize()`, which are needed to carry out the loading and saving of the configuration. The underscore at the beginning of their names indicates that they are for internal use only, an easy way to flag protected methods. Since in JavaScript we cannot declare a method as abstract, we simply define them as **stubs**, throwing an exception if they are invoked (in other words, if they are not overridden by a concrete subclass).

Let's now create a concrete class using our template, for example, one that allows us to load and save the configuration using the JSON format:

```
const util = require('util');
const ConfigTemplate = require('./configTemplate');

class JsonConfig extends ConfigTemplate {

    _deserialize(data) {
      return JSON.parse(data);
    };

    _serialize(data) {
      return JSON.stringify(data, null, '  ');
    }
}
module.exports = JsonConfig;
```

The `JsonConfig` class extends from our template, the `ConfigTemplate` class, and provides a concrete implementation for the `_deserialize()` and `_serialize()` methods.

The `JsonConfig` class can now be used as a standalone configuration object without the need to specify a strategy for serialization and deserialization, as it is *baked in* the class itself:

```
const JsonConfig = require('./jsonConfig');

constjsonConfig = new JsonConfig();
jsonConfig.read('samples/conf.json');
jsonConfig.set('nodejs', 'design patterns');
jsonConfig.save('samples/conf_mod.json');
```

With minimal effort, the Template pattern allowed us to obtain a new, fully-working configuration manager by reusing the logic and the interface inherited from the parent template class and providing only the implementation of a few abstract methods.

In the wild

This pattern should not sound entirely new to us. We already encountered it in `Chapter 5`, *Coding with Streams*, when we were extending the different stream classes to implement our custom streams. In that context, the template methods were the `_write()`, `_read()`, `_transform()`, or `_flush()` methods, depending on the stream class that we wanted to implement. To create a new custom stream, we needed to inherit from a specific abstract stream class, providing an implementation for the template methods.

Middleware

One of the most distinctive patterns in Node.js is definitely **middleware**. Unfortunately, it's also one of the most confusing for the inexperienced, especially for developers coming from the enterprise programming world. The reason for the disorientation is probably connected to the meaning of the term middleware, which in enterprise architecture jargon represents the various software suites that help to abstract lower-level mechanisms such as OS APIs, network communications, memory management, and so on, allowing the developer to focus only on the business case of the application. In this context, the term middleware recalls topics such as CORBA, Enterprise Service Bus, Spring, JBoss, but in its more generic meaning it can also define any kind of software layer that acts like a glue between lower-level services and the application (literally the *software in the middle*).

Middleware in Express

Express (`http://expressjs.com`) popularized the term middleware in the Node.js world, binding it to a very specific design pattern. In Express, in fact, middleware represents a set of services, typically functions, that are organized in a pipeline and are responsible for processing incoming HTTP requests and relative responses.

Express is famous for being a very non-opinionated and minimalist web framework. Using the middleware pattern is an effective strategy for allowing developers to easily create and distribute new features that can be easily added to the current application, without the need to grow the minimalistic core of the framework.

An Express middleware has the following signature:

```
function(req, res, next) { ... }
```

Here, `req` is the incoming HTTP request, `res` is the response, and `next` is the callback to be invoked when the current middleware has completed its tasks and that in turn triggers the next middleware in the pipeline.

Examples of the tasks carried out by Express middleware include the following:

- Parsing the body of the request
- Compressing/decompressing requests and responses
- Producing access logs
- Managing sessions
- Managing encrypted cookies
- Providing **Cross-site Request Forgery (CSRF)** protection

If we think about it, these are all tasks that are not strictly related to the main functionality of an application, nor essential parts of a minimal core of a web server; rather, they are accessories, components providing support to the rest of the application and allowing the actual request handlers to focus only on their main business logic. Essentially, those tasks are software in the middle.

Middleware as a pattern

The technique used to implement middleware in Express is not new; in fact, it can be considered the Node.js incarnation of the Intercepting Filter pattern and the Chain of Responsibility pattern. In more generic terms, it also represents a processing **pipeline**, which reminds us about streams. Today, in Node.js the word middleware is used well beyond the boundaries of the Express framework, and indicates a particular pattern whereby a set of processing units, filters, and handlers, under the form of functions, are connected to form an asynchronous sequence in order to perform the preprocessing and postprocessing of any kind of data. The main advantage of this pattern is *flexibility*; in fact, this pattern allows us to obtain a plugin infrastructure with incredibly little effort, providing an unobtrusive way for extending a system with new filters and handlers.

If you want to know more about the Intercepting Filter pattern, the following article is a good starting point: `http://www.oracle.com/technetwork/java/interceptingfilter -142169.html`. A nice overview of the Chain of Responsibility pattern is available at this URL: `http://java.dzone.com/articles/design-patterns-uncovered- chain-of-responsibility`.

The following diagram shows the components of the middleware pattern:

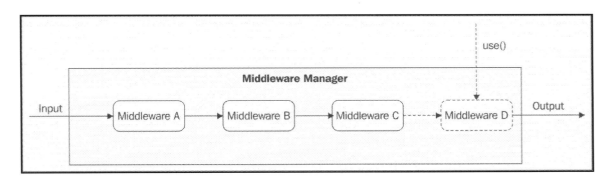

The essential component of the pattern is the **Middleware Manager**, which is responsible for organizing and executing the middleware functions. The most important implementation details of the pattern are as follows:

- New middleware can be registered by invoking the `use()` function (the name of this function is a common convention in many implementations of this pattern, but we can choose any name). Usually, new middleware can only be appended at the end of the pipeline, but this is not a strict rule.

- When new data is received for processing, the registered middleware is invoked in an asynchronous sequential execution flow. Each unit in the pipeline receives the result of the execution of the previous unit as input.

- Each piece of middleware can decide to stop further processing of the data by simply not invoking its callback or by passing an error to the callback. An error situation usually triggers the execution of another sequence of middleware that is specifically dedicated to handling errors.

There is no strict rule on how the data is processed and propagated in the pipeline. The strategies include:

- Augmenting the data with additional properties or functions
- Replacing the data with the result of some kind of processing
- Maintaining the immutability of the data and always returning fresh copies as result of processing

The right approach depends on the way the Middleware Manager is implemented and on the type of processing carried out by the middleware itself.

Creating a middleware framework for ØMQ

Let's now demonstrate the pattern by building a middleware framework around the **ØMQ** (`http://zeromq.org`) messaging library. ØMQ (also known as ZMQ, or ZeroMQ) provides a simple interface for exchanging atomic messages across the network using a variety of protocols; it shines for its performance, and its basic set of abstractions are specifically built to facilitate the implementation of custom messaging architectures. For this reason, ØMQ is often chosen to build complex distributed systems.

> In `Chapter 11`, *Messaging and Integration Patterns*, we will have the chance to analyze the features of ØMQ in more detail.

The interface of ØMQ is pretty low-level; it only allows us to use strings and binary buffers for messages, so any encoding or custom formatting of data has to be implemented by the users of the library.

In the next example, we are going to build a middleware infrastructure to abstract the preprocessing and post processing of the data passing through a ØMQ socket, so that we can transparently work with JSON objects, but also seamlessly compress messages traveling over the wire.

> Before continuing with the example, please make sure to install the ØMQ native libraries following the instructions at this URL: `http://zeromq.org/intro:get-the-software`. Any version in the 4.0 branch should be enough to work on this example.

The Middleware Manager

The first step toward building a middleware infrastructure around ∅MQ is to create a component that is responsible for executing the middleware pipeline when a new message is received or sent. For this purpose, let's create a new module called zmqMiddlewareManager.js and let's define it:

```
module.exports = class ZmqMiddlewareManager {
  constructor(socket) {
    this.socket = socket;
    this.inboundMiddleware = [];                    //[1]
    this.outboundMiddleware = [];
    socket.on('message', message => {               //[2]
      this.executeMiddleware(this.inboundMiddleware, {
        data: message
      });
    });
  }

  send(data) {
    constmessage = {
      data: data
    };

    this.executeMiddleware(this.outboundMiddleware, message,
      () => {
        this.socket.send(message.data);
      }
    );
  }

  use(middleware) {
    if (middleware.inbound) {
      this.inboundMiddleware.push(middleware.inbound);
    }
    if (middleware.outbound) {
      this.outboundMiddleware.unshift(middleware.outbound);
    }
  }

  executeMiddleware(middleware, arg, finish) {
    function iterator(index) {
      if (index === middleware.length) {
        return finish && finish();
      }
      middleware[index].call(this, arg, err => {
        if (err) {
```

```
            return console.log('There was an error: ' + err.message);
          }
          iterator.call(this, ++index);
        });
      }

      iterator.call(this, 0);
    }
};
```

In the first part of the class, we define the constructor for this new component. It accepts a ØMQ socket as an argument and:

1. Creates two empty lists that will contain our middleware functions, one for the inbound messages and another one for the outbound messages.

2. It immediately starts listening for new messages coming from the socket by attaching a new listener to the 'message' event. In the listener, we process the inbound message by executing the inboundMiddleware pipeline.

The next method of the ZmqMiddlewareManager class, send, is responsible for executing the middleware when a new message is sent through the socket.

This time the message is processed using the filters in the outboundMiddleware list and then passed to socket.send() for the actual network transmission.

Now, let's talk about the use method. This method is necessary for appending new middleware functions to our pipelines. Each middleware comes in pairs; in our implementation it's an object that contains two properties, inbound and outbound, that contain the middleware functions to be added to the respective list.

It's important to observe here that the inbound middleware is *pushed* to the end of the inboundMiddleware list, while the outbound middleware is *inserted* (using unshift) at the beginning of the outboundMiddleware list. This is because complementary inbound/outbound middleware functions usually need to be executed in an inverted order. For example, if we want to decompress and then deserialize an inbound message using JSON, it means that for the outbound, we should instead first serialize and then compress.

 It's important to understand that this convention for organizing the middleware in pairs is not strictly part of the general pattern, but only an implementation detail of our specific example.

The last function, `executeMiddleware`, represents the core of our component, it's the function that is responsible for executing the middleware functions. The code from this function should look very familiar; in fact, it is a simple implementation of the asynchronous sequential iteration pattern that we learned in Chapter 3, *Asynchronous Control Flow Patterns with Callbacks*. Each function in the `middleware` array received as input is executed one after the other, and the same `arg` object is provided as an argument to each middleware function; this is the trick that makes it possible to propagate the data from one middleware to the next. At the end of the iteration, the `finish()` callback is invoked.

 For brevity we are not supporting an error middleware pipeline. Normally, when a middleware function propagates an error, another set of middleware specifically dedicated to handling errors is executed. This can be easily implemented using the same technique that we are demonstrating here.

A middleware to support JSON messages

Now that we have implemented our Middleware Manager, we can create a pair of middleware functions to demonstrate how to process inbound and outbound messages. As we said, one of the goals of our middleware infrastructure is to have a filter that serializes and deserializes JSON messages, so let's create new middleware to take care of this. In a new module called `jsonMiddleware.js`, let's include the following code:

```
module.exports.json = () => {
  return {
    inbound: function (message, next) {
      message.data = JSON.parse(message.data.toString());
      next();
    },
    outbound: function (message, next) {
      message.data = new Buffer(JSON.stringify(message.data));
      next();
    }
  }
};
```

The `json` middleware that we just created is very simple:

- The `inbound` middleware deserializes the message received as an input and assigns the result back to the `data` property of `message`, so that it can be further processed along the pipeline
- The `outbound` middleware serializes any data found into `message.data`

Please note how the middleware supported by our framework is quite different from the one used in Express; this is totally normal and a perfect demonstration of how we can adapt this pattern to fit our specific need.

Using the ØMQ middleware framework

We are now ready to use the middleware infrastructure that we just created. To do that, we are going to build a very simple application, with a client sending a *ping* to a server at regular intervals and the server echoing back the message received.

From an implementation perspective, we are going to rely on a request/reply messaging pattern using the req/rep socket pair provided by ØMQ (`http://zguide.zeromq.org/page:all#Ask-and-Ye-Shall-Receive`). We will then wrap the sockets with our `zmqMiddlewareManager` to get all the advantages from the middleware infrastructure that we built, including the middleware for serializing/deserializing JSON messages.

The server

Let's start by creating the server side (`server.js`). In the first part of the module, we initialize our components:

```
const zmq = require('zmq');
const ZmqMiddlewareManager = require('./zmqMiddlewareManager');
const jsonMiddleware = require('./jsonMiddleware');
const reply = zmq.socket('rep');
reply.bind('tcp://127.0.0.1:5000');
```

In the preceding code, we loaded the required dependencies and bind a ØMQ `'rep'` (reply) socket to a local port. Next, we initialize our middleware:

```
const zmqm = new ZmqMiddlewareManager(reply);
zmqm.use(jsonMiddleware.json());
```

We created a new `ZmqMiddlewareManager` object and then added two items of middleware, one for compressing/decompressing the messages and another one for parsing/serializing JSON messages.

 For brevity, we did not show the implementation of the `zlib` middleware, but you can find it in the sample code that is distributed with the book.

Now we are ready to handle a request coming from the client; we will do this by simply adding more middleware, this time using it as a request handler:

```
zmqm.use({
  inbound: function (message, next) {
    console.log('Received: ', message.data);
    if (message.data.action === 'ping') {
      this.send({action: 'pong', echo: message.data.echo});
    }
    next();
  }
});
```

Since this last item of middleware is defined after the `zlib` and `json` middleware, we can transparently use the decompressed and deserialized message that is available in the `message.data` variable. On the other hand, any data passed to `send()` will be processed by the outbound middleware, which in our case will serialize then compress the data.

The client

On the client side of our little application, `'client.js'`, we will first have to initiate a new ØMQ `'req'` (request) socket connected to the port `5000`, the one used by our server:

```
const zmq = require('zmq');
const ZmqMiddlewareManager = require('./zmqMiddlewareManager');
const jsonMiddleware = require('./jsonMiddleware');

const request = zmq.socket('req');
request.connect('tcp://127.0.0.1:5000');
```

Then, we need to set up our middleware framework in the same way that we did for the server:

```
const zmqm = new ZmqMiddlewareManager(request);
zmqm.use(jsonMiddleware.json());
```

Next, we create an inbound item of middleware to handle the responses coming from the server:

```
zmqm.use({
  inbound: function (message, next) {
    console.log('Echoed back: ', message.data);
    next();
  }
});
```

In the preceding code, we simply intercept any inbound response and print it to the console.

Finally, we set up a timer to send some ping requests at regular intervals, always using the `zmqMiddlewareManager` to get all the advantages of our middleware:

```
setInterval( () => {
  zmqm.send({action: 'ping', echo: Date.now()});
}, 1000);
```

Note that we are defining all our `inbound` and `outbound` functions explicitly using the `function` keyword, avoiding the usage of the arrow function syntax. This is intentional because, as we learned in Chapter 1, *Welcome to the Node.js Platform*, the arrow function declaration blocks the function scope to its lexical scope. Using `call` on a function defined with an arrow function will not alter its internal scope. In other words, if we use an arrow function, our middleware will not recognize `this` as an instance of `zmqMiddlewareManager` and a "TypeError: `this.send is not a function`" will be raised.

We can now try our application by first starting the server:

node server

We can then start the client with the following command:

node client

At this point, we should see the client sending messages and the server echoing them back.

Our middleware framework did its job; it allowed us to decompress/compress and deserialize/serialize our messages transparently, leaving the handlers free to focus on their business logic!

Middleware using generators in Koa

In the previous paragraphs we saw how it's possible to implement the middleware pattern with callbacks and an example applied to a messaging system.

As we saw when we introduced it, the middleware pattern really shines in web frameworks as a handy mechanism to build "layers" of logic that can deal with input and output as data flows throughout the core of the application.

Apart from Express, another web framework which makes heavy use of the middleware pattern is Koa (`http://koajs.com/`). Koa is an extremely interesting framework mostly because of its radical choice to implement the middleware pattern only using ES2015 generator functions rather than using callbacks. We will see in a moment how this choice dramatically simplifies the way middleware can be written, but before moving to some code let's picture another way to visualize the middleware pattern, specific for this web framework:

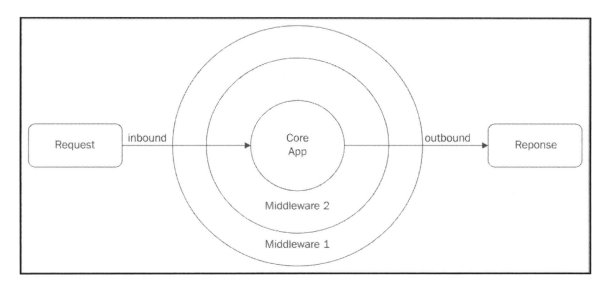

In this representation, we have an incoming request that, before getting into the core of our app, traverses a number of middlewares. This part of the flow is called **inbound** or **downstream**. After the flow reaches the core of the app, it traverses all the middlewares again, but this time in an inverse order. This allows the middlewares to perform other actions after the main logic of the app has been executed and the response is ready to be sent to the user. This part of the flow is called **outbound** or **upstream**.

The representation above is sometime called "the onion" among programmers because of the way middleware wraps the core app, which reminds us of the layers of an onion.

Now let's create a new web application with Koa to see how we can easily write a custom middleware with generator functions.

Our app will be a very simple JSON API that returns the current timestamp in our server.

First of all, we need to install Koa:

```
npm install koa
```

Then we can write our new `app.js`:

```
const app = require('koa')();

app.use(function *(){
  this.body = {"now": new Date()};
});

app.listen(3000);
```

It's important to notice that the core of our application is defined with a generator function within an `app.use` call. We will see in a moment that middlewares are added to the app in the exact same way and we will realize that the core of our app is, nonetheless, the last middleware added to the application (and which doesn't need to yield to another following item of middleware).

The first draft of our app is ready. We can now run it:

```
node app.js
```

We then point our browser to `http://localhost:3000` to see it in action.

Notice that Koa takes care of converting the response to a JSON string and adds the correct `content-type` header when we set a JavaScript object to be the body of the current response.

Our API works great, but now we might decide that we would like to protect it from people abusing it and make sure people don't make more than one request in less than one second. This logic can be considered external to the business logic of our API, so we should add it by simply writing a new dedicated item of middleware. Let's write it as a separate module called `rateLimit.js`:

```
const lastCall = new Map();

module.exports = function *(next) {

  // inbound
  const now = new Date();
  if (lastCall.has(this.ip) && now.getTime() -
      lastCall.get(this.ip).getTime() < 1000) {
    return this.status = 429; // Too Many Requests
  }
```

```
      yield next;

      // outbound
      lastCall.set(this.ip, now);
      this.set('X-RateLimit-Reset', now.getTime() + 1000);
    };
```

Our module exports a generator function that implements the logic for our middleware.

The first thing to notice is that we are using a `Map` object to store the time we received the last call from a given IP address. We will use this `Map` as a sort of in-memory database to be able to check whether a specific user is overloading our server with more than one request per second. Of course this implementation is just a dummy example and it's not ideal in a real case scenario, where it is better to just use external storage such as *Redis* or *Memcache* and a more refined logic to detect overloads.

We can see that the body of the middleware is divided in two logical parts, *inbound* and *outbound*, separated from the `yield next` call. In the inbound part, we haven't hit the core of the application yet, so it's the place where we need to check whether the user is exceeding our rate limit. If that is the case, we simply set the HTTP status code of the response to *429* (too many requests) and we return to stop the execution of the flow.

Another way we can progress to the next item of middleware is by calling `yield next`. This is where the magic happens: using generator functions and yield, the execution of the middleware is suspended to execute all the other middlewares in the list sequentially and only when the last item of middleware is executed (the real core of the app) the outbound flow can start and control is given back to every middleware in an inverted order, until the first middleware is called again.

When our middleware again receives control and the generator function is resumed, we take care of storing the timestamp for the successful call, and adding a `X-RateLimit-Reset` header to the request, to signal when the user will be able to make a new request.

 If you need a more complete and reliable implementation of rate-limit middleware, you can have a look at the `koajs/ratelimit` module: `https://github.com/koajs/ratelimit`

To enable this middleware, we need to add the following line in our `app.js` before the existing `app.use` which contains the core logic of our app:

```
app.use(require('./rateLimit'));
```

Now to see our new app in action, we need to restart our server and open our browser again. If we refresh the page quickly a few times, we will probably hit the rate limit and we should see the descriptive error message *"Too Many Requests"*. This message is automatically added by Koa as a consequence of setting the status code to 429 and having an empty response body.

 If you are interested in reading the actual implementation of the middleware pattern, based on generators used within the Koa framework, you can have a look at the koajs/compose repository (https://github.com/koajs/compose), which is the core module used to transform an array of generators into a new generator which executes the original ones in a pipeline.

Command

Another design pattern with huge importance in Node.js is **Command**. In its most generic definition, we can consider a Command as any object that encapsulates all the information necessary to perform an action at a later time. So, instead of invoking a method or a function directly, we create an object representing the intention to perform such an invocation; it will then be the responsibility of another component to materialize the intent, transforming it into an actual action. Traditionally, this pattern is built around four major components, as shown in the following figure:

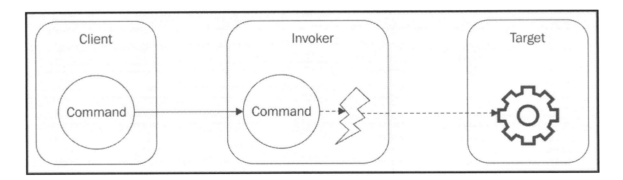

The typical organization of the Command pattern can be described as follows:

- **Command**: This is the object encapsulating the information necessary to invoke a method or function.
- **Client**: This creates the command and provides it to the Invoker.
- **Invoker**: This is responsible for executing the command on the target.
- **Target** (or **Receiver**): This is the subject of the invocation. It can be a lone function or the method of an object.

As we will see, these four components can vary a lot depending on the way we want to implement the pattern; this should not sound new at this point.

Using the Command pattern instead of directly executing an operation has several advantages and applications:

- A command can be scheduled for execution at a later time.
- A command can be easily serialized and sent over the network. This simple property allows us to distribute jobs across remote machines, transmit commands from the browser to the server, create RPC systems, and so on.
- Commands make it easy to keep a history of all the operations executed on a system.
- Commands are an important part of some algorithms for data synchronization and conflict resolution.
- A command scheduled for execution can be cancelled if it's not yet executed. It can also be reverted (undone), bringing the state of the application to the point before the command was executed.
- Several commands can be grouped together. This can be used to create atomic transactions or to implement a mechanism whereby all the operations in the group are executed at once.
- Different kinds of transformation can be performed on a set of commands, such as duplicate removal, joining and splitting, or applying more complex algorithms such as **Operational Transformation** (**OT**), which is the base for most of today's real-time collaborative software, such as collaborative text editing.

A great explanation of how OT works can be found at
`http://www.codecommit.com/blog/java/understanding-and-applying-operational-transformation`.

The preceding list clearly shows us how important this pattern is, especially in a platform such as Node.js where networking and asynchronous execution are essential players.

A flexible pattern

As we already mentioned, the **Command** pattern in JavaScript can be implemented in many different ways; we are now going to demonstrate only a few of them just to give an idea of its scope.

The task pattern

We can start off with the most basic and trivial implementation: the **task pattern**. The easiest way in JavaScript to create an object representing an invocation is, of course, by creating a closure:

```
function createTask(target, args) {
  return () => {
    target.apply(null, args);
  }
}
```

This should not look new at all; we have used this pattern already so many times throughout the book, and in particular in Chapter 3, *Asynchronous Control Flow Patterns with Callbacks*. This technique allowed us to use a separate component to control and schedule the execution of our tasks, which is essentially equivalent to the Invoker of the Command pattern. For example, do you remember how we were defining tasks to pass to the async library? Or even better, do you remember how we were using *thunks* in combination with generators? The callback pattern itself can be considered a very simple version of the Command pattern.

A more complex command

Let's now work on an example of a more complex command; this time we want to support *undo* and *serialization*. Let's start with the *target* of our commands, a little object that is responsible for sending status updates to a service like Twitter. We use a mock-up of such a service for simplicity:

```
const statusUpdateService = {
  statusUpdates: {},
  sendUpdate: function(status) {
    console.log('Status sent: ' + status);
```

```
      let id = Math.floor(Math.random() * 1000000);
      statusUpdateService.statusUpdates[id] = status;
      return id;
    },

    destroyUpdate: id => {
      console.log('Status removed: ' + id);
      delete statusUpdateService.statusUpdates[id];
    }
};
```

Now, let's create a command to represent the posting of a new status update:

```
function createSendStatusCmd(service, status) {
  let postId = null;

  const command = () => {
    postId = service.sendUpdate(status);
  };

  command.undo = () => {
    if(postId) {
      service.destroyUpdate(postId);
      postId = null;
    }
  };

  command.serialize = () => {
    return {type: 'status', action: 'post', status: status};
  };

  return command;
}
```

The preceding function is a factory that produces new *sendStatus* commands. Each command implements the following three functionalities:

1. The command itself is a function that, when invoked, will trigger the action; in other words, it implements the *task* pattern that we have seen before. The command when executed will send a new status update using the methods of the target service.

2. An undo() function, attached to the main task, that reverts the effects of the operations. In our case, we are simply invoking the destroyUpdate() method on the target service.

3. A serialize() function that builds a JSON object that contains all the necessary information to reconstruct the same command object.

After this, we can build an Invoker; we can start by implementing its constructor and its `run()` method:

```
class Invoker {

  constructor() {
    this.history = [];
  }

  run (cmd) {
    this.history.push(cmd);
    cmd();
    console.log('Command executed', cmd.serialize());
  }
}
```

The `run()` method that we defined earlier is the basic functionality of our `Invoker`; it is responsible for saving the command into the `history` instance variable and then triggering the execution of the command itself. Next, we can add a new method that delays the execution of a command:

```
delay (cmd, delay) {
  setTimeout(() => {
    this.run(cmd);
  }, delay)
}
```

Then, we can implement an `undo()` method that reverts the last command:

```
undo () {
  const cmd = this.history.pop();
  cmd.undo();
  console.log('Command undone', cmd.serialize());
}
```

Finally, we also want to be able to run a command on a remote server, by serializing and then transferring it over the network using a web service:

```
runRemotely (cmd) {
  request.post('http://localhost:3000/cmd',
    {json: cmd.serialize()},
    err => {
      console.log('Command executed remotely', cmd.serialize());
    }
  );
}
}
```

Now that we have the Command, the Invoker, and the Target, the only component missing is the Client. Let's start with instantiating `Invoker`:

```
const invoker = new Invoker();
```

Then, we can create a command using the following line of code:

```
const command = createSendStatusCmd(statusUpdateService, 'HI!');
```

We now have a command representing the posting of a status message; we can then decide to dispatch it immediately:

```
invoker.run(command);
```

Oops, we made a mistake; let's revert to the state of our timeline as it was before sending the last message:

```
invoker.undo();
```

We can also decide to schedule the message to be sent in an hour from now:

```
invoker.delay(command, 1000 * 60 * 60);
```

Alternatively, we can distribute the load of the application by migrating the task to another machine:

```
invoker.runRemotely(command);
```

The little example that we have just created shows how wrapping an operation in a command can open a world of possibilities, and that's just the tip of the iceberg.

As the last remarks, it is worth noticing that a fully-fledged Command pattern has been used only when really needed. We saw, in fact, how much additional code we had to write to simply invoke a method of `statusUpdateService`; if all that we need is only an invocation, then a complex command would be overkill. If, however, we need to schedule the execution of a task, or run an asynchronous operation, then the simpler *task pattern* offers the best compromise. If instead, we need more advanced features such as undo support, transformations, conflict resolution, or one of the other fancy use cases that we described previously, using a more complex representation for the command is almost necessary.

Summary

In this chapter, we learned how some of the traditional GoF design patterns can be applied to JavaScript and, in particular, to the Node.js philosophy. Some of them were transformed, some were simplified, others renamed or adapted as part of their assimilation by the language, the platform, and the community. We emphasized how simple patterns such as factory can greatly improve the flexibility of our code and how with Proxy, Decorator, and Adapter we can manipulate, extend, and adapt the interface of existing objects. Strategy, State, and Template, instead, have shown us how to split a bigger algorithm into its static and variable parts, allowing us to improve the code reuse and extensibility of our components. By learning the Middleware pattern, we are now able to process our data using a simple, extensible, and elegant paradigm. Finally, the Command pattern provided us with a simple abstraction to make any operation more flexible and powerful.

Apart from observing the JavaScript reincarnation of these widely accepted design patterns, we also discovered some new design patterns born and raised specifically in the JavaScript community, such as the *Revealing constructor* and the *Composable factory function* patterns. These patterns help to deal with specific aspects of the JavaScript language such as *asynchronicity* and *prototype-based programming*.

Finally, we acquired more evidence of how JavaScript is about getting things done and building software by composing different reusable objects or functions instead of extending many little classes or interfaces. Also, for developers coming from other object-oriented languages, it might have looked weird to see how different some design patterns become when implemented in JavaScript; some might feel lost knowing that there might not be only one, but rather many different ways of implementing a design pattern.

JavaScript is a pragmatic language, we said; it allows us to get things done quickly, however, without any kind of structure or guidelines, we are asking for trouble. That's where this book and, in particular, this chapter comes in useful. It tries to teach the right balance between creativity and rigor. It shows not only that there are patterns that can be reused to improve our code, but also that their implementation is not the most important detail; it can vary a lot, or even overlap with other patterns. What really matters is the blueprint, the guidelines, and the idea at the base of the pattern. This is the real reusable piece of information that we can exploit to design better Node.js applications in a fun way.

In the next chapter, we will analyze some more design patterns by focusing on one of the most opinionated aspects of programming: how to organize and connect modules together.

7
Wiring Modules

The Node.js module system brilliantly fills an old gap in the JavaScript language: the lack of a native way of organizing code into different self-contained units. One of its biggest advantages is the ability to link these modules together using the `require()` function (as we have seen in `Chapter 2`, *Node.js Essential Patterns*), a simple yet powerful approach. However, many developers new to Node.js might find this confusing; one of the most frequently asked questions is in fact: *what's the best way to pass an instance of component X into module Y?*

Sometimes, this confusion results in a desperate quest for the Singleton pattern in the hope of finding a more familiar way to link our modules together. On the other hand, some might overuse the Dependency Injection pattern, leveraging it to handle any type of dependency (even stateless) without a particular reason. It should not be surprising that the art of **module wiring** is one of the most controversial and opinionated topics in Node.js. There are many schools of thought influencing this area, but none of them can be considered to possess the undisputed truth. Every approach, in fact, has its pros and cons and they often end up mixed together in the same application, adapted, customized, or used in disguise under other names.

In this chapter, we're going to analyze the various approaches for wiring modules and highlight their strengths and weaknesses so that we can rationally choose and mix them together depending on the balance between simplicity, reusability, and extensibility that we want to obtain. In particular, we're going to present the most important patterns related to this topic, which are as follows:

- Hardcoded dependency
- Dependency Injection
- Service locator
- Dependency Injection containers

We will then explore a closely related problem, namely, how to wire plugins. This can be considered a specialization of module wiring and it mostly presents the same traits, but the context of its application is slightly different and presents its own challenges, especially when a plugin is distributed as a separate Node.js package. We will learn the main techniques to create a plugin-capable architecture and we will then focus on how to integrate these plugins into the flow of the main application.

At the end of this chapter, the obscure art of Node.js module wiring should not be a mystery to us anymore.

Modules and dependencies

Every modern application is the result of the aggregation of several components and, as the application grows, the way we connect these components becomes a win or lose factor. It's not only a problem related to technical aspects such as extensibility, but it's also a concern with the way we perceive the system. A tangled **dependency graph** is a *liability* and it adds to the **technical debt** of the project; in such a situation, any change in the code aimed to either modify or extend its functionality can result in tremendous effort.

In the worst case, the components are so tightly connected together that it becomes impossible to add or change anything without refactoring or even completely rewriting entire parts of the application. This, of course, does not mean that we have to over-engineer our design starting from the very first module, but surely finding a good balance from the very beginning can make a huge difference.

Node.js provides a great tool for organizing and wiring the components of an application together: it's the CommonJS module system. However, the module system alone is not a guarantee of success; if on the one hand, it adds a convenient *level of indirection* between the client module and the dependency, then on the other, it might introduce a tighter *coupling* if not used properly. In this section, we will discuss some fundamental aspects of dependency wiring in Node.js.

The most common dependency in Node.js

In software architecture, we can consider any entity, state, or data format which influences the behavior or structure of a component as a *dependency*. For example, a component might use the services offered by another component, rely on a particular global state of the system, or implement a specific communication protocol in order to exchange information with other components, and so on. The concept of dependency is very broad and sometimes hard to evaluate.

In Node.js, though, we can immediately identify one essential type of dependency, which is the most common and easy to identify; of course, we are talking about the **dependency between modules**. Modules are the fundamental mechanism at our disposal to organize and structure our code; it's unreasonable to build a large application without relying on the module system at all. If used properly to group the various elements of an application, it can bring a lot of advantages. In fact, the properties of a module can be summed up as follows:

- A module is more readable and understandable because (ideally) it's more focused
- Being represented as a separate file, a module is easier to identify
- A module can be more easily reused across different applications

A module represents the perfect level of granularity for performing **information hiding** and offers an effective mechanism to expose only the public interface of a component (using `module.exports`).

However, simply spreading the functionality of an application or a library across different modules is not enough for a successful design—it has to be done right. One of the fallacies is ending up in a situation where the relationship between our modules becomes so strong we create a unique monolithic entity, where removing or replacing a module would reverberate across most of the architecture. We are immediately able to recognize that the way we organize our code into modules and the way we connect them together play a strategic role. And, as with any problem in software design, it's a matter of finding the right balance between different measures.

Cohesion and coupling

The two most important properties to balance when building modules are **cohesion** and **coupling**. They can be applied to any type of a component or subsystem in software architecture, so we can use them as guidelines when building Node.js modules as well. These two properties can be defined as follows:

- **Cohesion**: This is a measure of the correlation between the functionalities of a component. For example, a module that does *only one thing*, where all its parts contribute to that one single task has a *high cohesion*. A module that contains functions to save any type of object into a database—`saveProduct()`, `saveInvoice()`, `saveUser()`, and so on has a *low cohesion*.

- **Coupling**: This measures how much a component is dependent on the other components of a system. For example, a module is *tightly coupled* to another module when it directly reads or modifies the data of the other module. Also, two modules that interact via a global or shared state are tightly coupled. On the other hand, two modules that communicate only via the passing of parameters are *loosely coupled*.

The desirable scenario is to have a high cohesion and a loose coupling, which usually results in more understandable, reusable, and extensible modules.

Stateful modules

In JavaScript, everything is an object. We don't have abstract concepts such as pure interfaces or classes; its dynamic typing already provides a natural mechanism to decouple the **interface** (or **policy**) from the **implementation** (or **detail**). That's one of the reasons why some of the design patterns that we have seen in Chapter 6, *Design Patterns*, looked so different and simplified compared to their traditional implementation.

In JavaScript, we have minimal problems in separating interfaces from implementations; however, by simply using the Node.js module system, we are already introducing a hardcoded relationship with one particular implementation. Under normal conditions, there is nothing wrong with this, but if we use require() to load a module that exports a stateful instance, such as a db handle, an HTTP server instance, the instance of a service, or in general any object which is not stateless, we are actually referencing something very similar to a Singleton, thus inheriting its pros and cons, with the addition of some caveats.

The Singleton pattern in Node.js

A lot of people new to Node.js get confused about how to implement the Singleton pattern correctly, most of the time with the simple intent of sharing an instance across the various modules of an application. However, the answer in Node.js is easier than what we might think; simply exporting an instance using module.exports is already enough to obtain something very similar to the Singleton pattern. Consider, for example, the following line of code:

```
//'db.js' module
module.exports = new Database('my-app-db');
```

By simply exporting a new instance of our database, we can already assume that within the current package (which can easily be the entire code of our application), we are going to have only one instance of the db module. This is possible because, as we know, Node.js will cache the module after the first invocation of `require()`, making sure to not execute it again at any subsequent invocation, returning instead the cached instance. For example, we can easily obtain a shared instance of the db module that we defined earlier, with the following line of code:

```
const db = require('./db');
```

But there is a caveat; the module is cached using its full path as lookup key, therefore it is guaranteed to be a Singleton only within the current package. We saw in Chapter 2, *Node.js Essential Patterns*, that each package might have its own set of private dependencies inside its `node_modules` directory, which might result in multiple instances of the same package and therefore of the same module, with the result that our Singleton might not be *single* anymore. Consider, for example, the case where the db module is wrapped into a package named `mydb`. The following lines of code will be in its `package.json` file:

```
{
  "name": "mydb",
  "main": "db.js"
}
```

Now consider the following package dependency tree:

```
app/
`-- node_modules
    |-- packageA
    |   `-- node_modules
    |       `-- mydb
    `-- packageB
        `-- node_modules
            `-- mydb
```

Both `packageA` and `packageB` have a dependency on the `mydb` package; in turn, the `app` package, which is our main application, depends on `packageA` and `packageB`. The scenario we just described will break the assumption about the uniqueness of the database instance; in fact, both `packageA` and `packageB` will load the database instance using a command such as the following:

```
const db = require('mydb');
```

However, `packageA` and `packageB` will actually load two different instances of our pretending Singleton because the `mydb` module will resolve to a different directory depending on the package it is required from.

At this point, we can easily say that the Singleton pattern, as described in the literature, does not exist in Node.js, unless we don't use a real *global variable* to store it, something such as the following:

```
global.db = new Database('my-app-db');
```

This would guarantee that the instance will be the only one and shared across the entire application, not just the same package. However, this is a practice to avoid at all costs; most of the time, we don't really need a pure Singleton, and anyway, as we will see later, there are other patterns that we can use to share an instance across the different packages.

 Throughout this book, for simplicity, we will use the term Singleton to describe a stateful object exported by a module, even if this doesn't represent a real Singleton in the strict definition of the term. We can surely say, though, that it shares the same practical intent with the original pattern: to easily share a state across different components.

Patterns for wiring modules

Now that we have discussed some basic theory around dependencies and coupling, we are ready to dive into some more practical concepts. In this section, in fact, we are going to present the main module wiring patterns. Our focus will be mainly pointed towards the wiring of stateful instances, which are, without any doubt, the most important type of dependencies in an application.

Hardcoded dependency

We start our analysis by looking at the most *conventional* relationship between two modules, which is the **hardcoded dependency**. In Node.js, this is obtained when a client module explicitly loads another module using `require()`. As we will see in this section, this way of establishing module dependencies is simple and effective, but we have to pay additional attention to hardcoding dependencies with stateful instances, as this would limit the reusability of our modules.

Building an authentication server using hardcoded dependencies

Let's start our analysis by looking at the structure represented by the following figure:

The preceding figure shows a typical example of layered architecture; it describes the structure of a simple authentication system. `AuthController` accepts the input from the client, extracts the login information from the request, and performs some preliminary validation. It then relies on `AuthService` to check whether the provided credentials match with the information stored in the database; this is done by executing some specific queries using the `db` module handle, as a means to communicate with the database. The way these three components are connected together will determine their level of reusability, testability, and maintainability.

The most natural way to wire these components together is by requiring the `db` module from `AuthService` and then requiring `AuthService` from `AuthController`. This is the hardcoded dependency that we are talking about.

Let's demonstrate this in practice by actually implementing the system that we just described. Let's then design a simple **authentication server**, which exposes the following two HTTP APIs:

- POST `'/login'`: This receives a JSON object that contains a `username` and `password` pair to authenticate. On success, it returns a **JSON Web Token (JWT)**, which can be used in subsequent requests to verify the identity of the user.

  JSON Web Token is a format for representing and sharing *claims* between parties. Its popularity is growing with the explosion of **Single Page Applications** and **Cross-origin resource sharing (CORS)** as a more flexible alternative to cookie-based authentication. To know more about JWT, you can refer to its specification (currently in draft) at `http://self-issued.info/docs/draft-ietf-oauth-json-web-token.html`

- GET '/checkToken': This reads a token from a GET query parameter and verifies its validity.

For this example, we are going to use several technologies; some of them are not new to us. In particular, we are going to use express (https://npmjs.org/package/express) to implement the Web API and levelup (https://npmjs.org/package/levelup) to store the user's data.

The db module

Let's start by building our application from the bottom up; the very first thing we need is a module that exposes a levelUp database instance. Let's do this by creating a new file named lib/db.js and including the following content:

```
const level = require('level');
const sublevel = require('level-sublevel');

module.exports = sublevel(
  level('example-db', {valueEncoding: 'json'})
);
```

The preceding module simply creates a connection to a LevelDB database stored in the ./example-db directory, then it decorates the instance using the sublevel plugin (https://npmjs.org/package/level-sublevel), which adds the support to create and query separate sections of the database (it can be compared to a SQL table or MongoDB collection). The object exported by the module is the database handle itself, which is a stateful instance; therefore, we are creating a singleton.

The authService module

Now that we have the db singleton, we can use it to implement the lib/authService.js module, which is the component responsible for checking a user's credentials against the information in the database. The code is as follows (only the relevant parts are shown):

```
// ...
const db = require('./db');
const users = db.sublevel('users');

const tokenSecret = 'SHHH!';

exports.login = (username, password, callback) => {
  users.get(username, function(err, user) {
    // ...
  });
```

```
};

exports.checkToken = (token, callback) => {
  // ...
    users.get(userData.username, function(err, user) {
      // ...
    });
};
```

The `authService` module implements the `login()` service, which is responsible for checking a username/password pair against the information in the database, and the `checkToken()` service, which takes in a token and verifies its validity.

The preceding code also shows the first example of a hardcoded dependency with a stateful module. We are talking about the `db` module, which we load by simply requiring it. The resulting `db` variable contains an already initialized database handle that we can use straight away to perform our queries.

At this point, we can see that all the code that we created for the `authService` module does not really necessitate one particular instance of the `db` module—any instance will simply work. However, we hardcoded the dependency to one particular `db` instance, and this means that we will be unable to reuse `authService` in combination with another database instance without touching its code.

The authController module

Continuing to go up in the layers of the application, we are now going to see what the `lib/authController.js` module looks like. This module is responsible for handling the HTTP requests, and it's essentially a collection of the Express routes; the module's code is the following:

```
const authService = require('./authService');

exports.login = (req, res, next) => {
  authService.login(req.body.username, req.body.password,
    (err, result) => {
      // ...
    }
  );
};

exports.checkToken = (req, res, next) => {
  authService.checkToken(req.query.token,
    (err, result) => {
      // ...
```

```
    }
  );
};
```

The `authController` module implements two Express routes: one for performing the login and returning the corresponding authentication token (`login()`) and another for checking the validity of the token (`checkToken()`). Both the routes delegate most of their logic to `authService`, so their only job is to deal with the HTTP request and response.

We can see that, in this case too, we are hardcoding the dependency with a stateful module: `authService`. Yes, the `authService` module is stateful by transitivity because it depends directly on the db module. With this, we should start to understand how a hardcoded dependency can easily propagate across the structure of the entire application: the `authController` module depends on the `authService` module, which in turn depends on the db module; transitively, this means that the `authService` module itself is indirectly linked to one particular db instance.

The app module

Finally, we can put all the pieces together by implementing the entry point of the application. Following the convention, we will place this logic in a module named `app.js`, sitting in the root of our project as follows:

```
const express = require('express');
const bodyParser = require('body-parser');
const errorHandler = require('errorhandler');
const http = require('http');

const authController = require('./lib/authController');

const app = module.exports = express();
app.use(bodyParser.json());

app.post('/login', authController.login);
app.get('/checkToken', authController.checkToken);

app.use(errorHandler());
http.createServer(app).listen(3000, () => {
  console.log('Express server started');
});
```

As we can see, our `app` module is really basic; it contains a simple Express server, which registers some middleware and the two routes exported by `authController`. Of course, the most important line of code for us is where we require `authController` to create a hardcoded dependency with its stateful instance.

Running the authentication server

Before we can try the authentication server that we just implemented, we advise you to populate the database with some sample data using the `populate_db.js` script, which is provided in the code samples. After doing this, we can fire up the server by running the following command:

```
node app
```

We can then try to invoke the two web services that we created; we can use a REST client to do this or, alternatively, the good old `curl` command. For example, to execute a login, we can run the following command:

```
curl -X POST -d '{"username": "alice", "password":"secret"}'
http://localhost:3000/login -H "Content-Type: application/json"
```

The preceding command should return a token that we can use to test the `/checkLogin` web service (just replace <TOKEN HERE> in the following command):

```
curl -X GET -H "Accept: application/json"
http://localhost:3000/checkToken?token=<TOKEN HERE>
```

The preceding command should return a string such as the following, which confirms that our server is working as expected:

```
{"ok":"true","user":{"username":"alice"}}
```

Pros and cons of hardcoded dependencies

The sample we just implemented demonstrates the conventional way of wiring modules in Node.js, leveraging the full power of its module system to manage the dependencies between the various components of the application. We exported stateful instances from our modules, letting Node.js manage their life cycle, and then we required them directly from other parts of the application. The result is an immediately intuitive organization, easy to understand and debug, where each module initializes and wires itself without any external intervention.

On the other hand, however, hardcoding the dependency on a stateful instance limits the possibility of wiring the module against other instances, which makes it less reusable and harder to unit test. For example, reusing `authService` in combination with another database instance would be close to impossible, as its dependency is hardcoded with one particular instance. Similarly, testing `authService` in isolation can be a difficult task because we cannot easily mock the database used by the module.

As a last consideration, it's important to see that most of the disadvantages of using hardcoded dependencies are associated with stateful instances. This means that if we use `require()` to load a stateless module, for example, a factory, constructor, or a set of stateless functions, we don't incur the same kind of problems. We will still have a tight coupling with a specific implementation, but in Node.js, this usually does not impact the reusability of a component, as it does not introduce a coupling with a particular state.

Dependency Injection

The **Dependency Injection** (DI) pattern is probably one of the most misunderstood concepts in software design. Many associate the term with frameworks and DI containers such as Spring (for Java and C#) or Pimple (for PHP), but in reality it is a much simpler concept. The main idea behind the Dependency Injection pattern is the dependencies of a component being *provided as input* by an external entity.

Such an entity can be a client component or a *global container*, which centralizes the wiring of all the modules of the system. The main advantage of this approach is an improved decoupling, especially for modules depending on stateful instances. Using DI, each dependency, instead of being hardcoded into the module, is received from the outside. This means that the module can be configured to use any dependency, and therefore can be reused in different contexts.

To demonstrate this pattern in practice, we are now going to refactor the authentication server that we built in the previous section, using DI to wire its modules.

Refactoring the authentication server to use DI

Refactoring our modules to use DI involves the use of a very simple recipe: instead of hardcoding the dependency to a stateful instance, we will instead create a factory, which takes a set of dependencies as arguments.

Let's start immediately with this refactoring; let's work on the `lib/db.js` module, given as follows:

```
const level = require('level');
const sublevel = require('level-sublevel');

module.exports = dbName => {
  return sublevel(
    level(dbName, {valueEncoding: 'json'})
  );
};
```

The first step in our refactoring process is to transform the db module into a factory. The result is that we can now use it to create as many database instances as we want; this means that the entire module is now reusable and stateless.

Let's move on and implement the new version of the `lib/authService.js` module:

```
const jwt = require('jwt-simple');
const bcrypt = require('bcrypt');

module.exports = (db, tokenSecret) => {
  const users = db.sublevel('users');
  const authService = {};

  authService.login = (username, password, callback) => {
    //...same as in the previous version
  };

  authService.checkToken = (token, callback) => {
    //...same as in the previous version
  };

  return authService;
};
```

Also, the `authService` module is now stateless; it doesn't export any particular instance anymore, just a simple factory. The most important detail, though, is that we made the `db` dependency *injectable* as an argument of the factory function, removing what was previously a hardcoded dependency. This simple change enables us to create a new `authService` module by wiring it to any database instance.

We can refactor the `lib/authController.js` module in a similar way as follows:

```
module.exports = (authService) => {
  const authController = {};

  authController.login = (req, res, next) => {
    //...same as in the previous version
  };

  authController.checkToken = (req, res, next) => {
    //...same as in the previous version
  };

  return authController;
};
```

The `authController` module does not have any hardcoded dependency at all, not even stateless! The only dependency, the `authService` module, is provided as input to the factory at the moment of its invocation.

Okay, now it's time to see where all these modules are actually created and wired together; the answer lies in the `app.js` module, which represents the topmost layer in our application. Its code is the following:

```
// ...
const dbFactory = require('./lib/db');                          //[1]
const authServiceFactory = require('./lib/authService');
const authControllerFactory = require('./lib/authController');

const db = dbFactory('example-db');                             //[2]
const authService = authServiceFactory(db, 'SHHH!');
const authController = authControllerFactory(authService);

app.post('/login', authController.login);                      //[3]
app.get('/checkToken', authController.checkToken);
// ...
```

The previous code can be summed up as follows:

1. Firstly, we load the factories of our services; at this point, they are still stateless objects.
2. Next, we instantiate each service by providing the dependencies it requires. This is the phase where all the modules are created and wired.
3. Finally, we register the routes of the `authController` module with the Express server as we would normally do.

Our authentication server is now wired using DI and ready to be used again.

The different types of DI

The example we just presented demonstrated only one type of DI (**factory injection**), but there are a couple more worth mentioning:

- **Constructor injection**: In this type of DI, the dependencies are passed to a constructor at the moment of its creation; one possible example can be the following:

```
const service = new Service(dependencyA, dependencyB);
```

- **Property injection**: In this type of DI, the dependencies are *attached* to an object after its creation, as demonstrated by the following code:

```
const service = new Service();  //works also with a factory
service.dependencyA = anInstanceOfDependencyA;
```

Property injection implies that an object is created in an *inconsistent* state because it's not wired to its dependencies, so it's the least robust, but it may sometimes be useful when there are cycles between the dependencies. For example, if we have two components, *A* and *B*, both using factory or constructor injection and both depending on each other, we cannot instantiate either of them because both would require the other to exist in order to be created. Let's consider a simple example, as follows:

```
function Afactory(b) {
  return {
    foo: function() {
      b.say();
    },
    what: function() {
      return 'Hello!';
    }
  }
}
```

```
    }

    function Bfactory(a) {
      return {
        a: a,
        say: function() {
          console.log('I say: ' + a.what);
        }
      }
    }
```

The dependency deadlock between the two preceding factories can be resolved only using property injection, for example, by first creating an incomplete instance of *B*, which then can be used to create *A*. Finally, we will inject *A* into *B* by setting the relative property as follows:

```
    const b = Bfactory(null);
    const a = Afactory(b);
    a.b = b;
```

 In some rare circumstances, a cycle in the dependency graph is not easily avoidable; however, it is important to remember that often it is a symptom of bad design.

Pros and cons of DI

In the authentication server example using DI, we were able to decouple our modules from a particular dependency instance. The result is that we can now reuse each module with minimal effort and without any change in their code. Testing a module that uses the DI pattern is also greatly simplified; we can easily provide mocked dependencies and test our modules in isolation from the state of the rest of the system.

Another important aspect to be highlighted from the example we presented earlier is that we *shifted* the dependency wiring responsibility from the bottom to the top of our architecture. The idea is that high-level components are by nature less reusable than low-level components, and that's because the more we go up in the layers of an application, the more a component becomes specific.

Starting from this assumption, we can then understand that the conventional way to see an application architecture where high-level components own their lower-level dependencies can be inverted, so that the lower-level components depend only on an interface (in JavaScript, it's just the interface that we expect from a dependency), while the ownership of defining the implementation of a dependency is given to the higher-level components. In our authentication server, in fact, all the dependencies are instantiated and wired in the topmost component, the `app` module, which is also the less reusable and so is the most expendable in terms of coupling.

All these advantages in terms of decoupling and reusability, though, come with a price to pay. In general, the inability to resolve a dependency at *coding time* makes it more difficult to understand the relationship between the various components of a system. Also, if we look at the way we instantiated all the dependencies in the `app` module, we can see that we had to follow a specific order; we practically had to manually build the dependency graph of the entire application. This can become unmanageable when the number of modules to wire becomes high.

A viable solution to this problem is to split the dependency ownership between multiple components, instead of having it centralized all in one place. This can reduce the complexity involved in managing the dependencies exponentially, as each component would be responsible only for its particular dependency subgraph. Of course, we can also choose to use DI only locally, just when necessary, instead of building the entire application on top of it.

We will see later in the chapter that another possible solution to simplify the wiring of modules in complex architectures is to use a DI container, a component exclusively responsible for instantiating and wiring all the dependencies of an application.

Using DI surely increases the complexity and verbosity of our modules, but as we saw earlier, there are many good reasons for doing this. It is up to us to choose the right approach, depending on the balance between simplicity and reusability that we want to obtain.

 DI is often mentioned in combination with the *Dependency Inversion principle* and *Inversion of Control*; however, they all are different concepts (even though correlated).

Service locator

In the previous section, we learned how DI can literally transform the way we wire our dependencies by obtaining reusable and decoupled modules. Another pattern with very similar intent is **service locator**. Its core principle is to have a central registry in order to manage the components of the system and to act as a mediator whenever a module needs to load a dependency. The idea is to ask the service locator for the dependency instead of hardcoding.

It is important to understand that by using a service locator, we are introducing a dependency on it, so the way we wire it to our modules determines their level of coupling and, therefore, their reusability. In Node.js, we can identify three types of service locators, depending on the way they are wired to the various components of the system:

- Hardcoded dependency on service locator
- Injected service locator
- Global service locator

The first is definitely the one offering the fewest advantages in terms of decoupling, as it consists of directly referencing the instance of the service locator using `require()`. In Node.js, this can be considered an anti-pattern because it introduces a tight coupling with the component supposedly meant to provide a better decoupling. In this context, a service locator clearly does not provide any value in terms of reusability, only adding another level of indirection and complexity.

On the other hand, an *injected service locator* is referenced by a component through DI. This can be considered a more convenient way of injecting an entire set of dependencies at once, instead of providing them one by one. And as we will see its advantages do not end here.

The third way of referencing a service locator is directly from the global scope. This has the same disadvantages as that of the hardcoded service locator, but since it is global, it is a *real singleton* and can therefore be easily used as a pattern for sharing instances between packages. We will see how this works later in the chapter, but for now we can certainly say that there are very few reasons for using a global service locator.

> The Node.js module system already implements a variation of the service locator pattern, with `require()` representing the global instance of the service locator itself.

All the considerations discussed here will become clearer once we start using the service locator pattern in a real example. Let's now refactor the authentication server again to apply what we learned.

Refactoring the authentication server to use a service locator

We are now going to convert the authentication server to use an injected service locator. To do this, the first step is to implement the service locator itself; we will use a new module, `lib/serviceLocator.js`:

```javascript
module.exports = function() {
  const dependencies = {};
  const factories = {};
  const serviceLocator = {};

  serviceLocator.factory = (name, factory) => {      //[1]
    factories[name] = factory;
  };

  serviceLocator.register = (name, instance) => {    //[2]
    dependencies[name] = instance;
  };

  serviceLocator.get = (name) => {                   //[3]
    if(!dependencies[name]) {
      const factory = factories[name];
      dependencies[name] = factory && factory(serviceLocator);
      if(!dependencies[name]) {
        throw new Error('Cannot find module: ' + name);
      }
    }
    return dependencies[name];
  };

  return serviceLocator;
};
```

Our `serviceLocator` module is a factory returning an object with three methods:

- `factory()` is used to associate a component name against a factory.
- `register()` is used to associate a component name directly with an instance.
- `get()` retrieves a component by its name. If an instance is already available, it simply returns it; otherwise, it tries to invoke the registered factory to obtain a new instance. It is very important to observe that the module factories are invoked by injecting the current instance of the service locator (`serviceLocator`). This is the core mechanism of the pattern that allows the dependency graph for our system to be built automatically and on-demand. We will see how this works in a moment.

A simple pattern, closely resembling a service locator, is to use an object as
a namespace for a set of dependencies:

```
const dependencies = {};
const db = require('./lib/db');
const authService = require('./lib/authService');
dependencies.db = db();
dependencies.authService = authService(dependencies);
```

Let's now convert the `lib/db.js` module straight away to demonstrate how our
`serviceLocator` works:

```
const level = require('level');
const sublevel = require('level-sublevel');

module.exports = (serviceLocator) => {
  const dbName = serviceLocator.get('dbName');

  return sublevel(
    level(dbName, {valueEncoding: 'json'})
  );
}
```

The db module uses the service locator received in input to retrieve the name of the
database to instantiate. This is an interesting point to highlight; a service locator can be used
not only to return component instances but also to provide configuration parameters that
define the behavior of the entire dependency graph that we want to create.

The next step is to convert the `lib/authService.js` module:

```
// ...
module.exports = (serviceLocator) => {
  const db = serviceLocator.get('db');
  const tokenSecret = serviceLocator.get('tokenSecret');

  const users = db.sublevel('users');
  const authService = {};

  authService.login = (username, password, callback) => {
    //...same as in the previous version
  }

  authService.checkToken = (token, callback) => {
    //...same as in the previous version
  }

  return authService;
};
```

Also, the `authService` module is a factory that takes the service locator as the input. The two dependencies of the module, the `db` handle and `tokenSecret` (which is another configuration parameter), are retrieved using the `get()` method of the service locator.

In a similar way, we can convert the `lib/authController.js` module:

```
module.exports = (serviceLocator) => {
  const authService = serviceLocator.get('authService');
  const authController = {};

  authController.login = (req, res, next) => {
    //...same as in the previous version
  };

  authController.checkToken = (req, res, next) => {
    //...same as in the previous version
  };

  return authController;
}
```

Now we are ready to see how the service locator is instantiated and configured. This happens, of course, in the `app.js` module:

```
//...
const svcLoc = require('./lib/serviceLocator')();        //[1]

svcLoc.register('dbName', 'example-db');                  //[2]
svcLoc.register('tokenSecret', 'SHHH!');
svcLoc.factory('db', require('./lib/db'));
svcLoc.factory('authService', require('./lib/authService'));
svcLoc.factory('authController', require('./lib/authController'));

const authController = svcLoc.get('authController');      //[3]

app.post('/login', authController.login);
app.all('/checkToken', authController.checkToken);
// ...
```

This is how the wiring works using our new service locator:

1. We instantiate a new service locator by invoking its factory.
2. We register the configuration parameters and module factories against the service locator. At this point, all our dependencies are not instantiated yet; we just registered their factories.
3. We load `authController` from the service locator; this is the entry point that triggers the instantiation of the entire dependency graph of our application. When we ask for the instance of the `authController` component, the service locator invokes the associated factory by injecting an instance of itself, then the `authController` factory will try to load the `authService` module, which in turn instantiates the `db` module.

It's interesting to see the *lazy* nature of the service locator; each instance is created only when needed. But there is another important implication: we can see, in fact, that every dependency is automatically wired without the need to manually do it in advance. The advantage is that we don't have to know in advance what the right order for instantiating and wiring the modules is—it all happens automatically and *on-demand*. This is much more convenient compared to the simple DI pattern.

 Another common pattern is to use an Express server instance as a simple service locator. This can be achieved using `expressApp.set(name, instance)` to register a service and `expressApp.get(name)` to then retrieve it. The convenient part of this pattern is that the server instance, which acts as a service locator, is already injected into each middleware and is accessible through the `request.app` property. You can find an example of this pattern in the samples distributed with the book.

Pros and cons of a service locator

Service locator and **Dependency Injection** have a lot in common: both shift the dependency ownership to an entity external to the component. But the way we wire the service locator determines the flexibility of our entire architecture. It is not by chance that we chose an injected service locator to implement our example, as opposed to a hardcoded or global service locator. These last two variations almost nullify the advantages of this pattern. In fact, the result would be that, instead of coupling a component directly to its dependencies using `require()`, we would be coupling it to one particular instance of the service locator. It's also true that a hardcoded service locator will still give more flexibility in configuring what component to associate with a particular name, but this still does not give any big advantage in terms of reusability.

Also, like DI, using a service locator makes it harder to identify the relationship between the components as they are resolved at runtime. In addition, it also makes it more difficult to know exactly what dependency a particular component is going to require. With DI, this is expressed in a much clearer way: by declaring the dependencies in the factory or constructor arguments. With a service locator, this is much less clear and would require a code inspection or an explicit statement in the documentation explaining what dependencies a particular component will try to load.

As a final note, it is important to know that often a service locator is incorrectly mistaken for a DI container because it shares the same role of service registry with it; however, there is a big difference between the two. With a service locator, each component loads its dependencies explicitly from the service locator itself. When using a DI container instead, the component has no knowledge of the container.

The difference between these two approaches is noticeable for two reasons:

- **Reusability**: A component relying on a service locator is less reusable because it requires that a service locator is available in the system
- **Readability**: As we have already said, a service locator obfuscates the dependency requirements of a component

In terms of reusability, we can say that the service locator pattern sits inbetween hardcoded dependencies and DI. In terms of convenience and simplicity, it is definitely better than manual DI, as we don't have to manually take care of building the entire dependency graph.

Under these assumptions, a DI container definitely offers the best compromise in terms of reusability of the components and convenience. We are going to better analyze this pattern in the next section.

Dependency Injection container

The step to transform a service locator into a Dependency Injection (DI) container is not big, but as we have already mentioned, it makes a huge difference in terms of decoupling. With this pattern, in fact, each module doesn't have to depend on the service locator, it can simply express its need in terms of dependencies and the DI container will do the rest seamlessly. As we will see, the big leap forward of this mechanism is that every module can be reused even without the container.

Declaring a set of dependencies to a DI container

A DI container is essentially a service locator with the addition of one feature: it identifies the dependency requirements of a module before instantiating it. For this to be possible, a module has to declare its dependencies in some way, and as we will see, we have multiple options for doing this.

The first, and probably the most popular, technique consists of injecting a set of dependencies based on the arguments' names used in a factory or constructor. Let's take, for example, the `authService` module:

```
module.exports = (db, tokenSecret) => {
  //...
}
```

As we defined it, the preceding module will be instantiated by our DI container using the dependencies with names `db` and `tokenSecret`—a very simple and intuitive mechanism. However, to be able to read the names of the arguments of a function, it's necessary to use a little trick. In JavaScript, we have the possibility to serialize a function, obtaining at runtime its source code; this is as easy as invoking `toString()` on the function reference. With regular expressions, obtaining the arguments list is certainly not black magic.

 This technique of injecting a set of dependencies using the names of the arguments of a function was popularized by AngularJS (`http://angularjs.org`), a client-side JavaScript framework developed by Google and entirely built on top of a DI container.

The biggest problem of this approach is that it doesn't play well with **minification**, a practice used extensively in client-side JavaScript which consists of applying particular code transformations to reduce to the minimum the size of the source code. Many minificators apply a technique known as **name mangling**, which essentially renames any local variable to reduce its length, usually to a single character. The bad news is that function arguments are local variables and are usually affected by this process, causing the mechanism that we described for declaring dependencies to fall apart. Even though minification is not really necessary in server-side code, it's important to consider that often Node.js modules are shared with the browser, and this is an important factor to consider in our analysis.

Luckily, a DI container might use other techniques to know which dependencies to inject. These techniques are given as follows:

- We can use a special property attached to the factory function, for example, an array explicitly listing all the dependencies to inject:

```
module.exports = (a, b) => {};
module.exports._inject = ['db', 'another/dependency'];
```

- We can specify a module as an array of dependency names followed by the factory function:

```
module.exports = ['db', 'another/depencency',(a, b) => {}];
```

- We can use a comment annotation that is appended to each argument of a function (however, this also doesn't play well with minification):

```
module.exports = function(a /*db*/, b /*another/depencency*/) {};
```

All these techniques are quite opinionated, so for our example, we are going to use the most simple and popular, which is to obtain the dependency names using the arguments of a function.

Refactoring the authentication server to use a DI container

To demonstrate how a DI container is much less invasive than a service locator, we are now going to again refactor our authentication server, and to do so we are going to use as a starting point the version in which we were using the plain DI pattern. In fact, what we are going to do is just leave untouched all the components of the application except for the app.js module, which is going to be the module responsible for initializing the container.

But first, we need to implement our DI container. Let's do that by creating a new module called diContainer.js under the lib/ directory. This is its initial part:

```
const fnArgs= require('parse-fn-args');

module.exports = function() {
  const dependencies = {};
  const factories = {};
  const diContainer = {};

  diContainer.factory = (name, factory) => {
    factories[name] = factory;
```

```
  };

  diContainer.register = (name, dep) => {
    dependencies[name] = dep;
  };

  diContainer.get = (name) => {
    if(!dependencies[name]) {
      const factory = factories[name];
      dependencies[name] = factory &&
          diContainer.inject(factory);
      if(!dependencies[name]) {
        throw new Error('Cannot find module: ' + name);
      }
    }
    return dependencies[name];
  };
  //...to be continued
```

The first part of the `diContainer` module is functionally identical to the service locator we have seen previously. The only notable differences are:

- We require a new npm module called `args-list` (`https://npmjs.org/package/args-list`), which we will use to extract the names of the arguments of a function
- This time, instead of directly invoking the module factory, we rely on another method of the `diContainer` module called `inject()`, which will resolve the dependencies of a module and use them to invoke the factory

Let's see how the `diContainer.inject()` method looks:

```
  diContainer.inject = (factory) => {
    const args = fnArgs(factory)
    .map(dependency => diContainer.get(dependency));
      return factory.apply(null, args);
    };

}; //end of module.exports = function() {
```

The preceding method is what makes the DI container different from a service locator. Its logic is very straightforward:

1. We extract the arguments list from the factory function we receive as the input, using the `parse-fn-args` library.
2. We then map each argument name to the correspondent dependency instance retrieved using the `get()` method.
3. At the end, all we have to do is just invoke the factory by providing the dependency list that we just generated.

That's really it for our `diContainer`. As we saw, it's not that much different from a service locator, but the simple step of instantiating a module by injecting its dependencies makes a dramatic difference (as compared to injecting the entire service locator).

To complete the refactoring of the authentication server, we also need to tweak the `app.js` module:

```
// ...
const diContainer = require('./lib/diContainer')();

diContainer.register('dbName', 'example-db');
diContainer.register('tokenSecret', 'SHHH!');
diContainer.factory('db', require('./lib/db'));
diContainer.factory('authService', require('./lib/authService'));
diContainer.factory('authController', require('./lib/authController'));

const authController = diContainer.get('authController');

app.post('/login', authController.login);
app.get('/checkToken', authController.checkToken);
// ...
```

As we can see, the code of the `app` module is identical to the one that we used to initialize the service locator in the previous section. We can also notice that to bootstrap the DI container, and therefore trigger the loading of the entire dependency graph, we still have to use it as a service locator by invoking `diContainer.get('authController')`. From that point on, every module registered with the DI container will be instantiated and wired automatically.

Pros and cons of a DI container

A DI container assumes that our modules use the DI pattern and therefore inherit most of its pros and cons. In particular, we have an improved decoupling and testability, but on the other hand more complexity, because our dependencies are resolved at runtime. A DI container also shares many properties with the service locator pattern, but it has on its side the fact that it doesn't force the modules to depend on any extra service except its actual dependencies. This is a huge advantage because it allows each module to be used even without the DI container, using a simple manual injection.

That's essentially what we demonstrated in this section: we took the version of the authentication server where we used the plain DI pattern, and then without modifying any of its components (except for the app module), we were able to automatize the injection of every dependency.

 On npm, you can find a lot of DI containers to reuse or take inspiration from at
https://www.npmjs.org/search?q=dependency%20injection.

Wiring plugins

The dream architecture of a software engineer is the one having a small, minimal core, extensible as needed through the use of **plugins**. Unfortunately, this is not always easy to obtain, since most of the time it has a cost in terms of time, resources, and complexity. Nonetheless, it's always desirable to support some kind of *external extensibility*, even if limited to just some parts of the system. In this section, we are going to plunge into this fascinating world and focus on a dualistic problem:

- Exposing the services of an application to a plugin
- Integrating a plugin into the flow of the parent application

Plugins as packages

Often in Node.js, the plugins of an application are installed as packages into the node_modules directory of a project. There are two advantages for doing this. Firstly, we can leverage the power of npm to distribute the plugin and manage its dependencies. And secondly, a package can have its own private dependency graph, which reduces the chances of having conflicts and incompatibilities between dependencies, as opposed to letting the plugin use the dependencies of the parent project.

The following directory structure gives an example of an application with two plugins distributed as packages:

```
application
'-- node_modules
    |-- pluginA
    '-- pluginB
```

In the Node.js world, this is a very common practice. Some popular examples are `express` (`http://expressjs.com`) with its middleware, `gulp` (`http://gulpjs.com`), `grunt` (`http://gruntjs.com`), `nodebb` (`http://nodebb.org`), and `docpad` (`http://docpad.org`).

However, the benefits of using packages are not only limited to *external plugins*. In fact, one popular pattern is to build entire applications by wrapping their components into packages, as if they were *internal plugins*. So, instead of organizing the modules in the main package of the application, we can create a separate package for each big chunk of functionality and install it into the `node_modules` directory.

 A package can be private and not necessarily available on the public npm registry. We can always set the `private` flag into the `package.json` to prevent accidental publication to npm. Then, we can commit the packages into a version control system such as git or leverage a private npm server to share them with the rest of the team.

Why follow this pattern? First of all, convenience: people often find it impractical or too verbose to reference the local modules of a package using the relative path notation. Let's, for example, consider the following directory structure:

```
application
|-- componentA
|   '-- subdir
|       '-- moduleA
'-- componentB
    '-- moduleB
```

If we want to reference `moduleB` from `moduleA`, we have to write something like this:

```
require('../../componentB/moduleB');
```

Instead, we can leverage the properties of the resolving algorithm of `require()` (as we have studied it in `Chapter 2`, *Node.js Essential Patterns*) and put the entire `componentB` directory into a package. By installing it into the `node_modules` directory, we can then write something such as the following (from anywhere in the main package of the application):

```
require('componentB/module');
```

The second reason for splitting a project into packages is, of course, reusability. A package can have its own private dependencies, and it forces the developer to think in terms of what to expose to the main application and what instead to keep private, with beneficial effects on the decoupling and information hiding of the entire application.

Pattern
Use packages as a means to organize your application, not just for distributing code in combination with npm.

The use cases we have just described make use of a package not just as a stateless, reusable library (like most of the packages on npm), but more as an integral part of a particular application, providing services, extending its functionality, or modifying its behavior. The main difference is that these types of packages are *integrated* inside an application rather than just used.

For simplicity, we will use the term plugin to describe any package meant to integrate with a particular application.

As we will see, the common problem that we are going to face when deciding to support this type of architecture is exposing parts of the main application to plugins. In fact, we cannot think of only stateless plugins—this is, of course, the aim for a perfect extensibility, because sometimes the plugin has to use some of the services of the parent application in order to carry out its tasks. This aspect might depend a lot on the technique used to wire modules in the parent application.

Extension points

There are literally infinite ways to make an application extensible. For example, some of the design patterns we studied in `Chapter 6`, *Design Patterns*, are meant exactly for this: using Proxy or Decorator we are able to change or augment the functionality of a service; with Strategy, we can swap parts of an algorithm; with middleware, we can insert processing units in an existing pipeline. Also, streams can provide great extensibility thanks to their composable nature.

On the other hand, **EventEmitters** allow us to decouple our components using events and the publish/subscribe pattern. Another important technique is to explicitly define in the application some points where new functionalities can be attached or the existing ones modified; these points in an application are commonly known as hooks. To summarize, the most important ingredient to support plugins is a set of extension points.

The way we wire our components also plays a decisive role because it can affect the way we expose the services of the application to the plugin. In this section, we are mainly going to focus on this aspect.

Plugin-controlled vs application-controlled extension

Before we go ahead and present some examples, it is important to understand the background of the technique we are going to use. There are mainly two approaches for extending the components of an application:

- Explicit extension
- Extension through Inversion of Control (**IoC**)

In the first case, we have a more specific component (the one providing the new functionality) explicitly extending the infrastructure, while in the second case, it is the infrastructure to control the extension by loading, installing, or executing the new specific component. In the second scenario, the flow of control is inverted, as shown in the following image:

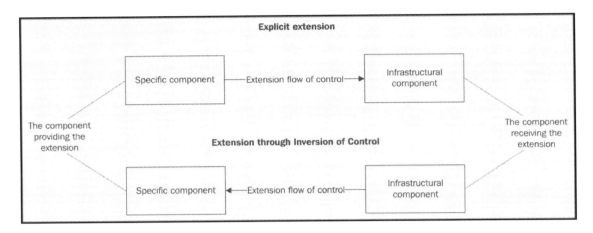

IoC is a very broad principle that can be applied not only to the problem of application extensibility. In fact, in more general terms it can be said that by implementing some form of IoC, instead of the custom code controlling the infrastructure, the infrastructure controls the custom code. With IoC, the various components of an application trade off their power of controlling the flow in exchange for an improved level of decoupling. This is also known as the **Hollywood principle** or *"don't call us, we'll call you"*.

For example, a DI container is a demonstration of the IoC principle applied to the specific case of dependency management. The Observer pattern is another example of IoC applied to state management. Template, Strategy, State, and Middleware are also more localized manifestations of the same principle. The browser implements the IoC principle when dispatching UI events to the JavaScript code (it's not the JavaScript code actively polling the browser for events), and guess what, Node.js itself follows the IoC principle when controlling the execution of the various callbacks for us.

 To know more about the IoC principle, we advise you to study the topic directly from the words of its master, Martin Fowler, at `http://martinfowler.com/bliki/InversionOfControl.html`.

Applying this concept to the specific case of plugins, we can then identify two forms of extension:

- Plugin-controlled extension
- Application-controlled extension (IoC)

In the first case, it is the plugin that taps into the components of the application to extend them as needed, while in the second case, the control is in the hands of the application, which integrates the plugin into one of its extension points.

To make a quick example, let's consider a plugin that extends the Express application with a new route. By using a plugin-controlled extension, this would look like the following:

```
//in the application:
const app = express();
require('thePlugin')(app);

//in the plugin:
module.exports = function plugin(app) {
  app.get('/newRoute', function(req, res) {...})
};
```

If, instead, we want to use an application-controlled extension (IoC), the same preceding example would look like the following:

```
//in the application:
const app = express();
const plugin = require('thePlugin')();
app[plugin.method](plugin.route, plugin.handler);

//in the plugin:
module.exports = function plugin() {
  return {
    method: 'get',
    route: '/newRoute',
    handler: function(req, res) {...}
  }
}
```

In the last code fragment, we saw how the plugin is only a passive player in the extension process; the control is in the hands of the application, which implements the framework to receive the plugin.

Based on the preceding example, we can immediately identify a few important differences between the two approaches:

- **Plugin-controlled extension** is more powerful and flexible, as often we have access to the internals of the application and we can move freely as if the plugin was actually a part of the application itself. However, this sometimes can be more of a liability than an advantage. In fact, any change in the application would have repercussions on the plugins more readily, requiring constant updates as the main application evolves.
- Application-controlled extension requires a **plugin infrastructure** in the main application. With a plugin-controlled extension, the only requirement is that the components of the application are extensible in some way.
- With a plugin-controlled extension, it becomes essential to share the internal services of the application with the plugin (in the preceding small example, the service to share was the `app` instance); otherwise, we would not be able to extend them. With an application-controlled extension, it might still be necessary to access some of the services of the application, not to extend but rather to use them. For example, we might want to query the `db` instance in our plugin or leverage the logger of the main application, just to name a few scenarios.

This last point should allow us to think about the importance of exposing the services of an application to the plugin—that's what we are mainly interested in exploring. The best way of doing this is to show a practical example of a plugin-controlled extension, which requires minimal effort in terms of infrastructure and we can emphasize more on the problem of sharing the application's state with the plugins.

Implementing a logout plugin

Let's now start to work on a small plugin for our authentication server. With the way we originally created the application, it is not possible to explicitly invalidate a token; it simply becomes invalid when it expires. Now we want to add support for this feature, namely *logout*, and we want to do that by not modifying the code of the main application but rather delegating the task to an external plugin.

To support this new feature, we need to save each token in the database after it is created and then check for its existence every time we want to validate it. To invalidate a token, we simply need to remove it from the database.

To do this, we are going to use a plugin-controlled extension to proxy the calls to `authService.login()` and `authService.checkToken()`. We then need to *decorate* the `authService` with a new method called `logout()`. After doing this, we also want to register a new route against the main Express server to expose a new endpoint (`/logout`), which we can use to invalidate a token using an HTTP request.

We are going to implement the plugin we just described in four different variations:

- Using hardcoded dependencies
- Using dependency injection
- Using a service locator
- Using a DI container

Using hardcoded dependencies

The first variation of the plugin we are now going to implement covers the case in which our application mainly uses hardcoded dependencies for wiring its stateful modules. In this context, if our plugin lives in a package under the `node_modules` directory, to use the services of the main application we have to gain access to the parent package. We can do this in two ways:

- Using `require()` and navigating to the application's root using relative or absolute paths.
- Using `require()` by impersonating a module in the parent application—usually the module instantiating the plugin. This will allow us to easily gain access to all the services of the application by using `require()`, as if it was invoked by the parent application and not from the plugin.

The first technique is less robust as it assumes that the package is aware of the position of the main application. The module impersonation pattern can instead be used regardless of where the package is required from, and for this reason, this is the technique that we are going to use to implement the next demo.

To build our plugin, we first need to create a new package under the node_modules directory, named authsrv-plugin-logout. Before we start coding, we need to create a minimal package.json to describe the package, filling in only the essential parameters (the complete path to the file is : node_modules/authsrv-plugin-logout/package.json):

```
{
  "name": "authsrv-plugin-logout",
  "version": "0.0.0"
}
```

Now we are ready to create the main module of our plugin, we will use the file index.js, as it is the default module that Node.js will try to load when requiring the package (if no main property is defined in the package.json). As always, the initial lines of the module are dedicated to loading the dependencies; pay attention to how we are going to require them (file node_modules/authsrv-plugin-logout/index.js):

```
const parentRequire = module.parent.require;

const authService = parentRequire('./lib/authService');
const db = parentRequire('./lib/db');
const app = parentRequire('./app');

const tokensDb = db.sublevel('tokens');
```

The first line of code is what makes the difference. We obtain a reference to the require() function of the parent module, which is the one that loads the plugin. In our case, the parent is going to be the app module in the main application, and this means that every time we use parentRequire(), we are loading a module as if we were doing it from app.js.

The next step is creating a proxy for the authService.login() method. After studying this pattern in Chapter 6, *Design Patterns*, we should already know how it works:

```
const oldLogin = authService.login;                          //[1]
authService.login = (username, password, callback) => {
  oldLogin(username, password, (err, token) => {             //[2]
    if(err) return callback(err);                            //[3]

    tokensDb.put(token, {username: username}, () => {
      callback(null, token);
    });
  });
}
```

In the preceding code, the steps performed are explained as follows:

1. We first save a reference to the old `login()` method and we then override it with our proxied version.
2. In the proxy function, we invoke the original `login()` method by providing a custom callback so that we can intercept the original return value.
3. If the original `login()` returns an error, we simply forward it to the callback; otherwise, we save the token into the database.

Similarly, we need to intercept the calls to `checkToken()` so that we can add our custom logic:

```
const oldCheckToken = authService.checkToken;

authService.checkToken = (token, callback) => {
  tokensDb.get(token, function(err, res) {
    if(err) return callback(err);

    oldCheckToken(token, callback);
  });
}
```

This time, we first want to check whether the token exists in the database before giving control to the original `checkToken()` method. If the token is not found, the `get()` operation returns an error; this means that our token was invalidated and so we immediately return the error back to the callback.

To finalize the extension of the `authService`, we now need to decorate it with a new method, which we will use to invalidate a token:

```
authService.logout = (token, callback) => {
  tokensDb.del(token, callback);
}
```

The `logout()` method is very simple: we just delete the token from the database.

Finally, we can attach a new route to the Express server to expose the new functionality through a web service:

```
app.get('/logout', (req, res, next) => {
  authService.logout(req.query.token, function() {
    res.status(200).send({ok: true});
  });
});
```

Now our plugin is ready to be attached to the main application. To do this we just need to go back to the main directory of the application and edit the `app.js` module:

```
// ...
let app = module.exports = express();
app.use(bodyParser.json());

require('authsrv-plugin-logout');

app.post('/login', authController.login);
app.all('/checkToken', authController.checkToken);
// ...
```

As we can see, to attach the plugin we only need to require it. As soon as this happens—during the startup of the application—the flow of control is given to the plugin, which in turn will extend the `authService` and the `app` modules, as we saw earlier.

Now our authentication server also supports the invalidation of the token. We did that in a reusable way, the core of the application remained almost untouched, and we were able to easily apply the Proxy and Decorator patterns to extend its functionalities.

We can now try to start the application again:

```
node app
```

Then, we can verify that the new `/logout` web service actually exists and works as expected. Using `curl`, we can now try to obtain a new token using `/login`:

```
curl -X POST -d '{"username": "alice", "password":"secret"}'
http://localhost:3000/login -H "Content-Type: application/json"
```

Then, we can check whether the token is valid using `/checkToken`:

```
curl -X GET -H "Accept: application/json"
http://localhost:3000/checkToken?token=<TOKEN HERE>
```

Then, we can pass the token to the `/logout` endpoint to invalidate it; with `curl`, this can be done with a command such as this:

```
curl -X GET -H "Accept: application/json"
http://localhost:3000/logout?token=<TOKEN HERE>
```

Now, if we try to check the validity of the token again, we should get a negative response, confirming that our plugin is working perfectly.

Even with a small plugin like the one we just implemented, the advantages of supporting plugin-based extensibility are clear. We also learned how to gain access to the services of the main application from another package using the module impersonation.

The module impersonation pattern is used by quite a few NodeBB plugins; you might want to check a couple of them in order to have an idea of how this is used in a real application. These are the links to some notable examples:

nodebb-plugin-poll:
https://github.com/Schamper/nodebb-plugin-poll/blob/b4a46
561aff279e19c23b7c635fda5037c534b84/lib/nodebb.js
nodebb-plugin-mentions:
https://github.com/julianlam/nodebb-plugin-mentions/blob/
9638118fa7e06a05ceb24eb521427440abd0dd8a/library.js#L4-13

Module impersonation is, of course, a form of hardcoded dependency and shares with it strengths and weaknesses. From one side, it allows us to access any service of the main application with little effort and minimal infrastructural requirements, but from the other, it creates a tight coupling, not only with a particular instance of a service but also with its location, which more easily exposes the plugin to changes and refactoring in the main application.

Exposing services using a service locator

Similar to module impersonation, the service locator is also a good choice if we want to expose all the components of an application to its plugins, but on top of that, it has a major advantage, because a plugin can use the service locator to expose its own services to the application or even to other plugins.

Let's now refactor our logout plugin again to use a service locator. We'll refactor the main module of the plugin in the node_modules/authsrv-plugin-logout/index.js file:

```
module.exports = (serviceLocator) => {
  const authService = serviceLocator.get('authService');
  const db = serviceLocator.get('db');
  const app = serviceLocator.get('app');

  const tokensDb = db.sublevel('tokens');

  const oldLogin = authService.login;
  authService.login = (username, password, callback) => {
    //...same as in the previous version
  }
```

```
const oldCheckToken = authService.checkToken;
authService.checkToken = (token, callback) => {
  //...same as in the previous version
}

authService.logout = (token, callback) => {
  //...same as in the previous version
}

app.get('/logout', (req, res, next) => {
  //...same as in the previous version
});
};
```

Now that our plugin receives the service locator of the parent application as the input, it can access any of its services as needed. This means that the application does not have to know in advance what the plugin is going to need in terms of dependencies; this is surely a major advantage when implementing a plugin-controlled extension.

The next step is to execute the plugin from the main application, and to do that, we have to modify the app.js module. We will use the version of the authentication server already based on the service locator pattern. The required changes are given in the following block of code:

```
// ...
const svcLoc = require('./lib/serviceLocator')();
svcLoc.register(...);
// ...

svcLoc.register('app', app);
const plugin = require('authsrv-plugin-logout');
plugin(svcLoc);

// ...
```

The changes are highlighted in the preceding code; those changes enabled us to:

- Register the app module itself in the service locator, as the plugin might want to have access to it
- Require the plugin
- Invoke the plugin's main function by providing the service locator as an argument

As we already said, the main strength of the service locator is that it provides a simple way to expose all the services of an application to its plugins, but it can also be used as a mechanism for sharing services from the plugin back into the parent application or even other plugins. This last consideration is probably the main strength of the service locator pattern in the context of plugin-based extensibility.

Exposing services using DI

Using DI to propagate services to a plugin is as easy as using it in the application itself. This pattern becomes almost a requirement if it's already the `main` method for wiring dependencies in the parent application, but nothing prevents us from using it when the prevalent form of dependency management is hardcoded dependencies or a service locator. DI is also an ideal choice when we want to support an application-controlled extension because it provides better control over what is shared with the plugin.

To test these assumptions, let's immediately try to refactor the logout plugin to use DI. The changes required are minimal, so let's start from the main module of the plugin (node_modules/authsrv-plugin-logout/index.js):

```
module.exports = (app, authService, db) => {
  const tokensDb = db.sublevel('tokens');

  const oldLogin = authService.login;
  authService.login = (username, password, callback) => {
    //...same as in the previous version
  }

  let oldCheckToken = authService.checkToken;
  authService.checkToken = (token, callback) => {
    //...same as in the previous version
  }

  authService.logout = (token, callback) => {
    //...same as in the previous version
  }

  app.get('/logout', (req, res, next) => {
    //...same as in the previous version
  });
};
```

All we did is wrap the plugin's code into a factory that receives the services of the parent application as the input; the rest of it remains unchanged.

To complete our refactoring, we also need to change the way we attach the plugin from the parent application; let's then change that one line where we require the plugin in the app.js module:

```
// ...
const plugin = require('authsrv-plugin-logout');
plugin(app, authService, authController, db);
// ...
```

We intentionally didn't show how these dependencies were obtained. In fact, it doesn't really make any difference, any method will equally work; we might use hardcoded dependencies or obtain the instances from factories or from a service locator—it doesn't really matter. This proves that DI is a flexible pattern when wiring plugins that can be used regardless of the way we wire the services in the parent application.

But the differences are much more profound. DI is definitely the cleanest way of providing a set of services to a plugin, but most importantly, it offers the best level of control over what's exposed to it, resulting in better information hiding and better protection against overly aggressive extensions. However, this can be also considered a drawback, because the main application can't always know what services the plugin is going to need, so we end up either injecting every service, which is impractical, or only a subset of them, for example, only the essential core services of the parent application. For this reason, DI is not the ideal choice if we mainly want to support plugin-controlled extensibility; however, the use of a DI container can easily solve these issues.

Grunt (http://gruntjs.com), a task runner for Node.js, uses DI to provide each plugin with an instance of the core Grunt service. Each plugin can then extend it by attaching new tasks, using it to retrieve the configuration parameters, or running other tasks. A Grunt plugin looks like the following:

```
module.exports = function(grunt) {
  grunt.registerMultiTask('taskName', 'description',
    function(...) {...}
  );
};
```

Exposing services using a DI container

Taking the previous example as a starting point, we can use a DI container in combination with our plugin by applying a small change to the `app` module, as shown in the following code:

```
// ...
const diContainer = require('./lib/diContainer')();
diContainer.register(...);
// ...
//initialize the plugin
diContainer.inject(require('authsrv-plugin-logout'));
// ...
```

After registering the factories or the instances of our application, all we have to do is instantiate the plugin, which is done by injecting its dependencies using the DI container. This way, each plugin can require its own set of dependencies without the parent application needing to know. All the wiring is again carried out automatically by the DI container.

Using a DI container also means that each plugin can potentially access any service of the application, reducing the information hiding and the control over what can be used or extended. A possible solution to this problem is to create a separate DI container registering only the services that we want to expose to plugins; this way, we can control what each plugin can see of the main application. This demonstrates that a DI container can also be a very good choice in terms of encapsulation and information hiding.

This concludes our last refactoring of the logout plugin and the authentication server.

Summary

The topic of dependency wiring is certainly one of the most opinionated in software engineering, but in this chapter, we tried to keep the analysis as factual as possible to give an objective overview of the most important wiring patterns. We cleared some of the most common doubts around Singletons and instances in Node.js, and we learned how to connect modules using hardcoded dependencies, DI, and service locators. We practiced each technique using the authentication server as a playground, allowing us to identify the pros and cons of each approach.

In the second part of the chapter, we learned how an application can support plugins, but most importantly, how we can wire those plugins into the main application. We applied the same techniques presented in the first part of the chapter but analyzed them from another perspective. We discovered how important it can be for a plugin to have access to the right services of the main application and how much this can impact its capabilities.

By the end of this chapter, we should feel comfortable in choosing the best approach for the level of decoupling, reusability, and simplicity we want to obtain in our application. We can also consider using more than one pattern in the same application. For example, we can use hardcoded dependencies as the main technique and then use a service locator when it comes to linking plugins; there are really no limits to what we can do now that we know the best use case for each approach.

So far in this book, we have focused our analysis on highly generic and customizable patterns, but from the next chapter onwards, we will shift our attention to solving more specific technical problems. What comes next is, in fact, a collection of *recipes* which can be used to solve specific issues related to CPU-bound tasks, asynchronous caching, and sharing code with the browser.

8
Universal JavaScript for Web Applications

JavaScript was born in 1995 with the original goal of giving web developers the power to execute code directly in the browser and build more dynamic and interactive websites.

Since then, JavaScript has grown up a lot and it is today one of the most famous and widespread languages in the world. If, at the very beginning, JavaScript was a very simple and limited language, today it can be considered a complete general purpose language that can be used even outside the browser to build almost any kind of application. In fact, JavaScript now powers frontend applications, web servers, and mobile applications, as well as embedded devices such as wearable devices, thermostats, and flying drones.

This availability across platforms and devices is fostering a new trend among JavaScript developers, which is being able to simplify code reuse across different environments in the same project. The most meaningful case in relation to Node.js regards the opportunity to build web applications where it is easy to share code between the server (backend) and the browser (frontend). This quest for code reuse was originally identified with the term **Isomorphic JavaScript**, but it's now widely recognized as **Universal JavaScript**.

In this chapter, we are going to explore the wonders of Universal JavaScript, specifically in the field of web development, and discover many tools and techniques to be able to share most of our code between the server and the browser.

In particular, we are going to learn how modules can be used both on the server and the client and how to use tools such as **Webpack** and **Babel** to package them for the browser. We will adopt the React library and other famous modules to build the web interface and share the state of the web server with the frontend, and finally we are going to explore some interesting solutions to enable universal routing and universal data retrieval within our apps.

At the end of this chapter, we should be able to write React-powered **Single-Page Applications (SPAs)** that reuse most of the code that is already present in our Node.js server, resulting in applications that are consistent, easy to reason about, and easy to maintain.

Sharing code with the browser

One of the main selling points of Node.js is the fact that it's based on JavaScript and runs on V8, an engine that actually powers one of the most popular browsers: Chrome. We might think that that's enough to conclude that sharing code between Node.js and the browser is an easy task; however, as we will see, this is not always true, unless we want to share only small, self-contained, and generic fragments of code. Developing code for both the client and the server requires a non-negligible level of effort in making sure that the same code can run properly in two environments that are intrinsically different. For example, in Node.js we don't have the DOM or long-living views, while in the browser we surely don't have the filesystem or the ability to start new processes. Moreover, we need to consider that we can safely use many of the new ES2015 features in Node.js. We cannot do the same in the browser, as the majority of browsers are still stuck with ES5, and running ES5 code in the client will remain the safest option for a relatively long time before ES2015-enabled web browsers are ubiquitous.

So, most of the effort required when developing for both platforms is making sure to reduce those differences to a minimum. This can be done with the help of abstractions and patterns that enable the application to switch, dynamically or at build time, between the browser-compatible code and the Node.js code.

Luckily, with the rising interest in this new mind-blowing possibility, many libraries and frameworks in the ecosystem have started to support both environments. This evolution is also backed by a growing number of tools supporting this new kind of workflow, which over the years have been refined and perfected. This means that if we are using an npm package on Node.js, there is a good probability that it will work seamlessly on the browser as well. However, this is often not enough to guarantee that our application can run without problems on both the browser and Node.js. As we will see, a careful design is always needed when developing cross-platform code.

In this section, we are going to explore the fundamental problems we might encounter when writing code for both Node.js and the browser, and we are going to propose some tools and patterns that can help us in tackling this new and exciting challenge.

Sharing modules

The first wall we hit when we want to share some code between the browser and the server is the mismatch between the module system used by Node.js and the heterogeneous landscape of the module systems used in the browser. Another problem is that in the browser, we don't have a `require()` function or the filesystem from which we can resolve modules. So, if we want to write large portions of code that can work on both platforms and we want to continue to use the CommonJS module system, we need to take an extra step—we need a tool to help us in bundling all the dependencies together at build time and abstracting the `require()` mechanism on the browser.

Universal Module Definition

In Node.js, we know perfectly well that the CommonJS modules are the default mechanism for establishing dependencies between components. The situation in *browser-space* is unfortunately way more fragmented:

- We might have an environment with no module system at all, which means that globals are the main mechanism to access other modules
- We might have an environment based on an **Asynchronous Module Definition** (**AMD**) loader, for example, RequireJS (`http://requirejs.org`)
- We might have an environment abstracting the CommonJS module system

Luckily, there is a pattern called **Universal Module Definition** (**UMD**) that can help us abstract our code from the module system used in the environment.

Creating an UMD module

UMD is not quite standardized yet, so there might be many variations that depend on the needs of the component and the module systems it has to support. However, there is one form that is probably the most popular and also allows us to support the most common module systems, such as AMD, CommonJS, and browser globals.

Let's see a simple example of how it looks. In a new project, let's create a new module called `umdModule.js`:

```
(function(root, factory) {                              //[1]
  if(typeof define === 'function' && define.amd) {      //[2]
    define(['mustache'], factory);
  } else if(typeof module === 'object' &&               //[3]
      typeof module.exports === 'object') {
    var mustache = require('mustache');
```

```
      module.exports = factory(mustache);
    } else {                                            //[4]
      root.UmdModule = factory(root.Mustache);
    }
  }(this, function(mustache) {                          //[5]
    var template = '<h1>Hello <i>{{name}}</i></h1>';
    mustache.parse(template);

    return {
      sayHello:function(toWhom) {
        return mustache.render(template, {name: toWhom});
      }
    };
  }));
```

The preceding example defines a simple module with one external dependency: `mustache` (`http://mustache.github.io`), which is a simple template engine. The final product of the preceding UMD module is an object with one method called `sayHello()` that will render a `mustache` template and return it to the caller. The goal of UMD is integrating the module with other module systems available on the environment. This is how it works:

1. All the code is wrapped in an anonymous self-executing function, very similar to the **Revealing Module** pattern we have seen in `Chapter 2`, *Node.js Essential Patterns*. The function accepts a root that is the global namespace object available on the system (for example, `window` on the browser). This is needed mainly for registering the dependency as a global variable, as we will see in a moment. The second argument is `factory()` of the module, a function returning an instance of the module and accepting its dependencies as input (Dependency Injection).

2. The first thing we do is check whether AMD is available on the system. We do this by verifying the existence of the `define` function and its `amd` flag. If found, it means that we have an AMD loader on the system, so we proceed with registering our module using `define` and requiring the dependency `mustache` to be injected into `factory()`.

3. We then check whether we are in a Node.js-flavored CommonJS environment by checking the existence of the `module` and `module.exports` objects. If that's the case, we load the dependencies of the module using `require()` and provide them to the `factory()`. The return value of the factory is then assigned to `module.exports`.

4. Lastly, if we have neither AMD nor CommonJS, we proceed with assigning the module to a global variable, using the `root` object, which in a browser environment will usually be the `window` object. In addition, you can see how the dependency, `Mustache`, is expected to be in the global scope.

5. As a final step, the wrapper function is self-invoked, providing the `this` object as `root` (in the browser, it will be the `window` object) and providing our module factory as a second argument. You can see how the factory accepts its dependencies as arguments.

It's also worth underlining that in the module, we haven't used any ES2015 feature. This is to guarantee that the code will run fine even in the browser without any modification.

Now, let's see how we can use this UMD module in both Node.js and the browser.

First of all, we create a new `testServer.js` file:

```
const umdModule = require('./umdModule');
console.log(umdModule.sayHello('Server!'));
```

If we execute this script, it will output the following:

`<h1>Hello <i>Server!</i></h1>`

If we want to use our freshly baked module on the client as well, we can create a `testBrowser.html` page with the following content:

```
<html>
  <head>
    <script src="node_modules/mustache/mustache.js"></script>
    <script src="umdModule.js"></script>
  </head>
  <body>
    <div id="main"></div>
    <script>
        document.getElementById('main').innerHTML =
          UmdModule.sayHello('Browser!');
    </script>
  </body>
</html>
```

This will produce a page with a big fancy **Hello Browser!** as the title of the page.

What has happened here is that we included our dependencies (`mustache` and our `umdModule`) as regular scripts in the head of the page and we then created a small inline script that uses `UmdModule` (available as a global variable in the browser) to generate some HTML code that was then placed inside the `main` block.

In the code examples available for this book on the Packt Publishing website, you can find other examples showing how the UMD module we just created can also be used in combination with an AMD loader and a CommonJS system.

Considerations on the UMD pattern

The UMD pattern is an effective and simple technique used for creating a module compatible with the most popular module systems out there. However, we have seen that it requires a lot of boilerplate, which can be difficult to test in each environment and is inevitably error-prone. This means that writing the UMD boilerplate manually can make sense for wrapping a single module which has already been developed and tested. It is not a practice to use when we are writing a new module from scratch; it is unfeasible and impractical, so in these situations, it is better to leave the task to tools that can help us automate the process. One of those tools is Webpack, which we will use in this chapter.

We should also mention that AMD, CommonJS, and browser globals are not the only module systems out there. The pattern we have presented will cover most of the use cases, but it requires adaptations to support any other module system. For example, the ES2015 module specification is something that we are going to discuss in the next section of the chapter as it offers a number of advantages over other solutions and it is already part of the new ECMAScript standard (even if at the time of writing it is not natively supported in Node.js).

You can find a broad list of formalized UMD patterns at
`https://github.com/umdjs/umd`.

ES2015 modules

One of the features introduced by the ES2015 specification is a **built-in module system**. This is the first time we will encounter it in this book because, unfortunately, at the time of writing, ES2015 modules are still not supported in the current version of Node.js.

We will not describe this feature in detail here but it is important to know about it because it will most likely become the go-to module syntax for years to come. Apart from being standard, ES2015 modules introduce a nicer syntax and a number of advantages over the other module systems we just discussed.

The goal for ES2015 modules was to take the best out of CommonJS and AMD modules:

- Like CommonJS, this specification provides a compact syntax, a preference for single exports, and support for cyclic dependencies
- Like AMD, it offers direct support for asynchronous loading and configurable module loading

Moreover, thanks to the declarative syntax, it is possible to use static analyzers to perform tasks such as static checking and optimizations. For instance, it is possible to analyze the dependency tree of a script and create a bundled file for the browser where all the unused functions of the imported modules are stripped, thus providing a more compact file on the client and reducing load times.

 To learn more about the syntax of the ES2015 modules you can have a look at the ES2015 specification: `http://www.ecma-international.org/ecma-262/6.0/#sec-scripts-and-modules`.

Today, you can also use the new module syntax in Node.js, adopting a transpiler such as Babel. Actually, many developers are advocating it while presenting their own solutions for building Universal JavaScript apps. It's generally a good idea to be future-proof, especially because this feature is already standardized and will eventually be part of the Node.js core. For the sake of simplicity, we will stick to the CommonJS syntax also all over this chapter.

Introducing Webpack

When writing a Node.js application, the last thing we want to do is to manually add support for a module system different from the one offered as default by the platform. The ideal situation would be to continue writing our modules as we have always done, using `require()` and `module.exports`, and then use a tool to transform our code into a bundle that can easily run in the browser. Luckily, this problem has already been solved by many projects, among which Webpack (`https://webpack.github.io`) is one of the most popular and broadly adopted.

Webpack allows us to write modules using the Node.js module conventions, and then, thanks to a compilation step, it creates a bundle (a single JavaScript file) that contains all the dependencies our modules need for working in the browser (including an abstraction of the `require()` function). This bundle can then be easily included into a web page and executed inside a browser. Webpack recursively scans our sources and looks for references of the `require()` function, resolving and then including the referenced modules into the bundle.

Webpack is not the only tool we have for creating browser bundles from Node.js modules. Other popular alternatives are Browserify (http://browserify.org), RollupJs (http://rollupjs.org) and Webmake (https://npmjs.org/package/webmake). In addition, require.js allows us to create modules for both the client and Node.js but it uses AMD in place of CommonJS (http://requirejs.org/docs/node.html).

Exploring the magic of Webpack

To quickly demonstrate how this magic works, let's see how umdModule, we created in the previous section looks, if we use Webpack. First, we need to install Webpack itself; we can do so with a simple command:

```
npm install webpack -g
```

The -g option will tell npm to install Webpack globally so that we can access it using a simple command from the console, as we will see in a moment.

Next, let's create a fresh project and let's try to build a module equivalent to the umdModule we created before. This is how it looks if we had to implement it in Node.js (file sayHello.js):

```
var mustache = require('mustache');
var template = '<h1>Hello <i>{{name}}</i></h1>';
mustache.parse(template);
module.exports.sayHello = function(toWhom) {
  return mustache.render(template, {name: toWhom});
};
```

Definitely simpler than applying a UMD pattern, isn't it? Now, let's create a file called main.js, that is, the entry point of our browser code:

```
window.addEventListener('load', function(){
  var sayHello = require('./sayHello').sayHello;
  var hello = sayHello(Browser!');
  var body = document.getElementsByTagName("body")[0];
  body.innerHTML = hello;
});
```

In the preceding code, we require the sayHello module in exactly the same way as we would do in Node.js so, no more annoyances for managing dependencies or configuring paths; a simple require() does the job.

Next, let's make sure to have `mustache` installed in the project:

```
npm install mustache
```

Now comes the magical step. In a terminal, let's run the following command:

```
webpack main.js bundle.js
```

The previous command will compile the `main` module and bundle all the required dependencies into a single file called `bundle.js`, which is now ready to be used in the browser!

To quickly test this assumption, let's create an HTML page called `magic.html` that contains the following code:

```
<html>
  <head>
    <title>Webpack magic</title>
    <script src="bundle.js"></script>
  </head>
    <body>
    </body>
</html>
```

This is enough for running our code in the browser. Try to open the page and see it with your eyes. Boom!

 During development, we don't want to manually run Webpack at every change we make to our sources. What we want instead is an automatic mechanism to regenerate the bundle when our sources change. To do that, we can use the `--watch` option when running the Webpack command. This option will keep Webpack running continuously and it will take care to re-compile our bundle every time one of the related source files changes.

The advantages of using Webpack

The magic of Webpack doesn't stop here. This is a (incomplete) list of features that make sharing code with the browser a simpler and seamless experience:

- Webpack automatically provides a version for many of the Node.js core modules that are compatible with the browser. This means that we can use modules such as `http`, `assert`, or `events`, and many more, in the browser!

The `fs` module is among those not supported.

- If we have a module that is incompatible with the browser, we can exclude it from the build or replace it with an empty object or with another module providing an alternative and browser-compatible implementation. This is a crucial feature and we will have the chance to use it in the example we are going to see shortly.
- Webpack can generate bundles for different modules.
- Webpack allows us to perform additional processing of the source files using third-party **loaders** and **plugins**. There are loaders and plugins for almost everything one might need, from CoffeeScript, TypeScript, or ES2015 compilation, to support for loading AMD, Bower (`http://bower.io`), and Component (`http://component.github.io`) packages using `require()`, from minification to the compilation and bundling of other assets such as templates and stylesheets.
- We can easily invoke Webpack from task managers such as Gulp (`https://npmjs.com/package/gulp-webpack`) and Grunt (`https://npmjs.org/package/grunt-webpack`).
- Webpack allows you to manage and pre-process all your project's resources, not just JavaScript files but also stylesheets, images, fonts, and templates.
- We can also configure Webpack to split the dependency tree and organize it into different chunks that can be loaded on demand whenever the browser needs them.

The power and flexibility of Webpack are so captivating that many developers started to use it even to manage client-side only code. This is also made possible by the fact that many client-side libraries are starting to support CommonJS and npm by default, opening new and interesting scenarios. For example, we can install jQuery as follows:

```
npm install jquery
```

And then, we can load it into our code with a simple line of code:

```
const $ = require('jquery');
```

You will be surprised at how many client-side libraries already support CommonJS and Webpack.

Using ES2015 with Webpack

As we said in the previous paragraph, one of the main advantages of Webpack is the ability to use loaders and plugins to transform the source code before bundling it.

Throughout this book we have been using many of the new handy features offered by the ES2015 standard, and we would love to keep using it even when working on a universal JavaScript application. In this section, we are going to see how to leverage the loader feature of Webpack to re-write the previous example using the ES2015 syntax within our source modules. With the proper configuration, Webpack will take care to transpile the resulting code for the browser to ES5 to guarantee the maximum compatibility with all the currently available browsers.

First of all, let's move our modules to a new `src` folder. This will make it easier for us to organize our code and separate the transpiled code from the original source code. This separation will also make it easier for us to configure Webpack properly and simplify the way we invoke Webpack from the command line.

Now we are ready to rewrite our modules. The ES2015 of our `src/sayHello.js` will look like this:

```
const mustache = require('mustache');
const template = '<h1>Hello <i>{{name}}</i></h1>';
mustache.parse(template);
module.exports.sayHello = toWhom => {
  return mustache.render(template, {name: toWhom});
};
```

Notice that we are using `const`, `let`, and the arrow function syntax.

We can now update our `src/main.js` file to ES2015. Our `src/main.js` file instead can be re-written as follows:

```
window.addEventListener('load', () => {
  const sayHello = require('./sayHello').sayHello;
  const hello = sayHello('Browser!');
  const body = document.getElementsByTagName("body")[0];
  body.innerHTML = hello;
});
```

Now we are ready to define the `webpack.config.js` file:

```
const path = require('path');

module.exports = {
  entry:  path.join(__dirname, "src", "main.js"),
```

```
  output: {
    path: path.join(__dirname, "dist"),
    filename: "bundle.js"
  },
  module: {
    loaders: [
      {
        test: path.join(__dirname, "src"),
        loader: 'babel-loader',
        query: {
          presets: ['es2015']
        }
      }
    ]
  }
};
```

This file is a module that exports a configuration object that will be read by Webpack when we invoke it from the command line without any argument.

In the configuration object, we are defining the entry point as our `src/main.js` file and the destination for our bundle file as `dist/bundle.js`.

This part was quite self-explanatory, so let's now have a look at the loaders array. This optional array allows us to specify a set of loaders that can alter the content of our source files while Webpack constructs our bundle file. The idea is that every loader represents a specific transformation (in this case, ES2015 to ES5 using `babel-loader`) and it is applied only if the current source file matches the specific `test` expression defined for the loader. In this example, we are telling Webpack to use `babel-loader` on all the files coming from our `src` folder and to apply the `es2015` preset as Babel option.

Now we are almost ready; the only missing step before running Webpack is to install Babel and the ES2015 preset with the following command:

```
npm install babel-core babel-loader babel-preset-es2015
```

Now, to generate your bundle, you can simply run:

```
webpack
```

Remember to reference the new `dist/bundle.js` in your `magic.html` file. You should be able to open it in the browser and see that everything is still working properly.

If you are curious, you can read the content of the freshly generated bundle file and you will discover that all the ES2015 features we used in the source files have been converted to the equivalent code valid in ES5, which every browser on the market can execute just fine.

Fundamentals of cross-platform development

When developing for different platforms, the most common problem we have to face is sharing the common parts of a component while providing different implementations for details that are platform-specific. We will now explore some of the principles and the patterns to use when facing this challenge.

Runtime code branching

The most simple and intuitive technique for providing different implementations based on the host platform is to dynamically branch our code. This requires that we have a mechanism to recognize at runtime the host platform and then switch dynamically the implementation with an `if...else` statement. Some generic approaches involve checking global variables that are available only on Node.js or only in the browser. For example, we can check the existence of the `window` global:

```
if(typeof window !== "undefined" && window.document) {
  //client side code
  console.log('Hey browser!');
} else {
  //Node.js code
  console.log('Hey Node.js!');
}
```

Using a runtime branching approach for switching between Node.js and the browser is definitely the most intuitive and simple pattern we can use for the purpose; however, there are some inconveniences:

- The code for both the platforms is included in the same module and therefore in the final bundle, increasing its size with unreachable code.
- If used too extensively, it can considerably reduce the readability of the code, as business logic would be mixed with logic meant only to add cross-platform compatibility.

- Using dynamic branching to load a different module depending on the platform will result in all the modules being added to the final bundle regardless of their target platform. For example, if we consider the next code fragment, both `clientModule` and `serverModule` will be included in a bundle generated with Webpack, unless we don't explicitly exclude one of them from the build:

```
if(typeof window !== "undefined" && window.document) {
  require('clientModule');
} else {
  require('serverModule');
}
```

This last inconvenience is due to the fact that bundlers have no sure way of knowing the value of a runtime variable at build time (unless the variable is a constant), so they include any module regardless of whether it's required from reachable or unreachable code.

A consequence of this last property is that modules required dynamically using variables are not included in the bundle. For example, from the following code, no module will be bundled:

```
moduleList.forEach(function(module) {
  require(module);
});
```

It's worth underlining that Webpack overcomes some of these limitations and, under certain specific circumstances, it is able to guess all the possible values for a dynamic requirement. For instance, if you have a snippet of code like the following:

```
function getController(controllerName) {
  return require("./controller/" + controllerName);
}
```

It will put all the modules available in the `controller` folder.

It's heavily recommended to have a look at the official documentation to understand all the supported cases.

Build-time code branching

In this section, we are going to see how to use Webpack to remove, at build time, all the parts of the code that we want only the server to use. This allows us to obtain lighter bundle files and to avoid accidentally exposing sensible code that should live only on the server.

Apart from loaders, Webpack also offers support for plugins, which allows us to extend our processing pipeline used to build the bundle file. To perform build-time code branching, we can use a pipeline of two built-in plugins called DefinePlugin and UglifyJsPlugin.

DefinePlugin can be used to replace specific code occurrences in our source files with custom code or variables. Instead, UglifyJsPlugin allows us to compress the resulting code and remove unreachable statements (dead code).

Let's see a practical example to better understand these concepts. Let's assume we have the following content in our main.js file:

```
if (typeof __BROWSER__ !== "undefined") {
  console.log('Hey browser!');
} else {
  console.log('Hey Node.js!');
}
```

Then, we can define the following webpack.config.js file:

```
const path = require('path');
const webpack = require('webpack');

const definePlugin = new webpack.DefinePlugin({
  "__BROWSER__": "true"
});

const uglifyJsPlugin = new webpack.optimize.UglifyJsPlugin({
  beautify: true,
  dead_code: true
});

module.exports = {
  entry: path.join(__dirname, "src", "main.js"),
  output: {
    path: path.join(__dirname, "dist"),
    filename: "bundle.js"
  },
  plugins: [definePlugin, uglifyJsPlugin]
};
```

The important parts of the code here are the definition and configuration of the two plugins that we introduced.

The first plugin, `DefinePlugin`, allows us to replace specific parts of the source code with dynamic code or constant values. The way it is configured is a bit tricky but this example should help with understanding how it works. In this case, we are configuring the plugin to look for all the occurrences of __BROWSER__ in the code and to replace them with `true`. Every value in the configuration object (in our case, `"true"` as a string and not as a boolean) represents a piece of code that will be evaluated at build time and then used to replace the currently matched snippet of code. This allows us to put in the bundle external dynamic values containing, for instance, the content of an environment variable, the current timestamp, or the hash of the last git commit. After occurrence of __BROWSER__ is replaced, the first `if` statement will internally look like `if (true !== "undefined")`, but Webpack is smart enough to understand that this expression will always be evaluated as `true`, so it transforms the resulting code again to be `if (true)`.

The second plugin (`UglifyJsPlugin`) is instead used to obfuscate and minify the JavaScript code of the bundle file using **UglifyJs** (`https://github.com/mishoo/UglifyJS`). With the `dead_code` option provided to the plugin, UglifyJs is able to remove all the dead code, so our currently processed code that will look like this:

```
if (true) {
  console.log('Hey browser!');
} else {
  console.log('Hey Node.js!');
}
```

can be easily converted only in:

```
console.log('Hey browser!');
```

The `beautify: true` option is used to avoid removing all the indentation and whitespaces so that, if you are curious, you can go and read the resulting bundle file. When creating bundles for production, it is better to avoid specifying this option, which is by default `false`.

 In the example code that you can download in addition to this book, you will find an extra example that will show you how to use the Webpack `DefinePlugin` to replace specific constants with dynamic variables such as the timestamp of bundle generation, the current user, and the current operative system.

Even if this technique is way better than runtime code branching because it produces much leaner bundle files, it can still make our source code cumbersome when abused. You don't want to have statements that branches your server code from your browser code all around your application, right?

Module swapping

Most of the time, we already know at build time what code has to be included in the client bundle and what shouldn't. This means that we can take this decision upfront and instruct the bundler to replace the implementation of a module at build time. This often results in a leaner bundle, as we are excluding unnecessary modules, and a more readable code because we don't have all the if...else statements required by runtime and build-time branching.

Let's find out how to adopt module swapping with Webpack with a very simple example.

We are going to build a module that exports a function called alert, which simply shows an alert message. We will have two different implementations, one for the server and one for the browser. Let's start with alertServer.js:

```
module.exports = console.log;
```

Then, with the alertBrowser.js:

```
module.exports = alert;
```

The code is super simple. As you can tell, we are just using the default functions console.log for the server and alert for the browser. They both accept a string as an argument, but the first prints the string in the console while the seconds displays it in a window.

Now let's write our generic main.js code, which by default, uses the module for the server:

```
const alert = require('./alertServer');
alert('Morning comes whether you set the alarm or not!');
```

There's nothing crazy here—we are just importing the alert module and using it. If we run:

```
node main.js
```

it will just print Morning comes whether you set the alarm or not! in the console.

Now comes the interesting part, let's see how our webpack.config.js should look to be able to swap the require of alertServer with alertBrowser when we want to create the bundle for the browser:

```
const path = require('path');
const webpack = require('webpack');

const moduleReplacementPlugin =
  new webpack.NormalModuleReplacementPlugin(/alertServer.js$/,
```

```
      './alertBrowser.js');

module.exports = {
  entry:  path.join(__dirname, "src", "main.js"),
  output: {
    path: path.join(__dirname, "dist"),
    filename: "bundle.js"
  },
  plugins: [moduleReplacementPlugin]
};
```

We are using the `NormalModuleReplacementPlugin`, which accepts two arguments. The first argument is a regular expression and the second one is a string representing a path to a resource. At build time, if a resource matches the given regular expression, it is replaced with the one provided in the second argument.

In this example, we are providing a regular expression that matches our `alertServer` module and replaces it with `alertBrowser`.

 Notice that we used the `const` keyword in this example but for the sake of simplicity, we didn't add the configuration to transpile ES2015 functionalities to the equivalent ES5 code, so with the current configuration the resulting code might not work with old browsers.

Of course, we can use the same swapping technique also with external modules fetched from npm. Let's improve the previous example to see how to use one or more external modules together with module swapping.

Nobody wants to use the `alert` function today, and for good reason. This function in fact displays a very bad looking window, which blocks the browser until the user dismisses it. It would be much nicer to use a fancy *toast popup* to display our alert message. There are a number of libraries on npm that provide this toast functionality, and one of these is `toastr` (`https://npmjs.com/package/toastr`), which provides a very simple programmatic interface and an enjoyable look and feel.

`toastr` relies on jQuery, so the first thing that we need to do is to install both with:

```
npm install jQuery toastr
```

Now we can rewrite our `alertBrowser` module to use `toastr` instead of the native `alert` function:

```
const toastr = require('toastr');
module.exports = toastr.info;
```

The `toastr.info` function accepts a string as an argument and it will take care to display the given message as a box in the top right corner of the browser window once invoked.

Our Webpack configuration file remains the same but, this time, Webpack will resolve the full dependency tree for the new version of the `alertBrowser` module, thus including `jQuery` and `toastr` in the resulting bundle file.

In addition, the server version of the module and the `main.js` file remained unchanged, and this proves how this solution makes our code much easier to maintain.

 To make this example work nicely in the browser, we should take care to add the `toastr` CSS file to our HTML file.

Thanks to Webpack and the module replacement plugin, we can easily deal with structural differences between platforms. We can focus on writing separate modules that are meant to provide platform-specific code and we can then swap Node.js—only modules with browser-specific ones in the final bundle.

Design patterns for cross-platform development

Now that we know how to switch between Node.js and browser code, the remaining pieces of the puzzle are how to integrate this within our design and how we can create our components in such a way that some of their parts are interchangeable. These challenges should not sound new to us at all; in fact, all throughout the book we have seen, analyzed, and used patterns to achieve this very purpose.

Let's revise some of them and describe how they apply to cross-platform development:

- **Strategy and Template**: These two are probably the most useful patterns when sharing code with the browser. Their intent is, in fact, to define the common steps of an algorithm, allowing some of its parts to be replaced, which is exactly what we need! In cross-platform development, these patterns allow us to share the platform-agnostic part of our components, while allowing their platform-specific parts to be changed using a different strategy or template method (which can be changed using runtime or compile-time branching).

- **Adapter**: This pattern is probably the most useful when we need to swap an entire component. In Chapter 6, *Design Patterns*, we have already seen an example of how an entire module, incompatible with the browser, can be replaced with an adapter built on top of a browser-compatible interface. Do you remember the LevelUP adapter for the fs interface?

- **Proxy**: When code meant to run in the server runs in the browser, we often expect things that live on the server to be available in the browser as well. This is where the *remote* Proxy pattern comes into place. Imagine if we wanted to access the filesystem of the server from the browser: we could think of creating an fs object on the client that proxies every call to the fs module living on the server, using Ajax or Web Sockets as a way of exchanging commands and return values.

- **Observer**: The Observer pattern provides a natural abstraction between the component that emits the event and those that receive it. In cross-platform development, this means that we can replace the emitter with its browser-specific implementation without affecting the listeners and vice versa.

- **DI and service locator**: Both DI and service locator can be useful to replace the implementation of a module at the moment of its injection.

As we can see, the arsenal of patterns at our disposal is quite powerful, but the most powerful weapon is still the ability of the developer to choose the best approach and adapt it to the specific problem at hand. In the next section, we are going to put into action what we have learned, leveraging some of the concepts and patterns we have seen so far.

Introducing React

From this point on in the chapter, we are going to use **React** (sometimes referred to as **ReactJs**), a JavaScript library originally released by Facebook (http://facebook.github.io/react/) and focused on providing a comprehensive set of functions and tools to build the view layer in our applications. React offers a view abstraction focused on the concept of components, where a component could be a button, a form input, a simple container such as an HTML div, or any other element in your user interface. The idea is that you should be able to construct the user interface of your application by just defining and composing highly reusable components with specific responsibilities.

What makes React different from other view implementations for the web is that it is not bound to the DOM by design. In fact, it provides a higher level abstraction called **virtual DOM** that fits very well with the web but that can also be used in other contexts, for example, building mobile apps, modeling 3D environments, or even defining the interaction between hardware components.

> *"Learn it once, use it everywhere"*
> *- Facebook*

This is the motto often used by Facebook to introduce React. It intentionally mocks the famous Java motto,*"Write once, run it everywhere,"* with the clear intention to take distance from it and to state that every context is different and needs its own specific implementation but, at the same time, you can re-use some *convenient* principles and tools across contexts once you learn them.

If you are interested in looking at the applications of React in contexts not strictly related to the field of web development, you can have a look at the following projects:
React Native for mobile apps
(`https://facebook.github.io/react-native`)
React Three to create 3D scenes
(`https://github.com/Izzimach/react-three`)
React Hardware (`https://github.com/iamdustan/react-hardware`)

The main reason why React is so interesting in the context of Universal JavaScript development is because it allows you to render the view code both from the server and on the client using almost the same code. To put it in another way, with React we are able to render all the HTML code that is required to display the page that the user requested directly from a Node.js server, and then, when the page is loaded, any additional interaction and rendering will be performed directly in the browser. This allows us to build Single-Page Applications (SPAs), where most of the things happen on the browser and only the part of the page that needs to be changed is refreshed. At the same time, this gives us the benefit of serving the first page loaded by the user straight off from the server, thus resulting in a faster (perceived) loading time and in a greater and easier indexability of the content for search engines.

It's also worth mentioning that React Virtual DOM is capable of optimizing the way changes are rendered. This means that the DOM is not rendered in full after every change, and instead React uses a smart in-memory diffing algorithm that is able to pre-calculate the minimum number of changes to apply to the DOM in order to update the view. This results in a very efficient mechanism for fast browser rendering, and that's probably another important reason why React is gaining a lot of traction over other libraries and frameworks.

Without further ado, let's start to use React and jump to a concrete example.

First React component

To start playing with React, we are going to build a very simple widget component to show a list of elements in our browser window.

In this example, we will use some of the tools we have already seen throughout this chapter, such as Webpack and Babel, so before starting to write some code, let's install all the dependencies we are going to need:

```
npm install webpack babel-core babel-loader babel-preset-es2015
```

We also need React and the Babel preset to turn React code into the equivalent ES5 code:

```
npm install react react-dom babel-preset-react
```

Now we are ready to write our first react component in a module called src/joyceBooks.js:

```
const React = require('react');

const books = [
  'Dubliners',
  'A Portrait of the Artist as a Young Man',
  'Exiles and poetry',
  'Ulysses',
  'Finnegans Wake'
];

class JoyceBooks extends React.Component {
  render() {
    return (
      <div>
        <h2>James Joyce's major works</h2>
        <ul className="books">{
          books.map((book, index) =>
            <li className="book" key={index}>{book}</li>
```

```
            )
        }</ul>
      </div>
    );
  }
}

module.exports = JoyceBooks;
```

The first part of the code is very trivial; we are just importing the `React` module and defining a `books` array that contains book titles.

The second part is the most interesting one: it's the core of our component. Beware—if this is the first time you are looking at React code, it might look weird!

So, to define a React component, we need to create a class that extends from `React.Component`. This class must define a function called `render`, which is used to describe the part of the DOM for which the component is responsible.

But what is inside our `render` function? We are returning some sort of HTML with some sort of JavaScript code inside and we are not even wrapping all of it with quotes. Yes, in case you were wondering, this is not JavaScript, but it is **JSX**!

JSX, what?!

As we said before, React provides a high level API for generating and manipulating the virtual DOM. The DOM is a great concept by itself and it can be easily represented with XML or HTML, but if we have to dynamically manipulate its tree dealing with low level concepts such as nodes, parents, and children, it might quickly get very cumbersome. To deal with this intrinsic complexity, React introduced JSX as an intermediate format designed to describe and manipulate the virtual DOM.

Actually, JSX is not a language on its own, and it is in fact a superset of JavaScript that needs to be transpiled to plain JavaScript to be executed. However, it still gives the developer the advantage of using an XML-based syntax with JavaScript. When developing for the browser, JSX is used to describe the HTML code that defines our web components and, as you have seen in the previous example, we can put HTML tags directly in the middle of our JSX code as if they are a part of this enhanced JavaScript syntax.

This approach offers an intrinsic advantage, that is, our HTML code is now dynamically validated at build time and we will get an ahead of time error if we forgot, for instance, to close one tag.

Let's now analyze the `render` function from the previous example to understand some important details of JSX:

```
render() {
  return (
    <div>
      <h2>James Joyce's major works</h2>
      <ul className="books">{
        books.map((book, index) =>
          <li className="book" key={index}>{book}</li>
        )
      }</ul>
    </div>
  );
}
```

As you saw, we can insert a piece of HTML code at any point of our JSX code without having to put any particular indicator or wrapper around it. In this case, we simply defined a `div` tag, which acts as a container for our component.

We can also put some JavaScript logic within this HTML block; notice the curly brackets within the `ul` tag. This approach allows us to define parts of the HTML code dynamically in a similar fashion to what you can do with many templating engines. In this case, we are using the native JavaScript `map` function to iterate over all the available books in the array, and for every one of them we create another piece of HTML to add the book name to the list.

The curly brackets are used to define an expression within an HTML block, and the simplest use case is to use them to print the content of a variable, like we are doing here with `{book}`.

Finally, notice that we can again put another block of HTML code within this JavaScript content, so that HTML and JavaScript content can be mixed and nested at any level to describe the Virtual DOM.

It is not mandatory to use JSX when developing with React. JSX is just a nice interface on top of the React Virtual DOM JavaScript library. With some additional effort, you can achieve the same results by calling these functions directly and completely skipping JSX and its transpilation step. Just to give you an idea about how React code looks without JSX, have a look at the transpiled version of the `render` function of our example:

```
function render() {
  return React.createElement(
    'div',
    null,
```

```
React.createElement(
  'h2',
  null,
  'James Joyce's major works'
),
React.createElement(
  'ul',
  { className: 'books' },
  books.map(function (book) {
    return React.createElement(
      'li',
      { className: 'book' },
      book
    );
  })
)
);
}
```

As you can see, this code looks much less readable and more prone to errors, so most of the time it is better to rely on JSX and use a transpiler to generate the equivalent JavaScript code.

To complete our quick overview of JSX, let's have a look at how this code will be finally rendered to HTML when executed:

```
<div data-reactroot="">
  <h2>James Joyce's major works</h2>
    <ul class="books">
      <li class="book">Dubliners</li>
      <li class="book">A Portrait of the Artist as a Young Man</li>
      <li class="book">Exiles and poetry</li>
      <li class="book">Ulysses</li>
      <li class="book">Finnegans Wake</li>
    </ul>
</div>
```

One last thing to notice here is that in the JSX/JavaScript version of the code, we used the attribute `className` and it was here converted to `class`. It's important to underline that when we work with the virtual DOM, we must use the DOM equivalent attributes for HTML attributes; React will then take care to convert them when rendering the HTML code.

A list with all the supported tags and attributes in React is available in the official documentation at `https://facebook.github.io/react/docs/tags-and-attributes.html`.

If you are interested in knowing more about JSX syntax, you can read the official specification provided by Facebook: `https://facebook.github.io/jsx`.

Configuring Webpack to transpile JSX

In this section, we will see an example of Webpack configuration that we can use to be able to transpile JSX code to JavaScript code that can be executed in the browser:

```
const path = require('path');
module.exports = {
  entry:  path.join(__dirname, "src", "main.js"),
  output: {
    path: path.join(__dirname, "dist"),
    filename: "bundle.js"
  },
  module: {
    loaders: [
      {
        test: path.join(__dirname, "src"),
        loader: 'babel-loader',
        query: {
          cacheDirectory: 'babel_cache',
          presets: ['es2015', 'react']
        }
      }
    ]
  }
};
```

As you might have noticed, this configuration is almost identical to the one we saw in the previous ES2015 Webpack example. The only relevant differences are as follows:

- We are using the `react` preset in Babel.
- We are using the option `cacheDirectory`. This option allows Babel to use a specific directory as a cache folder (in this case, `babel_cache`) and be faster while building the bundle file. It is not mandatory but highly encouraged to speed up the development.

Rendering in the browser

Now that we have our first React component ready, we just need to use it and render it in the browser. Let's create our `src/main.js` JavaScript file to use our `JoyceBooks` component:

```
const React = require('react');
const ReactDOM = require('react-dom');
const JoyceBooks = require('./joyceBooks');

window.onload = () => {
  ReactDOM.render(<JoyceBooks/>, document.getElementById('main'))
};
```

The most important part of the code here is the `ReactDOM.render` function call. This function takes as arguments a JSX code block and a DOM element, and it will take care to render the JSX block to HTML code and apply it to the DOM node given as a second argument. Also notice that the JSX block we are passing here contains only a custom tag (`JoyceBooks`). Every time we require a component, it will be available as a JSX tag (where the name of the tag is given by the class name of the component) so that we can easily insert a new instance of this component in other JSX blocks. This is the base mechanism that allows the developer to split the interface into several cohesive components.

Now the last step we need to perform to see our first React example live is to create an `index.html` page:

```
<!DOCTYPE html>
<html>
  <head>
    <meta charset="utf-8" />
    <title>React Example - James Joyce books</title>
  </head>
  <body>
    <div id="main"></div>
    <script src="dist/bundle.js"></script>
  </body>
</html>
```

This is very simple and doesn't require much explanation. We are just adding our `bundle.js` file to a plain HTML page which contains `div` with the ID `main` that will act as a container for our React application.

You can now just launch `webpack` from the command line and then open the `index.html` page in your browser.

What is important to understand is what happens with client-side rendering when the user loads the page:

1. The HTML code of the page is downloaded by the browser and then rendered.
2. The bundle file is downloaded and its JavaScript content is evaluated.
3. The evaluated code takes care to generate the real content of our page dynamically and updates the DOM to display it.

This means that if this page is loaded by a browser which has JavaScript disabled (for example, a search engine bot), our webpage will look like a blank webpage without any meaningful content. This might be a very serious problem, especially in terms of SEO.

Later in this chapter, we will see how to render the same React component from the server to overcome this limitation.

The React Router library

In this section, we will improve our previous example of building a very simple navigable app consisting of several screens. We will have three different sections: an index page, the page of the books by James Joyce, and the page of the books by H. G. Wells. We will also have a page to show when the user tries to access a URL that does not exist.

To build this app, we will use the React Router library, (`https://github.com/reactjs/react-router`), a module that makes it easy to have navigable components in React. So, the first thing we need to do is to download React Router in our project with:

```
npm install react-router
```

Now we are ready to create all the components needed to build the sections of this new app. Let's start with `src/components/authorsIndex.js`:

```
const React = require('react');
const Link = require('react-router').Link;

const authors = [
  {id: 1, name: 'James Joyce', slug: 'joyce'},
  {id: 2, name: 'Herbert George Wells', slug: 'h-g-wells'}
];

class AuthorsIndex extends React.Component {
  render() {
    return (
      <div>
        <h1>List of authors</h1>
```

```
        <ul>{
          authors.map( author =>
            <li key={author.id}><Link to={`/author/${author.slug}`}>
                    {author.name}</Link></li>
          )
        }</ul>
      </div>
    )
  }
}

module.exports = AuthorsIndex;
```

This component represents the index of our application. It displays the name of the two authors. Notice that, again, to keep things simple, we are storing the data necessary to render this component in `authors`, an array of objects, each one representing an author. Another new element is the `Link` component. As you might have guessed, this component comes from the React Router library and allows us to render clickable links that can be used to navigate through the available sections of the app. What is important to understand is the property `to` of the `Link` component. It is used to specify a relative URI that indicates the specific route to display when the link is clicked. So, it is not very different than a regular HTML `<a>` tag, the only difference is that, instead of moving to a new page by refreshing the full page, React Router will take care to dynamically only refresh the part of the page that needs to be changed to display the component associated with the new URI. We will see better how this mechanism works when we write the configuration for our router. For now, let's focus on writing all the other components that we want to use in our app. So, now let's rewrite our `JoyceBooks` components that, this time, will be stored in `components/joyceBooks.js`:

```
const React = require('react');
const Link = require('react-router').Link;

const books = [
  'Dubliners',
  'A Portrait of the Artist as a Young Man',
  'Exiles and poetry',
  'Ulysses',
  'Finnegans Wake'
];

class JoyceBooks extends React.Component {
  render() {
    return (
      <div>
        <h2>James Joyce's major works</h2>
        <ul className="books">{
```

```
        books.map( (book, key) =>
          <li key={key} className="book">{book}</li>
        )
      }</ul>
      <Link to="/">Go back to index</Link>
    </div>
    );
  }
}


module.exports = JoyceBooks;
```

As we might have expected, this component looks very similar to its previous version. The only notable differences are that we are adding Link to go back to the index at the end of the component and that we are using the attribute key inside our map function. With this last change, we are telling React that the specific element is identified by a unique key (in this case, we are using the index of the array for simplicity) so that it can perform a number of optimizations whenever it needs to re-render the list. This last change is not mandatory but it is heavily recommended, especially in larger applications.

Now following the same schema, we can write our components/wellsBooks.js component:

```
const React = require('react');
const Link = require('react-router').Link;

const books = [
  'The Time Machine',
  'The War of the Worlds',
  'The First Men in the Moon',
  'The Invisible Man'
];

class WellsBooks extends React.Component {
  render() {
    return (
      <div>
        <h2>Herbert George Wells's major works</h2>
        <ul className="books">{
          books.map( (book, key) =>
            <li key={key} className="book">{book}</li>
          )
        }</ul>
        <Link to="/">Go back to index</Link>
      </div>
    );
  }
```

```
}

module.exports = WellsBooks;
```

This component is almost identical to the previous one and, of course, this should ring a bell! We could build a more generic AuthorPage component and avoid code duplication, but this will be the topic for the next section, here we want to focus only on routing.

We also want to have a components/notFound.js component that just displays an error message. We will skip this trivial implementation for the sake of brevity.

So, now let's move to the interesting part—the routes.js component which defines the logic of our routing:

```
const React = require('react');
const ReactRouter = require('react-router');
const Router = ReactRouter.Router;
const Route = ReactRouter.Route;
const hashHistory = ReactRouter.hashHistory;
const AuthorsIndex = require('./components/authorsIndex');
const JoyceBooks = require('./components/joyceBooks');
const WellsBooks = require('./components/wellsBooks');
const NotFound = require('./components/notFound');

class Routes extends React.Component {
  render() {
    return (
      <Router history={hashHistory}>
        <Route path="/" component={AuthorsIndex}/>
        <Route path="/author/joyce" component={JoyceBooks}/>
        <Route path="/author/h-g-wells" component={WellsBooks}/>
        <Route path="*" component={NotFound} />
      </Router>
    )
  }
}
module.exports = Routes;
```

The first thing to analyze here is the list of modules that we need to implement the routing component of our app. We are requiring the react-router, which in turn contains three modules that we want to use: Router, Route, and hashHistory.

`Router` is the main component that holds all the routing configuration. It's the element we use as the root node for our `Routes` component. The property `history` specifies the mechanism used to detect which route is active and how to update the URL in the browser bar every time the user clicks on a link. There are commonly two strategies: `hashHistory` and `browserHistory`. The first one uses the **fragment** part of the URL (the one delimited by the hash symbol). With this strategy, our links will look like this: `index.html#/author/h-g-wells`. The second strategy does not use the fragment but leverages the HTML5 **history API** (`https://developer.mozilla.org/en-US/docs/We b/API/History_API`) to display more realistic URLs. With this strategy, every path has its own full URI, such as `http://example.com/author/h-g-wells`.

In this example, we are using the `hashHistory` strategy as it is the simplest to set up and doesn't require a web server to refresh the page. We will have chance to use the `browserHistory` strategy later in this chapter.

The `Route` component allows us to define an association between a `path` and a `component`. This component will be rendered when the route is matched.

Inside our `render` function, we are summarizing and composing all these concepts and, now that you know the meaning of every component and option, you should be able to make sense of it.

What is important to understand here is the way the `Router` component works with this declarative syntax:

- It acts as a container; it doesn't render any HTML code but contains a list of `Route` definitions.
- Every `Route` definition is associated to a component. This time, the component is a graphical component, meaning that it will be rendered in the HTML code of the page, but only if the current URL of the page matches the route.
- Only one route can be matched for a given URI. In ambiguous cases, the router prefers the less generic routes (for example, `/author/joyce` over `/author`).
- It is possible to define a **catch-all** route with `*`, which is matched only when all the other routes are not matched. We are using it here to display our "not found" message.
- Now the last step to complete this example is to update our `main.js` to use the `Routes` component as the main component of our application:

```
const React = require('react');
const ReactDOM = require('react-dom');
const Routes = require('./routes');
```

```
window.onload = () => {
  ReactDOM.render(<Routes/>, document.getElementById('main'))
};
```

Now we just need to run Webpack to regenerate our bundle file and open the `index.html` to see our new app working.

Try to click around and see how the URL gets updated. Also, if you use any debug tool, you will notice how the transition between one section and another doesn't fully refresh the page neither trigger a new request. The app is in fact completely loaded when we open the index page and the router is used here to basically show and hide the right component given the current URI. Anyway, the router is smart enough that if we try to refresh the page with a specific URI (for example, `index.html#/author/joyce`), it will immediately display the correct component.

React Router is a very powerful component and it has a number of interesting features. For example, it allows you to have nested routes to represent multi-level user interfaces (components with nested sections). We will also see in this chapter how it can be extended to load components and data on demand. In the meantime, you can have a break and read the official documentation of the component to discover all the available features.

Creating a Universal JavaScript app

At this stage of the chapter, we should have got most of the basics that we need to transform our sample app into a full Universal JavaScript app. We met Webpack, ReactJs, and analyzed most of the patterns that help us to uniform and differentiate the code between platforms as needed.

In this section, we will keep improving our example by creating reusable components, by adding universal routing and rendering, and finally universal data retrieval.

Creating reusable components

In the previous example, we created two very similar components: `JoyceBooks` and `WellsBooks`. These two components are almost identical; the only difference between them is that they use different data. Now imagine a real case scenario where we might have hundreds or even thousands of authors… Yes, it wouldn't make much sense to keep having a dedicated component for every author.

In this section, we are going to create a more generic component and update our routing to be able to have parameterized routes.

Let's start by creating the generic `components/authorPage.js` component:

```
const React = require('react');
const Link = require('react-router').Link;
const AUTHORS = require('../authors');

class AuthorPage extends React.Component {
  render() {
    const author = AUTHORS[this.props.params.id];
    return (
      <div>
        <h2>{author.name}'s major works</h2>
        <ul className="books">{
          author.books.map( (book, key) =>
            <li key={key} className="book">{book}</li>
          )
        }</ul>
        <Link to="/">Go back to index</Link>
      </div>
    );
  }
}
module.exports = AuthorPage;
```

This component is, of course, very similar to the two components it is replacing. The two major differences here are that we need to have a way to fetch the data from within the component and a way to receive a parameter that indicates which author we want to display.

For the sake of simplicity, we require `authors.js` here, a module that exports a JavaScript object containing data about the authors that we use as a simple database. The variable `this.props.params.id` represents the identifier of the author we need to display. This parameter is populated by the router and we will see exactly how in a minute. So, we use this parameter to extract the author from the database object and then we have everything we need to render the component.

Just to make you understand how we are fetching the data, here is an example of how our `authors.js` module might look:

```
module.exports = {

  'joyce': {
    'name': 'James Joyce',
```

```
      'books': [
        'Dubliners',
        'A Portrait of the Artist as a Young Man',
        'Exiles and poetry',
        'Ulysses',
        'Finnegans Wake'
      ]
    },

    'h-g-wells': {
      'name': 'Herbert George Wells',
      'books': [
        'The Time Machine',
        'The War of the Worlds',
        'The First Men in the Moon',
        'The Invisible Man'
      ]
    }
};
```

It's a very simple object that indexes authors by a mnemonic string identifier.

Now the final step is to review our routes.js components:

```
const React = require('react');
const ReactRouter = require('react-router');
const Router = ReactRouter.Router;
const hashHistory = ReactRouter.hashHistory;
const AuthorsIndex = require('./components/authorsIndex');
const AuthorPage = require('./components/authorPage');
const NotFound = require('./components/notFound');

const routesConfig = [
  {path: '/', component: AuthorsIndex},
  {path: '/author/:id', component: AuthorPage},
  {path: '*', component: NotFound}
];

class Routes extends React.Component {
  render() {
    return<Router history={hashHistory} routes={routesConfig}/>;
  }
}
module.exports = Routes;
```

This time, we are using the new generic `AuthorPage` component in place of the two specific components we had in the previous example. We are also using an alternative configuration for the router; this time, we are using a plain JavaScript array to define our routes instead of putting the `Route` components within the render function of the `Routes` component. The object is then passed to the `routes` attribute of the `Router` component. This configuration is totally equivalent to the tag-based one we saw in the previous example and is sometimes easier to write. Other times, for instance when we have many nested routes, the tag-based configuration might be more comfortable to work with. The important change here is our new `/author/:id` route that is linked to our new generic component and which replaced our old specific routes. This route is parameterized (named parameters are defined with the "column-prefixed-syntax," as you can see here) and will match both our old routes `/author/joyce` and `/author/h-g-wells`. Of course, it will match any other route of this kind and the matched string for the `id` parameter is directly passed to the component, which will be able to access it by reading `props.params.id`.

This completes our example; to run it, you just need to regenerate the bundle file using Webpack and refresh the `index.html` page. This page and `main.js` remains unchanged.

Using generic components and parameterized routes, we have great flexibility and we should be able to build quite complex apps.

Server-side rendering

Let's make another small step forwards in our journey through Universal JavaScript. We said that one of the most interesting features of React is the ability to render components even on the server side. In this section, we are going to leverage this feature to update our simple app and render it directly from the server.

We are going to use **Express** (`http://expressjs.com`) as the web server and **ejs** (`https://npmjs.com/package/ejs`) as the internal template engine. We will also need to run our server script on top of Babel to be able to leverage JSX, so the first thing we need to do is to install all these new dependencies:

```
npm install express ejs babel-cli
```

All our components remain the same as they were in the previous example, so we are going to focus on the server. In the server, we will need to access to the routing configuration so, to make this task simpler, we are going to extract the routing configuration object from the `routes.js` file to a dedicated module called `routesConfig.js`:

```
const AuthorsIndex = require('./components/authorsIndex');
const AuthorPage = require('./components/authorPage');
```

```
const NotFound = require('./components/notFound');

const routesConfig = [
  {path: '/', component: AuthorsIndex},
  {path: '/author/:id', component: AuthorPage},
  {path: '*', component: NotFound}
];
module.exports = routesConfig;
```

We are also going to transform our static `index.html` file into an ejs template called `views/index.ejs`:

```
<!DOCTYPE html>
<html>
  <head>
    <meta charset="utf-8" />
    <title>React Example - Authors archive</title>
  </head>
  <body>
    <div id="main">
      <%- markup -%>
    </div>
    <!--<script src="dist/bundle.js"></script>-->
  </body>
</html>
```

Everything is simple here; there are only two details worth underlining:

- The `<%- markup -%>` tag is the part of the template that will be dynamically replaced with the React content that we will render on the server side before serving the page to the browser.
- We are commenting the inclusion of the bundle script for now because in this section we want to focus only on the server-side rendering. We will integrate a complete universal rendering solution in the next sections.

- We can now create our `server.js` script:

  ```
  const http = require('http');
  const Express = require('express');
  const React = require('react');
  const ReactDom = require('react-dom/server');
  const Router = require('react-router');
  const routesConfig = require('./src/routesConfig');

  const app = new Express();
  const server = new http.Server(app);
  ```

```
app.set('view engine', 'ejs');

app.get('*', (req, res) => {
  Router.match(
    {routes: routesConfig, location: req.url},
    (error, redirectLocation, renderProps) => {
      if (error) {
        res.status(500).send(error.message)
      } else if (redirectLocation) {
        res.redirect(302, redirectLocation.pathname +
          redirectLocation.search)
      } else if (renderProps) {
        const markup = ReactDom.renderToString(<Router.RouterContext
                       {...renderProps} />);
        res.render('index', {markup});
      } else {
        res.status(404).send('Not found')
      }
    }
  );
});

server.listen(3000, (err) => {
  if (err) {
    return console.error(err);
  }
  console.info('Server running on http://localhost:3000');
});
```

The important part of this code is the Express route defined with `app.get('*', (req, res) => {...})`. This is an **Express catch-all** route that will intercept all the GET requests to every URL in the server. Inside this route, we take care of delegating the routing logic to the React Router that we setup before for the client-side application.

Pattern
The server router component (Express built-in router) is here replaced by a universal router (React Router) that is able to match the routes both on the client and on the server.

To adopt the React Router in the server, we use the function `Router.match`. This function accepts two parameters: the first one is a **configuration object** and the second is a **callback function**. The configuration object must have two keys:

- `routes`: This is used to pass the React Router routes configuration. Here, we are passing the exact same configuration that we used for the client-side rendering, and that's the reason why we extracted it into a dedicated component at the beginning of this section.

- `location`: This is used to specify the currently requested URL on which the router will try to match one of the previously defined routes.

The callback function is called when a route is matched. It will receive three arguments, `error`, `redirectLocation`, and `renderProps`, that we will use to determine what exactly the result of the match operation was. We can have four different cases that we need to handle:

- The first case is when we have an error during the routing resolution. To handle this case, we simply return a **500 internal server error** response to the browser.
- The second case is when we match a route that is a redirect route. In this case, we need to create a server redirect message (**302 redirect**) to tell the browser to go to the new destination.
- The third case is when we match a route and we have to render the associated component. In this case, the argument `renderProps` is an object that contains some data we need to use to render the component. This is the core of our server-side routing mechanism and we use the `ReactDOM.renderToString` function to be able to render the HTML code that represents the component associated to the currently matched route. Then, we inject the resulting HTML into the `index.ejs` template we defined before to obtain the full HTML page that we send to the browser.
- The last case is when the route is not matched, and here we simply return a **404 not found** error to the browser.

So, definitively, the most important part of this code is the following line:

```
const markup = ReactDom.renderToString(<Router.RouterContext
{...renderProps} />
```

Let's see better how the `renderToString` function works:

- This function comes from the module `react-dom/server` and it is capable of rendering any React component to a string. It is used to render the HTML code in the server to be immediately sent to the browser, speeding up the page load time and making the page SEO friendly. React is smart enough that if we call `ReactDOM.render()` for the same component in the browser, it will not render the component again, it will just attach the event listeners to its existing DOM nodes.

- The component we are rendering is `RouterContext` (contained in the `react-router` module), which is responsible for rendering the component tree for a given router state. We pass to this component a set of attributes that are all the fields inside the `renderProps` object. To expand this object, we are using the JSX-spread attributes operator (`https://facebook.github.io/react/docs/jsx-spread.html#spread-attributes`), which extracts all the key/value pairs in the object to component attributes.

Now we are ready to run our `server.js` script with:

```
node server
```

Then, we can open the browser and point it to `http://localhost:3000` to see our server-rendered app up and running.

Remember that we disabled the inclusion of the bundle file, so at the moment, we have no client-side JavaScript code running and every interaction triggers a new server request that refreshes the page entirely. This is not so cool, right?

In the next section, we will see how to enable both client and server rendering, adding to our sample app an effective universal routing and rendering solution.

Universal rendering and routing

In this paragraph, we will update our sample app to leverage both server- and client-side rendering and routing. We have already shown the individual parts working, so now it's just a matter of polishing things up a bit.

The first thing that we are going to do is to uncomment the `bundle.js` inclusion in our main view file (`views/index.ejs`).

Then, we need to change the history strategy in our client-side app (`main.js`). Do you remember that we were using the hash history strategy? Well, this strategy doesn't play well with universal rendering because we want to have the exact same URLs both in the client and the server routing. In the server, we can only use the browser history strategy, so let's rewrite the `routes.js` module to use it in the client as well:

```
const React = require('react');
const ReactRouter = require('react-router');
const Router = ReactRouter.Router;
const browserHistory = ReactRouter.browserHistory;
const routesConfig = require('./routesConfig');
```

```
class Routes extends React.Component {
  render() {
    return<Router history={browserHistory} routes={routesConfig}/>;
  }
}
module.exports = Routes;
```

As you can see, the only relevant change is that we are now requiring the `ReactRouter.browserHistory` function and passing it to our `Router` component.

We are almost done; there is only a small change that we need to perform in our server app to be able to serve the `bundle.js` file to the client from our server as a static asset.

To do this, we can use the `Express.static` middleware that allows us to expose the content of a folder as static files from a specific path. In our case, we want to expose the `dist` folder, so we just need to add the following line before our main server routing configuration:

```
app.use('/dist', Express.static('dist'));
```

And that's pretty much it! Now to see our app live, we just need to regenerate our bundle file with Webpack and restart our server. Then you will be able to navigate through your app on `http://localhost:3000` as you were doing before. Everything will look the same, but if you use an inspector or a debugger, you will notice that, this time, only the first request will be fully rendered by the server, while others will be managed by browser. If you want to keep playing a bit, you can also try to force refresh the page on specific URIs to also test that the routing is working seamlessly both on the server and on the browser.

Universal data retrieval

Our sample app is now starting to get a solid structure in order to grow and become a more complete and scalable app. However, there is still a very fundamental point that we haven't yet addressed properly, and that is, data retrieval. Do you remember that we used a module that just contains JSON data? Currently, we use that module as a sort of database, but of course, this is a very suboptimal approach for a number of reasons:

- We are sharing the JSON file everywhere in our app and accessing the data directly across frontend, backend, and in every React component.

- Given that we access the data also on the frontend, we end up putting the full database also in the frontend bundle. This is risky because we might accidentally expose any sensitive information. Also, our bundle file will grow with the growth of our database and we will be forced to recompile it after every change on the data.

It's obvious that we need a better solution—a more decoupled and scalable one.

In this section, we will improve our example by building a dedicated REST API server that will allow us to fetch the data asynchronously and on demand: only when it is really needed and only the specific subset of data that we want to render to the current section of the app.

The API server

We want the API server to be completely separated by our backend server; ideally, it should be possible to scale this server independently from the rest of the application.

Without further ado, let's see the code of our `apiServer.js`:

```
const http = require('http');
const Express = require('express');

const app = new Express();
const server = new http.Server(app);
const AUTHORS = require('./src/authors');           // [1]

app.use((req, res, next) => {                        // [2]
  console.log(`Received request: ${req.method} ${req.url} from
    ${req.headers['user-agent']}`);
  next();
});

app.get('/authors', (req, res, next) => {            // [3]
  const data = Object.keys(AUTHORS).map(id => {
    return {
      'id': id,
      'name': AUTHORS[id].name
    };
  });

  res.json(data);
});

app.get('/authors/:id', (req, res, next) => {        // [4]
```

```
  if (!AUTHORS.hasOwnProperty(req.params.id)) {
    return next();
  }

  const data = AUTHORS[req.params.id];
  res.json(data);
});

server.listen(3001, (err) => {
  if (err) {
    return console.error(err);
  }
  console.info('API Server running on http://localhost:3001');
});
```

As you can see, we are again using Express as a web server framework, but let's still analyze the main parts of this code:

- Our data still lies in a module as a JSON file (`src/authors.js`). This is, of course, only for simplicity and works for the sake of our example, but in a real world scenario, it should be replaced with a real database such as MongoDB, MySql, or LevelDB. In this example, we will access the data directly from the required JSON object, while in a real case app we will make queries to the external data source when we want to read the data.

- We are using a middleware that prints in the console some useful information every time we receive a request. We will see later that these logs can help us to understand who is calling the API (the frontend or the backend) and to verify that the whole app is behaving as expected.

- We expose a GET endpoint identified by the URI /authors that returns a JSON array containing all the available authors. For every author, we are exposing the fields' id and name. Again, here, we are extracting data directly from the JSON file we imported as database; in a real-world scenario, we would prefer to perform a query to a real database here.

- We are also exposing another GET endpoint on the URI /authors/:id, where :id is a generic placeholder that will match the ID of the specific author for which we want to read the data. If the given ID is valid (there is an entry in our JSON file for that ID), the API returns an object containing the name of the author and an array of books.

We can now run our API server with:

node apiServer

It will be now accessible on `http://localhost:3001`, and if you want to test it, you can try to make a couple of curl requests:

```
curl http://localhost:3001/authors/
[{"id":"joyce","name":"James Joyce"},{"id":"h-g-wells","name":"Herbert
George Wells"}]
```

```
curl http://localhost:3001/authors/h-g-wells
{"name":"Herbert George Wells","books":["The Time Machine","The War of the
Worlds","The First Men in the Moon","The Invisible Man"]}
```

Proxying requests for the frontend

The API we just built should be accessible for both the backend and the frontend. The frontend will need to call the API with an AJAX request. You are probably aware of the security policies that allow the browser to make AJAX requests only to URLs in the domain where the page was loaded. That means that if we run our API server on `localhost:3001` and our web server on `localhost:3000`, we are actually using two different domains and the browser will fail to call the API endpoints directly. To overcome this limitation, we can create a proxy within our web server that will take care to expose the same endpoints of the API server locally using an internal convenience route (`localhost:3000/api`), as shown in the following picture:

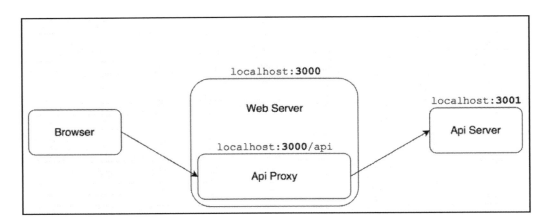

To build the proxy component in our web server, we are going to use the excellent `http-proxy` module (`https://npmjs.com/package/http-proxy`), so we need to install it with npm:

```
npm install http-proxy
```

We will see in a moment how it will be included in the web server and configured.

Universal API client

We will call the API using two different prefixes given the current environment:

- `http://localhost:3001` when we call the API from the web server
- `/api` when we call the API from the browser

We also need to consider that in the browser we have only the XHR/AJAX mechanism to make asynchronous HTTP requests, while on the server we have to use a library like `request` or the built-in `http` library.

To overcome all these differences and build a universal API client module, we can use a library called `axios` (`https://npmjs.com/package/axios`). This library works both on the client and on the server and abstracts the two different mechanisms that each environment uses to make HTTP requests to a single uniform API.

So, we need to install `axios` with:

```
npm install axios
```

Then, we also need to create a simple wrapper module that takes care to export a configured instance of `axios`. We call this module `xhrClient.js`:

```
const Axios = require('axios');

const baseURL = typeof window !== 'undefined' ? '/api' :
  'http://localhost:3001';
const xhrClient = Axios.create({baseURL});
module.exports = xhrClient;
```

In this module, we are basically checking if the `window` variable is defined to detect whether we are running the code on the browser or on the web server so that we can set the proper API prefix accordingly. Then, we simply export a new instance of the `axios` client, configured with the current value of the base URL.

Now we can simply import this module in our React components, and depending on whether they are executed on the server or on the browser, we will be able to use a universal interface and all the intrinsic differences of the two environments will be hidden within the code of the module.

Other widely appreciated universal HTTP clients are superagent (https
://npmjs.com/package/superagent) and isomorphic-fetch (https
://npmjs.com/package/isomorphic-fetch)

Asynchronous React components

Now that our components will have to use this new set APIs, they will need to be
asynchronously initialized. To be able to do so, we can use an extension of the React Router
called async-props (https://npmjs.com/package/async-props).

So, let's install this module with:

```
npm install async-props
```

Now we are ready to rewrite our components to be asynchronous. Let's start with
components/authorsIndex.js:

```
const React = require('react');
const Link = require('react-router').Link;
const xhrClient = require('../xhrClient');

class AuthorsIndex extends React.Component {
  static loadProps(context, cb) {
    xhrClient.get('authors')
      .then(response => {
        const authors = response.data;
        cb(null, {authors});
      })
      .catch(error => cb(error))
    ;
  }

  render() {
    return (
      <div>
        <h1>List of authors</h1>
        <ul>{
          this.props.authors.map(author =>
            <li key={author.id}>
              <Link to={`/author/${author.id}`}>{author.name}</Link>
            </li>
          )
        }</ul>
      </div>
    )
```

```
    }
}
module.exports = AuthorsIndex;
```

As you can see, in this new version of the module we require our new xhrClient in place of the old module containing the raw JSON data. Then, we add a new method in the component class called loadProps. This method accepts as arguments an object containing some context parameters that will be passed by the router (context) and a callback function (cb). Inside this method, we can perform all the asynchronous actions needed to retrieve the data necessary to initialize the component. When everything is loaded (or in case there is an error), we execute the callback function to propagate the data and notify the router that the component is ready. In this case, we are using xhrClient to fetch the data from the authors endpoint.

In the same fashion, we also update the components/authorPage.js component:

```
const React = require('react');
const Link = require('react-router').Link;
const xhrClient = require('../xhrClient');

class AuthorPage extends React.Component {
  static loadProps(context, cb) {
    xhrClient.get(`authors/${context.params.id}`)
      .then(response => {
        const author = response.data;
        cb(null, {author});
      })
      .catch(error => cb(error))
    ;
  }

  render() {
    return (
      <div>
        <h2>{this.props.author.name}'s major works</h2>
        <ul className="books">{
          this.props.author.books.map( (book, key) =>
            <li key={key} className="book">{book}</li>
          )
        }</ul>
        <Link to="/">Go back to index</Link>
      </div>
    );
  }
}
module.exports = AuthorPage;
```

The code here follows the same logic described in the previous component. The main difference is that, this time, we are calling the authors/:id API endpoint and we are taking the ID parameter from the context.params.id variable that will be passed by the router.

To be able to load these asynchronous components correctly, we need to also update our router definition for both the client and the server. For now, let's focus on the client and see how the new version of routes.js will look:

```
const React = require('react');
const AsyncProps = require('async-props').default;
const ReactRouter = require('react-router');
const Router = ReactRouter.Router;
const browserHistory = ReactRouter.browserHistory;
const routesConfig = require('./routesConfig');

class Routes extends React.Component {
  render() {
    return <Router
      history={browserHistory}
      routes={routesConfig}
      render={(props) => <AsyncProps {...props}/>}
    />;
  }
}
module.exports = Routes;
```

The two differences from the previous version are that we require the async-props module and that we are using it to redefine the render function of the Router component to use it. This approach actually hooks the logic of async-props module within the rendering logic of the router, enabling the support for asynchronous behavior.

The web server

Finally, the last task we need to complete in this example is to update our web server in order to use the proxy server to redirect the API calls to the real API server and to render the router using the async-props module.

We renamed our server.js to webServer.js to clearly distinguish it from the API server file. This will be the content of the new file:

```
const http = require('http');
const Express = require('express');
const httpProxy = require('http-proxy');
const React = require('react');
```

```
const AsyncProps = require('async-props').default;
const loadPropsOnServer = AsyncProps.loadPropsOnServer;
const ReactDom = require('react-dom/server');
const Router = require('react-router');
const routesConfig = require('./src/routesConfig');

const app = new Express();
const server = new http.Server(app);

const proxy = httpProxy.createProxyServer({
  target: 'http://localhost:3001'
});

app.set('view engine', 'ejs');
app.use('/dist', Express.static('dist'));
app.use('/api', (req, res) => {
  proxy.web(req, res, {target: targetUrl});
});

app.get('*', (req, res) => {
  Router.match({routes: routesConfig, location: req.url}, (error,
    redirectLocation, renderProps) => {
    if (error) {
      res.status(500).send(error.message)
    } else if (redirectLocation) {
      res.redirect(302, redirectLocation.pathname +
        redirectLocation.search)
    } else if (renderProps) {
      loadPropsOnServer(renderProps, {}, (err, asyncProps, scriptTag) => {
        const markup = ReactDom.renderToString(<AsyncProps {...renderProps}
          {...asyncProps} />);
        res.render('index', {markup, scriptTag});
      });
    } else {
      res.status(404).send('Not found')
    }
  });
});

server.listen(3000, (err) => {
  if (err) {
    return console.error(err);
  }
  console.info('WebServer running on http://localhost:3000');
});
```

Let's analyze one-by-one the changes from the previous version:

- First of all, we need to import some new modules: `http-proxy` and `async-props`.
- We initialize the `proxy` instance and we add it to our web server through middleware mapped to the requests that matches `/api`.
- We change the server-side rendering logic a bit. This time, we cannot directly call the `renderToString` function because we must ensure that all the asynchronous data has been loaded. The `async-props` module offers the function `loadPropsOnServer` to serve this purpose. This function executes all the necessary logic to load the data from the currently matched component asynchronously. When the loading finishes, a callback function is called, and only within this function is it safe to call the `renderToString` method. Also notice that, this time, we are rendering the `AsyncProps` component instead of `RouterContext`, passing it a set of synchronous and asynchronous attributes with the JSX-spread syntax. Another very important detail is that, in the callback, we are also receiving an argument called `scriptTag`. This variable will contain some JavaScript code that needs to be placed in the HTML code. This code will contain a representation of the asynchronous data loaded during the server-side rendering process, so that the browser will be able to directly access this data and will not need to make a duplicated API request. To put this script in the resulting HTML code, we pass it to the view along with the markup obtained from the component rendering process.

Our `views/index.ejs` template was also slightly modified to display the `scriptTag` variable we just mentioned:

```
<!DOCTYPE html>
<html>
  <head>
    <meta charset="utf-8"/>
    <title>React Example - Authors archive</title>
  </head>
  <body>
    <div id="main"><%- markup %></div>
    <script src="/dist/bundle.js"></script>
    <%- scriptTag %>
  </body>
</html>
```

As you can see, we are adding the `scriptTag` before closing the body of the page.

Now we are almost ready to execute this example; we just need to regenerate our bundle with Webpack and to start the web server with:

```
babel-cli server.js
```

Finally, you can open your browser and point it to `http://localhost:3000`. Again, everything will look the same, but what happens under the hood is now completely different. Open your inspector or debugger on the browser and try to figure out when an API request is made by the browser. You can also check the console where you started the API server and read the logs to understand who is requesting the data and when.

Summary

In this chapter, we explored the innovative and fast-moving world of Universal JavaScript. Universal JavaScript just opened up a lot of new opportunities in the field of web development, but it is still quite a fresh and immature field.

In this chapter, we focused on introducing all the basics of this subject, discussing topics such as component-oriented user interfaces, universal rendering, universal routing, and universal data retrieval. Throughout the process, we built a very simple application that demonstrates how to combine together all these concepts. We also added to our belt a new chain of powerful tools and libraries, such as Webpack and React.

Even though we discussed a lot of topics, we barely scratched the surface of this wide topic, and you should have gained all the necessary knowledge to keep exploring this world on your own if you are interested in knowing more. Given this immaturity, tools and libraries will probably change a lot in the next few years, but all the basic concepts should stay as they are, so don't be ashamed to keep exploring and experimenting. To become an expert on this topic is now just a matter of using the acquired knowledge to build a first real-world app with real, business-driven use cases.

It's also worth underlining that the knowledge acquired here might be useful for projects that cross the boundaries of web development, like mobile app development. If you are interested in this topic, React Native might be a good starting point.

In the next chapter, we are going to strengthen our knowledge of asynchronous design patterns and address some specific scenarios such as asynchronously initialized modules and asynchronous batching and caching. Are you ready for some more advanced and exciting topics?

9
Advanced Asynchronous Recipes

Almost all the design patterns we've seen so far can be considered generic and applicable to many different areas of an application. There is, however, a set of patterns that are more specific and focused on solving well-defined problems; we can call these patterns *recipes*. As in real-life cooking, we have a set of well-defined steps to follow that will lead us to an expected outcome. Of course, this doesn't mean that we can't use some creativity to customize the recipes to match the taste of our guests, but the outline of the procedure is usually the one that matters. In this chapter, we are going to provide some popular recipes to solve some specific problems we encounter in our everyday Node.js development. These recipes include the following:

- Requiring modules that are initialized asynchronously
- Batching and caching asynchronous operations to get a performance boost in busy applications, using only minimal development effort
- Running synchronous CPU-bound operations that can block the event loop and cripple the ability of Node.js to handle concurrent requests

Requiring asynchronously initialized modules

In `Chapter 2`, *Node.js Essential Patterns*, when we discussed the fundamental properties of the Node.js module system, we mentioned the fact that `require()` works synchronously and that `module.exports` cannot be set asynchronously.

This is one of the main reasons for the existence of synchronous API in the core modules and many npm packages, they are provided more as a convenient alternative, to be used primarily for initialization tasks rather than a substitute for asynchronous API.

Unfortunately, this is not always possible; a synchronous API might not always be available, especially for components using the network during their initialization phase, for example, to perform handshake protocols or to retrieve configuration parameters. This is the case for many database drivers and clients for middleware systems such as message queues.

Canonical solutions

Let's take an example: a module called db, which connects to a remote database. The db module will be able to accept requests only after the connection and the handshake with the server have been completed. In this scenario, we usually have two options:

- Making sure that the module is initialized before starting to use it, otherwise wait for its initialization. This process has to be done every time we want to invoke an operation on the asynchronous module:

```
const db = require('aDb'); //The async module

module.exports = function findAll(type, callback) {
  if(db.connected) {  //is it initialized?
    runFind();
  } else {
    db.once('connected', runFind);
  }
  function runFind() {
    db.findAll(type, callback);
  });
};
```

- Use **Dependency Injection** (**DI**) instead of directly requiring the asynchronous module. By doing this, we can delay the initialization of some modules until their asynchronous dependencies are fully initialized. This technique shifts the complexity of managing the module initialization to another component, usually the parent module. In the following example, this component is app.js:

```
//in the module app.js
const db = require('aDb'); //The async module
const findAllFactory = require('./findAll');
db.on('connected', function() {
  const findAll = findAllFactory(db);
```

```
    });

    //in the module findAll.js
    module.exports = db => {
      //db is guaranteed to be initialized
      return function findAll(type, callback) {
        db.findAll(type, callback);
      }
    }
```

We can immediately see that the first option can become highly undesirable, considering the amount of boilerplate code involved.

Also, the second option, which uses DI, is sometimes undesirable, as we have seen in Chapter 7, *Wiring Modules*. In big projects, it can quickly become over-complicated, especially if done manually and with asynchronously initialized modules. These problems would be mitigated if we were using a DI container designed to support asynchronously initialized modules.

As we will see, though, there is a third alternative that allows us to easily isolate the module from the initialization state of its dependencies.

Preinitialization queues

A simple pattern to decouple a module from the initialization state of a dependency involves the use of queues and the Command pattern. The idea is to save all the operations received by a module while it's not yet initialized and then execute them as soon as all the initialization steps have been completed.

Implementing a module that initializes asynchronously

To demonstrate this simple but effective technique, let's build a small test application; nothing fancy, just something to verify our assumptions. Let's start by creating an asynchronously initialized module called `asyncModule.js`:

```
const asyncModule = module.exports;

asyncModule.initialized = false;

asyncModule.initialize = callback => {
  setTimeout(function() {
    asyncModule.initialized = true;
    callback();
```

```
  }, 10000);
};

asyncModule.tellMeSomething = callback => {
  process.nextTick(() => {
    if(!asyncModule.initialized) {
      return callback(
        new Error('I don't have anything to say right now')
      );
    }
    callback(null, 'Current time is: ' + new Date());
  });
};
```

In the preceding code, `asyncModule` tries to demonstrate how an asynchronously initialized module works. It exposes an `initialize()` method, which after a delay of 10 seconds, sets the `initialized` variable to `true` and notifies its callback (10 seconds is a lot for a real application, but for us it's great for highlighting any race conditions). The other method, `tellMeSomething()`, returns the current time, but if the module is not yet initialized, it generates an error.

The next step is to create another module depending on the service we just created. Let's consider a simple HTTP request handler implemented in a file called `routes.js`:

```
const asyncModule = require('./asyncModule');

module.exports.say = (req, res) => {
  asyncModule.tellMeSomething((err, something) => {
    if(err) {
      res.writeHead(500);
      return res.end('Error:' + err.message);
    }
    res.writeHead(200);
    res.end('I say: ' + something);
  });
};
```

The handler invokes the `tellMeSomething()` method of `asyncModule`, then it writes the result into an HTTP response. As we can see, we are not performing any checks on the initialization state of `asyncModule`, and as we can imagine, this will likely lead to problems.

Now, let's create a very basic HTTP server using nothing but the core `http` module (the `app.js` file):

```
const http = require('http');
const routes = require('./routes');
const asyncModule = require('./asyncModule');

asyncModule.initialize(() => {
  console.log('Async module initialized');
});

http.createServer((req, res) => {
  if (req.method === 'GET' && req.url === '/say') {
    return routes.say(req, res);
  }
  res.writeHead(404);
  res.end('Not found');
}).listen(8000, () => console.log('Started'));
```

The preceding small module is the entry point of our application, and all it does is trigger the initialization of `asyncModule` and create an HTTP server that makes use of the request handler we created previously (`routes.say()`).

We can now try to fire up our server by executing the `app.js` module as usual. After the server is started, we can try to hit the URL, `http://localhost:8000/say`, with a browser and see what comes back from our `asyncModule`.

As expected, if we send the request just after the server is started, the result will be an error as follows:

```
Error:I don't have anything to say right now
```

This means that `asyncModule` is not yet initialized, but we still tried to use it. Depending on the implementation details of the asynchronously initialized module, we could have received a graceful error, lost important information, or even crashed the entire application. In general, the situation we just described has to always be avoided. Most of the time, a few failing requests might not be a concern or the initialization might be so fast that, in practice, it would never happen; however, for high load applications and cloud servers designed to *autoscale*, both of these assumptions might quickly get obliterated.

Wrapping the module with preinitialization queues

To add robustness to our server, we are now going to refactor it by applying the pattern we described at the beginning of the section. We will queue any operations invoked on `asyncModule` during the time it's not yet initialized and then flush the queue as soon we are ready to process them. This looks like a great application for the State pattern! We will need two states, one that queues all the operations while the module is not yet initialized, and another that simply delegates each method to the original `asyncModule` module, when the initialization is complete.

Often, we don't have the chance to modify the code of the asynchronous module; so, to add our queuing layer, we will need to create a proxy around the original `asyncModule` module.

Let's start to work on the code; let's create a new file named `asyncModuleWrapper.js` and let's start building it piece-by-piece. The first thing that we need to do is to create the object that delegates the operations to the active state:

```
const asyncModule = require('./asyncModule');

const asyncModuleWrapper = module.exports;

asyncModuleWrapper.initialized = false;
asyncModuleWrapper.initialize = () => {
  activeState.initialize.apply(activeState, arguments);
};

asyncModuleWrapper.tellMeSomething = () => {
  activeState.tellMeSomething.apply(activeState, arguments);
};
```

In the preceding code, `asyncModuleWrapper` simply delegates each of its methods to the currently active state. Let's see then what the two states look like, starting from `notInitializedState`:

```
const pending = [];
const notInitializedState = {

  initialize: function(callback) {
    asyncModule.initialize(() => {
      asyncModuleWrapper.initalized = true;
      activeState = initializedState;                 //[1]

      pending.forEach(req => {                         //[2]
        asyncModule[req.method].apply(null, req.args);
      });
```

```
      pending = [];

      callback();                                          //[3]
    });
  },

  tellMeSomething: callback => {
    return pending.push({
      method: 'tellMeSomething',
      args: arguments
    });
  }
};
```

When the `initialize()` method is invoked, we trigger the initialization of the original `asyncModule` module, providing a callback proxy. This allows our wrapper to know when the original module is initialized and consequently triggers the following operations:

1. Updates the `activeState` variable with the next state object in our flow—`initializedState`.
2. Executes all the commands that were previously stored in the `pending` queue.
3. Invokes the original callback.

As the module at this point is not yet initialized, the `tellMeSomething()` method of this state simply creates a new Command object and adds it to the queue of the `pending` operations.

At this point, the pattern should already be clear when the original `asyncModule` module is not yet initialized, our wrapper will simply queue all the received requests. Then, when we are notified that the initialization is complete, we execute all the queued operations and then switch the internal state to `initializedState`. Let's see then, what this last piece of the wrapper looks like:

```
let initializedState = asyncModule;
```

Without (probably) any surprise, the `initializedState` object is simply a reference to the original `asyncModule`! In fact, when the initialization is complete, we can safely route any request directly to the original module. Nothing more is required.

At last, we have to set the initial active state, which of course will be `notInitializedState`:

```
let activeState = notInitializedState;
```

We can now try to launch our test server again, but first, let's not forget to replace the references to the original `asyncModule` module with our new `asyncModuleWrapper` object; this has to be done in the `app.js` and `routes.js` modules.

After doing this, if we try to send a request to the server again, we will see that during the time the `asyncModule` module is not yet initialized, the requests will not fail; instead, they will hang until the initialization is completed and will only then be actually executed. We can surely affirm that this is a much more robust behavior.

Pattern

If a module is initialized asynchronously, queue every operation until the module is fully initialized.

Now, our server can start accepting requests immediately after it's started and it guarantees that none of these requests will ever fail because of the initialization state of its modules. We were able to obtain this result without using DI or requiring verbose and error-prone checks to verify the state of the asynchronous module.

In the wild

The pattern we just presented is used by many database drivers and ORM libraries. The most notable is Mongoose (`http://mongoosejs.com`), which is an ORM for **MongoDB**. With Mongoose, it's not necessary to wait for the database connection to open in order to be able to send queries, because each operation is queued and then executed later when the connection with the database is fully established. This clearly boosts the usability of its API.

Take a look at the code of Mongoose to see how every method in the native driver is proxied to add the preinitialization queue (it also demonstrates an alternative way of implementing this pattern). You can find the code fragment responsible for implementing the pattern at `https://github.com/LearnBoost/mongoose/blob/21f16c62e2f3230fe616745a40f22b4385a11b11/lib/drivers/node-mongodb-native/collection.js#L103-138`.

Asynchronous batching and caching

In high-load applications, **caching** plays a critical role and is used almost everywhere in the web, from static resources such as web pages, images, and stylesheets, to pure data such as the result of database queries. In this section, we are going to learn how caching applies to asynchronous operations and how a high request throughput can be turned to our advantage.

Implementing a server with no caching or batching

Before we start diving into this new challenge, let's implement a small demo server that we will use as a reference to measure the impact of the various techniques we are going to implement.

Let's consider a web server that manages the sales of an e-commerce company, in particular, we want to query our server for the sum of all the transactions of a particular type of merchandise. For this purpose, we are going to use LevelUP again for its simplicity and flexibility. The data model that we are going to use is a simple list of transactions stored in the `sales` sublevel (a section of the database), which is organized in the following format:

```
transactionId {amount, item}
```

The key is represented by `transactionId` and the value is a JSON object that contains the amount of the sale (`amount`) and the `item` type.

The data to process is really basic, so let's implement the API immediately in a file named `totalSales.js`, which will be as follows:

```
const level = require('level');
const sublevel = require('level-sublevel');
const db = sublevel(level('example-db', {valueEncoding: 'json'}));
const salesDb = db.sublevel('sales');

module.exports = function totalSales(item, callback) {
  console.log('totalSales() invoked');
  let sum = 0;
  salesDb.createValueStream()              // [1]
    .on('data', data => {
      if(!item || data.item === item) {   // [2]
        sum += data.amount;
      }
    })
```

```
      .on('end', () => {
        callback(null, sum);                    // [3]
      });
};
```

The core of the module is the `totalSales` function, which is also the only exported API; this is how it works:

1. We create a stream from the `salesDb` sublevel that contains the sales transactions. The stream pulls all the entries from the database.
2. The `data` event receives each sale transaction as it is returned from the database stream. We add the `amount` value of the current entry to the total `sum` value, but only if the `item` type is equal to the one provided in the input (or if no input is provided at all, allowing us to calculate the sum of all the transactions, regardless of the `item` type).
3. At last, when the `end` event is received, we invoke the `callback()` method by providing the final `sum` as result.

The simple query that we built is definitely not the best in terms of performance. Ideally, in a real-world application, we would have used an index to query the transactions by the `item` type, or even better, an incremental map/reduce to calculate the sum in real time; however, for our example, a slow query is actually better as it will highlight the advantages of the patterns we are going to analyze.

To finalize the *total sales* application, we only need to expose the `totalSales` API from an HTTP server; so, the next step is to build one (the `app.js` file):

```
const http = require('http');
const url = require('url');
const totalSales = require('./totalSales');

http.createServer((req, res) => {
  const query = url.parse(req.url, true).query;
  totalSales(query.item, (err, sum) => {
    res.writeHead(200);
    res.end(`Total sales for item ${query.item} is ${sum}`);
  });
}).listen(8000, () => console.log('Started'));
```

The server we created is very minimalistic; we only need it to expose the `totalSales` API.

Before we start the server for the first time, we need to populate the database with some sample data; we can do this with the `populate_db.js` script that is found in the code samples dedicated to this section. The script will create 100 K random sales transactions in the database.

Okay! Now, everything is ready. In order to start the server, as usual, we execute the following command:

```
node app
```

To query the server, simply navigate with a browser to the following URL:

```
http://localhost:8000?item=book
```

However, to have a better idea of the performance of our server, we will need more than one request; so, we will use a small script named `loadTest.js`, which sends requests at intervals of 200 ms. The script can be found in the code samples of the book and it's already configured to connect to the URL of the server, so, to run it, just execute the following command:

```
node loadTest
```

We will see that the 20 requests will take a while to complete; take note of the total execution time of the test, because we are now going to apply our optimizations and measure how much time we can save.

Asynchronous request batching

When dealing with asynchronous operations, the most basic level of caching can be achieved by **batching** together a set of invocations to the same API. The idea is very simple: if we are invoking an asynchronous function while there is still another one pending, we can attach callback to the already running operation, instead of creating a brand new request. Take a look at the following figure:

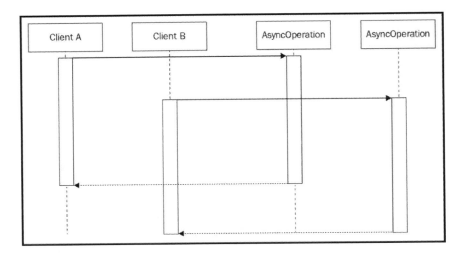

The previous image shows two clients (they can be two different objects, or two different web requests) invoking the same asynchronous operation with *exactly the same input*. Of course, the natural way to picture this situation is with the two clients starting two separate operations that will complete at two different moments, as shown by the preceding image. Now, consider the next scenario, depicted in the following figure:

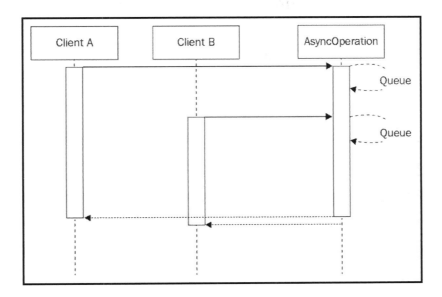

This second image shows us how the two requests—which invoke the same API with the same input—can be batched, or in other words, appended to the same running operation. By doing this, when the operation completes, both the clients will be notified. This represents a simple, yet extremely powerful, way to optimize the load of an application while not having to deal with more complex caching mechanisms, which usually require an adequate memory management and invalidation strategy.

Batching requests in the total sales web server

Let's now add a batching layer on top of our totalSales API. The pattern we are going to use is very simple: if there is already another identical request pending when the API is invoked, we will add the callback to a queue. When the asynchronous operation completes, all the callbacks in its queue are invoked at once.

Now, let's see how this pattern translates in code. Let's create a new module named totalSalesBatch.js. Here, we're going to implement a batching layer on top of the original totalSales API:

```
const totalSales = require('./totalSales');

const queues = {};
module.exports = function totalSalesBatch(item, callback) {
  if(queues[item]) {                              // [1]
```

```
      console.log('Batching operation');
      return queues[item].push(callback);
  }

  queues[item] = [callback];                              // [2]
  totalSales(item, (err, res) => {
    const queue = queues[item];                           // [3]
    queues[item] = null;
    queue.forEach(cb => cb(err, res));
  });
};
```

The `totalSalesBatch()` function is a proxy for the original `totalSales()` API, and it works as follows:

1. If a queue already exists for the `item` type provided as the input, it means that a request for that particular `item` is already running. In this case, all we have to do is simply append the `callback` to the existing queue and return from the invocation immediately. Nothing else is required.
2. If no queue is defined for the item, it means that we have to create a new request. To do this, we create a new queue for that particular `item` and we initialize it with the current `callback` function. Next, we invoke the original `totalSales()` API.
3. When the original `totalSales()` request completes, we iterate over all the callbacks that were added in the queue for that specific `item` and invoke them one by one with the result of the operation.

The behavior of the `totalSalesBatch()` function is identical to that of the original `totalSales()` API, with the difference that, now, multiple calls to the API using the same input are batched, thus saving time and resources.

Curious to know what the performance improvement compared to the raw, non-batched version of the `totalSales()` API is? Let's then replace the `totalSales` module used by the HTTP server with the one we just created (the `app.js` file):

```
//const totalSales = require('./totalSales');
const totalSales = require('./totalSalesBatch');

http.createServer(function(req, res) {
// ...
```

If we now try to start the server again and run the load test against it, the first thing we will see is that the requests are returned in *batches*. This is the effect of the pattern we just implemented and it's a great practical demonstration of how it works.

Besides that, we should also observe a considerable reduction in the total time for executing the test; it should be at least four times faster than the original test performed against the plain `totalSales()` API!

This is a stunning result, confirming the huge performance boost we can obtain by just applying a simple batching layer, without all the complexity of managing a full-fledged cache, and more importantly, without worrying about invalidation strategies.

 The request-batching pattern reaches its best potential in high-load applications and with slow APIs, because it's exactly in these circumstances that we can batch together a high number of requests.

Asynchronous request caching

One of the problems with the request-batching pattern is that the faster the API, the fewer batched requests we get. One can argue that if an API is already fast, there is no point in trying to optimize it; however, it still represents a factor in the resource load of an application that, when summed up, can still have a substantial impact. Also, sometimes we can safely assume that the result of an API invocation will not change so often; therefore, a simple request batching will not provide the best performance. In all these circumstances, the best candidate to reduce the load of an application and increase its responsiveness is definitely a more aggressive caching pattern.

The idea is simple: as soon as a request completes, we store its result in the cache, which can be a variable, an entry in the database, or in a specialized caching server. Hence, the next time the API is invoked, the result can be retrieved immediately from the cache, instead of spawning another request.

The idea of caching should not be new to an experienced developer, but what makes this pattern different in asynchronous programming is that it should be combined with the request batching, to be optimal. The reason is because multiple requests might run concurrently while the cache is not set, and when those requests complete, the cache will be set multiple times.

Based on these assumptions, the final structure of the asynchronous request-caching pattern is shown in the following figure:

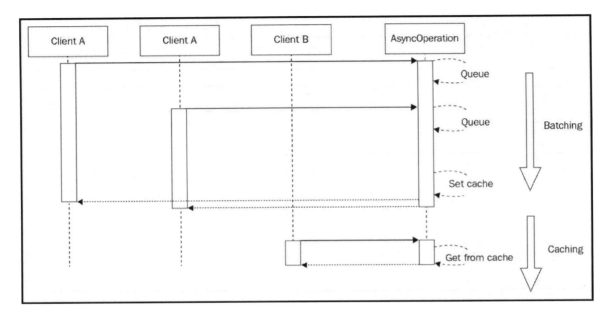

The preceding figure shows us the two phases of an optimal asynchronous caching algorithm:

- The first phase is totally identical to the batching pattern. Any request received while the cache is not set will be batched together. When the request completes, the cache is set, once.
- When the cache is finally set, any subsequent request will be served directly from it.

Another crucial detail to consider is the *unleashing Zalgo* anti-pattern (we have seen it in action in Chapter 2, *Node.js Essential Patterns*). As we are dealing with asynchronous APIs, we must be sure to always return the cached value asynchronously, even if accessing the cache involves only a synchronous operation.

Caching requests in the total sales web server

To demonstrate and measure the advantages of the asynchronous caching pattern, let's now apply what we've learned to the `totalSales()` API. As in the request-batching example, we have to create a proxy for the original API with the sole purpose of adding a caching layer.

Let's then create a new module named `totalSalesCache.js` that contains the following code:

```js
const totalSales = require('./totalSales');

const queues = {};
const cache = {};

module.exports = function totalSalesBatch(item, callback) {
  const cached = cache[item];
  if (cached) {
    console.log('Cache hit');
    return process.nextTick(callback.bind(null, null, cached));
  }

  if (queues[item]) {
    console.log('Batching operation');
    return queues[item].push(callback);
  }

  queues[item] = [callback];
  totalSales(item, (err, res) => {
    if (!err) {
      cache[item] = res;
      setTimeout(() => {
        delete cache[item];
      }, 30 * 1000); //30 seconds expiry
    }

    const queue = queues[item];
    queues[item] = null;
    queue.forEach(cb => cb(err, res));
  });
};
```

We should straight away see that the preceding code is in many parts identical to what we used for the asynchronous batching. In fact, the only differences are the following ones:

- The first thing that we need to do when the API is invoked is to check whether the cache is set and if that's the case, we will immediately return the cached value using `callback()`, making sure to defer it with `process.nextTick()`.

- The execution continues in batching mode, but this time, when the original API successfully completes, we save the result into the cache. We also set a timeout to invalidate the cache after 30 seconds. A simple but effective technique!

Now, we are ready to try the `totalSales` wrapper we just created; to do that, we only need to update the `app.js` module as follows:

```
//const totalSales = require('./totalSales');
//const totalSales = require('./totalSalesBatch');
const totalSales = require('./totalSalesCache');

http.createServer(function(req, res) {
  // ...
```

Now, the server can be started again and profiled using the `loadTest.js` script as we did in the previous examples. With the default test parameters, we should see a 10% reduction in the execution time as compared to simple batching. Of course, this is highly dependent on a lot of factors; for example, the number of requests received, and the delay between one request and the other. The advantages of using caching over batching will be much more substantial when the amount of requests is higher and spans a longer period of time.

 Memoization is the practice of caching the result of a function invocation. In npm, you can find many packages to implement asynchronous memoization with little effort; one of the most complete packages is memoizee (`https://npmjs.org/package/memoizee`).

Notes about implementing caching mechanisms

We must remember that in real-life applications, we might want to use more advanced invalidation techniques and storage mechanisms. This might be necessary for the following reasons:

- A large amount of cached values might easily consume a lot of memory. In this case, a **Least Recently Used (LRU)** algorithm can be applied to maintain constant memory utilization.

- When the application is distributed across multiple processes, using a simple variable for the cache might result in different results to be returned by each server instance. If that's undesired for the particular application we are implementing, the solution is to use a shared store for the cache. Popular solutions are Redis (`http://redis.io`) and Memcached (`http://memcached.org`).
- A manual cache invalidation, as opposed to a timed expiry, can enable a longer-living cache and at the same time provide more up-to-date data, but, of course, it would be a lot more complex to manage.

Batching and caching with promises

In `Chapter 4`, *Asynchronous Control Flow Patterns with ES2015 and Beyond,* we saw how promises can greatly simplify our asynchronous code, but they offer an even more interesting application when dealing with batching and caching. If we recall what we said about promises, there are two properties that can be exploited to our advantage in this circumstance:

- Multiple `then()` listeners can be attached to the same promise.
- The `then()` listener is guaranteed to be invoked at most once, and it works even if it's attached after the promise is already resolved. Moreover, `then()` is guaranteed to be invoked asynchronously, *always.*

In short, the first property is exactly what we need for batching requests, while the second means that a promise is already a cache for the resolved value and offers a natural mechanism for returning a cached value in a consistent asynchronous way. In other words, this means that batching and caching are extremely simple and concise with promises.

To demonstrate this, we can try to create a wrapper for the `totalSales()` API, using promises, and see what it takes to add a batching and caching layer. Let's see then what this looks like. Let's create a new module named `totalSalesPromises.js`:

```
const pify = require('pify');                    // [1]
const totalSales = pify(require('./totalSales'));

const cache = {};
module.exports = function totalSalesPromises(item) {
  if (cache[item]) {                             // [2]
    return cache[item];
  }

  cache[item] = totalSales(item)                 // [3]
```

```
      .then(res => {                                // [4]
        setTimeout(() => {delete cache[item]}, 30 * 1000); //30s expiry
        return res;
      })
      .catch(err => {                               // [5]
        delete cache[item];
        throw err;
      });
    return cache[item];                             // [6]
};
```

The first thing that strikes us is the simplicity and elegance of the solution we implemented in the preceding code. Promises are indeed a great tool, but for this particular application they offer a huge, out-of-the-box advantage. This is what happens in the preceding code:

1. First, we require a small module called pify (https://www.npmjs.com/packag e/pify) that allows us to apply a *promisification* to the original totalSales(). After doing this, totalSales() will return a ES2015 promise instead of accepting a callback.

2. When the totalSalesPromises() wrapper is invoked, we check whether a cached promise already exists for the given item type. If we already have such a promise, we return it back to the caller.

3. If we don't have a promise in the cache for the given item type, we proceed to create one by invoking the original (promisified) totalSales() API.

4. When the promise resolves, we set up a time to clear the cache (after 30 seconds) and we return res to propagate the result of the operation to any other then() listener attached to the promise.

5. If the promise rejects with an error, we immediately reset the cache and throw the error again to propagate it to the promise chain, so any other listener attached to the same promise will receive the error as well.

6. At last, we return the cached promise we just created.

Very simple and intuitive, and more importantly, we were able to achieve both batching and caching.

If we now want to try the totalSalesPromise() function, we will have to slightly adapt the app.js module as well, because now, the API is using promises instead of callbacks. Let's do it by creating a modified version of the app module named appPromises.js:

```
const http = require('http');
const url = require('url');
const totalSales = require('./totalSalesPromises');
```

```
http.createServer(function(req, res) {
  const query = url.parse(req.url, true).query;
  totalSales(query.item).then(function(sum) {
    res.writeHead(200);
    res.end(`Total sales for item ${query.item} is ${sum}`);
  });
}).listen(8000, () => console.log('Started'));
```

Its implementation is almost identical to the original `app` module, with the difference that now we use the promise-based version of the batching/caching wrapper; therefore, the way we invoke it is also slightly different.

That's it! We are now ready to try this new version of the server by running the following command:

```
node appPromises
```

Using the `loadTest` script, we can verify that the new implementation is working as expected. The execution time should be the same as when we tested the server using the `totalSalesCache()` API.

Running CPU-bound tasks

The `totalSales()` API, even though expensive in terms of resources, was not affecting the ability of the server to accept concurrent requests. What we learned about the event loop in `Chapter 1`, *Welcome to the Node.js Platform*, should provide an explanation for this behavior: invoking an asynchronous operation causes the stack to unwind back to the event loop, leaving it free to handle other requests.

However, what happens when we run a long, synchronous task that never gives back the control to the event loop? This kind of task is also known as CPU-bound, because its main characteristic is that it is heavy on CPU utilization rather than being heavy on I/O operations.

Let's work immediately on an example to see how these types of task behave in Node.js.

Solving the subset sum problem

Let's now choose a computationally expensive problem to use as a base for our experiment. A good candidate is the subset sum problem that consists of deciding whether a set (or multiset) of integers contains a non-empty subset that has a sum equal to zero. For example, if we had as input the set [1, 2, -4, 5, -3], the subsets satisfying the problem are [1, 2, -3] and [2, -4, 5, -3].

The simplest algorithm is the one that checks every possible combination of subsets of any size, and it has a computational cost of $O(2^n)$, or in other words, it grows exponentially with the size of the input. This means that a set of 20 integers would require up to 1,048,576 combinations to be checked, not bad for testing our assumptions. Of course, the solution might be found a lot sooner than that; so, to make things harder, we are going to consider the following variation of the subset sum problem: given a set of integers, we want to calculate all the possible combinations whose sum is equal to a given arbitrary integer.

Let's then work to build such an algorithm; let's create a new module called `subsetSum.js`. We will start by creating a class called `SubsetSum`:

```
const EventEmitter = require('events').EventEmitter;

class SubsetSum extends EventEmitter {
  constructor(sum, set) {
    super();
    this.sum = sum;
    this.set = set;
    this.totalSubsets = 0;
  }
//...
```

The `SubsetSum` class is extending from the `EventEmitter` class; this allows us to produce an event every time we find a new subset matching the sum received as input. As we will see, this will give us a lot of flexibility.

Next, let's see how we can generate all the possible combinations of subsets:

```
_combine(set, subset) {
  for(let i = 0; i < set.length; i++) {
    let newSubset = subset.concat(set[i]);
    this._combine(set.slice(i + 1), newSubset);
    this._processSubset(newSubset);
  }
}
```

We will not go into too much detail about the algorithm, but there are two important things to notice:

- The `_combine()` method is completely synchronous; it recursively generates every possible subset without ever giving back the control to the event loop. If we think about it, this is perfectly normal for an algorithm not requiring any I/O.
- Every time a new combination is generated, we provide it to the `_processSubset()` method for further processing.

The `_processSubset()` method is responsible for verifying that the sum of the elements of the given subset is equal to the number we are looking for:

```
_processSubset(subset) {
  console.log('Subset', ++this.totalSubsets, subset);
  const res = subset.reduce((prev, item) => (prev + item), 0);
  if(res == this.sum) {
    this.emit('match', subset);
  }
}
```

Trivially, the `_processSubset()` method applies a `reduce` operation to the subset in order to calculate the sum of its elements. Then, it emits an event of type `'match'` when the resulting sum is equal to the one we are interested in finding (`this.sum`).

Finally, the `start()` method puts all the preceding pieces together:

```
start() {
  this._combine(this.set, []);
  this.emit('end');
}
```

The preceding method triggers the generation of all the combinations by invoking `_combine()`, and lastly, emits an `'end'` event signaling that all the combinations were checked and any possible match has already been emitted. This is possible because `_combine()` is synchronous; therefore, the `'end'` event will be emitted as soon as the function returns, which means that all the combinations were calculated.

Next, we have to expose the algorithm we just created over the network, as always we can use a simple HTTP server for the task. In particular, we want to create an endpoint in the format `/subsetSum?data=<Array>&sum=<Integer>` that invokes the `SubsetSum` algorithm with the given array of integers and sum to match.

Let's then implement this simple server in a module named `app.js`:

```
const http = require('http');
const SubsetSum = require('./subsetSum');

http.createServer((req, res) => {
  const url = require('url').parse(req.url, true);
  if(url.pathname === '/subsetSum') {
    const data = JSON.parse(url.query.data);
    res.writeHead(200);
    const subsetSum = new SubsetSum(url.query.sum, data);
    subsetSum.on('match', match => {
      res.write('Match: ' + JSON.stringify(match) + '\n');
    });
    subsetSum.on('end', () => res.end());
    subsetSum.start();
  } else {
    res.writeHead(200);
    res.end('I\m alive!\n');
  }
}).listen(8000, () => console.log('Started'));
```

Thanks to the fact that the `SubsetSum` object returns its results using events, we can stream the matching subsets as soon as they are generated by the algorithm, in real time. Another detail to mention is that our server responds with the text `I'm Alive!` every time we hit a URL different from `/subsetSum`. We will use this for checking the responsiveness of our server, as we will see in a moment.

We are now ready to try our subset sum algorithm. Curious to know how our server will handle it? Let's fire it up then:

```
node app
```

As soon as the server starts, we are ready to send our first request; let's try with a set of 17 random numbers, which will result in the generation of 131,071 combinations, a nice amount to keep our server busy for a while:

```
curl -G http://localhost:8000/subsetSum --data-urlencode "data=[116,
119,101,101,-116,109,101,-105,-102,117,-115,-97,119,-116,-104,-105,115]" --
data-urlencode "sum=0"
```

We will start to see the results streaming live from the server, but if we try the following command in another terminal while the first request is still running, we will spot a huge problem:

```
curl -G http://localhost:8000
```

We will immediately see that this last request hangs until the subset sum algorithm of the first request has finished; the server is unresponsive! This was kind of what we expected. The Node.js event loop runs in a single thread, and if this thread is blocked by a long synchronous computation, it will be unable to execute even one more cycle in order to respond with a simple `I'm alive!`

We quickly understand that this behavior does not work for any kind of application meant to *serve multiple requests*. But don't despair in Node.js, we can tackle this type of situation in several ways. Let's analyze the two most important ones.

Interleaving with setImmediate

Usually, a CPU-bound algorithm is built upon a set of steps. It can be a set of recursive invocations, a loop, or any variation/combination of those. So, a simple solution to our problem would be to give back the control to the event loop after each one of these steps completes (or after a certain number of them). This way, any pending I/O can still be processed by the event loop in those intervals where the long-running algorithm yields the CPU. A simple way to achieve this is to schedule the next step of the algorithm to run after any pending I/O requests. This sounds like the perfect use case for the `setImmediate()` function (we already introduced this API in `Chapter 2, Node.js Essential Patterns`).

Pattern

Interleave the execution of a long-running synchronous task with `setImmediate()`.

Interleaving the steps of the subset sum algorithm

Let's now see how this pattern applies to the subset sum algorithm. All we have to do is slightly modify the `subsetSum.js` module. For convenience, we are going to create a new module called `subsetSumDefer.js`, taking the code of the original `subsetSum` class as a starting point.

The first change we are going to make is to add a new method called `_combineInterleaved()`, which is the core of the pattern we are implementing:

```
_combineInterleaved(set, subset) {
  this.runningCombine++;
  setImmediate(() => {
    this._combine(set, subset);
    if(--this.runningCombine === 0) {
```

```
      this.emit('end');
    }
  });
}
```

As we can see, all we had to do is defer the invocation of the original (synchronous) _combine() method with setImmediate(). However, now it becomes more difficult to know when the function has finished generating all the combinations because the algorithm is not synchronous anymore. To fix this, we have to keep track of all the running instances of the _combine() method using a pattern very similar to the asynchronous parallel execution we have seen in Chapter 3, *Asynchronous Control Flow Patterns with Callbacks*. When all the instances of the _combine() method have finished running, we can emit the end event notifying any listener that the process has completed.

To finalize the refactoring of the subset sum algorithm, we need a couple more tweaks. First, we need to replace the recursive step in the _combine() method with its deferred counterpart:

```
_combine(set, subset) {
  for(let i = 0; i < set.length; i++) {
    let newSubset = subset.concat(set[i]);
    this._combineInterleaved(set.slice(i + 1), newSubset);
    this._processSubset(newSubset);
  }
}
```

With the preceding change, we make sure that each step of the algorithm will be queued in the event loop using setImmediate() and therefore executed after any pending I/O request instead of running synchronously.

The other small tweak is in the start() method:

```
start() {
  this.runningCombine = 0;
  this._combineInterleaved(this.set, []);
}
```

In the preceding code, we initialize the number of running instances of the _combine() method to 0. We also replaced the call to _combine() with a call to _combineInterleaved() and removed the emission of the 'end' event, because now this is handled asynchronously in _combineInterleaved().

With this last change, our subset sum algorithm should now be able to run its CPU-bound code in steps interleaved by intervals where the event loop can run and process any other pending request.

The last missing bit is updating the `app.js` module so that it can use the new version of the SubsetSum API. This is actually a trivial change:

```
const http = require('http');
//const SubsetSum = require('./subsetSum');
const SubsetSum = require('./subsetSumDefer');

http.createServer(function(req, res) {
  // ...
```

We are now ready to try this new version of the subset sum server. Let's start the `app` module by using the following command:

```
node app
```

Then, try to send a request again to calculate all the subsets matching a given sum:

```
curl -G http://localhost:8000/subsetSum --data-urlencode "data=[116,
119,101,101,-116,109,101,-105,-102,117,-115,-97,119,-116,-104,-105,115]" --
data-urlencode "sum=0"
```

While the request is running, we might now want to see whether the server is responsive:

```
curl -G http://localhost:8000
```

Cool! The second request now should return immediately, even while a SubsetSum task is running, confirming that our pattern is working well.

Considerations on the interleaving pattern

As we saw, running a CPU-bound task while preserving the responsiveness of an application is not that complicated, it just requires the use of `setImmediate()` to schedule the next step of an algorithm after any pending I/O. However, this is not the best pattern in terms of efficiency; in fact, deferring a task introduces a small overhead that, multiplied by all the steps that an algorithm has to run, can have a significant impact. This is usually the last thing we want when running a CPU-bound task, especially if we have to return the result directly to the user, which should happen in a reasonable amount of time. A possible solution to mitigate the problem would be using `setImmediate()` only after a certain number of steps—instead of using it at every single step—but still this would not solve the root of the problem.

Bear in mind that this does not mean that the pattern we have just seen should be avoided at all costs, in fact, if we look at the bigger picture, a synchronous task does not necessarily have to be extremely long and complex to create troubles. In a busy server, even a task that blocks the event loop for 200 milliseconds can create undesirable delays. In those situations where the task is executed sporadically or in the background and does not have to run for too long, using `setImmediate()` to interleave its execution is probably the simplest and most effective way to avoid blocking the event loop.

`process.nextTick()` cannot be used to interleave a long-running task. As we saw in Chapter 1, *Welcome to the Node.js Platform*, `nextTick()` schedules an operation before any pending I/O, and this can eventually cause I/O starvation in the case of repeated calls. You can verify that by yourself by replacing `setImmediate()` with `process.nextTick()` in the previous sample. You might also want to know that this behavior was introduced with Node.js 0.10; in fact, with Node.js 0.8, `process.nextTick()` can still be used as an interleaving mechanism. Take a look at this GitHub issue to know more about the history and motivations of this change at `https://github.com/joyent/node/issues/3335`.

Using multiple processes

Deferring the steps of an algorithm is not the only option we have for running CPU-bound tasks; another pattern for preventing the event loop from blocking is using **child processes**. We already know that Node.js gives its best when running I/O-intensive applications such as web servers, which allows us to optimize resource utilization thanks to its asynchronous architecture.

So, the best way we have to maintain the responsiveness of an application is to not run expensive CPU-bound tasks in the context of the main application and instead, use separate processes. This has three main advantages:

- The synchronous task can run at full speed, without the need to interleave the steps of its execution
- Working with processes in Node.js is simple, probably easier than modifying an algorithm to use `setImmediate()`, and allows us to easily *use multiple processors* without the need to scale the main application itself
- If we really need maximum performance, the external process might be created in lower-level languages, such as good old C (always use the best tool for the job!)

Node.js has an ample tool belt of APIs for interacting with external processes. We can find all we need in the `child_process` module. Moreover, when the external process is just another Node.js program, connecting it to the main application is extremely easy and we don't even feel like we are running something external to the local application. The magic happens thanks to the `child_process.fork()` function, which creates a new child Node.js process and also automatically creates a communication channel with it, allowing us to exchange information using an interface very similar to an `EventEmitter`. Let's see how this works by refactoring our subset sum server again.

Delegating the subset sum task to other processes

The goal for the refactoring of the `SubsetSum` task is to create a separate child process responsible for handling the synchronous processing, leaving the event loop of the server free to handle requests coming from the network. This is the recipe we are going to follow to make this possible:

1. We will create a new module named `processPool.js` that will allow us to create a pool of running processes. Starting a new process is expensive and requires time, so keeping them constantly running and ready to handle requests allows us to save time and CPU. Also, the pool will help us limit the number of processes running at the same time to avoid exposing the application to **denial-of-service (DoS)** attacks.

2. Next, we will create a module called `subsetSumFork.js` responsible for abstracting a `SubsetSum` task running in a child process. Its role will be communicating with the child process and exposing the results of the task as if they were coming from the current application.

3. At last, we need a **worker** (our child process), a new Node.js program with the only goal of running the subset sum algorithm and forwarding its results to the parent process.

A DoS attack is an attempt to make a machine or network resource unavailable to its intended users, such as to temporarily or indefinitely interrupt or suspend services of a host connected to the Internet.

Implementing a process pool

Let's start by building the `processPool.js` module piece by piece:

```
const fork = require('child_process').fork;

class ProcessPool {
  constructor(file, poolMax) {
    this.file = file;
    this.poolMax = poolMax;
    this.pool = [];
    this.active = [];
    this.waiting = [];
  }
  //...
```

In the first part of the module, we import the `child_process.fork()` function that we will use to create new processes. Then, we define the `ProcessPool` constructor that accepts a `file` parameter representing the Node.js program to run and the maximum number of running instances in the pool (`poolMax`). We then define three instance variables:

- `pool` is the set of running processes ready to be used
- `active` contains the list of the processes currently being used
- `waiting` contains a queue of callbacks for all those requests that could not be fulfilled immediately because of the lack of an available process

The next piece of the `ProcessPool` class is the `acquire()` method, which is responsible for returning a process ready to be used:

```
acquire(callback) {
  let worker;
  if(this.pool.length > 0) {                       // [1]
    worker = this.pool.pop();
    this.active.push(worker);
    return process.nextTick(callback.bind(null, null, worker));
  }

  if(this.active.length >= this.poolMax) {  // [2]
    return this.waiting.push(callback);
  }

  worker = fork(this.file);                        // [3]
  this.active.push(worker);
  process.nextTick(callback.bind(null, null, worker));
}
```

Its logic is very simple and is explained as follows:

1. If we have a process in `pool` ready to be used, we simply move it to the `active` list and then return it by invoking `callback` (in a deferred fashion... remember Zalgo?).
2. If there are no available processes in `pool` and we already have reached the maximum number of running processes, we have to wait for one to be available. We achieve this by queuing the current callback in the `waiting` list.
3. If we haven't yet reached the maximum number of running processes, we will create a new one using `child_process.fork()`, add it to the `active` list, and then return it to the caller using the `callback`.

The last method of the `ProcessPool` class is `release()`, whose purpose is to put a process back in `pool`:

```
release(worker) {
  if(this.waiting.length > 0) {                        // [1]
    const waitingCallback = this.waiting.shift();
    waitingCallback(null, worker);
  }
  this.active = this.active.filter(w => worker !==  w);  // [2]
  this.pool.push(worker);
}
```

The preceding code is also very simple and its explanation is as follows:

- If there is a request in the `waiting` list, we simply reassign the `worker` being released by passing it to the callback at the head of the `waiting` queue.
- Otherwise, we remove the worker from the `active` list and put it back into `pool`.

As we can see, the processes are never stopped but just reassigned, allowing us to save time by not restarting them at each request. However, it's important to observe that this might not always be the best choice and this greatly depends on the requirements of our application. Possible tweaks for reducing long-term memory usage and adding robustness to our process pool are as follows:

- Terminate idle processes to free memory after a certain time of inactivity
- Add a mechanism to kill non-responsive processes or restart those that have simply crashed

But in this example, we will keep the implementation of our process pool simple, as the details we might want to add are really endless.

Communicating with a child process

Now that our `ProcessPool` class is ready, we can use it to implement the `SubsetSumFork` wrapper whose role is to communicate with the worker and expose the results it produces. As we said, starting a process with `child_process.fork()` also gives us a simple message-based communication channel, so let's see how this works by implementing the `subsetSumFork.js` module:

```
const EventEmitter = require('events').EventEmitter;
const ProcessPool = require('./processPool');
const workers = new ProcessPool(__dirname + '/subsetSumWorker.js', 2);

class SubsetSumFork extends EventEmitter {
  constructor(sum, set) {
    super();
    this.sum = sum;
    this.set = set;
  }

  start() {
    workers.acquire((err, worker) => {              // [1]
      worker.send({sum: this.sum, set: this.set});

      const onMessage = msg => {
        if (msg.event === 'end') {                  // [3]
          worker.removeListener('message', onMessage);
          workers.release(worker);
        }

        this.emit(msg.event, msg.data);             // [4]
      };

      worker.on('message', onMessage);              // [2]
    });
  }
}
module.exports = SubsetSumFork;
```

The first thing to notice is that we initialized a `ProcessPool` object using a file named `subsetSumWorker.js` as the target which represents our child worker. We also set the maximum capacity of the pool to 2.

Another point worth mentioning is that we tried to maintain the same public API of the original SubsetSum class. In fact, SubsetSumFork is an EventEmitter whose constructor accepts sum and set, while the start() method triggers the execution of the algorithm, which runs on a separate process this time. This is what happens when the start() method is invoked:

1. We try to acquire a new child process from the pool. When this happens, we immediately use the worker handle to send the child process a message with the input of the job to run. The send() API is provided automatically by Node.js to all processes that start with child_process.fork(), this is essentially the communication channel that we were talking about.

2. We then start listening for any message returned from the worker process, using the on() method to attach a new listener (this is also a part of the communication channel provided by all processes that start with child_process.fork()).

3. In the listener, we first check whether we received an end event, which means that the SubsetSum task has finished, in which case we remove the onMessage listener and release the worker, putting it back into the pool.

4. The worker produces messages in the format {event, data} allowing us to seamlessly re-emit any event produced by the child process.

That's it for the SubsetSumFork wrapper; let's now implement the worker application.

 It is good to know that the send() method available on a child process instance can also be used to propagate a socket handle from the main application to a child process (look at the documentation at: http://nodejs.org/api/child_process.html#child_process_child_send_message_sendhandle). This is actually the technique used by the cluster module to distribute the load of an HTTP server across multiple processes (as of Node.js 0.10). We will see this in more detail in the next chapter.

Communicating with the parent process

Let's now create the subsetSumWorker.js module, our worker application, the entire content of this module will run in a separate process:

```
const SubsetSum = require('./subsetSum');

process.on('message', msg => {                      // [1]
  const subsetSum = new SubsetSum(msg.sum, msg.set);
```

```
    subsetSum.on('match', data => {                    // [2]
      process.send({event: 'match', data: data});
    });

    subsetSum.on('end', data => {
      process.send({event: 'end', data: data});
    });

    subsetSum.start();
  });
```

We can immediately see that we are reusing the original (and synchronous) SubsetSum as it is. Now that we are in a separate process, we don't have to worry about blocking the event loop anymore, all the HTTP requests will continue to be handled by the event loop of the main application, without disruptions.

When the worker is started as a child process, this is what happens:

1. It immediately starts listening for messages coming from the parent process. This can be easily done with the process.on() function (also, a part of the communication API provided when the process starts using child_process.fork()). The only message we expect from the parent process is the one providing the input to a new SubsetSum task. As soon as such a message is received, we create a new instance of a SubsetSum class and register the listeners for the match and end events. Lastly, we start the computation with subsetSum.start().

2. Every time an event is received from the running algorithm, we wrap it in an object with the format, {event, data}, and send it to the parent process. These messages are then handled in the subsetSumFork.js module, as we have seen in the previous section.

As we can see, we just had to wrap the algorithm we already built, without modifying its internals. This clearly shows that any portion of an application can be easily put in an external process by simply using the pattern we have just seen.

When the child process is not a Node.js program, the simple communication channel we just described is not available. In these situations, we can still establish an interface with the child process by implementing our own protocol on top of the standard input and standard output streams, which are exposed to the parent process.

To find out more about all the capabilities of the `child_process` API, you can refer to the official Node.js documentation at `http://nodejs.or g/api/child_process.html`.

Considerations on the multiprocess pattern

As always, to try this new version of the subset sum algorithm, we simply have to replace the module used by the HTTP server (file `app.js`):

```
const http = require('http');
//const SubsetSum = require('./subsetSum');
//const SubsetSum = require('./subsetSumDefer');
const SubsetSum = require('./subsetSumFork');
//...
```

We can now start the server again and try to send a sample request:

```
curl -G http://localhost:8000/subsetSum --data-urlencode
"data=[116,119,101,101,-116,109,101,-105,-102,117,-115,-97,119,-116,-104,-1
05,115]" --data-urlencode "sum=0"
```

Similar to the interleaving pattern we have seen before, with this new version of the `subsetSum` module the event loop is not blocked while running the CPU-bound task. This can be confirmed by sending another concurrent request as follows:

```
curl -G http://localhost:8000
```

The preceding command line should immediately return a string as follows:

```
I'm alive!
```

More interestingly, we can also try to start two `subsetSum` tasks concurrently, we can see that they will use the full power of two different processors in order to run (if our system has more than one processor, of course). Instead, if we try to run three `subsetSum` tasks concurrently, the result should be that the last one to start will hang. This is not because the event loop of the main process is blocked, but because we set a concurrency limit of two processes for the `subsetSum` task, which means that the third request will be handled as soon as at least one of the two processes in the pool becomes available again.

As we saw, the multiprocess pattern is definitely more powerful and flexible than the interleaving pattern; however, it's still not scalable as the amount of resources offered by a single machine is still a hard limit. The answer in this case is to distribute the load across multiple machines, but this is another story and falls under the category of distributed architectural patterns which we will explore in the next chapters.

> It is worth mentioning that threads can be a possible alternative to processes when running CPU-bound tasks. Currently, there are a few npm packages that expose an API for working with threads to userland modules; one of the most popular is `webworker-threads` (`https://npmjs.org/package/webworker-threads`). However, even if threads are more lightweight, fully-fledged processes can offer more flexibility and a better level of isolation in the case of problems such as freezing or crashing.

Summary

This chapter added some great new weapons to our tool belt, and as we can see, our journey is getting more focused on specific problems and we have started to delve deeply into more advanced solutions. Often, we reused some of the patterns we have analyzed in the previous chapters: State, Command, and Proxy to provide an effective abstraction for asynchronously initialized modules, asynchronous control flow patterns to add batching and caching to our APIs, deferred execution and events to help us run CPU-bound tasks.

This chapter gave us not only a set of recipes to reuse and customize for our needs, but also some great demonstrations of how mastering a few principles and patterns can help us tackle the most complex problems in Node.js development.

The next two chapters represent the peak of our journey. After studying the various tactics, we are now ready to move to the strategies, and explore the patterns for scaling and distributing our Node.js applications.

10
Scalability and Architectural Patterns

In its early days, Node.js was mainly a non-blocking web server; its original name was in fact *web.js*. Its creator, *Ryan Dahl*, soon realized the potential of the platform and started extending it with tools to enable the creation of any type of server-side application on top of the duo JavaScript/non-blocking paradigm. The characteristics of Node.js were perfect for the implementation of distributed systems, made of nodes orchestrating their operations through the network. Node.js was born to be distributed. Unlike other web platforms, the word scalability enters the vocabulary of a Node.js developer very early in the life of an application, mainly because of its single-threaded nature, incapable of exploiting all the resources of a machine, but often there are more profound reasons. As we will see in this chapter, scaling an application does not only mean increasing its capacity, enabling it to handle more requests faster; it's also a crucial path to achieving high availability and tolerance to errors. Amazingly, it can also be a way to split the complexity of an application into more manageable pieces. Scalability is a concept with multiple faces, six to be precise, as many as the faces of a cube—the *scale cube*.

In this chapter, we will learn the following topics:

- What the scale cube is
- How to scale by running multiple instances of the same application
- How to leverage a load balancer when scaling an application
- What a service registry is and how it can be used
- How to design a microservice architecture out of a monolithic application
- How to integrate a large number of services through the use of some simple architectural patterns

An introduction to application scaling

Before we dive into some practical patterns and examples, it is worth saying a few words about the reasons for scaling an application and how it can be achieved.

Scaling Node.js applications

We already know that most of the tasks of a typical Node.js application run in the context of a single thread. In `Chapter 1`, *Welcome to the Node.js Platform*, we learned that this is not really a limitation but rather an advantage, because it allows the application to optimize the usage of the resources necessary to handle concurrent requests, thanks to the non-blocking I/O paradigm. A single thread fully exploited by non-blocking I/O works wonderfully for applications handling a moderate number of requests per second, usually a few hundred per second (this greatly depends on the application). Assuming we are using commodity hardware, the capacity that a single thread can support is limited no matter how powerful a server can be, therefore, if we want to use Node.js for high-load applications, the only way is to *scale* it across multiple processes and machines.

However, workload is not the only reason to scale a Node.js application; in fact, with the same techniques, we can obtain other desirable properties such as **availability** and **tolerance to failures**. Scalability is also a concept applicable to the size and the complexity of an application; in fact, building architectures that can grow big is another important factor when designing software. JavaScript is a tool to be used with caution, the lack of type checking and its many *gotchas* can be an obstacle to the growth of an application, but with discipline and an accurate design, we can turn this into an advantage. With JavaScript, we are often pushed to keep the application simple and split it into manageable pieces, making it easier to scale and distribute.

The three dimensions of scalability

When talking about scalability, the first fundamental principle to understand is **load distribution**, the *science* of splitting the load of an application across several processes and machines. There are many ways to achieve this, and the book *The Art of Scalability* by *Martin L. Abbott* and *Michael T. Fisher* proposes an ingenious model to represent them, called the **scale cube**. This model describes scalability in terms of the following three dimensions:

- *x*-**axis**: Cloning
- *y*-**axis**: Decomposing by service/functionality
- *z*-**axis**: Splitting by data partition

These three dimensions can be represented as a cube, as shown in the following figure:

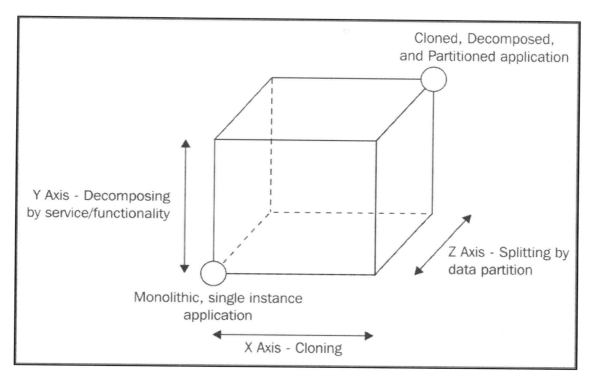

The bottom-left corner of the cube represents the applications having all their functionalities and services in a single codebase (monolithic applications) and running on a single instance. This is a common situation for applications handling small workloads or at the early stages of development.

The most intuitive evolution of a monolithic, unscaled application is moving right along the x– axis, which is simple, most of the time inexpensive (in terms of development cost), and highly effective. The principle behind this technique is elementary, that is, cloning the same application n times and letting each instance handle $1/n$th of the workload.

Scaling along the *y*-axis means decomposing the application based on its functionalities, services, or use cases. In this instance, *decomposing* means creating different, standalone applications, each with its own codebase, sometimes with its own dedicated database, or even with a separate UI. For example, a common situation is separating the part of an application responsible for the administration from the public-facing product. Another example is extracting the services responsible for user authentication, creating a dedicated authentication server. The criteria to split an application by its functionalities depend mostly on its business requirements, the use cases, the data, and many other factors, as we will see later in this chapter. Interestingly, this is the scaling dimension with the biggest repercussions, not only on the architecture of an application, but also on the way it is managed from a development perspective. As we will see, microservice is a term that at the moment is most commonly associated with a fine-grained *y*-axis scaling.

The last scaling dimension is the *z*-axis, where the application is split in such a way that each instance is responsible for only a portion of the whole data. This is a technique mainly used in databases and also takes the name of **horizontal partitioning** or **sharding**. In this setup, there are multiple instances of the same application, each of them operating on a partition of the data, which is determined using different criteria. For example, we could partition the users of an application based on their country (*list partitioning*), or based on the starting letter of their surname (*range partitioning*), or by letting a hash function decide the partition each user belongs to (*hash partitioning*). Each partition can then be assigned to a particular instance of our application. The use of data partitions requires each operation to be preceded by a lookup step to determine which instance of the application is responsible for a given datum. As we said, data partitioning is usually applied and handled at the database level because its main purpose is overcoming the problems related to handling large monolithic datasets (limited disk space, memory, and network capacity). Applying it at the application level is worth considering only for complex, distributed architectures or for very particular use cases as, for example, when building applications relying on custom solutions for data persistence, when using databases not supporting partitioning, or when building applications at Google scale. Considering its complexity, scaling an application along the *z*-axis should be taken into consideration only after the *x*-and *y*-axes of the scale cube have been fully exploited.

In the next sections, we will focus on the two most common and effective techniques to scale Node.js applications, namely, **cloning** and **decomposing** by functionality/service.

Cloning and load balancing

Traditional, multithreaded web servers are usually scaled only when the resources assigned to a machine cannot be upgraded any more or when doing so would involve a higher cost than simply launching another machine. By using multiple threads, traditional web servers can take advantage of all the processing power of a server, using all the available processors and memory. However, with a single Node.js process it is harder to do that, being single-threaded and having by default a memory limit of 1.7 GB on 64-bit machines (which needs a special command-line option called `--max_old_space_size` to be increased). This means that Node.js applications are usually scaled much sooner compared to traditional web servers, even in the context of a single machine, to be able to take advantage of all its resources.

> In Node.js, **vertical scaling** (adding more resources to a single machine) and **horizontal scaling** (adding more machines to the infrastructure) are almost equivalent concepts; both in fact involve similar techniques to leverage all the available processing power.

Don't be fooled into thinking about this as a disadvantage. On the contrary, being almost *forced* to scale has beneficial effects on other attributes of an application, in particular availability and fault-tolerance. In fact, scaling a Node.js application by cloning is relatively simple and it's often implemented even if there is no need to harvest more resources, just for the purpose of having a redundant, fail-tolerant setup.

This also pushes the developer to take into account scalability from the early stages of an application, making sure the application does not rely on any resource that cannot be shared across multiple processes or machines. In fact, an absolute prerequisite to scaling an application is that each instance does not have to store common information on resources that cannot be shared, usually hardware, such as memory or disk. For example, in a web server, storing the session data in memory or on disk is a practice that does not work well with scaling; instead, using a shared database will assure that each instance will have access to the same session information, wherever it is deployed.

Let's now introduce the most basic mechanism for scaling Node.js applications: the `cluster` module.

The cluster module

In Node.js, the simplest pattern to distribute the load of an application across different instances running on a single machine is by using the `cluster` module, which is part of the core libraries. The `cluster` module simplifies the *forking* of new instances of the same application and automatically distributes incoming connections across them, as shown in the following figure:

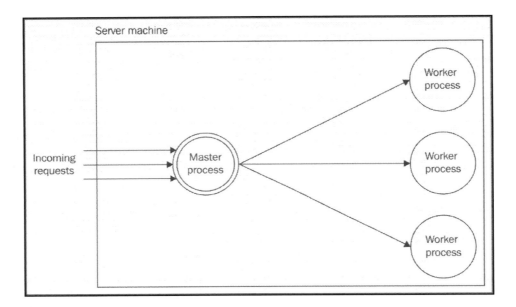

The **Master process** is responsible for spawning a number of processes (**workers**), each representing an instance of the application we want to scale. Each incoming connection is then distributed across the cloned workers, spreading the load across them.

Notes on the behavior of the cluster module

In Node.js 0.8 and 0.10, the `cluster` module shares the same server socket across the workers and leaves to the operating system, the job of *load-balancing* incoming connections across the available workers. However, there is a problem with this approach; in fact, the algorithms used by the operating system to distribute the load across the workers are not meant to load-balance network requests, but rather to schedule the execution of processes. As a result, the distribution is not always uniform across all the instances; often, a fraction of workers receive most of the load. This type of behavior can make sense for the operating system scheduler because it focuses on minimizing the context switches between different processes. The short story is that the `cluster` module does not work at its full potential in Node.js <= 0.10.

However, the situation changes starting from version 0.11.2, where an explicit round robin load-balancing algorithm is included inside the master process, which makes sure the requests are evenly distributed across all the workers. The new load-balancing algorithm is enabled by default on all platforms except Windows, and it can be globally modified by setting the variable `cluster.schedulingPolicy`, using the constants `cluster.SCHED_RR` (round robin) or `cluster.SCHED_NONE` (handled by the operating system).

The round robin algorithm distributes the load evenly across the available servers on a rotational basis. The first request is forwarded to the first server, the second to the next server in the list, and so on. When the end of the list is reached, the iteration starts again from the beginning. This is one of the simplest and most used load balancing algorithms; however, it's not the only one. More sophisticated algorithms allow assigning priorities, selecting the least loaded server or the one with the fastest response time. You can find more details about the evolution of the `cluster` module in these two Node.js issues:
https://github.com/nodejs/node-v0.x-archive/issues/3241
https://github.com/nodejs/node-v0.x-archive/issues/4435

Building a simple HTTP server

Let's now start working on an example. Let's build a small HTTP server, cloned and load-balanced using the `cluster` module. First of all, we need an application to scale; for this example we don't need too much, just a very basic HTTP server.

Let's create a file called `app.js` containing the following code:

```
const http = require('http');
const pid = process.pid;

http.createServer((req, res) => {
  for (let i = 1e7; i> 0; i--) {}
  console.log(`Handling request from ${pid}`);
  res.end(`Hello from ${pid}\n`);
}).listen(8080, () => {
  console.log(`Started ${pid}`);
});
```

The HTTP server we just built responds to any request by sending back a message containing its PID; this will be useful to identify which instance of the application is handling the request. Also, to simulate some actual CPU work, we perform an empty loop 10 million times; without this, the server load would be almost nothing considering the small scale of the tests we are going to run for this example.

The `app` module we want to scale can be anything and can also be implemented using a web framework, for example, Express.

We can now check if all works as expected by running the application as usual and sending a request to `http://localhost:8080` using either a browser or `curl`.

We can also try to measure the requests per second that the server is able to handle using only one process; for this purpose, we can use a network benchmarking tool such as `siege` (`http://www.joedog.org/siege-home`) or Apache `ab` (`http://httpd.apache.org/docs/2.4/programs/ab.html`):

```
siege -c200 -t10S http://localhost:8080
```

With `ab`, the command line would be very similar:

```
ab -c200 -t10 http://localhost:8080/
```

The preceding commands will load the server with 200 concurrent connections for 10 seconds. As a reference, the result for a system with 4 processors is in the order of 90 transactions per second, with an average CPU utilization of only 20%.

Please remember that the load tests we will perform in this chapter are intentionally simple and minimal and are provided only for reference and learning purposes. Their results cannot provide a 100% accurate evaluation of the performance of the various techniques we are analyzing.

Scaling with the cluster module

Let's now try to scale our application using the `cluster` module. Let's create a new module called `clusteredApp.js`:

```
const cluster = require('cluster');
const os = require('os');

if(cluster.isMaster) {
  const cpus = os.cpus().length;
  console.log(`Clustering to ${cpus} CPUs`);
  for (let i = 0; i<cpus; i++) {        // [1]
    cluster.fork();
  }
} else {
  require('./app');                     // [2]
}
```

As we can see, using the `cluster` module requires very little effort. Let's analyze what is happening:

- When we launch `clusteredApp` from the command line, we are actually executing the master process. The `cluster.isMaster` variable is set to `true` and the only work we are required to do is forking the current process using `cluster.fork()`. In the preceding example, we are starting as many workers as the number of CPUs in the system to take advantage of all the available processing power.
- When `cluster.fork()` is executed from the master process, the current main module (`clusteredApp`) is run again, but this time in worker mode (`cluster.isWorker` is set to `true`, while `cluster.isMaster` is `false`). When the application runs as a worker, it can start doing some actual work. In our example, we load the `app` module, which actually starts a new HTTP server.

 It's important to remember that each worker is a different Node.js process with its own event loop, memory space, and loaded modules.

It's interesting to notice that the usage of the `cluster` module is based on a recurring pattern, which makes it very easy to run multiple instances of an application:

```
if(cluster.isMaster) {
  // fork()
} else {
  //do work
}
```

Under the hood, the `cluster` module uses the `child_process.fork()` API (we already met this API in Chapter 9, *Advanced Asynchronous Recipes*), therefore, we also have a communication channel available between the master and the workers. The instances of the workers can be accessed from the variable `cluster.workers`, so broadcasting a message to all of them would be as easy as running the following lines of code:
```
Object.keys(cluster.workers).forEach(id => {
  cluster.workers[id].send('Hello from the master');
});
```

Now, let's try to run our HTTP server in cluster mode. We can do that by starting the `clusteredApp` module as usual:

node clusteredApp

If our machine has more than one processor, we should see a number of workers being started by the master process, one after the other. For example, in a system with four processors, the terminal should look like this:

```
Started 14107
Started 14099
Started 14102
Started 14101
```

If we now try to hit our server again using the URL `http://localhost:8080`, we should notice that each request will return a message with a different PID, which means that these requests have been handled by different workers, confirming that the load is being distributed among them.

Now we can try to load test our server again:

siege -c200 -t10S http://localhost:8080

This way, we should be able to discover the performance increase obtained by scaling our application across multiple processes. As a reference, by using Node.js 6 in a Linux system with 4 processors, the performance increase should be around 3x (270 trans/sec versus 90 trans/sec) with an average CPU load of 90%.

Resiliency and availability with the cluster module

As we already mentioned, scaling an application also brings other advantages, in particular the ability to maintain a certain level of service even in the presence of malfunctions or crashes. This property is also known as **resiliency** and it contributes towards the availability of a system.

By starting multiple instances of the same application, we are creating a redundant system, which means that if one instance goes down for whatever reason, we still have other instances ready to serve requests. This pattern is pretty straightforward to implement using the cluster module. Let's see how it works!

Let's take the code from the previous section as the starting point. In particular, let's modify the app.js module so that it crashes after a random interval of time:

```
// ...
// At the end of app.js
setTimeout(() => {
  throw new Error('Ooops');
}, Math.ceil(Math.random() * 3) * 1000);
```

With this change in place, our server exits with an error after a random number of seconds between 1 and 3. In a real-life situation, this would cause our application to stop working, and of course, serve requests, unless we use some external tool to monitor its status and restart it automatically. However, if we only have one instance, there may be a non-negligible delay between restarts caused by the startup time of the application. This means that during those restarts, the application is not available. Having multiple instances instead will make sure we always have a backup system to serve an incoming request even when one of the workers fails.

With the cluster module, all we have to do is spawn a new worker as soon as we detect that one is terminated with an error code. Let's then modify the clusteredApp.js module to take this into account:

```
if(cluster.isMaster) {
  // ...

  cluster.on('exit', (worker, code) => {
```

```
      if(code != 0 && !worker.suicide) {
        console.log('Worker crashed. Starting a new worker');
        cluster.fork();
      }
    });
  } else {
    require('./app');
  }
```

In the preceding code, as soon as the master process receives an `'exit'` event, we check whether the process is terminated intentionally or as the result of an error; we do this by checking the status `code` and the flag `worker.exitedAfterDisconnect`, which indicates whether the worker was terminated explicitly by the master. If we confirm that the process was terminated because of an error, we start a new worker. It's interesting to notice that while the crashed worker restarts, the other workers can still serve requests, thus not affecting the availability of the application.

To test this assumption, we can try to stress our server again using `siege`. When the stress test completes, we notice that among the various metrics produced by `siege`, there is also an indicator that measures the availability of the application. The expected result would be something similar to this:

```
Transactions:              3027 hits
Availability:              99.31 %
[...]
Failed transactions:          21
```

Bear in mind that this result can vary a lot; it greatly depends on the number of running instances and how many times they crash during the test, but it should give a good indicator of how our solution works. The preceding numbers tell us that despite the fact that our application is constantly crashing, we only had 21 failed requests over 3,027 hits. In the example scenario we built, most of the failing requests will be caused by the interruption of already established connections during a crash. In fact, when this happens, `siege` will print an error like the following:

```
[error] socket: read error Connection reset by peer sock.c:479: Connection
reset by peer
```

Unfortunately, there is very little we can do to prevent these types of failures, especially when the application terminates because of a crash. Nonetheless, our solution proves to be working and its availability is not bad at all for an application that crashes so often!

Zero-downtime restart

A Node.js application might also need to be restarted when its code needs to be updated. So, also in this scenario, having multiple instances can help maintain the availability of our application.

When we have to intentionally restart an application to update it, there is a small window in which the application restarts and is unable to serve requests. This can be acceptable if we are updating our personal blog, but it's not even an option for a professional application with a **Service Level Agreement (SLA)** or one that is updated very often as part of a continuous delivery process. The solution is to implement a **zero-downtime restart** where the code of an application is updated without affecting its availability.

With the `cluster` module, this is again a pretty easy task; the pattern consists of restarting the workers *one at a time*. This way, the remaining workers can continue to operate and maintain the services of the application available.

Let's then add this new feature to our clustered server; all we have to do is add some new code to be executed by the master process (the `clusteredApp.js` file):

```
if (cluster.isMaster) {
  // ...

  process.on('SIGUSR2', () => { //[1]
    const workers = Object.keys(cluster.workers);

    function restartWorker(i) { //[2]
      if (i >= workers.length) return;
      const worker = cluster.workers[workers[i]];
      console.log(`Stopping worker: ${worker.process.pid}`);
      worker.disconnect(); //[3]

      worker.on('exit', () => {
        if (!worker.suicide) return;
        const newWorker = cluster.fork(); //[4]
        newWorker.on('listening', () => {
          restartWorker(i + 1); //[5]
        });
      });
    }
    restartWorker(0);
  });
} else {
  require('./app');
}
```

This is how the preceding block of code works:

1. The restarting of the workers is triggered on receiving the SIGUSR2 signal.
2. We define an iterator function called restartWorker(). This implements an asynchronous sequential iteration pattern over the items of the cluster.workers object.
3. The first task of the restartWorker() function is stopping a worker gracefully by invoking worker.disconnect().
4. When the terminated process exits, we can spawn a new worker.
5. Only when the new worker is ready and listening for new connections can we proceed with restarting the next worker by invoking the next step of the iteration.

 As our program makes use of UNIX signals, it will not work properly on Windows systems (unless you are using the recent Windows subsystem for Linux in Windows 10). Signals are the simplest mechanism to implement our solution. However, this isn't the only one; in fact, other approaches include listening for a command coming from a socket, a pipe, or the standard input.

Now we can test our zero-downtime restart by running the clusteredApp module and then sending a SIGUSR2 signal. However, first we need to obtain the PID of the master process; the following command can be useful to identify it from the list of all the running processes:

```
ps af
```

The master process should be the parent of a set of node processes. Once we have the PID we are looking for, we can send the signal to it:

```
kill -SIGUSR2 <PID>
```

Now the output of the clusteredApp application should display something like this:

```
Restarting workers
Stopping worker: 19389
Started 19407
Stopping worker: 19390
Started 19409
```

We can try to use `siege` again to verify that we don't have any considerable impact on the availability of our application during the restart of the workers.

> pm2 (`https://github.com/Unitech/pm2`) is a small utility, based on `cluster`, which offers load balancing, process monitoring, zero-downtime restarts, and other goodies.

Dealing with stateful communications

The `cluster` module does not work well with stateful communications where the state maintained by the application is not shared between the various instances. This is because different requests belonging to the same stateful session may potentially be handled by a different instance of the application. This is not a problem limited only to the `cluster` module, but in general it applies to any kind of stateless, load balancing algorithm. Consider, for example, the situation described by the following figure:

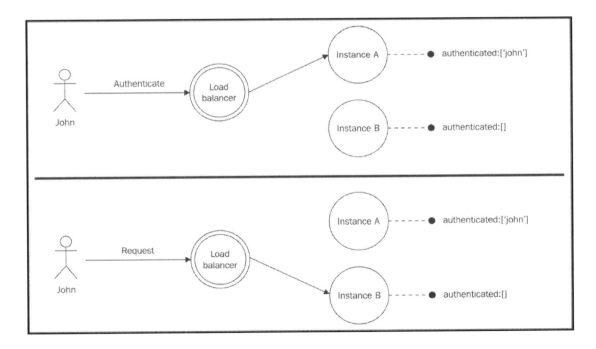

The user **John** initially sends a request to our application to authenticate himself, but the result of the operation is registered locally (for example, in memory), so only the instance of the application that receives the authentication request (**Instance A**) knows that John is successfully authenticated. When John sends a new request, the load balancer might forward it to a different instance of the application, which actually doesn't possess the authentication details of John, hence refusing to perform the operation. The application we just described cannot be scaled as it is, but luckily, there are two easy solutions we can apply to solve the problem.

Sharing the state across multiple instances

The first option we have to scale an application using stateful communications is *sharing the state* across all the instances. This can be easily achieved with a shared datastore, as, for example, a database such as PostgreSQL (`http://www.postgresql.org`), MongoDB (`http://www.mongodb.org`), or CouchDB (`http://couchdb.apache.org`), or even better, we can use an in-memory store such as Redis (`http://redis.io`) or Memcached (`http://memcached.org`).

The following diagram outlines this simple and effective solution:

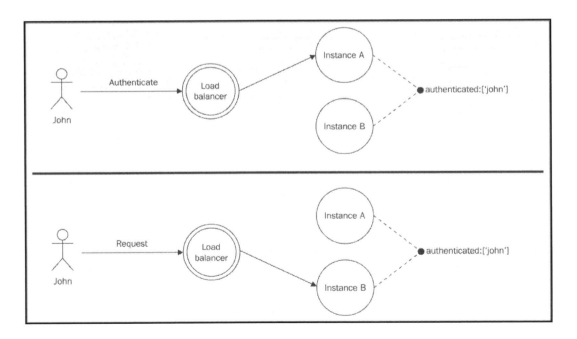

The only drawback of using a shared store for the communication state is that it's not always possible, for example, we might be using an existing library that keeps the communication state in memory; anyway, if we have an existing application, applying this solution requires a change in the code of the application (if it's not already supported). As we will see next, there is a less invasive solution.

Sticky load balancing

The other alternative we have to support stateful communications is having the load balancer always routing all of the requests associated with a session always to the same instance of the application. This technique is also called **sticky load balancing**.

The following figure illustrates a simplified scenario involving this technique:

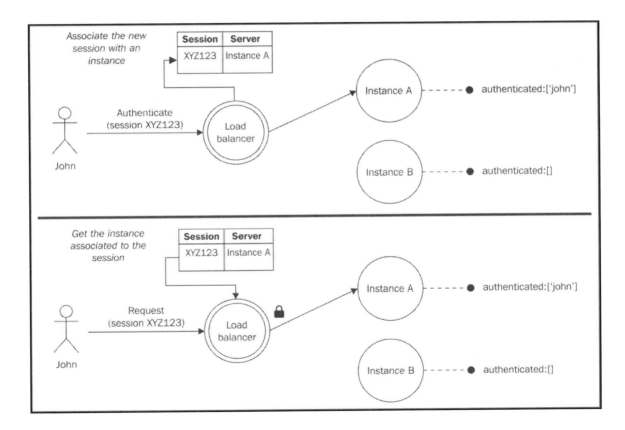

As we can see from the preceding figure, when the load balancer receives a request associated with a new session, it creates a mapping with one particular instance selected by the load-balancing algorithm. The next time the load balancer receives a request from that same session, it bypasses the load-balancing algorithm, selecting the application instance that was previously associated with the session. The particular technique we just described involves the inspection of the session ID associated with the requests (usually included in a cookie by the application or the load balancer itself).

A simpler alternative to associate a stateful connection to a single server is by using the IP address of the client performing the request. Usually, the IP is provided to a hash function that generates an ID representing the application instance designated to receive the request. This technique has the advantage of not requiring the association to be remembered by the load balancer. However, it doesn't work well with devices that frequently change IP as, for example, when roaming on different networks.

Sticky load balancing is not supported by default by the `cluster` module; however, it can be added with an npm library called `sticky-session` (`https://www.npmjs.org/package/sticky-session`).

One big problem with sticky load balancing is the fact that it nullifies most of the advantages of having a redundant system, where all the instances of the application are the same, and where an instance can eventually replace another one that stopped working. For these reasons, the recommendation is to always try to avoid sticky load balancing and building applications that maintain any session state in a shared store or that don't require stateful communications at all (for example, by including the state in the request itself) are preferred.

For a real example of a library requiring sticky load balancing, we can mention `Socket.io` (`http://socket.io/blog/introducing-socket-io-1-0/#scalability`).

Scaling with a reverse proxy

The `cluster` module is not the only option we have to scale a Node.js web application. In fact, more *traditional* techniques are often preferred because they offer more control and power in highly available production environments.

The alternative to using `cluster` is to start multiple *standalone instances* of the same application running on different ports or machines, and then use a *reverse proxy* (or *gateway*) to provide access to those instances, distributing the traffic across them. In this configuration, we don't have a master process distributing requests to a set of workers, but a set of distinct processes running on the same machine (using different ports) or scattered across different machines inside a network. To provide a single access point to our application, we can then use a reverse proxy, a special device or service placed between the clients and the instances of our application, which takes any request and forwards it to a destination server, returning the result to the client as if it was itself the origin. In this scenario, the reverse proxy is also used as a load balancer, distributing the requests among the instances of the application.

> For a clear explanation of the differences between a reverse proxy and a forward proxy, you can refer to the Apache HTTP server documentation at
> `http://httpd.apache.org/docs/2.4/mod/mod_proxy.html#forwa`
> `rdreverse`.

The next figure shows a typical multiprocess, multimachine configuration with a reverse proxy acting as a load balancer on the front:

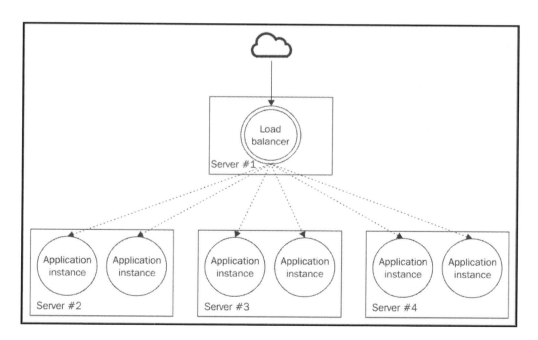

For a Node.js application, there are many reasons to choose this approach in place of the `cluster` module:

- A reverse proxy can distribute the load across several machines, not just several processes
- The most popular reverse proxies on the market support sticky load balancing
- A reverse proxy can route a request to any available server, regardless of its programming language or platform
- We can choose more powerful load balancing algorithms
- Many reverse proxies also offer other services such as URL rewrites, caching, SSL termination point, or even the functionality of fully-fledged web servers that can be used, for example, to serve static files

That said, the `cluster` module could also be easily combined with a reverse proxy if necessary; for example, using `cluster` to scale vertically inside a single machine and then using the reverse proxy to scale horizontally across different nodes.

Pattern
Use a reverse proxy to balance the load of an application across multiple instances running on different ports or machines.

We have many options to implement a load balancer using a reverse proxy; some popular solutions are the following:

- **Nginx** (`http://nginx.org`): This is a web server, reverse proxy, and load balancer, built upon the non-blocking I/O model.
- **HAProxy** (`http://www.haproxy.org`): This is a fast load balancer for TCP/HTTP traffic.
- **Node.js-based proxies**: There are many solutions for the implementation of reverse proxies and load balancers directly in Node.js. This might have advantages and disadvantages, as we will see later.
- **Cloud-based proxies**: In the era of cloud computing, it's not rare to utilize a load balancer as-a-service. This can be convenient because it requires minimal maintenance, it's usually highly scalable, and sometimes it can support dynamic configurations to enable on-demand scalability.

In the next few sections of this chapter, we will analyze a sample configuration using Nginx, and later on, we will also work on building our very own load balancer using nothing but Node.js!

Load balancing with Nginx

To give an idea of how dedicated reverse proxies work, we will now build a scalable architecture based on Nginx (`http://nginx.org`), but first we need to install it. We can do that by following the instructions at `http://nginx.org/en/docs/install.html`.

On the latest Ubuntu system, you can quickly install Nginx with the command:
sudo apt-get install nginx
On Mac OS X, you can use `brew` (`http://brew.sh`):
brew install nginx

As we are not going to use `cluster` to start multiple instances of our server, we need to slightly modify the code of our application so that we can specify the listening port using a command-line argument. This will allow us to launch multiple instances on different ports. Let's then consider again the main module of our example application (`app.js`):

```
const http = require('http');
const pid = process.pid;

http.createServer((req, res) => {
  for (let i = 1e7; i> 0; i--) {}
  console.log(`Handling request from ${pid}`);
  res.end(`Hello from ${pid}\n`);
}).listen(process.env.PORT || process.argv[2] || 8080, () => {
  console.log(`Started ${pid}`);
});
```

Another important feature we lack by not using `cluster` is the automatic restart in case of a crash. Luckily, this is easy to fix by using a dedicated supervisor, which is an external process monitoring our application and restarting it if necessary. Possible choices are the following:

- Node.js-based supervisors such as `forever` (`https://npmjs.org/package/forever`) or pm2 (`https://npmjs.org/package/pm2`)

- OS-based monitors such as upstart (`http://upstart.ubuntu.com`), systemd (`http://freedesktop.org/wiki/Software/systemd`) or runit (`http://smarden.org/runit/`)

- More advanced monitoring solutions such as monit
  (http://mmonit.com/monit) or supervisor (http://supervisord.org)

For this example, we are going to use forever, which is the simplest and most immediate for us to use. We can install it globally by running the following command:

```
npm install forever -g
```

The next step is to start the four instances of our application, all on different ports and supervised by forever:

```
forever start app.js 8081
forever start app.js 8082
forever start app.js 8083
forever start app.js 8084
```

We can check the list of the started processes using the command:

```
forever list
```

Now it's time to configure the Nginx server as a load balancer.

First, we need to identify the location of the nginx.conf file that can be found in one of the following locations, depending on your system /usr/local/nginx/conf, /etc/nginx, or /usr/local/etc/nginx.

Next, let's open the nginx.conf file and apply the following configuration, which is the very minimum required to get a working load balancer:

```
http {
  # ...
  upstream nodejs_design_patterns_app {
    server 127.0.0.1:8081;
    server 127.0.0.1:8082;
    server 127.0.0.1:8083;
    server 127.0.0.1:8084;
  }
  # ...
  server {
    listen 80;

    location / {
      proxy_pass http://nodejs_design_patterns_app;
    }
  }
  # ...
}
```

The configuration needs very little explanation. In the `upstream` `nodejs_design_patterns_app` section, we are defining a list of the backend servers used to handle the network requests, and then, in the `server` section, we specify the `proxy_pass` directive, which essentially tells Nginx to forward any request to the server group we defined before (`nodejs_design_patterns_app`). That's it, now we only need to reload the Nginx configuration with the command:

```
nginx -s reload
```

Our system should now be up and running, ready to accept requests and balance the traffic across the four instances of our Node.js application. Simply point your browser to the address `http://localhost` to see how the traffic is balanced by our Nginx server.

Using a service registry

One important advantage of modern cloud-based infrastructures is the ability to dynamically adjust the capacity of an application based on the current or predicted traffic; this is also known as **dynamic scaling**. If implemented properly, this practice can reduce the cost of the IT infrastructure enormously while still keeping the application highly available and responsive.

The idea is simple: if our application is experiencing a performance degradation caused by a peak in the traffic, we automatically spawn new servers to cope with the increased load. We could also decide to shut down some servers during certain hours, for example, at night, when we know that the traffic will be less, and restarting them again in the morning. This mechanism requires the load balancer to always be up-to-date with the current network topology, knowing at any time which server is up.

A common pattern to solve this problem is to use a central repository called a service registry, which keeps track of the running servers and the services they provide. The next figure shows a multiservice architecture with a load balancer on the front, dynamically configured using a service registry:

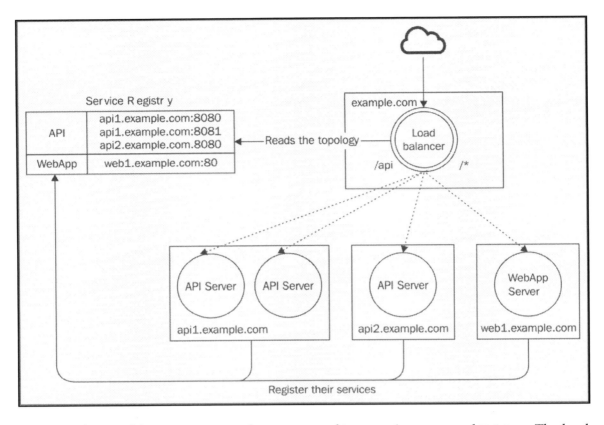

The preceding architecture assumes the presence of two services, API and WebApp. The load balancer distributes the requests arriving on the /api endpoint to all the servers implementing the API service, while the rest of the requests are spread across the servers implementing the WebApp service. The load balancer obtains the list of servers using the service registry.

For this to work in complete automation, each application instance has to register itself to the service registry the moment it comes up online, and unregister itself when it stops. This way, the load balancer can always have an up-to-date view of the servers and the services available on the network.

Pattern (service registry)
Use a central repository to store an always up-to-date view of the servers and the services available in a system.

This pattern can be applied not only to load balancing, but also more generally as a way to decouple a service type from the servers providing it. We can look at it as a service locator design pattern applied to network services.

Implementing a dynamic load balancer with http-proxy and Consul

To support a dynamic network infrastructure, we can use a reverse proxy such as **Nginx** or **HAProxy**; all we need to do is update their configuration using an automated service and then force the load balancer to pick the changes. For Nginx, this can be done using the following command line:

```
nginx -s reload
```

The same result can be achieved with a cloud-based solution, but we have a third and more familiar alternative that makes use of our favorite platform.

We all know that Node.js is a great tool to build any sort of network application; as we said, this is exactly one of its main design goals. So, why not build a load balancer using nothing but Node.js? This would give us much more freedom and power, and would allow us to implement any sort of pattern or algorithm straight into our custom-built load balancer, including the one we are now going to explore, dynamic load balancing using a service registry. In this example we are going to use Consul (https://www.consul.io) as the service registry.

For this example, we want to replicate the multiservice architecture we saw in the figure of the previous section, and to do that, we are going to mainly use three npm packages:

- http-proxy (https://npmjs.org/package/http-proxy): This is a library to simplify the creation of proxies and load balancers in Node.js
- portfinder (https://npmjs.com/package/portfinder): This is a library that allows a free port in the system to be discovered
- consul (https://npmjs.org/package/consul): This is a library that allows to services to be registered in Consul

Let's start by implementing our services. They are simple HTTP servers like the ones we have used so far to test `cluster` and Nginx, but this time we want each server to register itself into the service registry the moment it starts.

Let's see how this looks (file `app.js`):

```
const http = require('http');
const pid = process.pid;
const consul = require('consul')();
const portfinder = require('portfinder');
const serviceType = process.argv[2];

portfinder.getPort((err, port) => {        // [1]
  const serviceId = serviceType+port;
  consul.agent.service.register({          // [2]
    id: serviceId,
    name: serviceType,
    address: 'localhost',
    port: port,
    tags: [serviceType]
  }, () => {

    const unregisterService = (err) => {   // [3]
      consul.agent.service.deregister(serviceId, () => {
        process.exit(err ? 1 : 0);
      });
    };

    process.on('exit', unregisterService); // [4]
    process.on('SIGINT', unregisterService);
    process.on('uncaughtException', unregisterService);

    http.createServer((req, res) => {      // [5]
      for (let i = 1e7; i> 0; i--) {}
      console.log(`Handling request from ${pid}`);
      res.end(`${serviceType} response from ${pid}\n`);
    }).listen(port, () => {
      console.log(`Started ${serviceType} (${pid}) on port ${port}`);
    });
  });
});
```

In the preceding code, there are some parts that deserve our attention:

- First, we use `portfinder.getPort` to discover a free port in the system (by default, `portfinder` starts to search from port 8000).
- Next, we use the Consul library to register a new service in the registry. The service definition needs several attributes: `id` (a unique name for the service), `name` (a generic name that identifies the service), `address` and `port` (to identify how to access the service), `tags` (an optional array of tags that can be used to filter and group services). We are using `serviceType` (that we get as a command-line argument) to specify the service name and to add a tag. This will allow us to identify all the services of the same type available in the cluster.
- At this point we define a function called `unregisterService` that allows us to remove the service we just registered in Consul.
- We use `unregisterService` as a cleanup function, so that when the program is closed (either intentionally or by accident), the service is unregistered from Consul.
- Finally, we start the HTTP server for our service on the port discovered by `portfinder`.

Now it's time to implement the load balancer. Let's do that by creating a new module called `loadBalancer.js`. First, we need to define a routing table to map URL paths to services:

```
const routing = [
  {
    path: '/api',
    service: 'api-service',
    index: 0
  },
  {
    path: '/',
    service: 'webapp-service',
    index: 0
  }
];
```

Each item in the `routing` array contains `service` used to handle the requests arriving on the mapped `path`. The `index` property will be used to *round robin* the requests of a given service.

Let's see how this works by implementing the second part of `loadbalancer.js`:

```
const http = require('http');
const httpProxy = require('http-proxy');
```

```
const consul = require('consul')();                    // [1]

const proxy = httpProxy.createProxyServer({});
http.createServer((req, res) => {
  let route;
  routing.some(entry => {                               // [2]
    route = entry;
    //Starts with the route path?
    return req.url.indexOf(route.path) === 0;
  });

  consul.agent.service.list((err, services) => {       // [3]
    const servers = [];
    Object.keys(services).filter(id => { //
      if (services[id].Tags.indexOf(route.service) > -1) {
        servers.push(`http://${services[id].Address}:${services[id].Port}`)
      }
    });

    if (!servers.length) {
      res.writeHead(502);
      return res.end('Bad gateway');
    }

    route.index = (route.index + 1) % servers.length; // [4]
    proxy.web(req, res, {target: servers[route.index]});
  });
}).listen(8080, () => console.log('Load balancer started on port 8080'));
```

This is how we implemented our Node.js-based load balancer:

1. First, we need to require consul so that we can have access to the registry. Next, we instantiate an http-proxy object and start a normal web server.

2. In the request handler of the server, the first thing we do is match the URL against our routing table. The result will be a descriptor containing the service name.

3. We obtain from consul the list of servers implementing the required service. If this list is empty, we return an error to the client. We use the Tag attribute to filter all the available services and find the address of the servers that implements the current service type.

4. At last, we can route the request to its destination. We update route.index to point to the next server in the list, following a round robin approach. We then use the index to select a server from the list, passing it to proxy.web() along with the request (req) and the response (res) objects. This will simply forward the request to the server we chose.

It is now clear how simple it is to implement a load balancer using only Node.js and a service registry and how much flexibility we can have by doing so. Now we should be ready to give it a go, but first, let's install the `consul` server by following the official documentation at: `https://www.consul.io/intro/getting-started/install.html`.

This allows us to start the `consul` service registry in our development machine with this simple command line:

```
consul agent -dev
```

Now we are ready to start the load balancer:

```
node loadBalancer
```

Now if we try to access some of the services exposed by the load balancer, we will notice that it returns an HTTP 502 error, because we didn't start any server yet. Try it yourself:

```
curl localhost:8080/api
```

The preceding command should return the following output:

```
Bad Gateway
```

The situation will change if we spawn some instances of our services, for example, two `api-service` and one `webapp-service`:

```
forever start app.js api-service
forever start app.js api-service
forever start app.js webapp-service
```

Now the load balancer should automatically see the new servers and start distributing requests across them. Let's try again with the following command:

```
curl localhost:8080/api
```

The preceding command should now return this:

```
api-service response from 6972
```

By running it again, we should now receive a message from another server, confirming that the requests are being distributed evenly among the different servers:

```
api-service response from 6979
```

The advantages of this pattern are immediate. We can now scale our infrastructure dynamically, on demand, or based on a schedule, and our load balancer will automatically adjust with the new configuration without any extra effort!

Peer-to-peer load balancing

Using a reverse proxy is almost a necessity when we want to expose a complex internal network architecture to a public network such as the Internet. It helps hide the complexity, providing a single access point that external applications can easily use and rely on. However, if we need to scale a service that is for internal use only, we can have much more flexibility and control.

Let's imagine having a **Service A** which relies on a **Service B** to implement its functionality. **Service B** is scaled across multiple machines and it's available only in the internal network. What we have learned so far is that **Service A** will connect to **Service B** using a reverse proxy, which will distribute the traffic to all the servers implementing **Service B**.

However, there is an alternative. We can remove the reverse proxy from the picture and distribute the requests directly from the client (**Service A**), which now becomes directly responsible for load balancing its connections across the various instances of **Service B**. This is possible only if **Server A** knows the details about the servers exposing **Service B**, and in an internal network, this is usually known information. With this approach we are essentially implementing **peer-to-peer load balancing**.

The following diagram compares the two alternatives we just described:

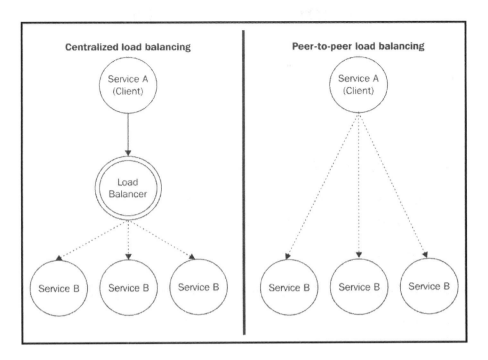

This is an extremely simple and effective pattern that enables truly distributed communications without bottlenecks or single points of failure. Besides that, it also does the following:

- Reduces the infrastructure complexity by removing a network node
- Allows faster communications, because messages will travel through one fewer node
- Scales better, because performances are not limited by what the load balancer can handle

On the other hand, by removing the reverse proxy, we are actually exposing the complexity of its underlying infrastructure. Also, each client has to be *smarter* by implementing a load-balancing algorithm and, possibly, also a way to keep its knowledge of the infrastructure up-to-date.

Peer-to-peer load balancing is a pattern used extensively in the ØMQ (`http://zeromq.org`) library.

Implementing an HTTP client that can balance requests across multiple servers

We already know how to implement a load balancer using only Node.js and distribute incoming requests across the available servers, so implementing the same mechanism on the client side should not be that different. All we have to do in fact is wrap the client API and augment it with a load-balancing mechanism. Take a look at the following module (balancedRequest.js):

```
const http = require('http');
const servers = [
  {host: 'localhost', port: '8081'},
  {host: 'localhost', port: '8082'}
];
let i = 0;

module.exports = (options, callback) => {
  i = (i + 1) % servers.length;
  options.hostname = servers[i].host;
  options.port = servers[i].port;

  return http.request(options, callback);
};
```

The preceding code is very simple and needs little explanation. We wrapped the original http.request API so that it overrides the hostname and port of the request with those selected from the list of available servers using a round robin algorithm.

The new wrapped API can then be used seamlessly (client.js):

```
const request = require('./balancedRequest');
for(let i = 10; i>= 0; i--) {
  request({method: 'GET', path: '/'}, res => {
    let str = '';
    res.on('data', chunk => {
      str += chunk;
    }).on('end', () => {
      console.log(str);
    });
  }).end();
}
```

To try the preceding code, we have to start two instances of the sample server provided:

```
node app 8081
node app 8082
```

Followed by the client application we just built:

```
node client
```

We should notice how each request is sent to a different server, confirming that we are now able to balance the load without a dedicated reverse proxy!

 An improvement to the wrapper we created before would be to integrate a service registry directly into the client and obtain the server list dynamically. You can find an example of this technique in the code distributed with the book.

Decomposing complex applications

So far in the chapter, we have mainly focused our analysis on the *x*-axis of the scale cube. We saw how it represents the easiest and most immediate way to distribute the load of an application, also improving its availability. In the following section, we are now going to focus on the *y*-axis of the scale cube, where applications are scaled by **decomposing** them by functionality and service. As we will learn, this technique allows us to scale not only the capacity of an application, but also, and most importantly, its complexity.

Monolithic architecture

The term monolithic might make us think of a system without modularity, where all the services of an application are interconnected and almost indistinguishable. However, this is not always the case. Often, monolithic systems have a highly modular architecture and a good decoupling between their internal components.

A perfect example is the Linux OS kernel, which is part of a category called **monolithic kernels** (in perfect opposition with its ecosystem and the Unix philosophy). Linux has thousands of services and modules that we can load and unload dynamically even while the system is running. However, they all run in *kernel mode*, which means that a failure in any of them might bring the entire OS down (have you ever seen a *kernel panic*?). This approach is opposite to the microkernel architecture, where only the core services of the operating system run in kernel mode, while the rest run in user mode, usually each one with its own process. The main advantage of this approach is that a problem in any of these services would more likely cause it to crash in isolation instead of affecting the stability of the entire system.

The Torvalds-Tanenbaum debate on kernel design is probably one of the most famous *flame wars* in the history of computer science, where one of the main points of dispute was exactly monolithic versus microkernel design. You can find a web version of the discussion (it originally appeared on Usenet) at
`https://groups.google.com/d/msg/comp.os.minix/wlhw16QWltI` `/P8isWhZ8PJ8J.`

It's remarkable how these design principles, more than 30 years old, can still be applied today and in totally different environments. Modern monolithic applications are comparable to monolithic kernels; if any of their components fail, the entire system is affected, which, translated into Node.js terms, means that all the services are part of the same codebase and run in a single process (when not cloned).

To make an example of a monolithic architecture, let's take a look at the following figure:

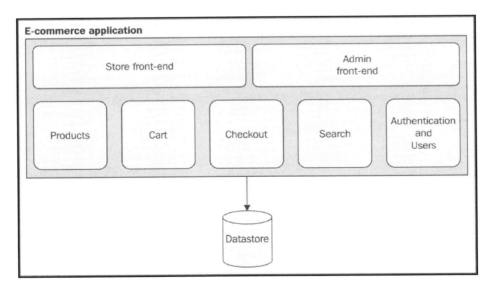

The preceding figure shows the architecture of a typical e-commerce application. Its structure is modular; we have two different frontends, one for the main store and another for the administration interface. Internally, we have a clear separation of the services implemented by the application, each one responsible for a specific portion of its business logic: **Products**, **Cart**, **Checkout**, **Search**, and **Authentication and Users**. However, the preceding architecture is monolithic; every module, in fact, is part of the same codebase and runs as part of a single application. A failure in any of its components, for example, an uncaught exception, can potentially tear down the entire online store.

Another problem with this type of architecture is the interconnection between its modules; the fact that they all live inside the same application makes it very easy for a developer to build interactions and coupling between modules. For example, consider the use case when a product is being purchased: the Checkout module has to update the availability of the **Product** object, and if those two modules are in the same application, it's too easy for a developer to just obtain a reference to a **Product** object and update its availability directly. Maintaining a low coupling between internal modules is very hard in a monolithic application, partly because the boundaries between them are not always clear or properly enforced.

A **high coupling** is often one of the main obstacles to the growth of an application and prevents its scalability in terms of complexity. In fact, an intricate dependency graph means that every part of the system is a liability; it has to be maintained for the entire life of the product, and any change should be carefully evaluated because every component is like a wooden block in a Jenga tower: moving or removing one of them can cause the entire tower to collapse. This often results in the building of conventions and development processes to cope with the increasing complexity of the project.

The microservice architecture

Now we are going to reveal the most important pattern in Node.js to write big applications: *avoid writing big applications*. This seems like a trivial statement, but it's an incredibly effective strategy to scale both the complexity and the capacity of a software system. So what's the alternative to writing big applications? The answer is in the y-axis of the scale cube, decomposition and splitting by service and functionality. The idea is to break down an application into its essential components, creating separate, independent applications. It is practically the opposite of monolithic architecture. This fits perfectly with the Unix philosophy, and the Node.js principles we discussed at the beginning of the book, in particular *"make each program do one thing well"*.

Microservice architecture is today, probably the main reference pattern for this type of approach, where a set of self-sufficient services replace big monolithic applications. The prefix micro means that the services should be as small as possible, but always within reasonable limits. Don't be misled by thinking that creating an architecture with a hundred different applications exposing only one web service is necessarily a good choice. In reality, there is no strict rule on how small or big a service should be. It's not the size that matters in the design of a microservice architecture; instead, it's a combination of different factors, mainly **loose coupling**, **high cohesion**, and **integration complexity**.

An example of microservice architecture

Let's now see what the monolithic e-commerce application would look like, using a microservice architecture:

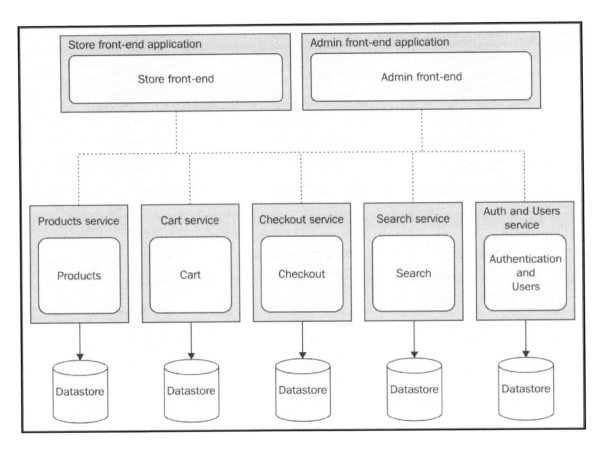

As we can see from the previous figure, each fundamental component of the e-commerce application is now a self-sustaining and independent entity, living in its own context, with its own database. In practice, they are all independent applications exposing a set of related services (high cohesion).

The **data ownership** of a service is an important characteristic of microservice architecture. This is why the database also has to be split to maintain the proper level of isolation and independence. If a unique shared database is used, it would become much easier for the services to work together; however, this would also introduce a coupling between the services (based on data), nullifying some of the advantages of having different applications.

The dashed line connecting all the nodes tells us that, in some way, they have to communicate and exchange information for the entire system to be fully functional. As the services do not share the same database, there is more communication involved to maintain the consistency of the whole system. For example, the **Checkout** application needs to know some information about **Products**, such as the price and restrictions on shipping, and at the same time, it needs to update the data stored in the **Products** service, for example, the product availability when the checkout is complete. In the preceding figure, we tried to keep the way the nodes communicate abstract. Surely, the most popular strategy is using web services, but as we will see later, this is not the only option.

Pattern (microservice architecture)
Split a complex application by creating several small, self-contained services.

Pros and cons of microservices

In this section we are going to highlight some of the advantages and disadvantages of implementing a microservice architecture. As we will see, this approach promises to bring a radical change in the way we develop our applications, revolutionizing the way we see scalability and complexity, but on the other hand, it introduces new nontrivial challenges as well.

Martin Fowler wrote a great article about microservices that you can find at http://martinfowler.com/articles/microservices.html.

Every service is expendable

The main technical advantage of having each service living in its own application context is that crashes, bugs, and breaking changes do not propagate to the entire system. The goal is to build truly independent services that are smaller, easier to change, or even *rebuild from scratch*. If, for example, the Checkout service of our e-commerce application suddenly crashes because of a serious bug, the rest of the system would continue to work as normal. Some functionality may be affected, for example, the ability to purchase a product, but the rest of the system would continue to work.

Also, imagine if we suddenly realized that the database or the programming language we used to implement a component was not a good design decision. In a monolithic application, there would be very little we could do to change things without affecting the entire system; instead, in a microservice architecture, we could more easily re-implement the entire service from scratch, using a different database or platform, and the rest of the system would not even notice it.

Reusability across platforms and languages

Splitting a big monolithic application into many small services allows us to create independent units that can be reused much more easily. **Elasticsearch** (http://www.elasticsearch.org) is a great example of a reusable search service; also, the authentication server we built in Chapter 7, *Wiring Modules*, is another example of a service that can be easily reused in any application, regardless of the programming language it's built in.

The main advantage is that the level of information hiding is usually much higher compared to monolithic applications. This is possible because the interactions usually happen through a remote interface such as a web service or a message broker, which makes it much easier to hide the implementation details and shield the client from changes in the way the service is implemented or deployed. For example, if all we have to do is invoke a web service, we are shielded from the way the infrastructure behind is scaled, from what programming language it uses, from what database it uses to store its data, and so on.

A way to scale the application

Going back to the scale cube, it's clear that microservices are equivalent to scaling an application along the *y*-axis, so it's already a means for the distribution of the load across multiple machines. Also, we should not forget that we can combine microservices with the other two dimensions of the cube to scale the application even further. For example, each service could be cloned to handle more traffic, and the interesting aspect is that they can be scaled independently, allowing better resource management.

The challenges of microservices

At this point, it would look like microservices are the solution to all our problems; however, this is far from being true. In fact, having more nodes to manage introduces a higher complexity in terms of integration, deployment, and code sharing; it fixes some of the pains of traditional architectures but it also opens up many new questions. How do we make the services interact? How can we deploy, scale, and monitor such a high number of applications? How can we share and reuse code between services? Fortunately, cloud services and modern DevOps methodologies can provide some answers to those questions, and also, Node.js can help a lot. Its module system is a perfect companion to share code between different projects. Node.js was made to be a *node* in a distributed system such as those implemented using a microservice architecture.

Although microservices can be built using any framework (or even just the core Node.js modules), there are a few solutions specialized for this purpose; among the most notable, we have **Seneca** (`https://npmjs.org/package/seneca`), **AWS Lambda** (`https://aws.amazon.com/lambda`), **IBM OpenWhisk** (`https://developer.ibm.com/openwhisk`) and **Microsoft Azure Functions** (`https://azure.microsoft.com/en-us/services/functions`). A useful tool to manage the deployment of microservices is **Apache Mesos** (`http://mesos.apache.org`).

Integration patterns in a microservice architecture

One of the toughest challenges of microservices is connecting all the nodes to make them collaborate. For example, the **Cart** service of our e-commerce application would make little sense without some **Products** to add, and the **Checkout** service would be useless without a list of products to buy (a cart). As we already mentioned, there are also other factors that necessitate an interaction between the various services. For example, the **Search** service has to know which **Products** are available and must also ensure it keeps its information up-to-date. The same can be said about the **Checkout** service, which has to update the information about **Product** availability when a purchase is completed.

When designing an integration strategy, it's also important to consider the *coupling* that it's going to introduce between the services in the system. We should not forget that designing a distributed architecture involves the same practices and principles that we use locally when designing a module or subsystem, therefore, we also need to take into consideration properties such as the reusability and extensibility of the service.

The API proxy

The first pattern we are going to show makes use of an **API Proxy** (also commonly identified as an **API Gateway**), a server that *proxies* the communications between a client and a set of remote APIs. In a microservice architecture, its main purpose is to provide a single access point for multiple API endpoints, but it can also offer load balancing, caching, authentication, and traffic limiting, all features that prove to be very useful to implement a solid API solution.

This pattern should not be new to us; we already saw it in action when we built the custom load balancer with `http-proxy` and `consul`. For that example, our load balancer was exposing only two services, and then, thanks to a Service Registry, it was able to map a URL path to a service and hence to a list of servers. An API proxy works in the same way; it is essentially a reverse proxy and often also a load balancer, specifically configured to handle API requests. The next figure shows how we can apply such a solution to our e-commerce application:

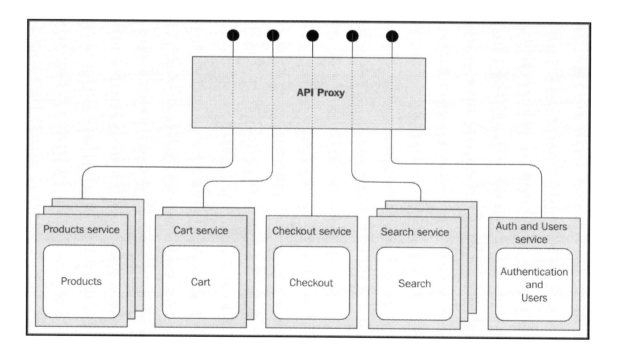

From the preceding figure, it should be clear how an API proxy can hide the complexity of its underlying infrastructure. This is really handy in a microservice infrastructure, as the number of nodes may be high, especially if each service is scaled across multiple machines. The integration achieved by an API Proxy is therefore only structural; there is no semantic mechanism. It simply provides a familiar monolithic view of a complex microservice infrastructure. This is opposed to the next pattern we are going to learn, where the integration is semantic instead.

API orchestration

The pattern we are going to describe next is probably the most natural and explicit way to integrate and compose a set of services, and it's called **API orchestration**. Daniel Jacobson, VP of Engineering for the Netflix API, in one of his blog posts (http://thenextweb.com/dd/2013/12/17/future-api-design-orchestration-la yer), defines API orchestration as follows:

> *"An API Orchestration Layer (OL) is an abstraction layer that takes generically-modeled data elements and/or features and prepares them in a more specific way for a targeted developer or application."*

The *generically modeled elements and/or features* fit the description of a service in a microservice architecture perfectly. The idea is to create an abstraction to connect those bits and pieces to implement new services specific to the application.

Let's make an example using the e-commerce application. Refer to the following figure:

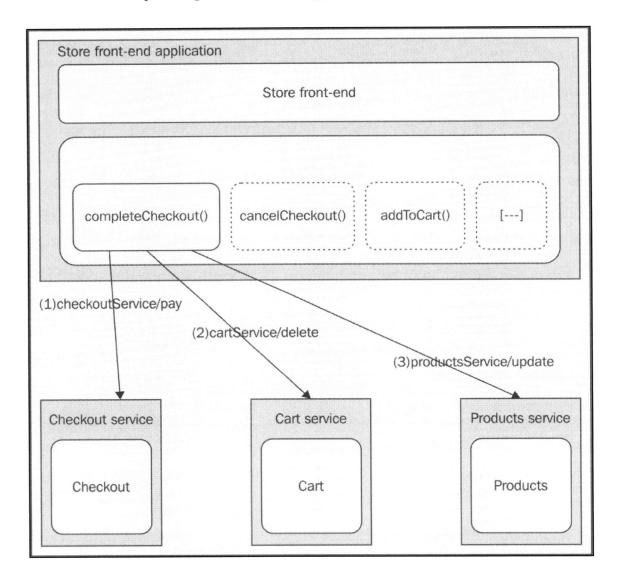

The preceding figure shows how the **Store front-end application** uses an orchestration layer to build more complex and specific features by composing and orchestrating existing services. The described scenario takes as example, a hypothetical `completeCheckout()` service that is invoked the moment a customer clicks the **Pay** button at the end of the checkout. The figure shows how `completeCheckout()` is a composite operation made of three different steps:

1. First, we complete the transaction by invoking `checkoutService/pay`.
2. Then, when the payment is successfully processed, we need to tell the cart service that the items were purchased and they can be removed from the cart. We do that by invoking `cartService/delete`.
3. Also, when the payment is complete, we need to update the availability of the products that were just purchased. This is done through `productsService/update`.

As we can see, we took three operations from three different services and we built a new API that coordinates the services to maintain the entire system in a consistent state.

Another common operation performed by the **API Orchestration Layer** is **data aggregation**, in other words, combining data from different services into a single response. Imagine if we wanted to list all the products contained in a cart. In this case, the orchestration would need to retrieve the list of product IDs from the **Cart** service and then retrieve the complete information about the products from the **Products** service. The ways in which we can combine and coordinate services are really infinite, but the important pattern to remember is the role of the orchestration layer, which acts as an abstraction between a number of services and a specific application.

The orchestration layer is a great candidate for a further functional splitting. It is in fact very common to have it implemented as a dedicated, independent service, in which case it takes the name of API Orchestrator. This practice is perfectly in line with the microservice philosophy.

The next figure shows this further improvement of our architecture:

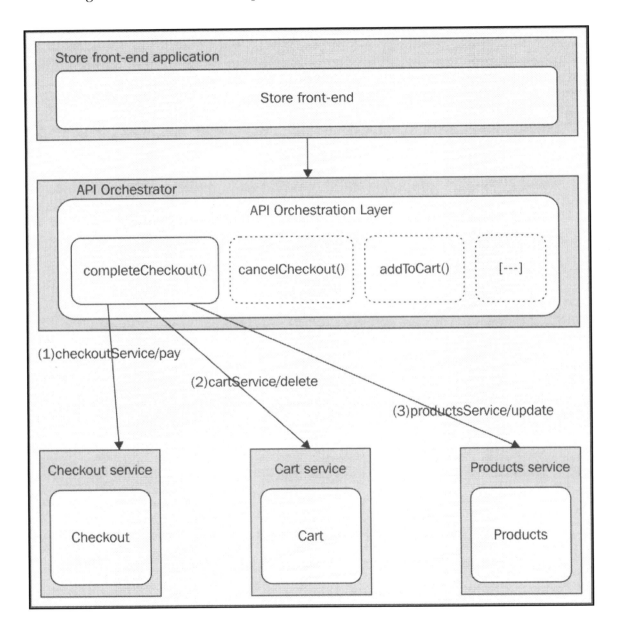

Creating a standalone orchestrator, as shown in the previous figure, can help in decoupling the client application (in our case, the **Store front-end**) from the complexity of the microservice infrastructure. This reminds us about the API Proxy; however, there is a crucial difference; an orchestrator performs a semantic integration of the various services; it's not just a naïve proxy, and it often exposes an API that is different from the one exposed by the underlying services.

Integration with a message broker

The orchestrator pattern gave us a mechanism to integrate the various services in an explicit way. This has both advantages and disadvantages. It is easy to design, easy to debug, and easy to scale, but unfortunately, it has to have a complete knowledge of the underlying architecture and how each service works. If we were talking about objects instead of architectural nodes, the orchestrator would be an anti-pattern called **God Object**, which defines an object that knows and does too much, which usually results in high coupling, low cohesion, but most importantly, high complexity.

The pattern we are now going to show tries to distribute, across the services, the responsibility of synchronizing the information of the entire system. However, the last thing we want to do is create direct relationships between services, which would result in high coupling and a further increase in the complexity of the system, due to the increasing number of interconnections between nodes. The goal is to have each service maintain its isolation; they should be able to work even without the rest of the services in the system or in combination with new services and nodes.

The solution is to use a message broker, a system capable of decoupling the sender from the receiver of a message, allowing us to implement a centralized publish/subscribe pattern, in practice an observer pattern for distributed systems (we will talk more about this pattern later in the book). The following diagram shows an example of how this applies to the e-commerce application:

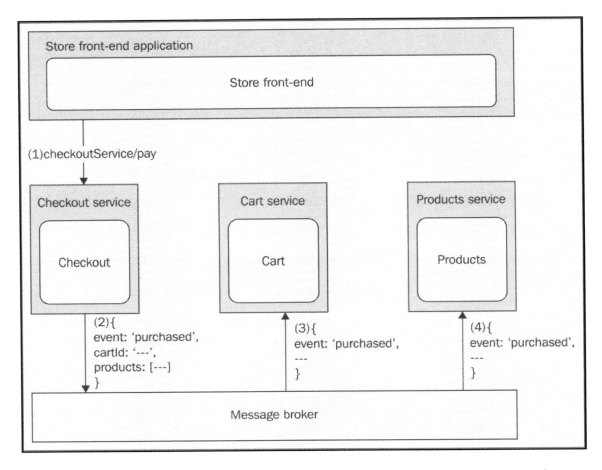

As we can see, the client of the **Checkout** service, which is the frontend application, does not need to carry out any explicit integration with the other services. All it has to do is invoke `checkoutService/pay` to complete the checkout and take the money from the customer; all the integration work happens in the background:

1. The **Store front-end** invokes the `checkoutService/pay` operation on the **Checkout** service.

2. When the operation completes, the **Checkout** service generates an event, attaching the details of the operation, that is, the `cartId` and the list of `products` that were just purchased. The event is published into the message broker. At this point, the **Checkout** service does not know who is going to receive the message.

3. The **Cart** service is subscribed to the broker, so it's going to receive the `purchased` event that was just published by the **Checkout** service. The **Cart** service reacts by removing from its database, the cart identified with the ID contained in the message.

4. The **Products** service was subscribed to the message broker as well, so it receives the same `purchased` event. It then updates its database based on this new information, adjusting the availability of the products included in the message.

The whole process happens without any explicit intervention from external entities such as an orchestrator. The responsibility for spreading the knowledge and keeping information in sync is distributed across the services themselves. There is no *god* service that has to know how to move the gears of the entire system; each service is in charge of its own part of the integration.

The message broker is a fundamental element to decouple the services and reduce the complexity of their interaction. It might also offer other interesting features, such as persistent message queues and guaranteed ordering of the messages. We will talk more about this in the next chapter.

Summary

In this chapter, we learned how to design Node.js architectures that scale both in capacity and complexity. We saw how scaling an application is not only about handling more traffic or reducing the response time, but it's also a practice to apply when we want better availability and tolerance to failures. We saw how these properties often are on the same wavelength and we understood that scaling early is not a bad practice, especially in Node.js, which allows us to do it easily and with few resources.

The scale cube taught us that applications can be scaled across three dimensions. We dived into the two most important of them, the *x*-and *y*-axes, allowing us to discover two essential architectural patterns, namely, load balancing and microservices. We should know by now how to start multiple instances of the same Node.js application, how to distribute the traffic across them, and how to exploit this setup for other purposes such as fail tolerance and zero-downtime restarts. We also analyzed how to handle the problem of dynamic and autoscaled infrastructures; we saw that a service registry can really come in useful for those situations. However, cloning and load balancing cover only one dimension of the scale cube, so we moved our analysis to another dimension, studying in more detail what it means to split an application by its constituent services, by building a microservice architecture. We saw how microservices enable a complete revolution in how a project is developed and managed, providing a natural way to distribute the load of an application and split its complexity. However, we learned that this also means shifting the complexity from *how to build a big monolithic application* to *how to integrate a set of services*. This last aspect is where we focused the last part of our analysis, showing some of the architectural solutions to integrate a set of independent services.

In the next chapter, we will have the chance to analyze in more detail, the messaging patterns we discussed in this chapter in addition to more advanced integration techniques, useful when implementing complex distributed architectures.

11
Messaging and Integration Patterns

If scalability is about splitting, systems integration is about rejoining. In the previous chapter, we learned how to distribute an apfunction is a simple iteration over all the connected clientsplication, fragmenting it across several machines. In order for it to work properly, all those pieces have to communicate in some way and, hence, they have to be integrated.

There are two main techniques to integrate a distributed application: one is to use a shared storage as a central coordinator and keeper of all the information, the other one is to use messages to disseminate data, events, and commands across the nodes of the system. This last option is what really makes the difference when scaling distributed systems, and it's also what makes this topic so fascinating and sometimes complex.

Messages are used in every layer of a software system. We exchange messages to communicate on the Internet, we can use messages to send information to other processes using pipes, we can use messages within an application as an alternative to direct function invocation (command pattern), and also device drivers use messages to communicate with the hardware. Any discrete and structured data that is used as a way to exchange information between components and systems can be seen as a *message*. However, when dealing with distributed architectures, the term **messaging system** is used to describe a specific class of solutions, patterns, and architectures that are meant to facilitate the exchange of information over the network.

As we will see, there are several traits that characterize these types of systems. We might choose to use a broker versus a peer-to-peer structure, we might use a request/reply or one-way communication, or we might use queues to deliver our messages more reliably; the scope of the topic is really broad. The book *Enterprise Integration Patterns* by *Gregor Hohpe* and *Bobby Woolf* gives you an idea about the vastness of the topic. It is considered the *Bible* of messaging and integration patterns and has more than 700 pages describing 65 different integration patterns. This chapter explores the most important of those well-known patterns, considering them from the perspective of Node.js and its ecosystem.

To sum up, in this chapter, we will learn about the following topics:

- The fundamentals of a messaging system
- The publish/subscribe pattern
- Pipelines and task distribution patterns
- Request/reply patterns

Fundamentals of a messaging system

When talking about messages and messaging systems, there are four fundamental elements to take into consideration; these are as follows:

- The direction of the communication, which can be one-way only or a request/reply exchange
- The purpose of the message, which also determines its content
- The timing of the message, which can be sent and received immediately or at a later time (asynchronously)
- The delivery of the message, which can happen directly or via a broker

In the sections that follow, we are going to formalize these aspects in order to provide a base for our later discussions.

One-way and request/reply patterns

The most fundamental aspect in a messaging system is the direction of the communication, which often also determines its semantics.

The most simple communication pattern is when the message is pushed *one-way* from a source to a destination; this is a trivial situation, and it doesn't need much explanation:

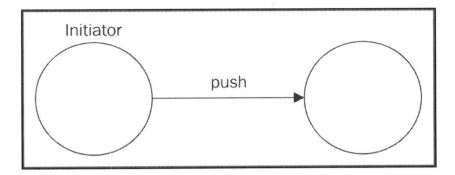

A typical example of one-way communication is an e-mail or a web server that sends a message to a connected browser using WebSockets, or a system that distributes tasks to a set of workers.

The request/reply pattern is, however, far more popular than the one-way only communication; a typical example is the invocation of a web service. The following figure shows this simple and well-known scenario:

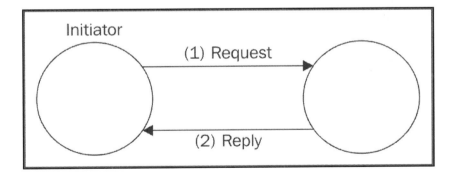

The request/reply pattern might seem a trivial pattern to implement; however, we will see that it becomes more complicated when the communication is asynchronous or involves multiple nodes. Take a look at the example in the following figure:

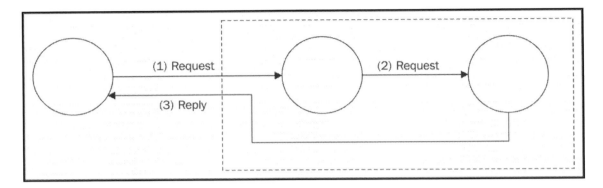

With the setup shown in the preceding diagram, we can appreciate the complexity of some request/reply patterns. If we consider the direction of the communication between any two nodes, we can surely say that it is one-way. However, from a global point of view, the initiator sends a request and in turn receives an associated response, even if from a different node. In these situations, what really differentiates a request/reply pattern from a bare one-way loop is the relationship between the request and the reply, which is kept in the initiator. The reply is usually handled in the same context of the request.

Message types

A **message** is essentially a means to connect different software components and there are different reasons for doing so: it might be because we want to obtain some information held by another system or a component, to execute operations remotely, or to notify some peers that something has just happened. The message content will also vary depending on the reason for the communication. In general, we can identify three types of messages, depending on their purpose:

- **Command Message**
- **Event Message**
- **Document Message**

Command Message

The **Command Message** is already familiar to us; it's essentially a serialized command object as we described it in `Chapter 6`, *Design Patterns*. The purpose of this type of message is to trigger the execution of an action or a task on the receiver. For this to be possible, our message has to contain the essential information to run the task, which is usually the name of the operation and a list of arguments to provide when it's executed. The Command Message can be used to implement **Remote Procedure Call** (**RPC**) systems, distributed computations, or more simply used to request some data. RESTful HTTP calls are simple examples of commands; each HTTP verb has a specific meaning and is associated with a precise operation: GET, to retrieve the resource; POST, to create a new one; PUT, to update it; and DELETE, to destroy it.

Event Message

An **Event Message** is used to notify another component that something has occurred. It usually contains the type of the event and sometimes also some details such as the context, the subject, or the actor involved. In web development, we are using an Event Message in the browser when using long-polling or WebSockets to receive notifications from the server that something has just happened, as, for example, changes in the data or, in general, the state of the system. The use of events is a very important integration mechanism in distributed applications, as it enables us to keep all the nodes of the system on the same page.

Document Message

The **Document Message** is primarily meant to transfer data between components and machines. The main characteristic that differentiates a document from a command (which might also contain data) is that the message does not contain any information that tells the receiver what to do with the data. On the other hand, the main difference from an Event Message is mainly the absence of an association with a particular occurrence, with something that happened. Often, the replies to the Command Messages are Document Messages, as they usually contain only the data that was requested or the result of an operation.

Asynchronous messaging and queues

As Node.js developers, we should already know the advantages of executing asynchronous operations. For messaging and communications, it's the same story.

We can compare synchronous communication to a phone call: the two peers must be connected to the same channel at the same time and they should exchange messages in real time. Normally, if we want to call someone else, we either need another phone or to close the ongoing communication in order to start a new one.

Asynchronous communication is similar to an SMS: it doesn't require the recipient to be connected to the network the moment we send it, we might receive a response immediately or after an unknown delay, or we might not receive a response at all. We might send multiple SMSes to multiple recipients one after the other, and receive their responses (if any) in any order. In short, we have a better parallelism with the use of fewer resources.

Another important advantage of asynchronous communications is that the messages can be stored and then delivered as soon as possible or at a later time. This might be useful when the receiver is too busy to handle new messages or when we want to guarantee delivery. In messaging systems, this is made possible using a **message queue**, a component that mediates the communication between the sender and the receiver, storing any message before it gets delivered to its destination, as shown in the following figure:

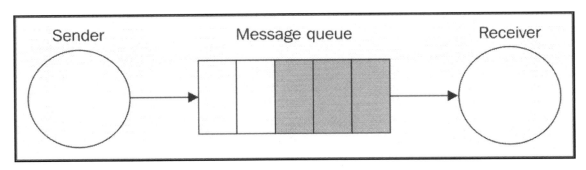

If for any reason the receiver crashes, disconnects from the network, or experiences a slowdown, the messages are accumulated in the queue and dispatched as soon as the receiver comes online and is fully working. The queue can be located in the sender, or split between the sender and receiver, or live in a dedicated external system acting as middleware for the communication.

Peer-to-peer or broker-based messaging

Messages can be delivered directly to the receiver, in a peer-to-peer fashion or through a centralized intermediary system called a **message broker**. The main role of the broker is to decouple the receiver of the message from the sender. The following figure shows the architectural difference between the two approaches:

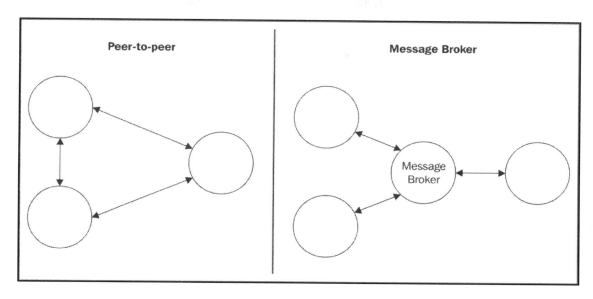

In a peer-to-peer architecture, every node is directly responsible for the delivery of the message to the receiver. This implies that the nodes have to know the address and port of the receiver and they have to agree on a protocol and message format. The broker eliminates these complexities from the equation: each node can be totally independent and can communicate with an undefined number of peers without directly knowing their details. A broker can also act as a bridge between the different communication protocols, for example, the popular RabbitMQ broker (`http://www.rabbitmq.com`) supports **Advanced Message Queuing Protocol** (**AMQP**), **Message Queue Telemetry Transport** (**MQTT**), and **Simple/Streaming Text Orientated Messaging Protocol** (**STOMP**), enabling multiple applications supporting different messaging protocols to interact.

MQTT (`http://mqtt.org`) is a lightweight messaging protocol, specifically designed for machine-to-machine communications (Internet of Things). AMQP (`http://www.amqp.org`) is a more complex protocol, which is designed to be an open source alternative to proprietary messaging middleware. STOMP (`http://stomp.github.io`) is a lightweight text-based protocol, which comes from *the HTTP school of design*. All three are application layer protocols, and based on TCP/IP.

Besides the decoupling and the interoperability, a broker can offer more advanced features such as persistent queues, routing, message transformations, and monitoring, without mentioning the broad range of messaging patterns that many brokers support out of the box. Of course, nothing stops us from implementing all these features using a peer-to-peer architecture, but unfortunately there is much more effort involved. Nonetheless, there might be different reasons to avoid a broker:

- Removing a single point of failure
- A broker has to be scaled, while in a peer-to-peer architecture we only need to scale the single nodes
- Exchanging messages without intermediaries can greatly reduce the latency of the transmission

If we want to implement a peer-to-peer messaging system, we also have much more flexibility and power, because we are not bound to any particular technology, protocol, or architecture. The popularity of ØMQ (`http://zeromq.org`), which is a low-level library for building messaging systems, is a great demonstration of the flexibility that we can have by building custom peer-to-peer or hybrid architectures.

Publish/subscribe pattern

Publish/subscribe (often abbreviated to pub/sub) is probably the best-known one-way messaging pattern. We should already be familiar with it, as it's nothing more than a distributed observer pattern. As in the case of observer, we have a set of *subscribers* registering their interest in receiving a specific category of messages. On the other side, the *publisher* produces messages that are distributed across all the relevant subscribers. The following figure shows the two main variations of the pub/sub pattern, the first peer-to-peer, the second using a broker to mediate the communication:

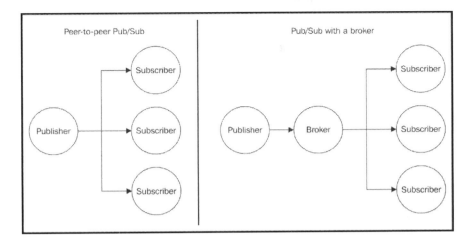

What makes pub/sub so special is the fact that the publisher doesn't know who the recipients of the messages are in advance. As we said, it's the subscriber which has to register its interest to receive a particular message, allowing the publisher to work with an unknown number of receivers. In other words, the two sides of the pub/sub pattern are *loosely coupled*, which makes this an ideal pattern to integrate the nodes of an evolving distributed system.

The presence of a broker further improves the decoupling between the nodes of the system because the subscribers interact only with the broker, not knowing which node is the publisher of a message. As we will see later, a broker can also provide a message queuing system, allowing reliable delivery even in the presence of connectivity problems between the nodes.

Now, let's work on an example to demonstrate this pattern.

Building a minimalist real-time chat application

To show a real example of how the pub/sub pattern can help us integrate a distributed architecture, we are now going to build a very basic real-time chat application using pure WebSockets. Then, we will try to scale it by running multiple instances and using a messaging system to put them in communication.

Implementing the server side

Now, let's take one step at a time. Let's first build our chat application; to do this, we will rely on the ws package (https://npmjs.org/package/ws), which is a pure WebSocket implementation for Node.js. As we know, implementing real-time applications in Node.js is pretty simple, and our code will confirm this assumption. Let's then create the server side of our chat; its content is as follows (in the app.js file):

```
const WebSocketServer = require('ws').Server;

//static file server
const server = require('http').createServer(        //[1]
  require('ecstatic')({root: `${__dirname}/www`})
);

const wss = new WebSocketServer({server: server});  //[2]
wss.on('connection', ws => {
  console.log('Client connected');
  ws.on('message', msg => {                          //[3]
    console.log(`Message: ${msg}`);
    broadcast(msg);
  });
});

function broadcast(msg) {                            //[4]
  wss.clients.forEach(client => {
    client.send(msg);
  });
}

server.listen(process.argv[2] || 8080);
```

That's it! That's all we need to implement our chat application on the server. This is the way it works:

1. We first create an HTTP server and attach middleware called ecstatic (https://npmjs.org/package/ecstatic) to serve static files. This is needed to serve the client-side resources of our application (JavaScript and CSS).

2. We create a new instance of the WebSocket server and we attach it to our existing HTTP server. We then start listening for incoming WebSocket connections, by attaching an event listener for the connection event.

3. Each time a new client connects to our server, we start listening for incoming messages. When a new message arrives, we broadcast it to all the connected

clients.

4. The `broadcast()` function is a simple iteration over all the connected clients, where the `send()` function is invoked on each one of them.

This is the magic of Node.js! Of course, the server that we implemented is very minimal and basic, but as we will see, it does its job.

Implementing the client side

Next, it's time to implement the client side of our chat; this is also a very small and simple fragment of code, essentially a minimal HTML page with some basic JavaScript code. Let's create this page in a file named `www/index.html` as follows:

```html
<html>
  <head>
    <script>
      var ws = new WebSocket('ws://' + window.document. location.host);
      ws.onmessage = function(message) {
        var msgDiv = document.createElement('div');
        msgDiv.innerHTML = message.data;
        document.getElementById('messages').appendChild(msgDiv);
      };

      function sendMessage() {
        var message = document.getElementById('msgBox').value;
        ws.send(message);
      }
    </script>
  </head>
  <body>
    Messages:
    <div id='messages'></div>
    <input type='text' placeholder='Send a message' id='msgBox'>
    <input type='button' onclick='sendMessage()' value='Send'>
  </body>
</html>
```

The HTML page we created doesn't really need many comments; it is just a piece of straightforward web development. We use the native WebSocket object to initialize a connection to our Node.js server, and then start listening for messages from the server, displaying them in new `div` elements as they arrive. For sending messages, instead, we use a simple textbox and a button.

When stopping or restarting the chat server, the WebSocket connection is closed and it will not reconnect automatically (as it would be using high-level libraries such as `Socket.io`). This means that it is necessary to refresh the browser after a server restart, to re-establish the connection (or implement a reconnection mechanism, which we will not cover here).

Running and scaling the chat application

We can try running our application immediately; just launch the server with a command such as the following:

```
node app 8080
```

To run this demo, you will need a recent browser which supports native WebSockets. There is a list of compatible browsers here: `http://caniuse.com/#feat=websockets`.

Pointing a browser to `http://localhost:8080` should present an interface similar to the following:

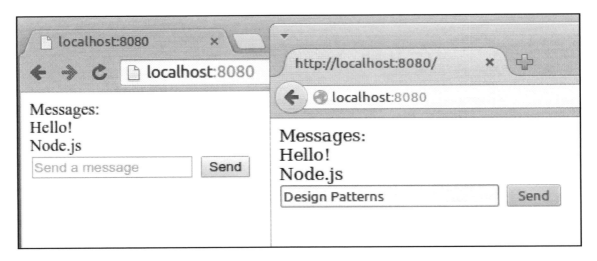

What we want to show now is what happens when we try to scale our application by launching multiple instances. Let's try to do this, let's start another server on another port:

```
node app 8081
```

The desired outcome of scaling our chat application should be that the two clients connecting to the two different servers should be able to exchange chat messages. Unfortunately, this is not what happens with our current implementation; we can try that by opening another browser tab to `http://localhost:8081`.

When sending a chat message on one instance, we broadcast a message locally, distributing it to only the clients connected to that particular server. In practice, the two servers don't talk to each other. We need to integrate them.

In a real application, we will use a load balancer to distribute the load across our instances, but for this demo, we will not use one. This allows us to access each server in a deterministic way to verify how it interacts with the other instances.

Using Redis as a message broker

We start our analysis of the most important pub/sub implementations by introducing **Redis** (`http://redis.io`), which is a very fast and flexible key/value store, also defined by many as a *data structure server*. Redis is more a database than a message broker; however, among its many features there is a pair of commands specifically designed to implement a centralized pub/sub pattern.

Of course, this implementation is very simple and basic, compared to more advanced message-oriented middleware, but this is one of the main reasons for its popularity. Often, in fact, Redis is already available in an existing infrastructure, for example, as a caching server or session store; its speed and flexibility make it a very popular choice for sharing data in a distributed system. So, as soon as the need for a publish/subscribe broker arises in a project, the most simple and immediate choice is to reuse Redis itself, avoiding the need to install and maintain a dedicated message broker. Let's work on an example to demonstrate its simplicity and power.

This example requires a working installation of Redis, listening on its default port. You can find more details at `http://redis.io/topics/quickstart`.

Our plan of action is to integrate our chat servers using Redis as a message broker. Each instance publishes any message received from its clients to the broker, and at the same time it subscribes for any message coming from other server instances. As we can see, each server in our architecture is both a subscriber and a publisher. The following figure shows a representation of the architecture that we want to obtain:

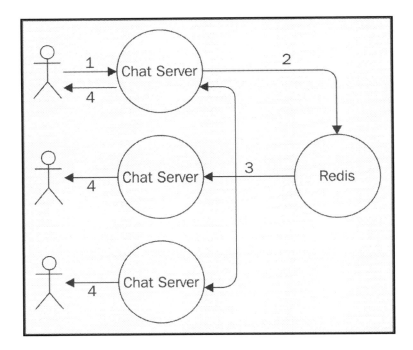

By looking at the preceding figure, we can sum up the journey of a message as follows:

1. The message is typed into the textbox of the web page and sent to the connected instance of our chat server.
2. The message is then published to the broker.
3. The broker dispatches the message to all the subscribers, which in our architecture are all the instances of the chat server.
4. In each instance, the message is distributed to all the connected clients.

> **Redis** allows publishing and subscribing to channels, which are identified by a string, for example, `chat.nodejs`. It also allows us to use glob-style patterns to define subscriptions that can potentially match multiple channels, for example, `chat.*`.

Let's see in practice how this works. Let's modify the server code by adding the publish/subscribe logic:

```
const WebSocketServer = require('ws').Server;
const redis = require("redis");                    // [1]
const redisSub = redis.createClient();
const redisPub = redis.createClient();

//static file server
const server = require('http').createServer(
  require('ecstatic')({root: `${__dirname}/www`})
);

const wss = new WebSocketServer({server: server});
wss.on('connection', ws => {
  console.log('Client connected');
  ws.on('message', msg => {
    console.log(`Message: ${msg}`);
    redisPub.publish('chat_messages', msg);       // [2]
  });
});

redisSub.subscribe('chat_messages');               // [3]
redisSub.on('message', (channel, msg) => {
  wss.clients.forEach((client) => {
    client.send(msg);
  });
});

server.listen(process.argv[2] || 8080);
```

The changes that we made to our original chat server are highlighted in the preceding code; this is how it works:

1. To connect our Node.js application to the Redis server, we use the `redis` package (`https://npmjs.org/package/redis`), which is a complete client that supports all the available Redis commands. Next, we instantiate two different connections, one used to subscribe to a channel, the other to publish messages. This is necessary in Redis, because once a connection is put in *subscriber mode*, only commands related to the subscription can be used. This means that we need a second connection for publishing messages.

2. When a new message is received from a connected client, we publish a message in the `chat_messages` channel. We don't directly broadcast the message to our clients because our server is subscribed to the same channel (as we will see in a moment), so it will come back to us through Redis. For the scope of this example, this is a simple and effective mechanism.

3. As we said, our server also has to subscribe to the `chat_messages` channel, so we register a listener to receive all the messages published into that channel (either by the current server or any other chat server). When a message is received, we simply broadcast it to all the clients connected to the current WebSocket server.

These few changes are enough to integrate all the chat servers that we might decide to start. To prove this, we can try starting multiple instances of our application:

```
node app 8080
node app 8081
node app 8082
```

We can then connect multiple browsers' tabs to each instance and verify that the messages we send to one server are successfully received by all the other clients connected to different servers. Congratulations! We just integrated a distributed real-time application using the publish/subscribe pattern.

Peer-to-peer publish/subscribe with ØMQ

The presence of a broker can considerably simplify the architecture of a messaging system; however, there are circumstances where it is not an optimal solution, such as, for example, when latency is critical, when scaling complex distributed systems, or when the presence of a single point of failure is not an option.

Introducing ØMQ

If our project falls in the category of possible candidates for a peer-to-peer message exchange, the best solution to evaluate is certainly **ØMQ** (`http://zeromq.org`, also known as zmq, ZeroMQ, or 0MQ); we already mentioned this library earlier in the book. ØMQ is a networking library that provides the basic tools to build a large variety of messaging patterns. It is low-level, extremely fast, and has a minimalistic API but it offers all the basic building blocks of a messaging system, such as atomic messages, load balancing, queues, and many more. It supports many types of transport, such as in-process channels (`inproc://`), inter-process communication (`ipc://`), multicast using the PGM protocol (`pgm://` or `epgm://`), and, of course, the classic TCP (`tcp://`).

Among the features of ØMQ, we can also find tools to implement a publish/subscribe pattern, exactly what we need for our example. So, what we are going to do now is remove the broker (Redis) from the architecture of our chat application and let the various nodes communicate in a peer-to-peer fashion, leveraging the publish/subscribe sockets of ØMQ.

 A ØMQ socket can be considered a network socket on steroids, which provides additional abstractions to help implement the most common messaging patterns. For example, we can find sockets designed to implement publish/subscribe, request/reply, or one-way communications.

Designing a peer-to-peer architecture for the chat server

When we remove the broker from our architecture, each instance of the chat application has to directly connect to the other available instances in order to receive the messages they publish. In ØMQ, we have two types of sockets specifically designed for this purpose: PUB and SUB. The typical pattern is to bind a PUB socket to a port that will start listening for subscriptions coming from the other SUB sockets.

A subscription can have a *filter* that specifies what messages will be delivered to the SUB sockets. The filter is a simple **binary buffer** (so it can also be a string), which will be matched against the beginning of the message (which is also a binary buffer). When a message is sent through the PUB socket it is broadcast to all the connected SUB sockets, but only after their subscription filters are applied. The filters will be applied to the publisher side only if a *connected* protocol is used, such as, for example, TCP.

The following figure shows the pattern applied to our distributed chat server architecture (with only two instances, for simplicity):

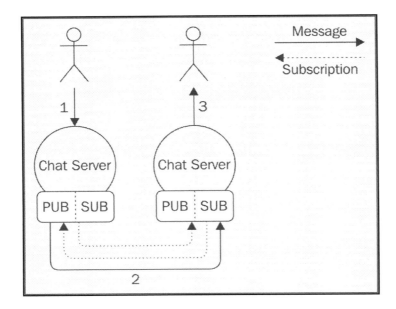

The preceding figure shows us the flow of information when we have two instances of the chat application, but the same concept can be applied for *N* instances. The architecture tells us that each node must be aware of the other nodes in the system, to be able to establish all the necessary connections. It also shows us how the subscriptions go from a SUB socket to a PUB socket, while messages travel in the opposite direction.

 To run the example in this section, you need to install the native ØMQ binaries on your system. You can find more information at `http://zeromq.org/intro:get-the-software`. Note: this example was tested against the 4.0 branch of ØMQ.

Using the ØMQ PUB/SUB sockets

Let's see how this works in practice by modifying our chat server (we will show you only the changed parts):

```
// ...
const args = require('minimist')(process.argv.slice(2));    //[1]
const zmq = require('zmq');
```

```
const pubSocket = zmq.socket('pub');                        //[2]
pubSocket.bind(`tcp://127.0.0.1:${args['pub']}`);

const subSocket = zmq.socket('sub');                        //[3]
const subPorts = [].concat(args['sub']);
subPorts.forEach(p => {
  console.log(`Subscribing to ${p}`);
  subSocket.connect(`tcp://127.0.0.1:${p}`);
});
subSocket.subscribe('chat');

// ...
ws.on('message', msg => {                                   //[4]
  console.log(`Message: ${msg}`);
  broadcast(msg);
  pubSocket.send(`chat ${msg}`);
});
//...

subSocket.on('message', msg => {                            //[5]
  console.log(`From other server: ${msg}`);
  broadcast(msg.toString().split(' ')[1]);
});

// ...
server.listen(args['http'] || 8080);
```

The preceding code clearly shows that the logic of our application became slightly more complicated; however, it's still straightforward considering that we are implementing a distributed and peer-to-peer publish/subscribe pattern. Let's see how all the pieces come together:

1. We require the zmq package (https://npmjs.org/package/zmq), which is essentially the Node.js binding for the ØMQ native library. We also require minimist (https://npmjs.org/package/minimist), which is a command-line argument parser; we need this to be able to easily accept named arguments.

2. We immediately create our PUB socket and bind it to the port provided in the --pub command-line argument.

3. We create the SUB socket and we connect it to the PUB sockets of the other instances of our application. The ports of the target PUB sockets are provided in the --sub command-line arguments (there might be more than one). We then create the actual subscription, by providing chat as a filter, which means that we will receive only the messages beginning with chat.

4. When a new message is received by our WebSocket, we broadcast it to all the connected clients but we also publish it through our PUB socket. We use `chat` as a prefix followed by a space, so the message will be published to all the subscriptions using `chat` as a filter.

5. We start listening for messages that arrive at our SUB socket, we do some simple parsing of the message to remove the `chat` prefix, and then we broadcast it to all the clients connected to the current WebSocket server.

We have now built a simple distributed system, integrated using a peer-to-peer publish/subscribe pattern!

Let's fire it up, let's start three instances of our application by making sure to connect their PUB and SUB sockets properly:

```
node app --http 8080 --pub 5000 --sub 5001 --sub 5002
node app --http 8081 --pub 5001 --sub 5000 --sub 5002
node app --http 8082 --pub 5002 --sub 5000 --sub 5001
```

The first command will start an instance with an HTTP server listening on port 8080, while binding a PUB socket on port 5000 and connecting the SUB socket to ports 5001 and 5002, which is where the PUB sockets of the other two instances should be listening at. The other two commands work in a similar way.

Now, the first thing we can see is that ØMQ will not complain if a port corresponding to a PUB socket is not available. For example, at the time of the first command, there is nobody listening on ports 5001 and 5002; however, ØMQ is not throwing any error. This is because ØMQ has a reconnection mechanism that will automatically try to establish a connection to these ports at regular time intervals. This feature also comes in particularly handy if any node goes down or is restarted. The same *forgiving* logic applies to the PUB socket: if there are no subscriptions, it will simply drop all the messages, but it will continue working.

At this point, we can try to navigate with a browser to any of the server instances that we started and verify that the messages are properly broadcast to all the chat servers.

In the previous example, we assumed a static architecture, where the number of instances and their addresses are known in advance. We can introduce a service registry, as explained in the previous chapter, to connect our instances dynamically. It is also important to point out that ØMQ can be used to implement a broker using the same primitives we demonstrated here.

Durable subscribers

An important abstraction in a messaging system is the **message queue** (MQ). With a message queue, the sender and the receiver(s) of the message don't necessarily need to be active and connected at the same time to establish a communication, because the queuing system takes care of storing the messages until the destination is able to receive them. This behavior is opposed to the set and forget paradigm, where a subscriber can receive messages only during the time it is connected to the messaging system.

A subscriber that is able to always reliably receive all the messages, even those sent when it's not listening for them, is called a **durable subscriber**.

The MQTT protocol defines a level of **Quality of Service (QoS)** for the messages exchanged between the sender and receiver. These levels are also very useful to describe the reliability of any other messaging system (not only MQTT). These are as follows:

- **QoS0, at most once**: Also known as set and forget, the message is not persisted, and the delivery is not acknowledged. This means that the message can be lost in cases of crashes or disconnections of the receiver.
- **QoS1, at least once**: The message is guaranteed to be received at least once, but duplicates might occur if, for example, the receiver crashes before notifying the sender. This implies that the message has to be persisted in the eventuality it has to be sent again.
- **QoS2, exactly once**: This is the most reliable QoS; it guarantees that the message is received once and only once. This comes at the expense of a slower and more data-intensive mechanism for acknowledging the delivery of messages.

Find out more in the MQTT specifications at
`http://public.dhe.ibm.com/software/dw/webservices/ws-mqtt`
`/mqtt-v3r1.html#qos-flows`.

As we said, to allow durable subscribers, our system has to use a message queue to accumulate the messages while the subscriber is disconnected. The queue can be stored in memory or persisted on disk to allow the recovery of its messages even if the broker restarts or crashes. The following figure shows a graphical representation of a durable subscriber backed by a message queue:

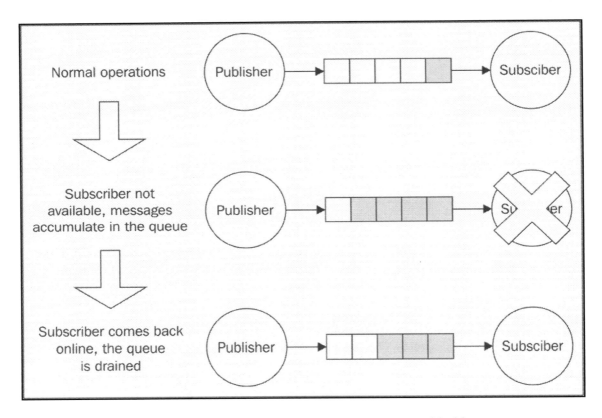

The durable subscriber is probably the most important pattern enabled by a message queue, but it's certainly not the only one, as we will see later in the chapter.

The Redis publish/subscribe commands implement a set and forget mechanism (QoS0). However, Redis can still be used to implement a durable subscriber using a combination of other commands (without relying directly on its publish/subscribe implementation). You can find a description of this technique in the following blog posts:
`http://davidmarquis.wordpress.com/2013/01/03/reliable-del`
`ivery-message-queues-with-redis`
`http://www.ericjperry.com/redis-message-queue`
ØMQ defines some patterns to support durable subscribers as well, but it's mostly up to us to implement this mechanism.

Introducing AMQP

A message queue is normally used in situations where message can't be lost, which includes mission-critical applications such as banking or financial systems. This usually means that the typical enterprise-grade message queue is a very complex piece of software, which utilizes bulletproof protocols and persistent storage to guarantee the delivery of the message even in the presence of malfunctions. For this reason, enterprise messaging middleware has been, for many years, a prerogative of giants such as Oracle and IBM, each one of them usually implementing its own proprietary protocol, resulting in a strong customer lock-in. Fortunately, it's been a few years now since messaging systems entered the mainstream, thanks to the growth of open protocols such as AMQP, STOMP, and MQTT. To understand how a message queuing system works, we are now going to give an overview of AMQP; this is fundamental to understand how to use a typical API based on this protocol.

AMQP is an open standard protocol supported by many message-queuing systems. Besides defining a common communication protocol, it also provides a model for describing routing, filtering, queuing, reliability, and security. In AMQP, there are three essential components:

- **Queue**: The data structure responsible for storing the messages consumed by the clients. The messages from a queue are pushed (or pulled) to one or more consumers essentially, our applications. If multiple consumers are attached to the same queue, the messages are load balanced across them. A queue can be one of the following:
    - **Durable**: This means that the queue is automatically recreated if the broker restarts. A durable queue does not imply that its contents are preserved as well; in fact, only messages that are marked as persistent are saved to the disk and restored in case of a restart.

- **Exclusive**: This means that the queue is bound to only one particular subscriber connection. When the connection is closed, the queue is destroyed.
- **Auto-delete**: This will cause the queue to be deleted when the last subscriber disconnects.

- **Exchange**: This is where a message is published. An exchange routes the messages to one or more queues depending on the algorithm it implements:
    - **Direct exchange**: It routes the messages by matching an entire routing key (for example, `chat.msg`).
    - **Topic exchange**: It distributes the messages using a glob-like pattern matched against the routing key (for example, `chat.#` matches all the routing keys starting with `chat`).
    - **Fanout exchange**: It broadcasts a message to all the connected queues, ignoring any routing key provided.

- **Binding**: This is the link between exchanges and queues. It also defines the routing key or the pattern used to filter the messages that arrive from the exchange.

These components are managed by a broker, which exposes an API for creating and manipulating them. When connecting to a broker, a client creates a channel—an abstraction of a connection—which is responsible for maintaining the state of the communication with the broker.

In AMQP, the durable subscriber pattern can be obtained by creating any type of queue that is not exclusive or auto-delete.

The following figure shows us all these components put together:

The AMQP model is way more complex than the messaging systems we have used so far (Redis and ØMQ); however, it offers a set of features and a reliability that would be very hard to obtain using only primitive publish/subscribe mechanisms.

> You can find a detailed introduction to the AMQP model on the RabbitMQ website:
> `https://www.rabbitmq.com/tutorials/amqp-concepts.html`.

Durable subscribers with AMQP and RabbitMQ

Let's now practice what we learned about durable subscribers and AMQP and work on a small example. A typical scenario where it's important to not lose any message is when we want to keep the different services of a microservice architecture in sync; we already described this integration pattern in the previous chapter. If we want to use a broker to keep all our services on the same page, it's important that we don't lose any information, otherwise we might end up in an inconsistent state.

Designing a history service for the chat application

Let's now extend our small chat application using a microservice approach. Let's add a history service that persists our chat messages inside a database, so that when a client connects, we can query the service and retrieve the entire chat history. We are going to integrate the history service with the chat server using the RabbitMQ broker (`https://www.rabbitmq.com`) and AMQP.

The next figure shows our planned architecture:

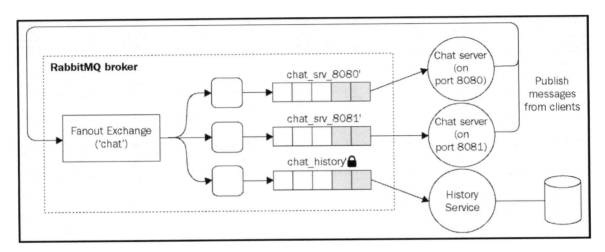

As described in the preceding architecture, we are going to use a single fanout exchange; we don't need any particular routing, so our scenario does not require any exchange more complex than that. Next, we will create one queue for each instance of the chat server. These queues are exclusive; we are not interested in receiving any missed message when a chat server is offline, that's the job of our history service, which eventually can also implement more complicated queries against the stored messages. In practice, this means that our chat servers are not durable subscribers and their queues will be destroyed as soon as the connection is closed.

On the contrary, the history service cannot afford to lose any messages; otherwise, it would not fulfill its very purpose. The queue we are going to create for it has to be durable, so that any message that is published while the history service is disconnected will be kept in the queue and delivered when it comes back online.

We are going to use the familiar LevelUP as the storage engine for the history service, while we will use the `amqplib` package (`https://npmjs.org/package/amqplib`) to connect to RabbitMQ using the AMQP protocol.

 The following example requires a working RabbitMQ server, listening on its default port. For more information, please refer to its official installation guide at `http://www.rabbitmq.com/download.html`.

Implementing a reliable history service using AMQP

Let's now implement our history service! We are going to create a standalone application (a typical microservice), which is implemented in the module `historySvc.js`. The module is made up of two parts: an HTTP server to expose the chat history to clients, and an AMQP consumer which is responsible for capturing the chat messages and storing them in a local database.

Let's see what this looks like in the code that follows:

```
const level = require('level');
const timestamp = require('monotonic-timestamp');
const JSONStream = require('JSONStream');
const amqp = require('amqplib');
const db = level('./msgHistory');

require('http').createServer((req, res) => {
  res.writeHead(200);
  db.createValueStream()
    .pipe(JSONStream.stringify())
    .pipe(res);
}).listen(8090);

let channel, queue;
amqp
  .connect('amqp://localhost')                               // [1]
  .then(conn => conn.createChannel())
  .then(ch => {
    channel = ch;
    return channel.assertExchange('chat', 'fanout');         // [2]
  })
  .then(() => channel.assertQueue('chat_history'))           // [3]
  .then((q) => {
    queue = q.queue;
    return channel.bindQueue(queue, 'chat');                 // [4]
  })
  .then(() => {
```

```
      return channel.consume(queue, msg => {              // [5]
        const content = msg.content.toString();
        console.log(`Saving message: ${content}`);
        db.put(timestamp(), content, err => {
          if (!err) channel.ack(msg);
        });
      });
    })
    .catch(err => console.log(err));
```

We can immediately see that AMQP requires a little bit of setting up, which is necessary to create and connect all the components of the model. It's also interesting to observe that amqplib supports Promises by default, so we leveraged them heavily to streamline the asynchronous steps of the application. Let's see in detail how it works:

1. We first establish a connection with the AMQP broker, which is RabbitMQ in our case. Then, we create a channel, which is similar to a session that will maintain the state of our communications.

2. Next, we set up our exchange, named chat. As we already mentioned, it is a fanout exchange. The assertExchange() command will make sure that the exchange exists on the broker, otherwise it will create it.

3. We also create our queue, called chat_history. By default, the queue is durable; not exclusive and not auto-delete, so we don't need to pass any extra options to support durable subscribers.

4. Next, we bind the queue to the exchange we previously created. Here, we don't need any other particular option, for example, a routing key or pattern, as the exchange is of the type fanout, so it doesn't perform any filtering.

5. Finally, we can begin to listen for messages coming from the queue we just created. We save every message that we receive in a LevelDB database using a monotonic timestamp as key (https://npmjs.org/package/monotonic-timestamp), to keep the messages sorted by date. It's also interesting to see that we are acknowledging every message using channel.ack(msg), and only after the message is successfully saved into the database. If the ACK (acknowledgment) is not received by the broker, the message is kept in the queue for being processed again. This is another great feature of AMQP for bringing the reliability of our service to a whole new level. If we are not interested in sending explicit acknowledgments, we can pass the option {noAck:true} to the channel.consume() API.

Integrating the chat application with AMQP

To integrate the chat servers using AMQP, we have to use a setup very similar to the one we implemented in the history service, so we are not going to repeat it here in full. However, it's still interesting to see how the queue is created and how a new message is published into the exchange. The relevant parts of the new `app.js` file are the following:

```
// ...
  .then(() => {
     return channel.assertQueue(`chat_srv_${httpPort}`, {exclusive: true});
  })
// ...
  ws.on('message', msg => {
     console.log(`Message: ${msg}`);
     channel.publish('chat', '', new Buffer(msg));
  });
// ...
```

As we mentioned, our chat server does not need to be a durable subscriber, a set and forget paradigm is enough. So when we create our queue, we pass the option `{exclusive:true}`, indicating that the queue is scoped to the current connection and therefore it will be destroyed as soon as the chat server shuts down.

Publishing a new message is also very easy; we simply have to specify the target exchange (`chat`) and a routing key, which in our case is empty (`''`) because we are using a fanout exchange.

We can now run our improved chat architecture; to do that, let's start two chat servers and the history service:

```
node app 8080
node app 8081
node historySvc
```

It is now interesting to see how our system, and in particular the history service, behaves in case of downtime. If we stop the history server and continue to send messages using the web UI of the chat application, we will see that when the history server is restarted, it will immediately receive all the messages it missed. This is a perfect demonstration of how the durable subscriber pattern works!

It is nice to see how the microservice approach allows our system to survive even without one of its components—the history service. There would be a temporary reduction of functionality (no chat history available) but people would still be able to exchange chat messages in real time. Awesome!

Pipelines and task distribution patterns

In Chapter 9, *Advanced Asynchronous Recipes*, we learned how to delegate costly tasks to multiple local processes, but even though this was an effective approach, it cannot be scaled beyond the boundaries of a single machine. In this section, we are going to see how it's possible to use a similar pattern in a distributed architecture, using remote workers located anywhere in a network.

The idea is to have a messaging pattern that allows us to spread tasks across multiple machines. These tasks might be individual chunks of work or pieces of a bigger task split using a *divide and conquer* technique.

If we look at the logical architecture represented in the following figure, we should be able to recognize a familiar pattern:

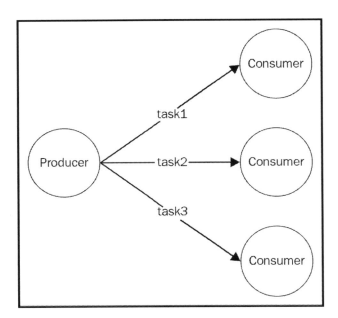

As we can see from the preceding diagram, the publish/subscribe pattern is not suitable for this type of application, as we absolutely don't want a task to be received by multiple workers. What we need instead is a message distribution pattern similar to a load balancer, that dispatches each message to a different consumer (also called worker, in this case). In the messaging system terminology, this pattern is known as **competing consumers**, fanout distribution, or **ventilator**.

One important difference with the HTTP load balancers we have seen in the previous chapter is that, here, the consumers have a more active role. In fact, as we will see later, most of the time it's not the producer that connects to the consumers, but the consumers themselves that connect to the task producer or the task queue in order to receive new jobs. This is a great advantage in a scalable system as it allows us to seamlessly increase the number of workers without modifying the producer or adopting a service registry.

Also, in a generic messaging system, we don't necessarily have a request/reply communication between the producer and workers. Instead, most of the time, the preferred approach is to use one-way asynchronous communication, which enables a better parallelism and scalability. In such an architecture, messages can potentially always travel in one direction, creating pipelines, as shown in the following figure:

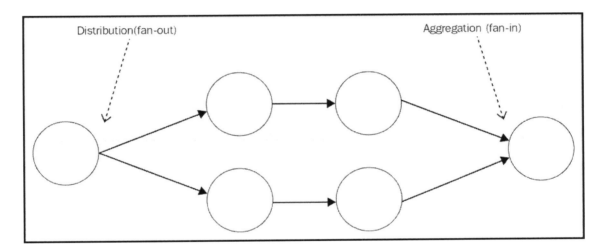

Pipelines allow us to build very complex processing architectures without the burden of a synchronous request/reply communication, often resulting in lower latency and higher throughput. In the preceding figure, we can see how messages can be distributed across a set of workers (fanout), forwarded to other processing units, and then aggregated into a single node (fanin), usually called **sink**.

In this section, we are going to focus on the building blocks of these kinds of architectures, by analyzing the two most important variations: peer-to-peer and broker-based.

 The combination of a pipeline with a task distribution pattern is also called a **parallel pipeline**.

The ØMQ fanout/fanin pattern

We have already discovered some of the capabilities of ØMQ for building peer-to-peer distributed architectures. In the previous section, we used PUB and SUB sockets to disseminate a single message to multiple consumers; now we are going to see how it's possible to build parallel pipelines using another pair of sockets called PUSH and PULL.

PUSH/PULL sockets

Intuitively, we can say that the PUSH sockets are made for *sending* messages, while the PULL sockets are meant for *receiving*. It might seem a trivial combination; however, they have some nice characteristics that make them perfect for building one-way communication systems:

- Both can work in *connect* mode or *bind* mode. In other words, we can build a PUSH socket and bind it to a local port listening for the incoming connections from a PULL socket, or vice versa, a PULL socket might listen for connections from a PUSH socket. The messages always travel in the same direction, from PUSH to PULL; it's only the initiator of the connection that can be different. The bind mode is the best solution for *durable* nodes, such as, for example, the task producer and the sink, while the connect mode is perfect for *transient* nodes, such as, for example, the task workers. This allows the number of transient nodes to vary arbitrarily without affecting the more durable nodes.
- If there are multiple PULL sockets connected to a single PUSH socket, the messages are evenly distributed across all the PULL sockets; in practice, they are load balanced (peer-to-peer load balancing!). On the other hand, a PULL socket that receives messages from multiple PUSH sockets will process the messages using a fair queuing system, which means that they are consumed evenly from all the sources—a round robin applied to inbound messages.
- The messages sent over a PUSH socket that doesn't have any connected PULL socket do not get lost; they are instead queued up on the producer until a node comes online and starts pulling the messages.

We are now starting to understand how ØMQ is different from traditional web services and why it's a perfect tool for building any kind of messaging system.

Building a distributed hashsum cracker with ØMQ

Now it's time to build a sample application to see in action the properties of the `PUSH/PULL` sockets we just described.

A simple and fascinating application to work with would be a *hashsum cracker*, a system that uses a brute-force technique to try to match a given hashsum (MD5, SHA1, and so on) to every possible variation of characters of a given alphabet. This is an *embarrassingly parallel* workload (`http://en.wikipedia.org/wiki/Embarrassingly_parallel`), which is perfect for building an example demonstrating the power of parallel pipelines.

For our application, we want to implement a typical parallel pipeline with a node to create and distribute tasks across multiple workers, plus a node to collect all the results. The system we just described can be implemented in ØMQ using the following architecture:

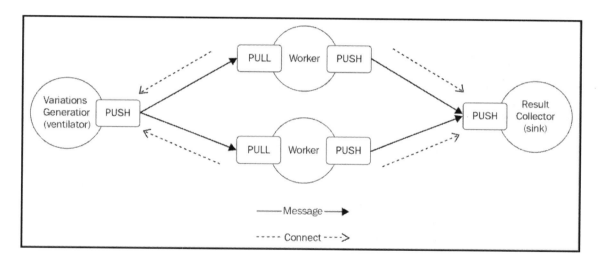

In our architecture, we have a *ventilator* generating all the possible variations of characters in a given alphabet and distributing them to a set of workers, which in turn calculate the hashsum of every given variation and try to match it against the hashsum given as the input. If a match is found, the result is sent to a results collector node (sink).

The durable nodes of our architecture are the ventilator and the sink, while the transient nodes are the workers. This means that each worker connects its `PULL` socket to the ventilator and its `PUSH` socket to the sink; this way, we can start and stop how many workers we want without changing any parameter in the ventilator or the sink.

Implementing the ventilator

Now, let's start to implement our system by creating a new module for the ventilator, in a file named `ventilator.js`:

```
const zmq = require('zmq');
const variationsStream = require('variations-stream');
const alphabet = 'abcdefghijklmnopqrstuvwxyz';
const batchSize = 10000;
const maxLength = process.argv[2];
const searchHash = process.argv[3];

const ventilator = zmq.socket('push');                  // [1]
ventilator.bindSync("tcp://*:5000");

let batch = [];
variationsStream(alphabet, maxLength)
  .on('data', combination => {
    batch.push(combination);
    if (batch.length === batchSize) {                   // [2]
      const msg = {searchHash: searchHash, variations: batch};
      ventilator.send(JSON.stringify(msg));
      batch = [];
    }
  })
  .on('end', () => {
    //send remaining combinations
    const msg = {searchHash: searchHash, variations: batch};
    ventilator.send(JSON.stringify(msg));
  });
```

To avoid generating too many variations, our generator uses only the lowercase letters of the English alphabet and sets a limit on the size of the words generated. This limit is provided in input as a command-line argument (`maxLength`) together with the hashsum to match (`searchHash`). We use a library called `variations-stream` (`https://npmjs.org/package/variations-stream`) to generate all the variations using a streaming interface.

But the part that we are most interested in analyzing is how we distribute the tasks across the workers:

1. We first create a PUSH socket and we bind it to local port `5000`; this is where the PULL socket of the workers will connect to receive their tasks.

2. We group the generated variations in batches of 10,000 items each and then we craft a message that contains the hash to match and the batch of words to check. This is essentially the task object that the workers will receive. When we invoke `send()` over the `ventilator` socket, the message will be passed to the next available worker, following a round robin distribution.

Implementing the worker

Now it's time to implement the worker (`worker.js`):

```
const zmq = require('zmq');
const crypto = require('crypto');
const fromVentilator = zmq.socket('pull');
const toSink = zmq.socket('push');

fromVentilator.connect('tcp://localhost:5016');
toSink.connect('tcp://localhost:5017');

fromVentilator.on('message', buffer => {
  const msg = JSON.parse(buffer);
  const variations = msg.variations;
  variations.forEach( word => {
    console.log(`Processing: ${word}`);
    const shasum = crypto.createHash('sha1');
    shasum.update(word);
    const digest = shasum.digest('hex');
    if (digest === msg.searchHash) {
      console.log(`Found! => ${word}`);
      toSink.send(`Found! ${digest} => ${word}`);
    }
  });
});
```

As we said, our worker represents a transient node in our architecture, therefore, its sockets should connect to a remote node instead of listening for the incoming connections. That's exactly what we do in our worker, we create two sockets:

- A PULL socket that connects to the ventilator, for receiving the tasks
- A PUSH socket that connects to the sink, for propagating the results

Besides this, the job done by our worker is very simple: for each message received, we iterate over the batch of words it contains, then for each word we calculate the SHA1 checksum and we try to match it against searchHash passed with the message. When a match is found, the result is forwarded to the sink.

Implementing the sink

For our example, the sink is a very basic result collector, which simply prints the messages received by the workers to the console. The contents of the file `sink.js` are as follows:

```
const zmq  = require('zmq');
const sink = zmq.socket('pull');
sink.bindSync("tcp://*:5017");

sink.on('message', buffer => {
  console.log('Message from worker: ', buffer.toString());
});
```

It's interesting to see that the sink (as the ventilator) is also a durable node of our architecture and therefore we bind its PULL socket instead of connecting it explicitly to the PUSH socket of the workers.

Running the application

We are now ready to launch our application; let's start a couple of workers and the sink:

```
node worker
node worker
node sink
```

Then it's time to start the ventilator, specifying the maximum length of the words to generate and the SHA1 checksum that we want to match. The following is a sample list of arguments:

```
node ventilator 4 f8e966d1e207d02c44511a58dccff2f5429e9a3b
```

When the preceding command is run, the ventilator will start generating all the possible words that have a length of, at most, four characters, distributing them to the set of workers we started, along with the checksum we provided. The results of the computation, if any, will appear in the terminal of the sink application.

Pipelines and competing consumers in AMQP

In the previous section, we saw how a parallel pipeline can be implemented in a peer-to-peer context. Now we are going to explore this pattern when applied to a fully-fledged message broker, such as RabbitMQ.

Point-to-point communications and competing consumers

In a peer-to-peer configuration, a pipeline is a very straightforward concept to picture in mind. With a message broker in the middle though, the relationship between the various nodes of the system are a little bit harder to understand; the broker itself acts as an intermediary for our communications and, often, we don't really know who is on the other side listening for messages. For example, when we send a message using AMQP, we don't deliver it directly to its destination, but instead to an exchange and then to a queue. Finally, it will be for the broker to decide where to route the message, based on the rules defined in the exchange, the bindings, and the destination queues.

If we want to implement a pipeline and a task distribution pattern using a system like AMQP, we have to make sure that each message is received by only one consumer, but this is impossible to guarantee if an exchange can potentially be bound to more than one queue. The solution, then, is to send a message directly to the destination queue, bypassing the exchange altogether; this way, we can make sure that only one queue will receive the message. This communication pattern is called **point-to-point**.

Once we are able to send a set of messages directly to a single queue, we are already halfway to implementing our task distribution pattern. In fact, the next step comes naturally: when multiple consumers are listening on the same queue, the messages will be distributed evenly across them, implementing a fan-out distribution. In the context of message brokers, this is better known as the **competing consumers** pattern.

Implementing the hashsum cracker using AMQP

We just learned that exchanges are the point in a broker where a message is multicast to a set of consumers, while queues are the place where messages are load balanced. With this knowledge in mind, let's now implement our brute-force hashsum cracker on top of an AMQP broker (such as, for example, RabbitMQ). The following figure gives an overview of the system we want to obtain:

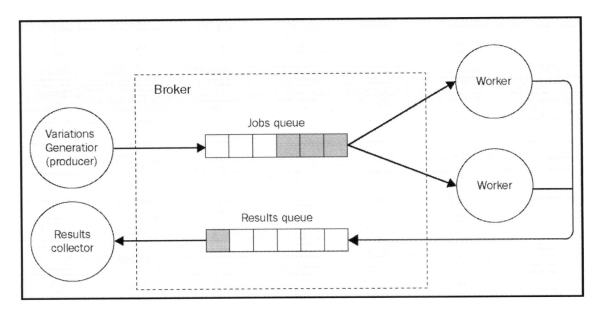

As we discussed, to distribute a set of tasks across multiple workers, we need to use a single queue. In the preceding figure, we called this the *jobs queue*. On the other side of the jobs queue, we have a set of workers, which are *competing consumers*; in other words, each one will pull a different message from the queue. The result is that multiple tasks will execute in parallel on different workers.

Any result generated by the workers is published into another queue, which we called the *results queue*, and then consumed by the results collector; this is actually equivalent to a sink, or fanin distribution. In the entire architecture, we don't make use of any exchange; we only send messages directly to their destination queue, implementing a point-to-point communication.

Implementing the producer

Let's see how to implement such a system, starting from the producer (the variation generator). Its code is identical to the sample we saw in the previous section except for the parts concerning the message exchange. The `producer.js` file will look as follows:

```
const amqp = require('amqplib');
//...

let connection, channel;
amqp
```

```
    .connect('amqp://localhost')
    .then(conn => {
      connection = conn;
      return conn.createChannel();
    })
    .then(ch => {
      channel = ch;
      produce();
    })
    .catch(err => console.log(err));

function produce() {
  //...
  variationsStream(alphabet, maxLength)
    .on('data', combination => {
      //...
      const msg = {searchHash: searchHash, variations: batch};
      channel.sendToQueue('jobs_queue',
        new Buffer(JSON.stringify(msg)));
      //...
    })
  //...
}
```

As we can see, the absence of any exchange or binding makes the setup of an AMQP communication much simpler. In the preceding code, we didn't even need a queue, as we are interested only in publishing a message.

The most important detail, though, is the `channel.sendToQueue()` API, which is actually new to us. As its name says, that's the API responsible for delivering a message straight to a queue—`jobs_queue` in our example—bypassing any exchange or routing.

Implementing the worker

On the other side of `jobs_queue`, we have the workers listening for the incoming tasks. Let's implement their code in a file called `worker.js`, as follows:

```
const amqp = require('amqplib');
//...

let channel, queue;
amqp
  .connect('amqp://localhost')
  .then(conn => conn.createChannel())
  .then(ch => {
    channel = ch;
```

```
      return channel.assertQueue('jobs_queue');
    })
    .then(q => {
      queue = q.queue;
      consume();
    })

//...

function consume() {
  channel.consume(queue, msg => {
    //...
    variations.forEach(word => {
      //...
      if(digest === data.searchHash) {
        console.log(`Found! => ${word}`);
        channel.sendToQueue('results_queue',
          new Buffer(`Found! ${digest} => ${word}`));
      }
      //...
    });
    channel.ack(msg);
  });
};
```

Our new worker is also very similar to the one we implemented in the previous section using ØMQ, except for the part related to the message exchange. In the preceding code, we can see how we first make sure that `jobs_queue` exists and then we start listening for incoming tasks using `channel.consume()`. Then, every time a match is found, we send the result to the collector via `results_queue`, using again a point-to-point communication.

If multiple workers are started, they will all listen on the same queue, resulting in the messages being load balanced between them.

Implementing the result collector

The results collector is again a trivial module, simply printing any message received to the console. This is implemented in the `collector.js` file, as follows:

```
//...
  .then(ch => {
    channel = ch;
    return channel.assertQueue('results_queue');
  })
  .then(q => {
    queue = q.queue;
```

```
channel.consume(queue, msg => {
    console.log('Message from worker: ', msg.content.toString());
  });
})
//...
```

Running the application

Now everything is ready to give our new system a try, we can start by running a couple of workers, which will both connect to the same queue (`jobs_queue`), so that every message will be load balanced between them:

```
node worker
node worker
```

Then, we can run the `collector` module and then `producer` (by providing the maximum word length and the hash to crack):

```
node collector
node producer 4 f8e966d1e207d02c44511a58dccff2f5429e9a3b
```

With this, we implemented a message pipeline and the competing consumers pattern using nothing but AMQP.

Request/reply patterns

Dealing with a messaging system often means using a one-way asynchronous communication; publish/subscribe is a perfect example.

One-way communications can give us great advantages in terms of parallelism and efficiency, but alone they are not able to solve all our integration and communication problems. Sometimes, a good old request/reply pattern might just be the perfect tool for the job. Therefore, in all those situations where an asynchronous one-way channel is all that we have, it's important to know how to build an abstraction that allows us to exchange messages in a request/reply fashion. That's exactly what we are going to learn next.

Correlation identifier

The first request/reply pattern we are going to learn is called **correlation identifier** and it represents the basic block for building a request/reply abstraction on top of a one-way channel.

The pattern consists of marking each request with an identifier, which is then attached to the response by the receiver; this way, the sender of the request can correlate the two messages and return the response to the right handler. This elegantly solves the problem with the presence of a one-way asynchronous channel, where messages can travel in any direction at any time. Let's take a look at the example in the following figure:

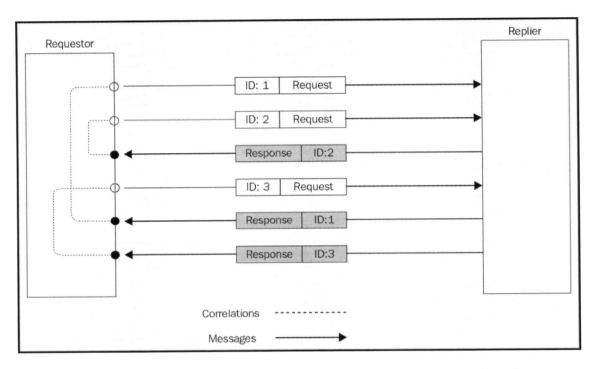

The preceding scenario shows how using a correlation ID allows us to match each response with the right request, even if those are sent and then received in a different order.

Implementing a request/reply abstraction using correlation identifiers

Let's now start working on an example by choosing the most simple type of one-way channel, one that is point-to-point (which directly connects two nodes of the system) and full-duplex (messages can travel in both directions).

In the *simple channel* category, we can find, for example, WebSockets: they establish a point-to-point connection between the server and browser, and the messages can travel in any direction. Another example is the communication channel that is created when a child process is spawned using `child_process.fork()`; we should already know about it, we saw this API in `Chapter 9`, *Advanced Asynchronous Recipes*. This channel too is asynchronous: it connects the parent only with the child process and it allows messages to travel in any direction. This is probably the most basic channel of this category, so that's what we are going to use in our next example.

The plan for the next application is to build an abstraction in order to wrap the channel created between the parent and child processes. This abstraction should provide a request/reply communication by automatically marking each request with a correlation identifier and then matching the ID of any incoming reply against the list of request handlers awaiting a response.

From `Chapter 9`, *Advanced Asynchronous Recipes*, we should remember that the parent process can access the channel with the child using two primitives:

- `child.send(message)`
- `child.on('message',callback)`

In a similar way, the child can access the channel to the parent process using:

- `process.send(message)`
- `process.on('message',callback)`

This means that the interface of the channel available in the parent is identical to the one available in the child; this will allow us to build a common abstraction, so that the requests can be sent from both ends of the channel.

Abstracting the request

Let's start building this abstraction by considering the part responsible for sending new requests; let's create a new file called `request.js`:

```
const uuid = require('node-uuid');

module.exports = channel => {
  const idToCallbackMap = {};                              // [1]

  channel.on('message', message => {                       // [2]
    const handler = idToCallbackMap[message.inReplyTo];
    if(handler) {
```

```
        handler(message.data);
      }
    });

    return function sendRequest(req, callback) {              // [3]
      const correlationId = uuid.v4();
      idToCallbackMap[correlationId] = callback;
      channel.send({
        type: 'request',
        data: req,
        id: correlationId
      });
    };
  };
```

This is how our request abstraction works:

1. The one that follows is a closure created around our `request` function. The magic of the pattern lies in the `idToCallbackMap` variable, which stores the association between the outgoing requests and their reply handlers.

2. As soon as the factory is invoked, the first thing we do is start listening for incoming messages. If the correlation ID of the message (contained in the `inReplyTo` property) matches any of the IDs contained in the `idToCallbackMap` variable, we know that we just received a reply, so we obtain the reference to the associated response handler and we invoke it with the data contained in the message.

3. Finally, we return the function we will use to send new requests. Its job is to generate a correlation ID using the `node-uuid` package (`https://npmjs.org/package/node-uuid`) and then wrap the request data in an envelope that allows us to specify the correlation ID and the type of the message.

That's it for the `request` module; let's move to the next part.

Abstracting the reply

We are just a step away from implementing the full pattern, so let's see how the counterpart of the `request.js` module works. Let's create another file called `reply.js`, which will contain the abstraction for wrapping the reply handler:

```
module.exports = channel =>
{
  return function registerHandler(handler) {
    channel.on('message', message => {
```

```
      if (message.type !== 'request') return;
      handler(message.data, reply => {
        channel.send({
          type: 'response',
          data: reply,
          inReplyTo: message.id
        });
      });
    });
  };
};
```

Our `reply` module is again a factory that returns a function to register new reply handlers. This is what happens when a new handler is registered:

1. We start listening for incoming requests and, when we receive one, we immediately invoke the handler by passing the data of the message and a callback function to collect the reply from the handler.

2. Once the handler has done its work, it will invoke the callback that we provided, returning its reply. We then build an envelope by attaching the correlation ID of the request (the `inReplyTo` property), then we put everything back into the channel.

The amazing thing about this pattern is that in Node.js, it comes very easily; everything for us is already asynchronous, so an asynchronous request/reply communication built on top of a one-way channel is not very different from any other asynchronous operation, especially if we build an abstraction to hide its implementation details.

Trying the full request/reply cycle

Now we are ready to try our new asynchronous request/reply abstraction. Let's create a sample *replier* in a file named `replier.js`:

```
const reply = require('./reply')(process);

reply((req, cb) => {
  setTimeout(() => {
    cb({sum: req.a + req.b});
  }, req.delay);
});
```

Our replier simply calculates the sum between the two numbers received and returns the result after a certain delay (which is also specified in the request). This will allow us to verify that the order of the responses can also be different from the order in which we sent the requests, to confirm that our pattern is working.

The final step to complete the sample is to create the requestor in a file named `requestor.js`, which also has the task of starting the replier using `child_process.fork()`:

```
const replier = require('child_process')
                .fork(`${__dirname}/replier.js`;
const request = require('./request')(replier);

request({a: 1, b: 2, delay: 500}, res => {
  console.log('1 + 2 = ', res.sum);
  replier.disconnect();
});

request({a: 6, b: 1, delay: 100}, res => {
  console.log('6 + 1 = ', res.sum);
});
```

The requestor starts the replier and then passes its reference to our `request` abstraction. We then run a couple of sample requests and verify that the correlation with the response they receive is right.

To try out the sample, simply launch the `requestor.js` module; the output should be something similar to the following:

```
6 + 1 =  7
1 + 2 =  3
```

This confirms that our pattern works perfectly well and that the replies are correctly associated with their own requests, no matter in what order they are sent or received.

Return address

The correlation identifier is the fundamental pattern for creating a request/reply communication on top of a one-way channel; however, it's not enough when our messaging architecture has more than one channel or queue, or when there can be potentially more than one requestor. In these situations, in addition to a correlation ID, we also need to know the *return address*, a piece of information which allows the replier to send the response back to the original sender of the request.

Implementing the return address pattern in AMQP

In AMQP, the return address is the queue where the requestor is listening for incoming replies. Because the response is meant to be received by only one requestor, it's important that the queue is private and not shared across different consumers. From these properties, we can infer that we are going to need a transient queue, scoped to the connection of the requestor and that the replier has to establish a point-to-point communication with the return queue, to be able to deliver its responses.

The following image gives us an example of this scenario:

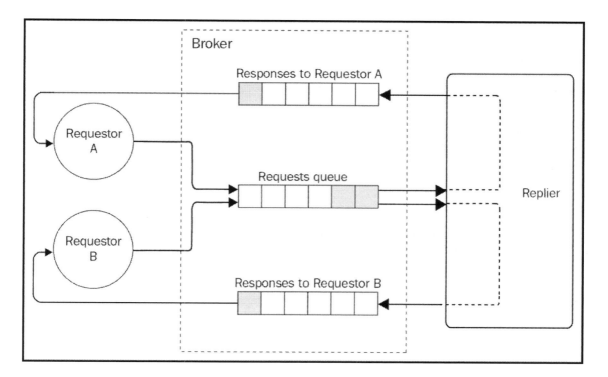

To create a request/reply pattern on top of AMQP, all that we need to do is to specify the name of the response queue in the message properties; this way, the replier knows where the response message has to be delivered. The theory seems very straightforward, so let's see how to implement this in a real application.

Implementing the request abstraction

Let's now build a request/reply abstraction on top of AMQP. We will use RabbitMQ as a broker, but any compatible AMQP broker should do the job. Let's start with the request abstraction (implemented in the `amqpRequest.js` module); we will show here only the relevant parts.

The first interesting thing to observe is how we create the queue to hold the responses; this is the code responsible for that:

```
channel.assertQueue('', {exclusive: true});
```

When we create the queue, we don't specify any name, which means that a random one will be chosen for us; in addition to this, the queue is *exclusive*, which means that it's bound to the active AMQP connection and it will be destroyed when the connection closes. There is no need to bind the queue to an exchange, as we don't need any routing or distribution to the multiple queues; this means that the messages have to be delivered straight into our response queue.

Next, let's see how we can generate a new request:

```
classAMQPRequest {
  //...
  request(queue, message, callback) {
    const id = uuid.v4();
    this.idToCallbackMap[id] = callback;
    this.channel.sendToQueue(queue, new Buffer(JSON.stringify(message)),
      {correlationId: id, replyTo: this.replyQueue}
    );
  }
}
```

The `request()` method accepts as input, the name of the request `queue` and the `message` to send. As we learned in the previous section, we need to generate a correlation ID and associate it to the `callback` function. Finally, we send the message, specifying the `correlationId` and the `replyTo` property as metadata.

It's interesting to see that for sending the message we are using the `channel.sentToQueue()` API instead of `channel.publish()`; this is because we are not interested in implementing any publish/subscribe distribution using exchanges, but a more basic point-to-point delivery straight into the destination queue.

In AMQP, we can specify a set of properties (or metadata) to be passed to the consumer, together with the main message.

The last important piece of our `amqpRequest` prototype is where we listen for incoming responses:

```
_listenForResponses() {
  return this.channel.consume(this.replyQueue, msg => {
    const correlationId = msg.properties.correlationId;
    const handler = this.idToCallbackMap[correlationId];
    if (handler) {
      handler(JSON.parse(msg.content.toString()));
    }
  }, {noAck: true});
}
```

In the preceding code, we listen for messages on the queue we created explicitly for receiving responses, then for each incoming message we read the correlation ID and we match it against the list of handlers awaiting a reply. Once we have the handler, we only need to invoke it by passing the reply message.

Implementing the reply abstraction

That's it for the `amqpRequest` module; now it's time to implement the response abstraction in a new module named `amqpReply.js`.

Here, we have to create the queue that will receive the incoming requests; we can use a simple durable queue for this purpose. We won't show this part, since it's again all AMQP boilerplate. What we are interested in seeing instead is how we handle a request and then send it back to the right queue:

```
class AMQPReply {
  //...

  handleRequest(handler) {
    return this.channel.consume(this.queue, msg => {
      const content = JSON.parse(msg.content.toString());
      handler(content, reply => {
        this.channel.sendToQueue(
          msg.properties.replyTo,
          new Buffer(JSON.stringify(reply)),
          {correlationId: msg.properties.correlationId}
        );
        this.channel.ack(msg);
```

```
      });
    });
  }
}
```

When sending back a reply, we use `channel.sendToQueue()` to publish the message straight into the queue specified in the `replyTo` property of the message (our return address). Another important task of our `amqpReply` object is to set a `correlationId` in the reply, so that the receiver can match the message with the list of pending requests.

Implementing the requestor and the replier

Everything is now ready to give our system a try, but first, let's build a sample requestor and replier to see how to use our new abstraction.

Let's start from the module `replier.js`:

```
const Reply = require('./amqpReply');
const reply = Reply('requests_queue');

reply.initialize().then(() => {
  reply.handleRequest((req, cb) => {
    console.log('Request received', req);
    cb({sum: req.a + req.b});
  });
});
```

It's nice to see how the abstraction we built allows us to hide all the mechanisms that handle the correlation ID and the return address; all we need to do is to initialize a new `reply` object, specifying the name of the queue where we want to receive our requests (`'requests_queue'`). The rest of the code is just trivial; our sample replier simply calculates the sum of the two numbers received as input and sends back the result using the provided callback.

On the other side, we have a sample requestor implemented in the `requestor.js` file:

```
const req = require('./amqpRequest')();

req.initialize().then(() => {
  for (let i = 100; i> 0; i--) {
    sendRandomRequest();
  }
});

function sendRandomRequest() {
  const a = Math.round(Math.random() * 100);
```

```
    const b = Math.round(Math.random() * 100);
    req.request('requests_queue', {a: a, b: b},
      res => {
        console.log(`${a} + ${b} = ${res.sum}`);
      }
    );
  }
```

Our sample requestor sends 100 random requests to the requests_queue queue. In this case too, it's interesting to see that our abstraction is doing its job perfectly, hiding all the details of the asynchronous request/reply pattern.

Now, to try out the system, simply run the replier module followed by the requestor module:

```
node replier
node requestor
```

We will see a set of operations published by the requestor and then received by the replier, which in turn will send back the responses.

Now we can try other experiments. Once the replier is started for the first time, it creates a durable queue; this means that, if we now stop it and then run the requestor again, no request will be lost. All the messages will be stored in the queue until the replier is started again!

Another nice feature that we get for free using AMQP is the fact that our replier is scalable out-of-the-box. To test this assumption, we can try to start two or more instances of the replier, and watch the requests being load balanced between them. This works because, every time a requestor starts, it attaches itself as a listener to the same durable queue, and as a result, the broker will load balance the messages across all the consumers of the queue (competing consumers pattern). Sweet!

 ØMQ has a pair of sockets specifically meant for implementing request/reply patterns (REQ/REP); however, they are synchronous (only one request/response at a time). More complex request/reply patterns are possible with more sophisticated techniques. For more information, you can read the official guide at http://zguide.zeromq.org/page:all#advanced-request-reply.

Summary

We have reached the end of this chapter. Here, we learned the most important messaging and integration patterns and the role they play in the design of distributed systems. We made our acquaintance with the three major types of message exchange patterns: publish/subscribe, pipelines, and request/reply, and we saw how they can be implemented using a peer-to-peer architecture or a message broker. We analyzed their pros and cons, and we saw that by using AMQP and a fully-fledged message broker, we can implement reliable and scalable applications with little developmental effort but at a cost of having one more system to maintain and scale. Also, we saw how ØMQ allows us to build distributed systems where we can have total control over every aspect of the architecture, fine tuning its properties around our very own requirements.

This chapter also closes the book; by now, we should have a tool belt full of patterns and techniques we can go and apply in our projects. We should also have a deeper understanding of how Node.js development works and what its strengths and weaknesses are. Throughout the book, we also had the chance to work with a myriad of packages and solutions developed by many extraordinary developers. In the end, this is the most beautiful aspect of Node.js: its people, a community where everybody plays their part in giving back something.

I hope you enjoyed our small contribution.

Index